Cisco CCNA Simplified
3rd Edition

Your Complete Guide to Passing the CCNA Exam
CCNA 640-802

What They Don't Teach You in Other Books

Paul Browning (LLB Hons)
CCNP, MCSE, NET+, A+

This study guide and/or material is not sponsored by, endorsed by or affiliated with Cisco Systems, Inc. Cisco®, Cisco Systems®, CCDA™, CCNA™, CCDP™, CCNP™, CCIE™, CCSI™, the Cisco Systems logo and the CCIE logo are trademarks or registered trademarks of Cisco Systems, Inc in the United States and certain other countries. All other trademarks are trademarks of their respective owners.

ISBN: 978-0-9557815-3-7

Published by:
Reality Press Ltd.
Midsummer Court
314 Midsummer Blvd.
Milton Keynes
MK9 2UB
help@reality-press.com

LEGAL NOTICE
The advice in this book is designed to help you achieve the standard of Cisco Certified Network Engineer which is Cisco's foundation internetworking examination. A CCNA is able to carry out basic router and switch installations and troubleshooting. Before you carry out more complex operations it is advisable to seek the advice of experts or Cisco Systems, Inc.

The practical scenarios in this book are meant to illustrate a technical point only and should be used on your privately owned equipment only and never on a live network.

Dedication

To aspiring Cisco engineers everywhere.
If I can do it, anyone can.
Paul Browning

"Train hard—Fight easy"
Roman Legions motto

FOREWORD

If you are reading this book, you are embarking upon the road toward becoming a Cisco certified networking engineer. Or at the least, you are contemplating the journey and are curious to know what lies ahead.

It was not too many years ago that the only technical certification Cisco Systems offered—indeed, the only serious internetworking certification anyone offered—was the CCIE. Acquiring the CCIE meant months of intensive study to tackle a hands-on lab, the details of which were mysterious to most. Those who passed the lab (few passed on their first, and often even second attempt) had lengthy hands-on experience in internetworking before even beginning their course of preparation. Only a very few intrepid individuals passed the CCIE lab without extensive prior experience.

Cisco Systems haves, since that time, added to their program a number of intermediate certifications to their program that can be used as stepping-stones toward the coveted CCIE. You must still, in the end, prove your expertise in the dreaded hands-on lab, but these intermediate certifications are wonderful for getting you acclimatized to the rigors of testing your skills and knowledge without having to step into the most difficult of them "cold."

The first milestone on the certification path is the CCNA, the subject of Paul Browning's outstanding preparation guide. Within these pages Paul imparts to you step-by-step, using abundant illustrations, examples, and exercises, the knowledge you need for passing the CCNA exam, step by step, using abundant illustrations, examples, and exercises. But beyond the coursework, you will find in this book you will find the practical advice necessary for gaining hands-on experience and for preparing for the certification exam that will benefit you not only for the CCNA but also through subsequent Cisco certifications to whatever objective you set for yourself.

Follow the advice and exercises Paul has provided for you here and you will have made an excellent start.

Jeff Doyle
CCIE #1919

ACKNOWLEDGMENTS

Thanks to Nick Osborne, Stuart "Stupot" Juggins, and Andy Barkl. Thanks also to the contributors below who volunteered their time and effort to make this a better book for you to read.

CONTRIBUTORS

Thanks to the below people who have all tech reviewed various chapters and provided valuable additions to the book.

Paul Casey (CCIE), Brian S Griffith, W. Alan Robertson (CCIE), Howard C Berkowitz, Joe Gagznos, Debbie Westall, Azeem M Suleman, Koen Pintens, Allen Garrett, Annu Roopa, Bill Creighton, Michael Woznicki.

THANKS

Special thanks are due to Mark Thompson, who helped project manage the book. Thanks also to Gary Schnabl from http://LivernoisYard.com for the book's layout and copyediting and to Stephen Wadeley for his proofreading.

BIOGRAPHIES

About the author

Paul Browning (LLB[Hons], CCNP, MCSE + I, A+, Network+) spent 12 years as a police officer in Coventry and Birmingham in the UK. He left for a career in IT in June 2000. He started out on an IT helpdesk and after passing his MCSE and CCNA he got a job working at the Cisco TAC north of London. The TAC was made redundant in March 2003. Paul then started his own IT consultancy and training company, Networks, Inc. Ltd.

Networks, Inc. Ltd. provides Cisco consulting and training to companies and individuals all over the UK. They also run Cisco weekend boot camps in the UK. So to find out more, go to www.networksinc.co.uk.

Paul also runs some other training sites and companies:

- www.howtonetwork.net is an online Cisco training portal which features streaming videos, exams, flash study cards and a very friendly discussion forum.
- www.BreakIntoIT.com helps people get a successful career in IT.
- www.subnetting.org is an online subnetting question generator.
- www.subnetting-secrets.com is an online subnetting training course.
- www.howtocontract.net shows you how to break into IT contracting

About the technical reviewers

Andy Barkl, CCNP, CCDP, CISSP, MCT, MVP, MCDST, MCSE: Security, MCSA: Security, MCSA: Messaging A+, CTT+, i-Net+, Network+, Security+, Server+, CNA, has over 20 years of experience in the IT field. He is the owner of MCT & Associates LLC, a technical training and consulting firm in Phoenix, Arizona. He enjoys dividing his time between teaching in the classroom, writing from his office and consulting on Cisco and Windows deployments. He is also the online editor for MCPMag.com, TCPMag.com, CertCities.com, and a contributing author and editor for Sybex and Cisco Press. He hosts a multitude of exam preparation chats monthly on MCPmag.com and CertCities.com. You can contact Andy by e-mail at: andy.barkl@WeTrainIT.com.

Stuart "Stupot" Juggins, CCNP, MCSE has 12 years experience in the IT industry. He has consulted for EDS, MICL and other large consultancy companies before working at the Cisco TAC, as well as providing WAN support for global companies.

Nick "The Oracle" Osborne, CCNP has 15 years experience in the IT industry. He has spent five years in the USA as a bounty hunter but then left that behind to work at IBM in the UK. He worked at the Cisco TAC north of London for three years providing ISDN dial support to global customers.

WHAT DO YOU THINK?

No matter how brilliant we think this course book is, the only opinion that really matters is that of you the readers. Is there something missing that we should really have covered? Do you think it is brilliant or not good enough? Have you found a mistake?

If so, please drop us a line at:
help@howtonetwork.net.

Your copy of this study guide comes with over $400 worth of free Cisco CCNA study software including cram guide, flash cards and practice exams. Please visit the link below to register your copy of this book and you will be e-mailed instructions on how to download your software:
http://www.HowToNetwork.net/public/539.cfm.

I am so confident that you will find in this book the practical to the best Cisco CCNA study manual you have ever used that if, within 30 days of buying it you are not completely delighted, you can send it back for a 100% refund.

Just post it back to us with the original receipt to:
Reality Press
Midsummer Court
314 Midsummer Blvd.
Milton Keynes
MK9 2UB

Make sure you include your home address (no PO boxes), e-mail address, and contact telephone number.

Paul Browning
Published by Reality Press Ltd.

INTRODUCTIONS

Introduction to the November 2009 version

If I can pass the CCNA, then anyone can. Believe me. When I started out on a helpdesk with a CCNA book in front of me I felt that I was at the bottom of a huge mountain. Six weeks of studying for three hours per day and I passed (on my second attempt). Three months later, I was working for Cisco and two years after that I was running my own Cisco consultancy.

All you need is a strong desire to pass and this book. That is it. You will need access to live Cisco equipment as well but we can provide that via our racks website at: http://racks.HowToNetwork.net.

The CCNA is a highly regarded qualification, and having it will improve your credibility as a network professional and bring respect from your peers. If you are looking to get a break into IT then it will get you the interviews you need. If you are feeling the pinch of recession, then the CCNA will set you apart from the competition and be the platform for you to launch a career as a network freelancer if you so choose.

In this new version of CCNA Simplified, you benefit from several updates and additions. You can enjoy new switching labs including STP, switch security, and inter-VLAN routing. There are new Security Device Manager (SDM) labs and wireless updates. The switching module has been completely revised and updated with more detail on spanning tree, switch security, and VLANs.

There have been over 500 tweaks and changes added to make this what I feel is the best CCNA book on the market. I have put my money where my mouth is and if you do not agree than post it back to me for a full refund. See the offer on page xii.

I admire you for taking the time and effort to better yourself. If I can help you in any way, then drop me a line.

Paul Browning
help@HowToNetwork.net

Introduction to the May 2009 version

Nothing lasts forever, and this certainly applies to the CCNA. Every few months you will see new topics added to the exam and others removed. In November 2007 Cisco stopped testing the 640-801 and moved to the 640-802. This change saw the removal of ISDN and RIP and the addition of several subjects including wireless networking, security device manager (SDM), IPv6, network security and a requirement for more detail in areas like DNS and DHCP.

This version of CCNA simplified is my attempt to match everything I think Cisco could throw at you in the exam. But it is much more than that. My objective is for you to pass your CCNA exams and apply what you have learned to the exciting world of Cisco internetworking. Working as a network engineer is certainly never boring and, with the skills you will learn in this book, you will be in a good position to deal with most day-to-day networking issues.

I have to be honest and say that due to all the new changes I feel that you are going to need something extra to help you get through the exam and give you even more confidence. For this reason, I have spent twelve months developing an interactive membership website for people like you. It features streaming videos, practice exams, networking tools, and a discussion forum where Cisco experts are available to answer your questions. It cost a huge amount to build and run, but I have kept the membership down to a few bucks per month and you can leave at any time.

You can find it at www.HowToNetwork.net.

Introduction

Hello and congratulations on your decision to purchase what is arguably the best Cisco study guide on the market. It takes the average person about 90 hours of dedicated study time to pass the CCNA. If you can manage three hours per day, that means you are about a month away from being a CCNA. If you can only manage about an hour, then it will be three months—plus extra time for forgetting what you revised during months one and two.

Passing the CCNA has nothing to do with how clever you are. It is simply a matter of dedication and discipline and doing what we tell you in this book. Make sure you read my *How To Pass Your CCNA* e-book on my www.HowToNetwork.net training website (you can find it in the free "Pass Your CCNA in 60 Days" section).

This guide was written out of frustration. Frustration that after having read just about every CCNA book available I still did not seem to have a grasp of the subject matter. I learned all about the OSI model, Ethernet frame types and ISDN reference points, but I just could not see what possible relevance it was to the real world of networking.

Eventually, after weeks and weeks of struggling and one failed attempt, I passed the CCNA. I still did not know how to apply what I had learned to the real world. What use was the knowledge I had gained from all those hours of studying and more importantly, how could I earn more money with the qualification?

Luckily, with this book in your hands, the outcome I expect for you is not only being able to pass the exam with relative ease but, if you use the advice in the book and the cool free tools on www. HowToNetwork.net, you will either be able to earn more money in your present IT role, break into IT or to consult as a network engineer. Confidence comes with knowledge and knowledge comes with practice and practice is the mother of all skills.

You have in your hands, everything you need to become a CCNA. You just need to follow the steps to get the result you want.

This course is a work in progress, as I am writing this paragraph on my computer I am still not completely satisfied with it and probably never will be. If you can see any way it can be improved or if you spot any mistakes no matter how small, then please let me know by contacting me at help@ howtonetwork.net. If I implement your suggestion, I will credit you with a mention as a contributor for the next version of the course.

Which exam?

You can pass the CCNA by taking one exam (640-802) or two (CCENT/ICND 640-822 and ICND2 640-816). The syllabus is the same, but the two exam route breaks it into two parts. We recommend taking the one exam route. You will be a CCNA after passing it and save money.

How to complete the course

You may be tempted to get out your hi-lighter and start reading through from page one. That is the hard way, if you want to waste weeks or months then go ahead—but this is the hard way. I recommend you quickly flick through all of the pages to get a feel for how the course progresses and then tuck into my free e-book—*How to Pass Your CCNA Exam*. Please ensure you access www.How-ToNetwork.net also which will really help you.

On www.HowToNetwork.net, you can sign up for the FREE CCNA question of the day, and there are free study tools, exams, and videos and, if you like, you can also join as a member for a few months. It only costs a few dollars.

Take your time to browse through the book several times without worrying about all of the facts and figures. I know this will be hard for some people to believe but the information will be assimilated by your subconscious mind as you look over the text and diagrams. If you really want to make light work of this book, buy a book on speed reading, it will be time well spent (trust me).

If you are struggling to get the information to sink be rest assured that almost every other CCNA student will find the same or different areas difficult to understand. Sometimes it is better to move on to another subject and come back to the difficult part later.

Throughout this book you will see different boxes.

 IN THE EXAM:

Information in this box will give you a warning that you need to remember this for the exam. I have no idea what questions you will be asked but some topics are more likely to be featured than others.

 IN THE REAL WORLD:

This is how what you have learned can be applied to the real world of networking. This is where knowledge converts into practical ability.

INSPIRATION:

Feeling like it is all too much? Wondering if you are the only one who finds it difficult. This box will encourage you to keep going and attain your goal.

The output from the router can be identified by the fact it is printed in a `monospaced font`. This will make it easier for you to identify router output. Sometimes, I insert explanatory notes next to the router output to make the configuration easier to understand.

I wish I'd had access to the information in *How to Pass Your CCNA Exam* and the rest of this course when I started studying to enhance my opportunities in the IT arena. I wish you every success with your studies.

How to do the labs

Success in the CCNA lab hinges upon your hands on Cisco skills. To this end the accompanying lab guide has hands on labs addressing all of the major areas you will be expected to know for the lab. The lab guide goes further than any other guide on the market I have seen by addressing trouble-shooting skills and guiding you through every step of the configuration so you really understand what it is you are doing.

Hands on experience is crucial to your success in the exam and to your credibility as a CCNA. Some vendors certifications used to attract a huge amount of kudos but as employers began to discover, many people were passing the exams by reading books and studying from brain dump sites. How would you like an operation to be performed on you by a surgeon who had only learned from books and exam cheat sources? Well the same goes for network engineers.

You have three options to attain the crucial hands on exposure to pass the practical part of the CCNA:

1. Buy two or more routers
2. Rent on line router time
3. Use a router simulator

The first is the best option, by far. Use the real equipment, putting in the cables and doing the labs over and over and over again until you feel like throwing the routers out of the window.

You should be able to pick up second hand routers from http://www.eBay.com or your countries version of eBay. Most of the labs in the accompanying lab book have been designed to work with only two routers. Any Cisco router with a serial interface connecting to another Cisco router with a serial interface will do. You should be able to pick up a 1700, 1800 or 2600 with a back-to-back serial cable for around $100 in total.

If you wish to purchase another router and a switch, you should budget for around $250 all in to get all of the equipment you need for the CCNA. I know that having a frame relay switch would be nice, but if you are on a budget then these are not necessary items.

I have no affiliations with any online companies. If you want to get the necessary hands on experience and cannot or do not want to get your own routers, then renting access to somebody else's kit is a great idea. You will need to have them set up the routers in the way you want, but there are several excellent companies available who have all the routers you need ready to use.

Members of www.HowToNetwork.net have access to racks of live Cisco routers and switches available 24 hours of the day / 365 days of the year. The URL is: racks.HowToNetwork.net. Non-members can buy rack hours at a very low price.

The quality of router simulators continues to impress me. There are simulators currently on the market, ranging from $20 to well over $250 (US dollars). It all comes down to your budget and how much functionality is available.

I would recommend that you look through the labs in the course and then look at what functionality you have with the router simulator. You will not get the benefit of having your own router but the look and feel of modern simulators is very close to the real thing. Chat to other students who have tried out the simulators and ask them what they think. The single best way to find out what is best is to get a referral.

Please note that if you want to work on real routers in the real world and make real money, you will need to be comfortable with using the real thing. Routers simulators are a great practice tool but you will be expected to be able to install and troubleshoot the real thing at some point.

One other thing, please avoid downloading illegal copies of any software. I have worked with several companies whilst developing this book and www.HowToNetwork.net. They usually consist of other one or only handful of people who have sank a lot of their time, effort and own money to produce a product to help you pass your exam. Please show your support by paying for the product, and one day you could be doing the same thing.

Paul Browning—help@HowToNetwork.net

TABLE OF CONTENTS

PART 1

CCNA Study Guide

CHAPTER 1

Module 1—Introduction to Internetworking

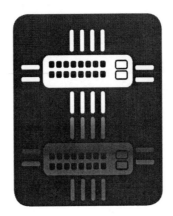

What you will learn in this in module	Timings
Overview of networking equipment	Theory: 80 minutes
Understand the OSI model	
Network topologies	Review: 10 minutes
How Ethernet networking works	
IEEE standards	
Understand the Cisco networking model	
How to select Cisco products	
How to cable the network	

OVERVIEW OF NETWORKING EQUIPMENT

The earlier versions of the CCNA exam did not focus on basic networking concepts and theory, but this has changed now. Cisco will expect you to have a good working knowledge of general networking, LAN and WAN topologies, and equipment.

If you are fairly new to the world of IT and in particular networking it would be a good idea to study some general networking or Network+ books. There is no need to take the Network+ exam but the information will stand you in good stead for the CCNA syllabus.

A computer network can be as small as two computers joined together by a single cable to the largest network in the world—the Internet. To get a large number of PCs connected, specialized equipment has been designed to carry out certain tasks such as preventing broadcast storms and keeping track of which networks are where.

PC / server

PCs and servers are the devices requesting and providing network services. Servers provide authentication for users logging onto the network, Internet access, firewall services, and many other functions.

Network card

Often referred to as the NIC (network interface card), these are used with PCs, servers, and printers to allow communication on the network to take place. Every single NIC has an address burned onto the chip that sits on the card. This address is known as a hardware or MAC address. The MAC address is also known as the BIA or burned-in address.

The NIC in Figure 1–1 has an old-fashioned BNC connector (left) and the more modern RJ-45 connector (right).

Figure 1–1: PCI network card

Hub

The most basic piece of networking equipment is a hub. A hub simply allows several networking devices to speak to each other. Each device plugs into a port on the hub using a network cable (more on these later). The simplest network you can build will be with some PCs connecting into a hub. Hubs have no memory or hard drive, so they can never remember which device is plugged into which port. This causes a lot of unnecessary traffic to pass on the network.

Figure 1–2: SnyOptics 16-port hub

Switch

One drawback of using hubs is that, because they have no memory, they can never keep a record of which PC is plugged into which port. For this reason, every time one PC wants to speak to another, every single PC plugged into the hub gets a copy of the frame sent out on the wire also.

A data frame sent to every device on a network is known as a broadcast. Too many broadcasts on a network can cause delays and dramatically reduce performance. A high amount of broadcasts causes an enormous amount of traffic to traverse the network at any one time.

Switches build up a list of which PCs are connected to which ports allowing the available bandwidth to be used a lot more efficiently. If a PC wants to speak to another PC that is not directly connected to it, the switch will send out a broadcast to find out where on the network the PC actually is. Switches and hubs are designed to forward broadcast traffic.

Because switches only forward broadcast information when the destination is unknown, they are used to create smaller collision domains. A collision occurs when a data frame, traveling along a network cable, collides with another frame. The collision causes the data inside the frame to become corrupted. This corrupted frame is sent out to every device within a collision domain. Smaller collision domains mean that traffic will move faster throughout the network.

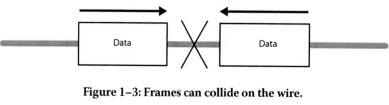

Figure 1–3: Frames can collide on the wire.

Figure 1–4: A corrupted frame is heard by every device in a collision domain.

A bridge is a similar device to a switch. However, they usually only have one or two ports, whereas a switch has several ports. A switch is basically a multiport bridge.

We will look at switching technology in Module 3.

Figure 1–5: Cisco 2950 Switch

Router

A router can be considered to be a large directory of networks. Rather than concerning itself about which PC is where, a router's job is to find out where different networks are. It then sends the traffic via the best path, this could be the fastest, most reliable or shortest. If the router does not know how to get to its intended destination, it will either drop the packet or forward it to another router who should know how to get there.

It is important to remember that by default, routers do not forward broadcasts. If they did, we would find that most networks including the Internet would be extremely slow because of all the broadcasts passing across them.

Figure 1–6: Cisco 1800 Model Router

By not forwarding broadcast information, routers are used to create broadcast domains.

 FOR THE EXAM:

Switches create collisions domains. Every port on the switch is a separate collision domain. Routers create broadcast domains, and every port on the router is a separate broadcast domain.

THE OPEN SYSTEMS INTERCONNECT (OSI) MODEL

In the 1980s, there was a huge increase in the amount of companies producing networking equipment and protocols. It was very difficult to connect networks together and almost impossible to do so using different equipment. The job of standardizing networking fell upon the International Standard Organization (ISO). The ISO created a model for every company to follow when designing networking hardware and software. The model was named the Open Standards Interconnect model or more commonly known as the OSI model.

The OSI model does not just serve as a reference, there is a practical value to using it. There has to be some way to order things so we know which devices do which job. What if your company wants to buy switches from a different vendor than the one they buy their routers from? How can they be sure the equipment will work together?

Advantages of using the OSI model are:

*   It allows different vendors equipment to work together.
*   It allows different types of network hardware and software to communicate.
*   A change made in one layer does not affect any of the other layers.

The OSI is made up from seven different layers; each layer has responsibility for a specific function or set of functions.

*   Application (layer 7)
*   Presentation (layer 6)
*   Session (layer 5)

- Transport (layer 4)
- Network (layer 3)
- Data link (layer 2)
- Physical (layer 1)

 IN THE REAL WORLD:

The application layer is also known as layer 7; it is never called layer 1. The physical layer is always known as layer 1 and so on.

An easy way to remember the order is to use the acronym: All People Seem To Need Data Processing (APSTNDP).

Encapsulation

As data passes down each OSI layer, a new header is added to it; this process is called encapsulation. As data is encapsulated while moving down the layers it will be known by a different name. This is necessary because each layer requires a different set of information and addressing to work properly. When the data is received at the destination, it is then de-encapsulated, a process of removing each header, and then the information is passed up to the next layer.

An easy way to remember the order of data encapsulation is to use the acronym: Don't Some People Fry Bacon (DSPFB).

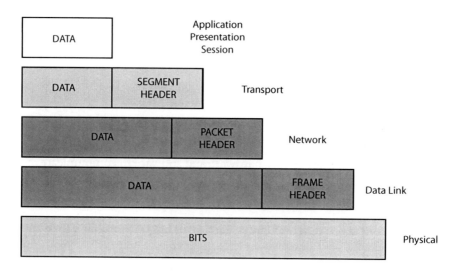

Figure 1–7: Five steps of data encapsulation

Data turns into Segment, which turns into Packet, which turns into Frame, which turns into Bits.

Application layer

This is where most users interact with the network. The application layer establishes whether the destination is available to communicate and determines if sufficient resources are available to do so.

There are many services that operate at the application layer. They include:

- **World Wide Web (WWW)**—connects millions of users to servers providing multimedia functions such as text, graphics, and sound.
- **E-mail (SMTP, POP)**—the standard used to send and receive e-mail all over the world.
- **File transfer protocol (FTP)**—provides a means to upload and download large files over networks. Imagine having to e-mail a colleague a 20 Mb file!
- **Telnet**—this is used to connect to networking devices remotely. Many network engineers connect to their networking equipment many miles away from the actual physical location.

Presentation layer

The function of the presentation layer is to present data to the application layer. It converts coded data into a format the application layer can understand. It is also responsible for data encryption and decryption and finally data compression.

The presentation layer converts many multimedia functions for the application layer including:

- **JPEG**—Joint Photographic Experts Group. A widely used image format.
- **MPEG**—Moving Pictures Experts Group. Format for video compression and coding.
- **QuickTime**—manages audio and video for Macintosh or PowerPCs.
- **ASCII**—American Standard Code for Information Interchange. The standard format for text and data.

 FOR THE EXAM:

Any protocol that will change the "look" of the data works at the Presentation layer. Aside from what is listed Graphic Image File (GIF), Bitmap (BMP), MP3 and EBCIDIC or mainframe language are some of the others.

Session layer

Here, sessions or dialogs between applications are set up, managed, and eventually terminated. A session is co-ordinated and synchronized to prevent different applications data from becoming mixed up during transfer.

Some of the protocols that operate at the session layer include:

- **Network file system (NFS)**—developed by Sun/IBM for use with TCP/IP and Unix to allow transparent remote access to resources.
- **Structured query language (SQL)**—provides a simple means of accessing system information on local or remote systems.
- **Remote procedure call (RPC)**—these are procedures created on a client and performed on a server.

Transport layer

Here, end-to-end reliable data transport services are provided to the upper OSI layers as well as error correction. The transport layer takes data from the upper layers and breaks it into smaller units called segments.

Before communication can take place an end-to-end logical connection called a virtual circuit has to be established. This is done by each end system agreeing that a connection is about to be initiated. This process is known as a three-way handshake. The handshake can be seen if the packets on the wire are read and can be identified by fields in the packet being marked as SYN, SYN ACK, and ACK.

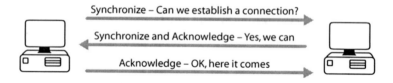

Figure 1–8: The three-way handshake

Data transfer at the transport layer is considered to be "reliable." This means that there is a guarantee that the data sent will reach the intended destination. This is accomplished by using three methods:

1. Flow control
2. Windowing
3. Acknowledgments

Flow control

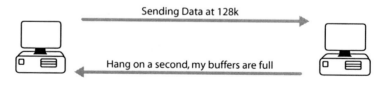

Figure 1–9: Flow control

If the receiving system is being sent more information than it can process it will ask the sending system to stop for a short time. This normally happens when one side uses broadband and the other a dial-up modem. The packet sent telling the other device to stop is known as a source quench message.

Windowing

Each system agrees how much data is to be sent before an acknowledgment is required. This "window" opens and closes as data moves along in order to maintain a constant flow.

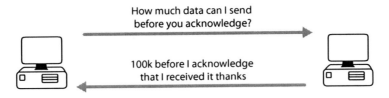

Figure 1–10: Windowing

Acknowledgments

When a certain amount of segments are received, the fact that they all arrived safely and in the correct order needs to be communicated to the sending system.

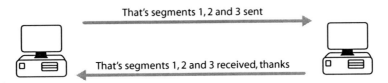

Figure 1–11: Acknowledgments

The transport layer includes several protocols, the most widely known are TCP and UDP which are part of the TCP/IP suite of protocols. This suite is well known because it is the standard used on the Internet. TCP is known as a reliable connection oriented protocol. It uses the three-way handshake, windowing, and other techniques to guarantee your data gets to its destination safely. Many protocols use TCP including Telnet, HTTPS, and FTP (although they sit at the application layer they do use TCP).

UDP on the other hand is known as a connectionless protocol. It numbers each packet and then sends them to the destination. It never checks to see if they arrived safely and will never set up a connection before sending the packet. Sometimes data is not that important and the application developer decides that you can always send the information again if it fails to get there.

Why is UDP used at all? TCP uses a lot of bandwidth on the network and there is a lot of traffic sent back and forth to set up the connection even before the data is sent. This all takes up valuable time and network resources. UDP packets are a lot smaller than TCP packets and are very useful if a really reliable connection is not that necessary. Protocols carried on UDP include DNS and TFTP.

Network layer

Table 1–1: Router B best-path routing table

Destination network	Next hop	Number of hops away
Network 1	None	Directly connected
Network 2	None	Directly connected
Network 3	Router A	1
Network 3	Router C	1
Network 4	Router A	1
Network 4	Router C	2

The role of the network layer is to determine the best path or route for data to take from one network to another. Data from the session layer are assembled into packets here. End-to-end delivery of packets occurs at the network layer.

Because networks need some way of identifying themselves we also find logical addressing takes place here. The most popular form of network addressing used today is IP addressing.

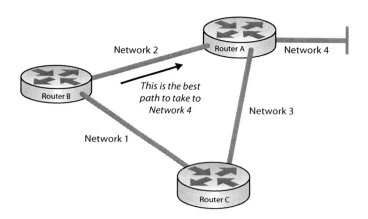

Figure 1–12: Best path is decided at the network layer.

In Figure 1–12 above, each router stores a table of which networks are directly attached and also how to get to the networks that are not directly attached. You can see the routing table for Router B in Table 1-1 above.

Routers operate exclusively at the network layer of the OSI. When a packet arrives at a router interface, the router looks at the network address and decides if that network is directly attached. If it is not, the router looks at its routing table to see which interface it should leave by.

Network layer addressing

Logical addressing for TCP/IP uses 32 binary bits to make up a network address. We write binary out in decimal to make it easier for us to read and understand. An example of a logical address for TCP/IP is 192.168.2.3; 192.168.2 identifies the network and the number 3 belongs to a host on that network.

We discuss IP addressing in far more detail in Module 4 and Appendix A.

Network 192.168.2.x

Host.2

Host.3

Host.1

Figure 1–13: Hosts on a network

Network layer protocols include IP, IPX, and AppleTalk.

Data link layer

The data link is divided into two sublayers—the LLC and MAC sublayers:

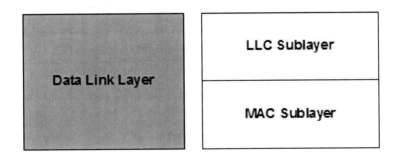

Data Link Layer

LLC Sublayer

MAC Sublayer

Figure 1–14: The data link layer

The data link layer takes packets from the network layer and divides them into smaller units known as frames. Frames are then transported across a physical medium (wires).

The data link layer has its own way of addressing known as hardware addressing. While the network layer determines where networks are located the data link layer determines where hosts are on a particular network.

Logical link control (LLC) sublayer—IEEE 802.2

The LLC layer interfaces with the network layer. The LLC sublayer provides Service Access Points (SAP); these allow the MAC sublayer to communicate with the upper layers of the OSI.

Media access control (MAC) sublayer—IEEE 802.3

The MAC layer directly interfaces with the physical layer. This is where the physical address of the interface or device is stored. A MAC address is a 48-bit address expressed as 12 hexadecimal digits. This address identifies the manufacturer of the device and the rest identifies the host.

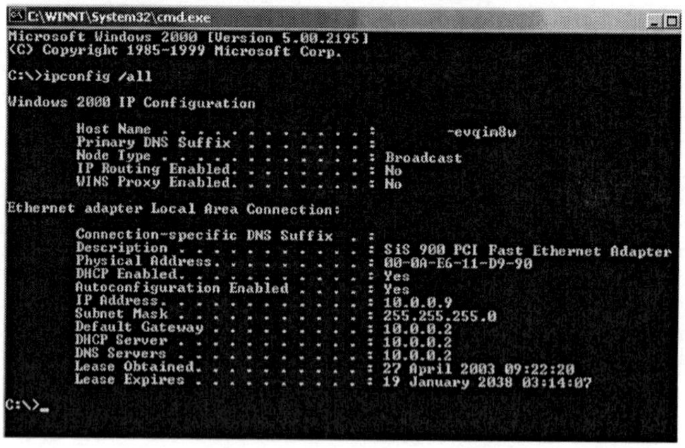

Figure 1–15: MAC address on a PC 00-0A-E6-11-D9-90

The best example of MAC addressing is the address hard coded onto the network card you find in PC or server. You can see the MAC address (shown as the physical address) of your network card by typing "ipconfig /all" at the command prompt on your windows PC.

The first six hexadecimal digits identify the vendor for the NIC and the last six identify the host address.

Switches and bridges operate at the data link layer of the OSI. A table of MAC addresses and which port they are connected to is built up by both devices.

Data link protocols

There are many protocols operating at the data link layer. Protocols are an agreed format for devices on a network to communicate with. The reason why protocols operate at the data link layer is twofold. Firstly, a connection has to take place before network layer communication can start. Secondly, data link layer communication is a lot faster than network layer. There is far less overhead involved in data link layer networking.

Data link protocols operate on both LANs and WANs.

LAN protocols

Local area networks all communicate at the data link layer. Once the packets reach your network the network layer information is stripped off leaving the data and the data link address. Data link protocols include Ethernet, token ring, and fiber distributed data interface (FDDI).

WAN protocols

Nearly all wide area network protocols operate at the data link layer. WAN protocols include frame relay, ISDN, PPP, and HDLC. We will look at WAN protocols in much more detail later.

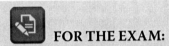

FOR THE EXAM:

Because you are using packets at the network layer and frames at the data link layer, remember YOU ROUTE PACKETS AND YOU FORWARD FRAMES.

Physical layer

The physical layer takes frames from the data link layer and converts them into bits. The physical layer has to use bits (binary digits) since data on a wire can only be sent as a pulse of electricity or light—i.e., only as one of two values, either a 1 or a 0.

Figure 1–16: Hubs and repeaters clean the signal on the wire.

The physical layer deals with the physical characteristics of the medium such as number of pins and their use. Physical layer specifications include IEEE 802.3, FDDI, Ethernet, RJ-45, and many more. Hubs operate at the physical layer of the OSI model. Hubs take the bits, clean up the signal if it has degraded and send it out to every device connected to the ports.

Summary—the OSI model

The OSI model can be summarized as:

Table 1–2: The OSI model summarized

Layer	Encapsulation	Function	Services	Device
7 Application	Data	Establishes availability of resources	FTP, SMTP, Telnet, POP3	
6 Presentation	Data	Compression, encryption, and decryption	JPEG, GIF, MPEG, ASCII	
5 Session	Data	Establishes, maintains, and terminates sessions	NFS, SQL, RPC	
4 Transport	Segment	Establishes end-to-end connection. Uses virtual circuits, buffering, windowing, and flow control	TCP, UDP, SPX	
3 Network	Packet	Determines best path for packets to take.	IP, IPX	Router
2 Data link (LLC MAC)	Frame	Transports data across a physical connection. Error detection	Frame relay, PPP, HDLC	Switch/bridge
1 Physical	Bits	Puts data onto the wire		Hub/repeater/concentrator/MAU

 FOR THE EXAM:

A thorough knowledge of the OSI model is vital for the exam. Know each level and encapsulation formats and which device sits where.

THE TCP/IP MODEL

There are different models of representation for Internetworking. After the OSI comes the TCP/IP model in terms of popularity. The TCP/IP model does not map directly to the OSI model.

Table 1–3: The TCP/IP and OSI models

OSI	TCP/IP
Application	
Presentation	Application
Session	
Transport	Host-to-host
Network	Internet
Data link	
Physical	Network interface

 FOR THE EXAM:

A gateway is a network device that operates at all seven layers. Gateways are the most complex piece of equipment on your network.

NETWORK TOPOLOGIES

 IN THE REAL WORLD:

Knowing the OSI layers can help you to quickly locate the source of any network faults.

A topology refers to how hosts on a network are arranged in order to communicate with each other. The topology you will use depends upon many factors such as cost, resilience, security, future expansion, ease of installation and the type of equipment you are using.

Point-to-point

Point-to-point topologies are used when only two hosts need to communicate directly. The most common example is a WAN link where two offices need to communicate.

Figure 1–17: Point-to-point topology

Bus

A bus topology uses a single wire (referred to as the backbone). It was first utilized for use with co-axial cable where a thick core cable was used to connect 10Base5 and 10Base 2 Ethernet devices.

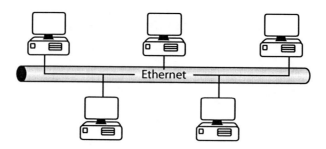

Figure 1–18: Ethernet bus

Star

In a star topology, hosts on the network connect to a central device, such as a hub or switch. This is the most current topology in use today. The media type associated with this topology is 10BaseT (more on media types later).

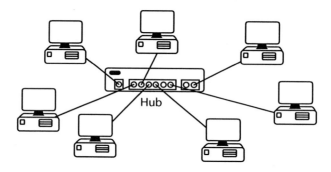

Figure 1–19: Star

Ring

As the name suggests, a ring topology is a circular shape. Token ring was the first network type to use this topology followed by fiber-distributed data interface (FDDI) which uses a dual ring. A dual ring is used for increased speed and resilience, in case one of the rings fail.

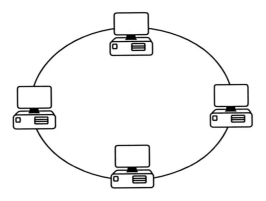

Figure 1–20: Ring

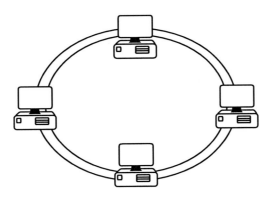

Figure 1–21: Dual ring

Mesh

When a fail-safe design is needed, the only option is a mesh topology. A mesh provides a connection to every device on the network so should a connection fail, an alternative connection exists. A mesh is commonly used on WAN connections where inter-office connectivity is vital for business continuity. Most businesses cannot function without a mesh or partial mesh for redundancy.

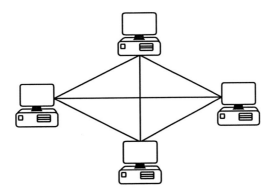

Figure 1–22: Mesh

Physical vs logical

When you can see the network equipment you are looking at the physical topology. This can be misleading because although the network appears to be wired in a star fashion it could, in fact be working logically as a ring.

A classic example is a ring network. Although the traffic circulates round the ring in a circular fashion, all of the devices plug into a hub. The ring is actually inside the token ring hub so you cannot see it from the outside.

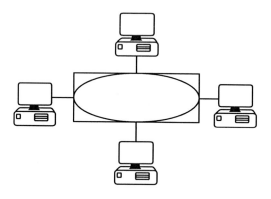

Figure 1–23: The ring is inside the hub

You may be asked to identify what type of networks the above are physically and logically. It is a good idea to remember that the physical topology is what you can see and the logical topology is what the network can see.

Table 1–4: Physical vs. logical topologies

Topology	Physical	Logical
Bus	Bus	Bus
Star	Star	Bus
Token ring	Star	Ring
Point-to-point	Bus	Bus
FDDI	Ring	Ring

ETHERNET NETWORKING

Ethernet has become the *de facto* standard in modern networking. Alternatives to Ethernet are token ring and FDDI, but these are fairly rare when compared to Ethernet.

Ethernet networking is known as a contention-access method meaning all of the hosts on the network segment are fighting to be heard. In order to control all of the traffic, a system known as carrier sense multiple access with collision detection (CSMA/CD) is employed. This ensures that when a network card (NIC) wishes to transmit data, it first listens to the wire to see if any other host is transmitting.

The very first implementation of Ethernet networking used coaxial cables which are only capable of sending or receiving a signal, but not at the same time. This was why CSMA/CD was invented.

The traditional method for Ethernet to work is to use half-duplex mode. This works in the same way as walkie-talkies, a host can only transmit or receive—it cannot do both at the same time. The reason for half duplex is that the sending device must reserve one wire to transmit and one to listen in case the frame collides with another frame. Half duplex is the method used when you have hubs on your network.

Full duplex allows the host to send and receive frames at the same time. This is achieved by giving a dedicated connection between devices on a LAN providing separate paths for the data to be transmitted on. Because a wire is not needed to listen for collisions, it is free to be used to send or receive frames.

 IN THE REAL WORLD:

A very large amount of late collisions showing on your Ethernet interface is a sure sign of duplex mismatch settings on your Ethernet ports.

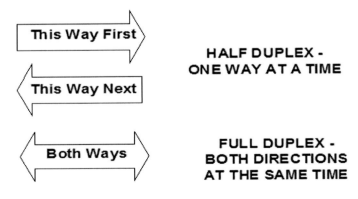

Figure 1–24: Duplex operations

In theory, a full-duplex Ethernet segment will run at twice the speed of half duplex. So, a 10 Mbps network "should" work at 20 Mbps and a 100 Mbps network at 200 Mbps. These are theoretical speeds though and are not normally possible.

Bandwidth

LANs and WANs both have something in common; they feature something known as bandwidth. Bandwidth is the measurement of how much traffic the device or network is capable of passing. The higher the bandwidth the more traffic that can be passed across the link.

Bandwidth is measured in how many units or bits per second that can flow across the link in a given amount of time, normally seconds. A bit is simply a pulse of electricity passing along a wire.

As technology advances, the amount of traffic we can pass across the link increases.

Table 1–5: Bandwidth measurements

Unit	Known as	Formula
Bits per second	bps	1 bps = single unit
Kilobits per second	kbps	1 kbps = 1000 bps or 10^3 bps
Megabits per second	Mbps	1 Mbps = 1,000,000 bps or 10^6 bps
Gigabits per second	Gbps	1 Gbps = 1,000,000,000 bps or 10^9 bps

Ethernet frames

Ethernet has four different frame types available.

1. Ethernet 802.3
2. Ethernet II
3. Ethernet 802.2 SAP
4. Ethernet 802.2 SNAP

The first two Ethernet standards deal with the framing used for communication between network cards. They cannot identify the upper-layer protocols which is where the 802.2 frames come in.

Preamble	SFD	Destination address	Source address	Length	Data	FCS

Figure 1–25: Ethernet 802.3 frame

The IEEE 802.3 Ethernet frame consists of specific fields that have been determined by the IEEE:

- Preamble—synchronizes and alerts the network card for the incoming data.
- Start-of-frame delimiter (SFD)—indicates the start of the frame.
- Destination address—the destination MAC address. Can be unicast, broadcast, or multicast.
- Source address—the MAC address of the sending host.
- Length—defines the length of the data field in the frame.
- Data—the payload in the frame. This is the data being transferred.
- Frame-check sequence (FCS)—provides a cyclic-redundancy check (CRC) on all data in the frame.

The Ethernet II frame is the same apart from the fact that length field is replaced with a type field. An Ethernet 802.2 SAP frame looks like this:

Destination SAP	Source SAP	Control	Data

Figure 1–26: Ethernet SAP frame

An Ethernet 802.2 SNAP frame looks like this:

Destination SAP AA	Source SAP AA	Control 03	OUI ID	Type	Data

Figure 1–27: Ethernet SNAP frame

The SNAP frame is easily identified by the AA in the source and destination field. Also, the control field is always 03.

The following URL contains some very useful info on Ethernet standards:
`http://www.geocities.com/SiliconValley/Vista/8672/network/index.html`.

LAN traffic

Traffic traveling within a LAN can be one of three types:

1. Unicast
2. Broadcast
3. Multicast

Unicast

Unicast traffic is a transmission from one host on the LAN to another host on the LAN.

Broadcast

Broadcast traffic is exclusive to LANs because broadcasts are not forwarded by routers. A broadcast is sent by a device on the LAN and heard by all other devices on that segment of the LAN. A LAN can be broken into segments by routers or VLANs (more on VLANs later). A broadcast frame appears as FF:FF:FF:FF:FF:FF in hexadecimal.

Multicast

Multicast traffic is transmitted from a host and sent to a specific set of hosts on the network. An example of a multicast is an OSPF TCP packet forwarded on address 224.0.0.5 (more on OSPF later).

IEEE STANDARDS

The Institute of Electrical and Electronics Engineers (IEEE) is a nonprofit group of professionals and, among other things, they are the leading authority in the field of computer engineering.

The IEEE publish standards for networking, one such standard is called the 802 project. These standards are constantly changing to keep pace with emerging technologies and developments in the industry.

The 802.3 standard deals with Ethernet networking and can be further broken down into 802.3u fast Ethernet and 802.3z gigabit Ethernet (1000BaseX) or 802.3ab gigabit Ethernet over copper wiring (1000BaseT).

 FOR THE EXAM:

Be very familiar with all of the 802 standards. You will be expected to know them.

Table 1–6: IEEE standards

Standard	Covers
802.1	Internetworking
802.2	Logical link control (LLC)
802.3	CSMA/CD
802.4	Token bus
802.5	Token ring
802.6	Metropolitan area networks (MAN)
802.7	Broadband
802.8	Fiber optics
802.9	Integrated voice and video
802.10	Security
802.11	Wireless
802.12	100BaseVG-AnyLAN

THE CISCO HIERARCHICAL NETWORKING MODEL

The Cisco approach to designing and building networks is to break networking into three distinct layers: core, distribution, and access layers. Each layer has very specific responsibilities to perform.

The core layer

Also known as the backbone of the network; this is the heart of the network and is responsible for switching huge amounts of traffic very reliably. In order to carry out this role, certain characteristics are associated with the core layer. It must offer high reliability, provide redundancy (i.e., if one part breaks another can pick up where it left off), provide fault tolerance and avoid slowing traffic down by filtering it in any way.

The distribution layer

Also known as the workgroup layer, the distribution layer allows communication between the core and access layers. Packets are manipulated at this layer. The distribution layer should perform certain services such as security, address summarization, workgroup access routing between LANs, traffic filtering, and redistribution.

The access layer

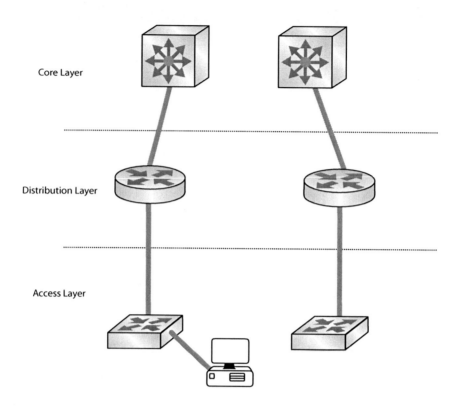

Figure 1–28: The Cisco layer model

Also known as the desktop layer, this is the point at which end users connect to the network. The access layer allows user access to local segments on the network. Functions performed here include creation of separate collision domains (segmenting the network into smaller chunks), sharing bandwidth and local policies for network traffic control.

Breaking networks down into specific layers helps us to understand how they work and also which devices should be performing which functions and features.

SELECTING CISCO PRODUCTS

Cisco is famous for being able to offer a complete networking solution from the smallest home office to the largest corporate enterprise network. Understanding the Cisco networking model will allow you to choose the correct Cisco product to match your business and IT needs.

The core hardware products offered by Cisco include hubs, switches, firewalls, wireless routers, and routers—but this list is by no means exhaustive.

Hubs

Most businesses are moving away from hubs now due to the affordability of switches. Cisco does still offer hubs that can auto sense the speed of the Ethernet device and allows several devices to access the network simultaneously.

Switches

Switches allow network devices to access the network at speeds of 10, 100, or 1000 Mbps. Lower-end switches simply allow better use of network bandwidth and allow LANs to be broken into smaller separate segments known as virtual LANs or VLANs. Higher-end switches can filter traffic; implement access lists, and perform more intelligent services.

Routers

The performance of Cisco routers is constantly changing due to customer requirements and demands of modern businesses. When deciding which product will suit your needs, you will need to analyze your current and future bandwidth needs along with what type of security features you may require. Some router models have fixed ports, and more cannot be added, whilst others are modular and you can swap the modules whenever your needs change.

www.cisco.com contains several tools to help you select the right tool for your needs.

 INSPIRATION:

Learning all of the fundamentals will give you a great head start in the world of networking. Learn the basics or you may become lost later on.

CABLING THE NETWORK

PCs, hubs, switches, routers, and all other types of networking equipment use different connector types. There are many reasons for this but the main two are that LAN and WAN connections send data in different formats, requiring the use of different cables. Also, as speeds have improved, certain cable types and network interfaces have become obsolete and been replaced by newer more efficiently designed components.

LAN cabling

LANs use several types of cable including coaxial and fiber optic however the industry standard is referred to as unshielded twisted pair or UTP (unshielded twisted pair) cable. UTP cable is rated into different categories or CAT in order to determine what speed the cable is capable of passing data across.

A UTP Ethernet connection consists of the UTP cable, an attachment for the end of the cable known as an RJ-45 male connector, and an RJ-45 female connector on the device the cable connects to.

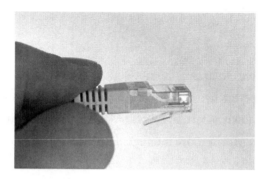

Figure 1–29: RJ-45 connector

Inside the cable are eight smaller wires that are color coded so they can be identified. You should not be expected to remember which color is associated with which pin (this could change), but you will be expected to know what you can do with these wires to make different types of UTP cable. Each standard or category is rated for a different purpose. In table 1-7 we list the IEEE speeds for the various cable specifications.

Table 1–7: Cat 1 to 7 capabilities

Category of cable	Transmission speed
Cat 1	Voice only (telephone cable)
Cat 2	4 Mbps
Cat 3	10 Mbps
Cat 4	16 Mbps
Cat 5	100 Mbps
Cat 5e	Gigabit Ethernet
Cat 6	155 Mbps
Cat 7	Up to 1 Gbps

IEEE and cabling standards

LAN cabling is a fairly detailed subject and for historical reasons there are many cable types. Each cable type has certain limitations and can only be used on certain topologies.

802.3 Ethernet

Standard Ethernet works at 10 Mbps; the IEEE 802.3 standard refers to this. Ethernet can be either a star or bus topology. The cabling used can be coaxial, Cat 3, or higher using twisted pair. Twisted pair cable is referred to as XBaseT, where X refers to the speed at which the media operates.

- **10BaseT**—10 Mbps twisted pair. Can be up to 100 meters long between segments.
- **10Base2**—10 Mbps coaxial cable. Can be up to 185 meters long between segments.
- **10Base5**—10 Mbps coaxial cable. Can be up to 500 meters long between segments.

802.3u fast Ethernet

This is the standard used by most modern networks. Fast Ethernet is a vast improvement on standard Ethernet. It uses a star topology and either Cat 5 twisted-pair or fiber-optic cable.

100BaseT—100 Mbps twisted pair. Can be up to 100 meters long between segments.

802.3z (or 802.3ab) Gigabit Ethernet

Gigabit Ethernet is an improvement upon fast Ethernet. It uses a star topology with twisted-pair (802.3ab/1000BaseT) and fiber-optic/shielded copper (802.3z /1000BaseX).

1000BaseT—1000 Mbps twisted pair or fiber. Can be 100 meters between segments.

 IN THE REAL WORLD:

Knowing the basics is essential for exam success and for success as a Cisco engineer. If you are new to networking you may want to invest in a good quality Network+ book which really covers all the basics in great detail.

Table 1–8: Ethernet cable specifications

Cable	Bandwidth (Mbps)	Max distance (meters)	Cable construction
10Base2	10	185	Thinnet coaxial
10Base5	10	500	Thicknet coaxial
10BaseT	10	100	UTP
100BaseT	100	100	UTP / fiber
1000BaseT	1000	100	UTP
1000BaseX	1000	varies	Fiber / shielded copper

Straight-through cable

When the color of each wire matches on both sides of the cable, then it is known as a straight-through cable. The diagrams below do not reflect accurate CAT-5 cable wire colors. They serve as an illustration of how the wires are changed for each cable type.

The colors indicated on the diagram below are (in order from pin 1 to pin 8): red, yellow, blue, green, cyan, purple, maroon, and lilac.

So you can see that the red wire on each side is found at pin 1, and the same goes for the other cables. This type of cable is used for connecting equipment to the network, such as a PC to a hub or switch.

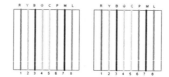

Figure 1–30: Straight-through cable

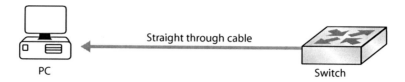

Figure 1–31: Straight-through cable from a PC to a switch

If we take the cable from pin 1 and put it to pin 3 at the other end and then pin 2 to pin 6, we will have made another type of cable known as a crossover cable.

Crossover cable

The main use of a crossover cable is to connect two PCs together without having to buy a hub or switch. However, other types of networking device can be connected using a crossover cable. You will need to remember these for the CCNA exam. The easy way to remember is that like to like device uses a crossover cable.

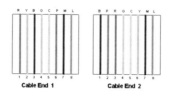

Figure 1–32: Crossover cable

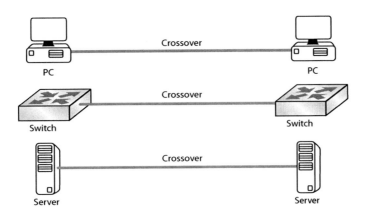

Figure 1–33: Crossover cable in use

Rollover cable

The last type of cable using UTP is a rollover, flat, or console cable. These are only used to connect to a special port on networking equipment known as the console port. You would connect to the console port to configure the networking equipment when you first install it or if there is a fault on the equipment and you cannot reach it over the network.

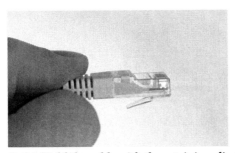

Figure 1–34: Hold the cable with the retaining clip facing down.

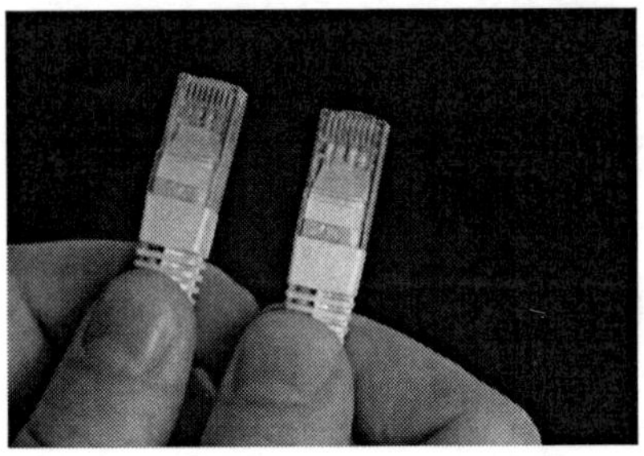

Figure 1–35: You can compare the colors of the wires.

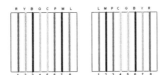

Figure 1–36: Rollover cable

On a rollover cable, pin 1 on one side goes to pin 8 on the other. Pin 2 goes to pin 7 and so on. As you hold the ends of the cables together with the retaining clips facing towards the floor, you can see that each wire is reversed.

Table 1–9: Which cable to use?

	PC/Server	Hub	Switch	Router
PC/Server	Crossover	Straight	Straight	Crossover
Hub	Straight	Crossover	Crossover	Straight
Switch	Straight	Crossover	Crossover	Straight
Router	Crossover	Straight	Straight	Crossover

Figure 1–37: Typical rollover cable

 IN THE REAL WORLD:

Always hold the RJ-45 connector with the retainer clip facing down towards the floor. You can then count the wires from 1–8 left to right.

WAN cabling

Cabling the wide area network is a lot more complicated than LAN cabling. There are many types of WAN service available, such as ISDN, Frame Relay, ATM, ADSL, and many others. Each type of service can have different connector types associated with it.

Most Cisco products use a 60-pin D-shaped connector for a WAN connection. The connector on the other side of the cable can vary, depending upon who is providing you with the WAN connection and what type of service you have asked for.

Figure 1–38: Cisco WAN DB-60 cable

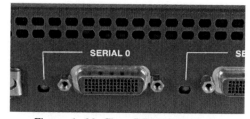

Figure 1–39: Cisco DB-60 WAN port

NETWORK DIAGRAM

When engineers draw diagrams of networks, they tend to use standard symbols so that when they speak to another engineer they know they are referring to the same thing.

Switches are normally used for LAN connectivity. There are switches that can perform some layer-three functions and some that can have routers slotted inside them, but they are outside the boundaries of the CCNA syllabus.

When connecting over a WAN, most companies have the choice of going out via the Internet by using broadband or a modem, for example. There are several security issues associated with this. You can connect to a telecommunications company (Telco), such as BT or AT&T, and they will allow you to use their bandwidth for a price.

Lastly, you can pay for a dedicated point-to-point connection that only your company has access to. These tend to be expensive, but you do not, however, have to share bandwidth with any other company. We discuss WAN connection types in Module 8.

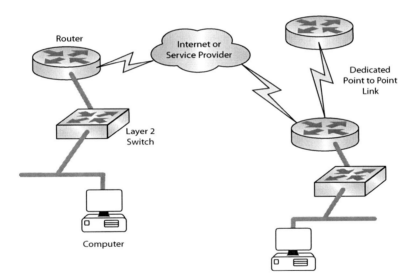

Figure 1–40: Simple network diagram

SUMMARY QUESTIONS

NOTE: The answers to the summary questions for the modules are located in Appendix B.

1. What type of address is burned onto a network card?
2. What common services are found at the application layer
3. What function does the network layer perform?
4. What are the steps of data encapsulation?
5. What are the three Cisco network design layers?
6. When would you use a crossover cable?
7. Describe the pin-out settings for a crossover cable
8. IEEE 802.3ab refers to which Ethernet standard?
9. TCP sits at which layer of the OSI model?
10. JPEGs sit at which layer of the OSI model?

CHAPTER 2

Module 2—Connecting and Configuring Cisco Devices

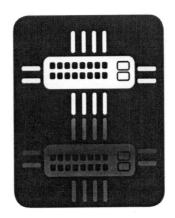

What you will learn in this module	Timings
Router interfaces and connectors	Theory: 80 minutes
Understanding router architecture	Review: 10 minutes
Router boot up sequence	
How to connect to a router	
Router modes	
Configuring a router	
Understand the config-register	

ROUTER INTERFACES AND CONNECTORS

There are many varieties of connectors that can be used with computers and networks. Cisco devices use different types of connectors depending upon which interface you want to use and which device you want to connect to the router. We are going to look at the most commonly used connector and interface types.

Ethernet

Also known as RJ-45 or registered jack, these connectors look similar to the type of cable associated with telephone connectors; however, there is a small plastic tab on the bottom to prevent it being pulled out of the interface. There is a connector used in the UK to plug into a phone socket; this is known as an RJ-11 connector. The RJ-45 connector has eight pins, while the RJ-11 only has four. RJ-45 connectors are used for LAN connectivity, console connections, and aux connections. Modern category 5e cable is used allowing speeds of around 1 Gbps to be achieved over LANs.

Figure 2–1: AUI interface

Figure 2–2: Ethernet AUI transceiver

Each pin in a UTP cable serves a specific purpose. Depending upon which way the pins inside the connector are arranged, you can use the UTP cable to connect different types of network device. There are older-style Ethernet connectors still used on some networking equipment (Figure 2–1). These use DB-15-type connectors and are called attachment unit interfaces or AUIs. If you have one of these, you can buy a a device called a transceiver (fig 2-2) that will convert the DB-15 presentation to an RJ-45 presentation. There are also connectors called BNCs, which are now almost obsolete.

Aux connectors

Short for auxiliary, the aux port on a router is used to dial in from a remote location. Rather than drive to the router location, a network administrator can connect remotely using a modem and configure the router. Aux ports use an RJ-45 connector. They can also be used for dial backup to the router via a modem.

Console connectors

When a router is first used, the only way to configure it is to connect to the console port using a rollover cable. It will also be used if there is ever a problem with the router and it cannot be reached over the network. The only way to perform any sort of disaster recovery is to connect to it via the console port.

The rollover cable connects directly into the console port; the other end of the cable connects to your COM port on your PC or laptop. If the presentation of your cable end is RJ-45, you will need an adapter to allow it to interface with your nine-pin COM port (see Figure 2–8 on page 46). See the " Connecting to a router " section later in this module for more information.

WAN connectors

There are many varieties of WAN connectors. Selecting the correct cable(s) for the type of service you are using can sometimes prove to be a challenge. All WAN cables use serial (one bit at a time) transmission, as opposed to parallel transmission (8 bits at a time). Average WAN speeds range from 56 kbps to around 2 Mbps, but far greater speeds are available.

Figure 2–3: Rear view Cisco 2509 model router.

From left to right: asynch port, DB-15 AUI interface, two DB-60 WAN interfaces, console port, Aux port, on / off switch, and power socket.

ROUTER ARCHITECTURE

Router memory

Cisco routers ship with several different types of memory. Each memory module performs a specific function, and you will be expected to know which does what for the exam.

ROM

Read only memory is used to store a tiny operating system called the bootstrap. This helps the router boot up and then pulls the main operating system or IOS into memory from the flash. ROM chips cannot usually be upgraded without being physically replaced.

DRAM

Dynamic RAM is used by a router to store the running configuration. The running configuration or config comprises the commands and instructions the router is currently using. Any changes you make to the routers configuration are automatically stored in DRAM. They will all be lost when the router is powered down which makes this type of memory volatile. In order to save the instructions, you have to tell the router to save the running config into NVRAM and rename it to startup-config. We will cover this in more detail later.

DRAM also is used as a buffer to temporarily store packets and routing tables. The main IOS is also loaded into DRAM while the router is running. You can see how the split is made when you issue the "show version" command, and see your DRAM is divided into two numbers. For example, my router (below) has 16 MB DRAM split into 14 MB and 2 MB. (14 MB is for the IOS, running configuration, and routing tables, and 2 MB for buffering packets that cannot be processed yet.)

This 75% / 25% split is normal in most models of the Cisco router and can be changed with the "memory size" command. This change is not recommended unless under the direction of a Cisco TAC.

When you issue a "show version" command on a router, you can see the DRAM memory split:

```
14336 KB / 2048 KB of memory
```

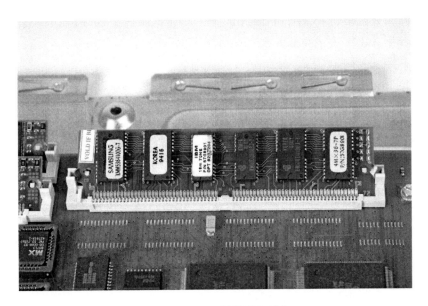

Figure 2–4: 16 MB DRAM

EEPROM or flash memory

Flash is used by the router to store the main operating system or IOS. Flash memory is normally in the form of SIMM chips on the motherboard. Flash memory can also be added to the router in the form of PCMCIA cards on some router models.

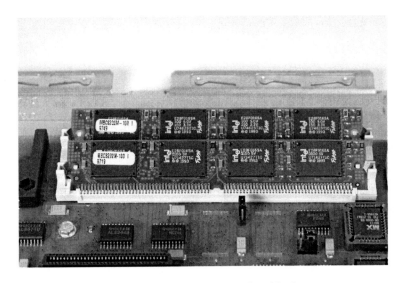

Figure 2–5: Two 8 MB sticks of flash

When the router boots, the IOS is decompressed out of flash memory and loaded into DRAM. An example of a flash image stored on the router is:

System image file is "`flash:c2500-is-l_122-4_T1.bin`".

C2500 refers to the model of router, in this case the 25xx series "i" refers to the fact it can run IP (internet protocol), and "s-1" refers to the features it can run. 122-4_T1 is the release version.

You can view the internetwork operating system (IOS) on a router with the "show flash" or the "show version" command, although this may differ depending upon your router model.

```
RouterA#show flash
System flash directory:
File  Length   Name/status
  1   14692012  c2500-js-1.121-17.bin
[14692076 bytes used, 2085140 available, 16777216 total]
16384K bytes of processor board System flash (Read ONLY)
```

You can delete the files on the flash with the "delete flash:filesystem" command.

```
RouterA#delete flash:c2500-js-1.121-17.bin
```

If you accidentally delete a flash file system, you can recover it with the "undelete" command. The specific steps depend upon the type of file system you have on your router.

 FOR THE EXAM:

You may be expected to know the IOS naming conventions for the CCNA exam.

NVRAM

Non-volatile RAM or NVRAM is used by the router to store the routers startup configuration. Imagine having to reconfigure the router every time you want to reload it. Because NVRAM is non-volatile, it will not lose information when power is removed. The startup config is transferred to DRAM every time you reload the router and named running config.

You can compress it with the "service compress-config" command, if you have a very large configuration file in NVRAM. It will, however, take longer for the image to decompress into DRAM.

```
Router(config)#service compress-config
```

 INSPIRATION:

Knowing which router config file belongs with which memory can save you a lot of time in the long run.

Table 2–1: Router memory and configuration file location

Memory	Usage
ROM	Bootstrap IOS
DRAM	Running config/routing tables/buffers
EEPROM/flash	IOS storage
NVRAM	Startup config

CPU

This is where all of the processing takes place on the router. Cisco CPUs are generally not upgradeable.

We can easily see the CPU type and how much memory we have on our router by typing the command "show version" at the router prompt. Some of the output below has been truncated.

```
Router#show version
Cisco Internetwork Operating System Software
IOS (tm) 2500 Software (C2500-IS-L), Version 12.2(4)T1, RELEASE SOFTWARE
Copyright (c) 1986-2001 by cisco Systems, Inc.
ROM: System Bootstrap, Version 11.0(10c), SOFTWARE ⇦ ROM code
BOOTLDR: 3000 Bootstrap Software (IGS-BOOT-R), Version 11.0(10c)
System image file is "flash:c2500-is-l_122-4_T1.bin" ⇦ Flash image
cisco 2522 (68030) processor ⇦ CPU
with 14336K/2048K bytes of memory. ⇦ DRAM
Processor board ID 18086064, with hardware revision 00000003
32K bytes of non-volatile configuration memory. ⇦ NVRAM
16384K bytes of processor System flash (Read ONLY) ⇦ EEPROM/FLASH
```

ROUTER BOOT-UP SEQUENCE

When you turn on the power switch for the router a series of steps occurs before you can start using the router. The router first performs a power on self-test or POST. This is a check of the router hardware to confirm that the devices interfaces and internal components are working correctly. The bootstrap is loaded and then the IOS is loaded from flash and placed into DRAM.

The router looks for a startup-configuration file in NVRAM. If it is there it loads this configuration that will consist of interface IP addresses and other parameters. If there is no startup-configuration file then the router will boot into setup mode (more on setup mode shortly).

CONNECTING TO A ROUTER

When you buy a router it normally comes with no configuration on it whatsoever. The network administrator must configure the router from scratch according to the particular requirements of his or her network.

To connect to a router console port a rollover cable is needed, one end (RJ-45 connector) is connected to the console port of the router and the other to the COM port on a PC or laptop using an RJ-45 to DB-9 converter. This is needed because normally PCs do not come with RJ-45 serial ports.

Please also note that with Windows Vista hyperterminal has been discontinued and with Internet Explorer version 6.0 telnet is disabled, by default. You can learn how to fix these issues on http://racks.howtonetwork.net.

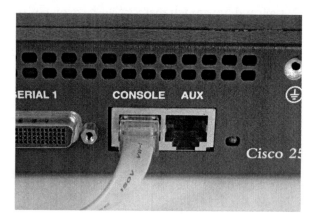

Figure 2–6: Connect one end to the router's console port.

Cisco does provide a preassembled cable with an RJ-45 at one end and a DB-9 on the other with all new routers (see fig 2-10).

Figure 2–7: RJ-45 to DB-9 adapter

Figure 2–8: Connect the console cable to the adapter.

Figure 2–9: The adapter connects to the PC's COM port.

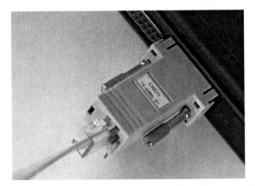

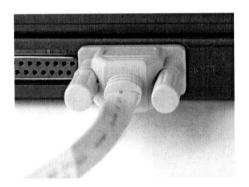

Figure 2–10: Connect the adapter or the fixed end (depending on your cable type).

To see free videos about how to connect to the router, please visit my YouTube link at: http://www.youtube.com/user/paulwbrowning.

Once the connection is made the PC has to be configured to communicate with the router. The most common method is to use the hyper terminal facility. This is available with all versions of Windows except Vista or Windows 7 and can be found via the Accessories menu on Windows. If it is not there, you may have to install it from the original CD ROM.

Figure 2–11: Start Programs > Accessories > Communications > HyperTerminal

Give your new connection a name.

Figure 2–12: Name your connection.

In the Connect using drop-down menu, click on the down arrow and choose whichever COM port you have plugged the DB-9 adapter into. You may have to try a few different COM ports to find the one logically connected to the router.

Figure 2–13: Choose the COM port.

The default properties have to be changed to:

- Bits per second: 9600
- Data bits: 8 is the default
- Parity: None is the default
- Stop bits: 1 is the default
- Flow control: must be None

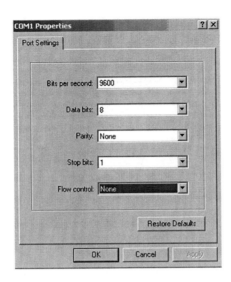

Figure 2–14: HyperTerminal settings

Turn on the router: It should then boot, and if all of the console settings have been configured correctly, you should (after a few seconds) see the boot-up text appear on the screen.

```
System Bootstrap, Version 11.0(10c), SOFTWARE
Copyright (c) 1986-1996 by cisco Systems
2500 processor with 14336 Kbytes of main memory
```

You will also see "Connected" on the bottom lower left hand corner of the HyperTerminal window. If it does not, wait a while longer (up to two minutes), press the Enter key a few times and then double-check your connection settings. If it still does not work, try different COM ports. After you try a different COM port, press the Enter key several times.

 IN THE REAL WORLD:

It is crucial that you know how to connect to a router using hyperterminal and which settings you need. You do not want to have to look in a book when your client is standing over your shoulder. Also, make sure you save your hyperterminal settings for future use.

When the router first begins to boot, it runs a diagnostic test known as power-on self-test (or POST). If no problems are found, the router will then look for its operating system, which is stored in flash memory also known as electrically erasable programmable read-only memory (EEPROM).

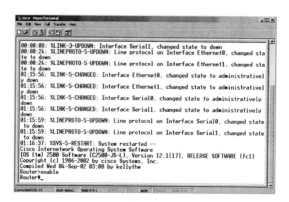

Figure 2–15: You can see the router boot-up text in the HyperTerminal window.

```
Cisco Internetwork Operating System Software
IOS (tm) 2500 Software (C2500-IS-L), Version 12.2(4)T1,  RELEASE SOFTWARE
(fc1)
TAC Support: http://www.cisco.com/tac
Copyright (c) 1986-2001 by Cisco Systems, Inc.
Compiled Thu 25-Oct-01 16:33 by ccai
Image text-base: 0x0306740C, data-base: 0x00001000
```

I highly recommend you use the free Putty utility for all your telnet and console connections. Putty has more features than HyperTerminal and needs no Registry changes to work with Windows Vista (or Internet Explorer 7 or later, which disables telnet by default and has no HyperTerminal facility). You can download Putty at: http://www.putty.org.

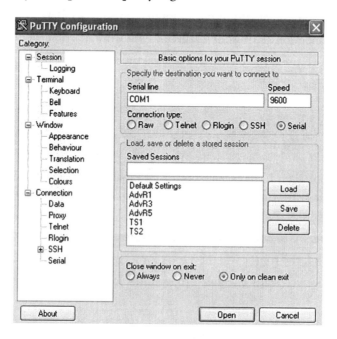

Figure 2–16: Use Putty for your console connection.

Once the operating system is pulled from EEPROM into RAM, the router then looks into non-volatile RAM or NVRAM to see if a previous configuration is present. If there is no configuration there, the router will then boot into set-up mode. Set-up mode allows you to answer various questions posed by the operating system in order to set the router up for use. You will never use set-up mode as a CCNA.

 IN THE REAL WORLD:

Avoid set-up mode. You could spend an hour answering all of the questions asked and still not have the router working the way you want.

When the router boots, you will be presented with a command-line interface (CLI). Everything you do with a router will be carried out at a CLI of some sort. If when you are first asked if you want to enter set-up mode, you enter the word "no" or the letter 'n', you will be presented with a command prompt, and be expected to configure the router yourself. To escape set-up mode, hold down both the Control (Ctrl) and C keys simultaneously.

```
Would you like to enter the initial configuration dialog? [yes/no]:
% Please answer 'yes' or 'no'.
Would you like to enter the initial configuration dialog? [yes/no]: n

Press RETURN to get started!
Router>
```

USB connection

Many laptops are now being built without a COM port. It is still possible to make a console connection to the router using a special type of USB cable which connects to a console cable. The USB cable ends in a 9-pin connector and should come with driver software to allow it to be accessed via the Device Manager.

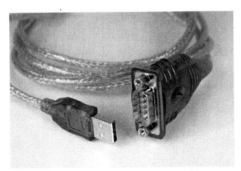

Figure 2–17: USB to DB-9 cable

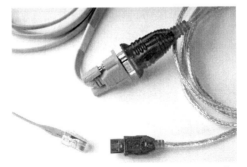

Figure 2–18: The USB cable connects to the rollover cable.

After the software is installed, you should go to Device Manager on your PC and check which COM port the USB cable has been allocated. You can then go into hyperterminal or putty and choose that COM port.

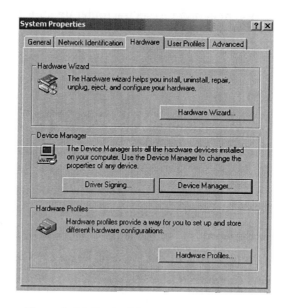

Figure 2–19: Device Manager (Windows 2000)

 IN THE REAL WORLD:

Router commands are not case sensitive, but stick to lowercase. If you are entering a password, then the characters ARE case sensitive.

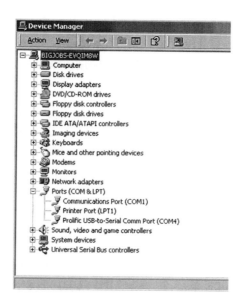

Figure 2–20: The USB cable has been allocated to COM4

FOR THE EXAM:

In the CCNA exam, you will be expected to be able to configure a "virtual" router so make sure you are comfortable with doing this. The virtual router experience is different to the real thing. You can try out the Cisco version of a virtual router at www.cisco.com/go/ccna.

ROUTER MODES

In order to pass the CCNA exam, you will need to understand which prompt you should be at to configure various router parameters. Whatever function you wish to perform, you will have to be in the correct mode. This is the biggest mistake people make when they are having problems configuring the router and cannot find the right command to use. Make sure you are in the correct mode.

User mode

The first mode you will be presented with is known as user mode or user exec mode. It has a very limited set of commands you can use with it but can be useful for looking at basic router elements. The default name of the router is "Router" but this can be changed as we will see later.

```
Router>
```

Privileged mode

Typing "enable" at the user prompt takes us into the next mode known as privileged or privileged exec mode. To get back to user mode you simply type "disable" or to quit out of the session altogether type "logout" or "exit".

```
Router>enable
Router#
Router#disable
Router>
```

Privileged mode is very useful for looking at the entire configuration of the router and statistics about how it is performing and even which modules you have connected to the router.

Global config mode

In order to actually configure anything on the router, you have to be in global configuration mode. To get to global config mode, you simply type "configure terminal" or "config t" for short at the privileged exec prompt. Alternatively, just type "config" and the router will ask you which mode you would like to enter. The default is terminal (the default options will show inside the brackets [ ]). If you press Enter, the command inside the brackets will be accepted.

```
Router#config
Configuring from terminal, memory, or network[terminal]? ⇦ Press "Enter"
Enter configuration commands, one per line. End with CNTL/Z.
Router(config)#
```

Interface configuration mode

This allows you to enter commands for individual router interfaces such as FastEthernet, Serial, etc. On a new router, all of the interfaces will be shut down by default and have no configuration present.

```
Router>enable
Router#config t
Enter configuration commands, one per line. End with CNTL/Z.
Router(config)#interface serial 0
Router(config-if)#
```

 INSPIRATION:

It is okay to read through this the first time, but it will make far more sense if you try all of the commands out on a real router.

Line configuration mode

Line configuration mode is used to make any changes to the console, telnet, or aux ports. You can control who can access the router via these ports as well as put passwords or a security feature called access lists on them.

```
Router#config t
Enter configuration commands, one per line. End with CNTL/Z.
Router(config)#line console 0
Router(config-line)#
```

You can also configure baud rates, exec levels, and a lot more in line configuration mode.

Router configuration mode

In order to configure a routing protocol onto the router so it can dynamically build up a picture of the network, you will need to be in router configuration mode.

```
Router#config t
Enter configuration commands, one per line. End with CNTL/Z.
Router(config)#router rip
Router(config-router)#
```

IN THE REAL WORLD:

Almost every command can be truncated to make life easier for you. It will also save a lot of time when you are doing router configurations at work or whilst consulting if you know the shortcuts. You can also use the tab key to finish off your commands.

 FOR THE EXAM:

You will be configuring a "virtual" router that may not recognize a lot of shortened commands. Make sure you use the full commands for the exam.

CONFIGURING A ROUTER

There are no menus available on a router, and you cannot use a mouse to navigate between the different modes. It is all done via the command line interface or CLI. There is, however, some help in the form of a "?". If you type a question mark at the router prompt, you will be presented with a list of all the available commands.

```
Router#?
Exec commands:
  access-enable      Create a temporary Access-List entry
  access-profile     Apply user-profile to interface
  access-template    Create a temporary Access-List entry
  alps               ALPS exec commands
  archive            manage archive files
  bfe                For manual emergency modes setting
  cd                 Change current directory
  clear              Reset functions
  clock              Manage the system clock
  cns                CNS subsystem
  configure          Enter configuration mode
  connect            Open a terminal connection
  copy               Copy from one file to another
  debug              Debugging functions (see also 'undebug')
  delete             Delete a file
  dir                List files on a
  disable            Turn off privileged commands
  disconnect         Disconnect an existing network connection
  enable             Turn on privileged commands
  erase              Erase a
  exit               Exit from the EXEC
  help               Description of the interactive help system
  -- More --
```

If there is too much information to display on the screen, you will see the `-- More --` tab. If you want to see the next page, press the space bar. If not, hold down the CTRL+Z keys (the Control (Ctrl) and the Z key together) or press the letter 'Q' to get back to the router prompt.

Also, if you have started to type a command but forget what else you need to type in, using the question mark will give a list of options available.

```
Router#cl?
clear clock
```

If you begin to type out a command, so long as there is only one possible word or command available with that syntax, you can press the TAB key to have it completed for you.

```
Router#copy ru ⇦ press the TAB key here
Router#copy running-config
```

FOR THE EXAM:

The "?" option may not be there for the virtual router in the exam. You must know the commands. Cisco is testing you for a certain amount of knowledge and want to ensure you know enough to be able to apply your knowledge for real.

The router has several modes to choose from. This is to make sure you do not make changes to parts of the router you do not want to. You can recognize which mode you are in by looking at the command prompt. For example, if we wanted to make some changes to one of the FastEthernet interfaces, we would need to be in interface-configuration mode.

```
Router#config t
Router(config)#
```

We then tell the router which interface we want to configure:

```
Router(config)#interface fastethernet 0
Router(config-if)#exit
Router(config)#
```

If you are not sure which way to enter the interface number, then use the "?". Do not worry about all of the choices you will be given. Most people only ever use the FastEthernet, serial, ISDN BRI, or loopback interfaces.

```
Router(config)#interface ?
  Async              Async interface
```

```
BRI                    ISDN Basic Rate Interface
BVI                    Bridge-Group Virtual Interface
CTunnel                CTunnel interface
Dialer                 Dialer interface
FastEthernet           IEEE 802.3u
Group-Async            Async Group interface
Lex                    Lex interface
Loopback               Loopback interface
Multilink              Multilink-group interface
Null                   Null interface
Serial                 Serial
Tunnel                 Tunnel interface
Vif                    PGM Multicast Host interface
Virtual-Template       Virtual Template interface
Virtual-TokenRing      Virtual TokenRing
range                  interface range command

Router(config)#interface fastethernet ?
  <0-0>  FastEthernet interface number

Router(config)#interface fastethernet 0
```

And the router drops into interface configuration mode:

```
Router(config-if)#
```

From here we can put an IP address on the interface, set the bandwidth, apply an access list, and a lot of other things.

If we ever need to exit out of configuration mode, we can simply type "exit". This takes us back to the next highest level. To quit out of any sort of configuration mode, simply press Ctrl+Z (hold down the Control and the Z keys) together.

```
Router(config-if)#exit
Router(config)#
```

Or using Ctrl+Z:

```
Router(config-if)# ^z
Router#
```

Loopback interfaces

Loopback interfaces are not normally covered in the CCNA syllabus but they are very useful in the real world and for practice labs. A loopback interface is a virtual or logical interface that you configure, but it does not physically exist. The router will let you ping this interface though which will save you having to connect the FastEthernet interfaces on the routers to try the labs.

An advantage of using loopback interfaces is that they always remain UP UP (physically up and logically up) if the router is working because they are logical; they can never go down. You cannot put a network cable into the loopback interface because it is a virtual interface.

```
RouterA#config t
RouterA#(config)#interface loopback 0
RouterA#(config-if)#ip address 192.168.20.1 255.255.255.0
RouterA#(config-if)#^z ⇦ press Ctrl+Z
Router#
Router#show ip interface brief
Interface      IP-Address     OK? Method Status     Protocol
Loopback0      192.168.20.1   YES manual up         up
```

Your output for this command will show all of the available interfaces on your router.

IN THE REAL WORLD:

If you need to, you can shut down a loopback interface with the "shutdown" command in interface configuration mode.

Loopback interfaces have to be given a valid IP address. You can then use them for routing protocols or testing that your router is permitting certain traffic. We will be using them a lot throughout the course.

Editing commands

It is possible to navigate your way around a line you have typed rather than deleting the whole line. Certain keystrokes will move the cursor to various places around the line.

Table 2–2: Keyboard shortcuts

Keystroke	Meaning
Ctrl+A	Moves to the beginning of the command line
Ctrl+E	Moves to the end of the line
Ctrl+B	Moves back one character
Ctrl+F	Moves forward one character
Esc+F	Moves forward one word
Esc+B	Moves back one word
Ctrl+P or up arrow	Recalls the previous command
Ctrl+N or down arrow	Recalls the next command

Ctrl+U	Deletes a line
Ctrl+W	Deletes a word
Tab	Finishes typing a command for you
Show history	Shows the last 10 commands entered by default
Backspace	Deletes a single character

Putting an IP address on an interface

In order for a router to communicate with other devices it will need to have an address on the connected interface. Putting an IP address on an interface is very straightforward although you have to remember to go into interface configuration mode first.

 IN THE REAL WORLD:

If you want to connect to another network, you have to have an IP address. It is like having no postal or zip code. We will look more at IP addressing later.

Do not worry about where we get the IP address from at the moment; we will look at this later on.

```
Router>enable ⇦ takes you from user to privileged mode
Router#config t ⇦ from privileged to config mode
Router(config)#interface serial 0 ⇦ and then into interface config mode
Router(config-if)#ip address 192.168.1.1 255.255.255.0
Router(config-if)#no shutdown ⇦ the interface is opened for traffic
Router(config-if)#exit ⇦ you could also hold down Ctrl and Z keys to exit
Router(config)#exit
Router#

A description can also be added to the interface.

RouterA(config)#interface serial 0
RouterA(config-if)#description To_Headquarters
RouterA(config-if)#^Z ⇦ press Ctrl+Z to exit
RouterA#show interface serial 0
Serial0 is up, line protocol is up
  Hardware is HD64570
  Description: To_Headquarters
  Internet address is 12.0.0.2/24
  MTU 1500 bytes, BW 1544 Kbit, DLY 20000 usec,
     reliability 255/255, txload 1/255, rxload 1/255
  Encapsulation HDLC, loopback not set
  Keepalive set (10 sec)
  Last input 00:00:02, output 00:00:03, output hang never
```

(Output restricted...)

Show commands

You can look at most of the settings on the router by simply using the "show X" command from privileged mode with x being the next command:

```
Router#show ?
  access-expression  List access expression
  access-lists       List access lists
  accounting         Accounting data for active sessions
  adjacency          Adjacent nodes
  aliases            Display alias commands
  alps               Alps information
  apollo             Apollo network information
  appletalk          AppleTalk information
  arap               Show AppleTalk Remote Access statistics
  arp                ARP table
  async               Information on terminal lines used as router interfaces
  backup             Backup status
  bridge             Bridge Forwarding/Filtering Database [verbose]
  bsc                BSC interface information
  bstun              BSTUN interface information
  buffers            Buffer pool statistics
  cca                CCA information
  cdapi              CDAPI information
  cdp                CDP information
  cef                Cisco Express Forwarding
  class-map          Show QoS Class Map
  clns               CLNS network information
--More—
```

Some of the more common show commands and their meanings are below:

Table 2–3: Common show commands

Show command	Result
show running-configuration	Shows configuration in DRAM
show startup-configuration	Shows configuration in NVRAM
show flash:	Shows which IOS is in flash
show ip interface brief	Shows brief summary of all interfaces
show interface serial 0	Shows serial interface statistics
show history	Shows last 10 commands entered

Examples

```
Router#show ip interface brief
Interface  Address    OK? Method  Status       Protocol
Ethernet0  10.0.0.1   YES manual  up           up
```

```
Ethernet1   unassigned    YES unset   administratively down down

Loopback0   172.16.1.1    YES manual  up                      up

Serial0     192.168.1.1   YES manual  down                    down

Serial1     unassigned    YES unset   administratively down down
```

The "method" tag indicates how the address has been assigned. It can state unset, manual, NVRAM, IPCP, or DHCP.

Routers can recall commands previously entered at the router prompt—the default is ten. The commands can be recalled by using the up arrow. Using this feature can save a lot of time and effort re-entering a long line. The "show history" command shows the buffer of the last ten commands.

```
Router#show history
  show ip interface brief
  show history
  show version
  show flash:
  conf t
  show access-lists
  show process cpu
  show buffers
  show logging
  show memory
You can increase the history buffer with the "terminal history size"
command.
Router#terminal history ?
  size  Set history buffer size
  <cr>

Router#terminal history size ?
  <0-256>  Size of history buffer

Router#terminal history size 20
```

 IN THE REAL WORLD:

The show commands are very powerful and an essential part of your troubleshooting tool bag. Ninety percent of all troubleshooting can be done without ever looking at the running configuration of the router. Learn the show commands.

Backing up files

Router configurations can be moved around the router or stored on a PC or server on the network. The running configuration on the router is stored in DRAM, any changes to the configuration will remain in DRAM and be lost if the router is reloaded for any reason.

If you need the existing configuration file to be loaded when the router next reloads then you need to copy the running configuration file to NVRAM with the "copy running-config startup-config".

We can save the running config into NVRAM so the router remembers it when we reboot:

```
Router(config)#copy running-config startup-config
```

We can copy the startup config into DRAM:

```
Router(config)#copy startup-config running-config ⇐ or copy start run
```

We can even copy the configuration onto a PC or server running TFTP server software (see the TFTP lab for more details):

```
Router(config)#copy startup-config tftp: ⇐ You need to include the colon
```

We can also copy our IOS to a TFTP server:

```
Router(config)#copy flash tftp:
```

There are some legacy commands left in the Cisco IOS code for backing up files (such as "write mem"), but you should stick to the new commands. A good reason for disregarding the older commands is that they may not be accepted by the router simulation software in the exam.

- "write memory" is now "copy running-config startup-config".
- "write terminal" is now "show running-config".
- "write erase" is now "erase nvram:" (or "erase startup-config").
- "show config" is now "show startup-config".
- "write network" is now "copy running-config tftp:".
- "config memory" is now "copy startup-config running-config".
- "config network" is now "copy tftp running-config".
- "config overwrite" is now "copy tftp startup-config".

 IN THE REAL WORLD:

Backing up your files and configurations is absolutely vital. Many companies have gone out of business because they did not bother to back up their startup configurations. By the time they get back on line they may have lost a huge sum of money. Do not ever let this happen to you or your client.

Booting options

There are several options available when the router boots. Usually there is one IOS image in flash memory so the router will boot using that. You may have more than one image or the image may be too big for the flash to hold so you prefer the router to boot from a TFTP server on the network which holds the IOS.

The commands differ slightly depending upon which boot options you want to configure. Try all of the options on a live router.

```
RouterA(config)#boot system ?

 WORD   TFTP filename or URL
 flash  Boot from flash memory
 ftp    Boot from a server via ftp
 mop    Boot from a Decnet MOP server
 rcp    Boot from a server via rcp
 tftp   Boot from a tftp server
```

For flash:

```
RouterB(config)#boot system flash ?
 WORD  System image filename
 <cr>
```

For TFTP:

```
Enter configuration commands, one per line.  End with CNTL/Z.
RouterB(config)#boot system tftp c2500-js-1.121-17.bin ?
  Hostname or A.B.C.D  Address from which to download the file
  <cr>

RouterB(config)#boot system tftp c2500-js-1.121-17.bin
```

Pipes

The command line interface for configuring Cisco devices using Cisco IOS has some features used by the Unix command line. A pipe (shown as '|' on the keyboard) can be used on the Cisco command line to give you some granularity when searching for certain commands or entries in the routers config.

 IN THE REAL WORLD:

Using pipes can save you time and effort, and possessing this knowledge will show you in a more professional light.

You can use several commands with pipes such as:

```
show {command} {begin | include | exclude} {regular expression}
```

Example

```
RouterA#show run ?
  interface  Show interface configuration
  |          Output modifiers
  <cr>

RouterA#show run | ?
  begin    Begin with the line that matches
  exclude  Exclude lines that match
  include  Include lines that match

RouterA#show run | include ?
  LINE  Regular Expression

RouterA#show run | include login
aaa authentication login default group tacacs+ line
 timeout login response 120
 timeout login response 120

RouterA#show run | begin interface
interface Ethernet0
 no ip address
 shutdown
!
interface Serial0
 no ip address
 shutdown
!
interface Serial1
 no ip address
 shutdown
!
ip classless
no ip http server
!
line con 0
line aux 0
line vty 0 4
!
end
```

 IN THE REAL WORLD:

When you want to find information on the Cisco website, use the Google search engine and put the word "cisco" in the search term, e.g., "cisco password recovery". Using Google will save a lot of time because it is easier to use than the search facility on Cisco's website.

THE CONFIG-REGISTER

How does the router know where to find the configuration file from when it boots up? The router checks the config-register field upon booting to determine which booting option to use. You can see which option has been set when you issue the "show version" command.

```
RouterA#show version
Cisco Internetwork Operating System Software
IOS (tm) 2500 Software (C2500-JS-L), Version 12.1(17), RELEASE SOFTWARE (fc1)
Copyright (c) 1986-2002 by cisco Systems, Inc.
Compiled Wed 04-Sep-02 03:08 by kellythw
Image text-base: 0x03073F40, data-base: 0x00001000

ROM: System Bootstrap, Version 11.0(10c)XB2, PLATFORM SPECIFIC RELEASE
SOFTWARE (fc1)
BOOTLDR: 3000 Bootstrap Software (IGS-BOOT-R), Version 11.0(10c)XB2, PLATFORM
SPECIFIC RELEASE SOFTWARE (fc1)

RouterA uptime is 46 minutes
System returned to ROM by power-on
System image file is "flash:c2500-js-l.121-17.bin"

cisco 2500 (68030) processor (revision L) with 14336K/2048K bytes of memory.
Processor board ID 01760497, with hardware revision 00000000
Bridging software.
X.25 software, Version 3.0.0.
SuperLAT software (copyright 1990 by Meridian Technology Corp).
TN3270 Emulation software.
2 Ethernet/IEEE 802.3 interface(s)
2 Serial network interface(s)
32K bytes of non-volatile configuration memory.
16384K bytes of processor board System flash (Read ONLY)

Configuration register is 0x2142.
```

When we are using routers for practicing labs, we do not want the configuration changes we make to stay there every time we boot up the routers. In order to be able to pass the practical tests in the lab you must practice over and over again. If we change the config-register setting we can prevent the router from looking at the startup configuration file when it boots. This will boot the router with no configuration file, i.e., a blank config to begin working on.

Having the router config-register set to 0x2102 tells it to look at the startup config file when it boots and pulls it into NVRAM. Changing it to 0x2142 tells the router to ignore it so it will boot with a blank config. This setting has to be entered if you ever forget the router password because the password sits in the startup config. The router will boot without any of the configuration including any passwords.

See the labs in Part II for information on how to do this. Part II contains specialized lab exercises, starting with Module 2.

Now go through the labs for Module 2. Feel free to watch the accompanying videos for the labs on: www.howtonetwork.net.

SUMMARY QUESTIONS

1. Which command takes you from user mode to privileged mode?
2. Which command shows you how much memory your router has installed?
3. Which command shows you a summary of your interfaces?
4. What are the hyper terminal settings to connect to the router?
5. How can you see which commands you recently entered?
6. COM 1 HyperTerminal connection will not work. What do you try next?
7. Which command copies the config from DRAM to NVRAM?
8. What check does the router perform on boot up?
9. EEPROM is also known as what?
10. Which protocol can copy the routers configuration onto a server?

RESOURCES

You can find more information at:

http://www.howtonetwork.net/public/1047.cfm

CHAPTER 3

Module 3—LAN Switching

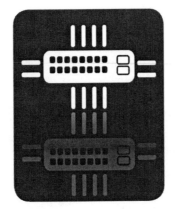

What you will learn in this module	Timings
Learn layer 2 switching functions	Theory: 60 minutes
How port security works	Practical: 60 minutes
How spanning tree protocol works	Review: 10 minutes
Understand switching methods	
Rapid Spanning Tree (RSTP+)	
Configuring the switch	
Learn the purpose of VLANs	
Configuring VLANs	
The frame tagging process	
Importance of trunking	
Inter-VLAN routing	
VLAN trunking protocol (VTP)	
Troubleshooting VLANs and trunks	
Configuring a 2950 switch	

LEARN LAYER 2 SWITCHING FUNCTIONS

Do you remember from Module 1 that switches operate at layer 2 of the OSI? Switches can only look at the MAC address of traffic and forward or block it based upon this address. Historically, because switches don't have to waste time examining layer 3 (IP) addresses they were considerably faster than routers. Now, due to advances in switching and routing technology, forwarding planes are of comparable speed.

LAN switching is usually referred to as layer 2 switching because more advanced switching methods have now been invented that can actually operate at layer 3 and above. These types of switches are not included in the CCNA syllabus yet, but do check before you book the exam.

Figure 3–1: Cisco Catalyst 2950 switch range

The most notable difference between a switch and a bridge is the commercial implementation. Switches are used for separating the LAN into smaller segments (micro-segmentation). In practice, they are more intelligent and can be used for services such as VLAN trunking protocol (VTP), virtual LANs (VLANs), and quality of service (QOS). Another notable difference is that a bridge uses software to store the CAM table whereas switch uses Application Specific Integrated Circuits (ASICs) to do this.

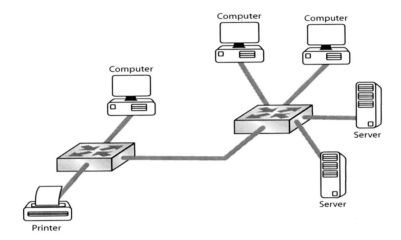

Figure 3–2: A simple switched network

Switches perform three main functions:

1. Learning MAC addresses
2. Filtering and forwarding frames
3. Preventing loops on the network

Learning MAC addresses

When a switch is first powered up it is not aware of the location of any of the hosts on the network. In a very short time, as hosts transmit data to other hosts, it learns the MAC address and remembers which hosts are connected to which port. If an address is not currently in the switches database it will send a broadcast message out of each port except the port that the request was received on.

Then when the switch receives a reply it will add the address and source port to its database. It can take only a matter of minutes to build this database, Cisco refers to this as the CAM (Content addressable memory) table.

The switch will store a table of MAC addresses for a limited amount of time. If no traffic is heard from that port for a predefined period of time then the entry is purged from memory. This is to free up memory space on the switch and also prevent entries from becoming out of date and inaccurate.

This time is known as the MAC address aging time. On the Cisco 2950 this time is 300 seconds by default and can be configured to be between 10 and 1,000,000 seconds. The switch can also be configured so as to not purge the addresses ever.

A hub will never remember which hosts are connected to which ports, and will always flood traffic out of each and every port. A hub is actually a layer 1 (OSI) device. This is where switches differ from hubs.

The command to see the CAM table of a switch is "`show mac-address-table`". Here is an example of the CAM table of a switch:

Table 3–1: Switch1#show mac-address-table

Vlan	MAC Address	Type	Ports
1	0014.a93f.838d	DYNAMIC	Fa0/16
1	0014.a93f.838e	DYNAMIC	Fa0/17
1	0014.a93f.838f	DYNAMIC	Fa0/18

Note that the switch stores the MAC address and the port where the host is connected. Do not worry about the VLAN column at the moment, as we will cover this later in the module. If you want to view only the dynamic MAC addresses that the switch has discovered, use the "`show mac-address-table dynamic`" command. Dynamic means that the address was discovered by the switch.

Filtering and forwarding frames

Whenever a frame arrives at a switch port the switch examines its database of MAC addresses. If the destination address is in the database, the frame will only be sent out of the interface the destination host is attached to. This process is known as frame filtering. If the address is not known, then the switch has no option but to flood the frame out all ports other than the one on which it arrived.

 IN THE REAL WORLD:

Broadcasts can also be caused by faulty network cards that can send out considerable amounts of traffic until the source can be found. Tracing the source of broadcast storms usually requires the use of a network sniffer.

Preventing loops on the network

Having multiple paths to destinations can be very useful in a network. If one path breaks, the traffic can take an alternative route. However, for switches this feature can often cause a lot of problems on the network. If a broadcast is sent out of one link, it will be flooded out of all links and could bring the network to a grinding halt due to congestion. This situation is known as a broadcast storm.

The least desired effect of a broadcast storm is when a switch sends out an incorrect broadcast frame. As a consequence, it also receives multiple replies from different hosts with incorrect answers and the broadcast process grows as further broadcasts are sent out. This will quickly cause the network to slow and produce lots of errors and time-outs. The switch prevents this using the Spanning Tree Protocol. We will look at this in depth shortly.

PORT SECURITY

Typically, the switch will learn the MAC address of the device directly connected to a particular port and allow traffic through. The CCNA syllabus now wants us to ask the question: "How do we control who and how many can connect to a switch port?" This is where port security can assist us. Cisco switches allow us to control which devices can connect to a switch port or how many of them can connect to it (such as when a hub or another switch is connected to the port).

Enabling port security

Port security is disabled by default. Before configuring the port security, we have to enable it. It can be enabled using the "switchport port-security" command. Here's how to do it:

```
Switch#config terminal
Switch(config)#interface fa0/1
Switch(config-if)#switchport port-security
```

 IN THE REAL WORLD:

As soon as port security is enabled, it will apply the default values which is one host permitted to connect at a time. If this rule is violated the port will shutdown.

Using the switchport's port security feature, we can specify:

- Who can connect to the switchport
- How many devices can connect to the switchport
- Violation action

Who can connect?

If you know that only a particular host should be connecting to a switchport, then you can restrict access on that port to the MAC address of that host. This will ensure that no one can unplug the authorized host and connect another one. This is a good option for secure locations. This is done using the following command:

```
switchport port-security mac-address <address>
```

Example: If we want only the host with MAC address 0001.14ac.3298 to connect to port fa0/1 on our switch, then the commands required will be:

```
Switch#config terminal
Switch(config)#interface fa0/1
Switch(config-if)#switchport port-security
Switch(config-if)#switchport port-security mac-address 0001.14ac.3298
```

 IN THE REAL WORLD:

This command will not add the MAC address to the CAM table. When a host connects to this port and sends the first packet, the source address of the packet is checked against the configured MAC address. If a match is found that the address is added to the CAM table. The address would be purged in the configured aging time if no traffic is seen for that host.

So, do we have to provide each host's MAC address manually? That's a huge task considering thousands of hosts that a network can have! Well, not really. Port security provides something called a sticky address. The switch will use the MAC address of the first host connected to the port as a static MAC address and only that host will be able to connect to the port subsequently. The command required is :

```
switchport port-security mac-address sticky
```

How many can connect?

Let's say we have only one switchport left free and we need to connect five hosts to it. What can we do? Connect a hub or switch to the free port!

Connecting a switch or a hub to a port has implications. It means that the network will have more traffic. If a switch or a hub is connected by a user instead of an administrator, then there are chances that loops will be created. So, it is best that number of hosts allowed to connect is restricted at the switch level. This can be done using the "switchport port-security maximum" command. This command configures the maximum number of MAC addresses that can source traffic through a port. Consider the following examples:

Examples

```
Switch(config-if)#switchport port-security maximum 1
Switch(config-if)#switchport port-security mac-address sticky
```

Allow only one host to connect to the port. Learn the MAC address of the allowed host automatically.

```
Switch(config-if)#switchport port-security maximum 3
Switch(config-if)#switchport port-security mac-address 001a.14e9.8a7d
```

Allow three hosts to connect at the same time out of which one MAC address is static and the other two can vary.

```
Switch(config-if)#switchport port-security maximum 5
```

Allow a maximum of five hosts to connect simultaneously. Hosts can vary.

Violation action

What happens if a violation of security occurs on a switchport? What if five hosts are allowed on a port, but six connect to it? The switch can take one of the three configured actions:

- Shut down the port.
- Keep the port up, but do not allow the offending host to send / receive data (protect).
- Keep the port up, but do not allow the offending host to send / receive data and notify the administrator through SNMP and/or syslog (restrict).

The three modes can be configured using the following command:

```
switchport port-security violation shutdown|protect|restrict
```

Let's verify our port security configuration using the "show port-security interface" command:

```
Switch# show port-security interface fastethernet0/1
Port Security              :Enabled
Port status               :SecureUp
Violation mode            :Shutdown
Maximum MAC Addresses     :5
Total MAC Addresses       :5
Configured MAC Addresses  :3
Aging time                :20 mins
Aging type                :Inactivity
SecureStatic address aging :Enabled
Security Violation count  :0
```

The above out shows that Fa0/1 has been configured with three static MAC Addresses and will allow a maximum of five hosts to connect to it. If a violation is detected, then the port (by default) will go into error-disabled mode and shut the port (switch interface) down. You can see this happening on the below switch where an unauthorized MAC address comes into the `fast Ethernet 0/2` port.

```
Switch#
00:55:59: %PM-4-ERR_DISABLE: psecure-violation error detected on Fa0/2,
putting Fa0/2 in err-disable state
Switch#
00:55:59: %PORT_SECURITY-2-PSECURE_VIOLATION: Security violation occurred,
caused by MAC address 1234.5678.489d on port FastEthernet0/2.
Switch#
00:56:00: %LINEPROTO-5-UPDOWN: Line protocol on Interface FastEthernet0/2,
changed state to down
00:56:01: %LINK-3-UPDOWN: Interface FastEthernet0/2, changed state to down
```

Another important command is "`show port-security`" command. This command provides an overview of all the ports which have port security configured:

```
Switch#show port-security
Secure Port  MaxSecureAddr  CurrentAddr  SecurityViolation  Security Action
             (Count)        (Count)      (Count)

Fa0/1        8              7            0                  Shutdown
Fa0/2        15             5            0                  Restrict
Fa0/3        5              4            0                  Protect
```

This brings us to the end of port security. For the CCNA exam, please ensure you know how to configure it, the extensions you can add to the "`switchport port-security mac-address`" command, and the show commands. The only way to do this properly is to configure them on a switch. You will learn far more about switch security when you follow the lab in the labs section and watch the videos on `www.howtonetwork.net`.

SPANNING TREE PROTOCOL (STP)

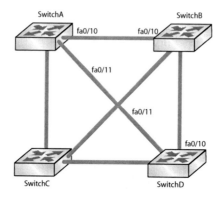

Figure 3–3: Full-mesh layer 2 network

Figure 3–3 shows a full-mesh network. A good redundant setup where, if one link fails, there would be two more links for traffic to go through. However, could this lead to any problems? Let's say a host is connected to port fa0/1 on SwitchA (not shown) and this switch sends a broadcast out to the network advertising this MAC. SwitchA has to forward this frame out every port except fa0/1. A part of what happens next is shown below:

1. SwitchB receives the packet on fa0/10 and sends it out on every port except that one.
2. SwitchD receives the packet on fa0/10 and sends it out on every port except that one but including fa0/11.
3. SwitchA receives the packet on fa0/11 and sends it out on every port except fa0/11 but including fa0/1 and fa0/10!

What we see here is that not only the original source received the frame back, but now SwitchA has to send the packet back out fa0/10 also. Back to the step one to three, which goes on forever.

What we have just seen is a loop. Such loops can bring a network to a grinding halt. Layer 2 LAN protocols have no method to stop traffic endlessly travelling around possibly carrying inaccurate information. At layer 3, we can make packets expire after a certain amount of time or after they have traveled a certain distance (using route poisoning for example—see the routing module for more info).

As layer 2 networks grew, it quickly became evident that a system to prevent loops was needed if LANs were to continue to function. Digital Equipment Corporation created a protocol called Spanning Tree Protocol (STP) to prevent broadcast storms and network loops at layer 2. STP is now regulated by the IEEE under standard 802.1d.

STP allows bridges and switches to communicate with each other so they can create a loop free topology. Each bridge runs the Spanning Tree Algorithm which calculates how the loop (as seen in the example above) can be prevented. When STP is applied to a looped LAN topology, all VLANs will be reachable but any open ports which would create a traffic loop are blocked. When it sees a loop in the network it blocks one or more redundant paths preventing a loop from forming. STP continually monitors the network always looking for failures on switch ports or changes in the network topology. If a change on the LAN is detected, STP can quickly make redundant ports available and close other ports to ensure the network continues to function normally.

Before we learn more about STP, we need to understand some of the common terms associated with it. To see some of the actual values on a switch, you would issue the "show spanning-tree vlan (vlan#)" command, which we will come to shortly.

Bridge ID: This is a unique identification number of each switch in the network. It consists of bridge priority and the base MAC address of the switch.

 IN THE REAL WORLD:

The default bridge priority of a Cisco switch is 32768. This is a configurable value between 0 to 61440, but the value has to be in increments of 4096. 4096, 8192, 12288, so on and so forth are acceptable values. Priority plays a very big role in STP and how well the network will function.

Root bridge: All switches in the network elect the root of the tree. Thereon all decision such as which redundant path to block and which to open, are taken from the perspective of the root switch. The election is won by the switch with the lowest Bridge ID. Switches which do not become root bridge are called non-root bridges.

BPDU: Bridge Protocol Data Unit (BPDU) is the information exchanged between switches to select root bridge as well as configure the network after that. A decision on which port to block is taken after examining BPDUs from the neighbors. Cisco switches send BPDUs every 2 seconds by default. This value can be configured from 1 second to 10 seconds.

Root port: Each switch has to have a path to the root bridge, if not directly connected. Root port is the directly connected link or the fastest path to the root bridge from a non-root bridge.

Port cost: Each port has a cost which is determined by the bandwidth of the link. Port cost determines which of the redundant links will not be blocked. The lower the cost, the better it is. Port cost also determines which port will become the root port if multiple paths to the root bridge exist. Default port costs are shown below.

Table 3–2: STP cost

Link speed	STP cost
4 Mbps	250
10 Mbps	100
16 Mbps	62
100 Mbps	19
1 Gbps	4
10 Gbps	2

Designated port: The bridges on a network segment collectively determine which bridge has the least-cost path from the network segment to the root. The port connecting this bridge to the network segment is then the designated port for the segment. Ports which are not selected designated port are called non-designated ports.

Port states in Spanning Tree

Switch ports running STP can be in one of five states. Please ensure you understand all of these for your CCNA exam:

1. Blocked
2. Listening
3. Learning
4. Forwarding
5. Disabled

1st State—Blocked

None of the ports will transmit or receive any data, but they will listen to BPDUs. The BPDU carries various pieces of information that are used by STP to determine what state the ports should be in, and what the STP topology should be.

2nd State—Listening

The switch listens for frames but does not learn or act on them. The switch does receive the frames but discards them before any action is taken. MAC addresses are not placed into the CAM table while the port is listening.

3rd State—Learning

The switch will start to learn MAC addresses it can see and will populate its CAM table with the addresses and the ports on which they were found. In this state, the switch will start to transmit its own BPDUs.

4th State—Forwarding

The switch has learned MAC addresses and corresponding ports and populates its CAM table with this. The switch can now forward traffic.

5th State—Disabled

In disabled state, the port will receive BPDUs but will not forward them to the switch processor. It discards all incoming frames from both the port and other forwarding ports on the switch.

The port states are transitional and allow other BPDUs to arrive in good time from other switches. Port transition times are typically:

- initialization to blocking
- blocking to listening (20 secs)
- listening to learning (15 secs)
- learning to forwarding (15 secs)
- forwarding to disabled (if there is a failure)

 IN THE REAL WORLD:

All ports start at blocking stage (except few exceptions discussed later). After STP convergence some ports will transition to listening, learning and finally forwarding and rest would remain in blocked state. Keeping this and the time, needed to transition from one stage to another, in mind we find that a layer 2 network running STP takes 50 seconds to start switching data!

STP convergence

Remember that Spanning tree works by selecting a root bridge on the LAN. It is selected by comparing Bridge ID of each switch.

STP can be considered to be converged after three steps have taken place:

1. Elect one root bridge
2. Elect root ports
3. Elect designated ports

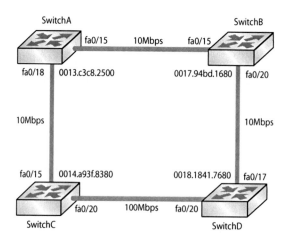

Figure 3–4: STP convergence

We will use the network shown in Figure 3–4 to go through the STP convergence process.

Elect one root bridge

The bridge with the lowest Bridge ID (BID) becomes the root bridge. The BID consists of two values in an 8-byte field. The bridge priority (32768 by default) which is two bytes and the MAC address of the backplane or supervisor module (depending upon the model of switch) which is six bytes. Many modern switches use an extended BID. When the extended BID is enabled, the root bridge priority becomes a multiple of 4096 plus the VLAN ID (see the below switch output).

The root bridge on a LAN is selected by an election. Each switch running STP passes information in a format known as bridge protocol data units (BPDUs). BPDUs are multicast* frames which can be thought of as hello messages between STP enabled switches, they are sent out every two seconds from every port. This is necessary to maintain a loop free topology. When the switch or bridge priorities combined with its MAC address are all exchanged the bridge with the lowest ID is selected as the root bridge.

*Multicast frames are similar to broadcast frames. They are sent from one host to many hosts, the difference is the destination address is received by a specific group of devices. This is better that a broadcast as not every device on the network needs to acknowledge the frame and cuts down on network consumption.

All ports on the root bridge are set as designated and so always set to forwarding state.

In our network, the priority of all the switches has been left at default. So the switch with the lowest MAC address will be selected the root bridge. In this case it will be SwitchA. To verify this, we issue the "show spanning tree vlan (vlan#)" command on SwitchA :

```
SwitchA#show spanning-tree vlan 5

VLAN0005
  Spanning tree enabled protocol ieee
  Root ID    Priority    32773 ⇦ 32768 plus 5 (the VLAN ID)
             Address     0013.c3e8.2500
             This bridge is the root
             Hello Time   2 sec  Max Age 20 sec  Forward Delay 15 sec

  Bridge ID  Priority    32773  (priority 32768 sys-id-ext 5)
             Address     0013.c3e8.2500
             Hello Time   2 sec  Max Age 20 sec  Forward Delay 15 sec
             Aging Time 300

Interface          Role Sts Cost      Prio.Nbr Type
------------------ ---- --- --------- -------- ------------------------
Fa0/15             Desg FWD 19        128.15   P2p
Fa0/18             Desg FWD 19        128.18   P2p
```

Note: Do not worry about the number 5 in vlan 5 right now. We will get to it shortly.

Now, if we want SwitchC to be the root bridge then we will need to give it better priority than 32773 using the following command:

```
Switch(config)#spanning-tree vlan 5 priority 8192
```

Let's check the "show spanning-tree" output now on SwitchC and SwitchA. The VLAN number is added to the priority in the output:

```
SwitchC#show spanning-tree vlan 5
VLAN0005
  Spanning tree enabled protocol ieee
  Root ID    Priority    8197
             Address     0014.a93f.8380
             This bridge is the root
             Hello Time   2 sec  Max Age 20 sec  Forward Delay 15 sec

  Bridge ID  Priority    8197   (priority 8192 sys-id-ext 5)
             Address     0014.a93f.8380
             Hello Time   2 sec  Max Age 20 sec  Forward Delay 15 sec
             Aging Time 300

SwitchA#show spanning-tree vlan 5

VLAN0005
  Spanning tree enabled protocol ieee
  Root ID    Priority    8197
             Address     0014.a93f.8380
             Cost        19
             Port        18 (FastEthernet0/18)
             Hello Time   2 sec  Max Age 20 sec  Forward Delay 15 sec

  Bridge ID  Priority    32773  (priority 32768 sys-id-ext 5)
             Address     0013.c3e8.2500
             Hello Time   2 sec  Max Age 20 sec  Forward Delay 15 sec
             Aging Time 300
```

 IN THE EXAM:

Please learn and use the "Switch#show spanning-tree vlan #" command because a good working knowledge of spanning tree is now required.

Please also learn the "Switch#show mac-address-table dynamic" command, which may be important for the exam.

Note that SwitchA now shows SwitchC's MAC address as the root bridge's MAC address and SwitchC says that it is the root bridge.

In case you are wondering why SwitchC's priority is 8197 instead of 8192, we will come to this point shortly.

Now, please set the priority on SwitchC back to 32768 and make SwitchA the root bridge for the next section.

Elect root ports

For non-root bridges, there will be only one root port. The root port will be the port with the lowest path cost to the root bridge. The root port will also be set to forwarding state.

Path cost is the cost of transmitting a frame to the root bridge, the value is set according to the bandwidth of the link on the LAN, the slower the link then the higher the cost is.

In our network, SwitchB and SwitchC's fa0/15 ports will be the root ports. Switch D has two options — fa0/17 towards SwitchB and fa0/20 towards SwitchC. The total cost of the link on fa0/17 is 200 (10 Mbps = 100). The total cost of the link on fa0/20 is 119 (10 Mbps = 100 and 100 Mbps = 19). So, fa0/20 will be the root port for SwitchD and fa0/17 will be blocked. For default costs, see Table 3–2 on page 75.

Let's verify SwitchD's root port using the "show spanning-tree" command:

```
SwitchD#show spanning-tree vlan 5

VLAN0005
  Spanning tree enabled protocol ieee
  Root ID    Priority     32773
             Address      0013.c3e8.2500
             Cost         119
             Port         20 (FastEhternet0/20)
             Hello Time   2 sec  Max Age 20 sec  Forward Delay 15 sec

  Bridge ID  Priority     32773  (priority 32768 sys-id-ext 5)
             Address      0018.1841.7680
             Hello Time   2 sec  Max Age 20 sec  Forward Delay 15 sec
             Aging Time 300

Interface          Role Sts Cost      Prio.Nbr Type
------------------ ---- --- --------- -------- ------------------------
fa0/17             Altn BLK 200       128.17   P2p
fa0/20             Root FWD 119       128.20   P2p
```

If we want to make fa0/17 on SwitchD as a root port instead of fa0/20, then we will need to change the cost on fa0/17 to something better (less) than 119. To do this, the "spanning-tree cost" command can be used on fa0/17. Look at the following output:

```
SwitchD(config)#int fa0/17
SwitchD(config-if)#spanning-tree cost 1
SwitchD(config-if)#do show spanning-tree vlan 5 ⇦ the "do" entry lets you
                                issue a show command while in config mode
--output truncated--

Interface           Role Sts Cost       Prio.Nbr Type
------------------- ---- --- ---------- -------- -------
fa0/17              Root LIS 1          128.17   P2p
fa0/20              Altn BLK 119        128.20   P2p
```

We see that fa0/17 becomes the root port with a Cost of 1 (as specified in the command) and fa0/20 goes into a blocking state.

Elect designated ports

If a switch has redundant ports connecting it to a LAN segment (another downstream switch or hub for example), then the port with the lowest cost will be elected the designated port. Designated ports forward BPDUs into the LAN segment and traffic to and from the LAN segment. In simple terms, the designated port becomes the only link for the LAN segment towards the rest of the network and the root bridge.

In our example, the fa0/20 port on SwitchC will be the designated port for the link to SwitchD. If there were multiple links, then an election would have taken place. Let's verify this on SwitchC:

```
SwitchC#show spanning-tree vlan 5

VLAN0005
  Spanning tree enabled protocol ieee
  Root ID    Priority    32773
             Address     0013.c3e8.2500
             Cost        19
             Port        15 (Fasthernet0/15)
             Hello Time   2 sec  Max Age 20 sec  Forward Delay 15 sec

  Bridge ID  Priority    32773  (priority 32768 sys-id-ext 5)
             Address     0014.a93f.8380
             Hello Time   2 sec  Max Age 20 sec  Forward Delay 15 sec
             Aging Time 300

Interface           Role Sts Cost       Prio.Nbr Type
------------------- ---- --- ---------- -------- --------------------------
fa0/15              Root FWD 100         128.15   P2p
fa0/20              Desg FWD 19          128.20   P2p
```

INSPIRATION:

It is very important to understand STP, so please revisit this section often and try out all of the commands on a live switch (not simulators).

Cisco's changes to STP

STP, as we know it, keeps the network loop free but at what cost? The exact cost to you and I is 50 seconds! That is a long, long time in networking terms. For almost a minute, data cannot flow across the network. In most cases this is a critical issue, especially for important network services. To deal with this issue (before the industry standard was ratified) Cisco added the following features to STP implementation on its switches:

- PortFast
- UplinkFast
- BackboneFast

PortFast

If you have a laptop or a server connected to a switchport, then you know that:

- It will not need to listen to BPDUs because it is not a layer 2 device
- It will not create loops because it has a single link to the layer 2 network

Therefore, you can safely disable Spanning Tree on such ports. It is very important to ensure that such ports never have a STP-enabled layer 2 device connected on them (Think port security!) or else a loop or a breakdown of the network is quite possible. You will even get a warning message on certain switches stating this when you enable PortFast on a switchport!

When you configure a switchport as PortFast, STP will be disabled on that port and it will transition to forwarding state when it comes up and will never be blocked.

The command to configure PortFast is "spanning-tree portfast":

```
SwitchA(config)#int fastethernet0/44
SwitchA(config-if)#spanning-tree portfast
%Warning: PortFast should only be enabled on ports connected to a single
host. Connecting hubs, concentrators, switches, bridges, etc... to this
interface when PortFast is enabled can cause temporary bridging loops.
Use with CAUTION
%PortFast has been configured on FastEthernet0/44 but will only  take effect
when the interface is in a nontrunking mode.
```

PortFast security

As we learned, PortFast disables STP on a switchport, but an important fact is that a PortFast switchport will keep listening for BDPUs. If someone adds a switch to a port that has been configured as PortFast, the consequences will be unpredictable and is in some cases disasterous.

To guard against this situation, Cisco provides the BPDU Guard and BPDU Filter features.

BPDU Guard

If a switch is plugged into a switchport configured as PortFast, it could change the STP topology without the administrator knowing and could even bring down the network. To prevent this, BPDU Guard can be configured on the switchport. With this configured, if BPDU is received on a switchport, it will be put into an error-disabled mode, and an administrator will have to bring the port up. This can be configured on the port using the "`spanning-tree bpduguard enable`" command.

BPDU Filter

When BPDU Filter is configured on a switchport that has been configured as PortFast, it will cause the port to lose the PortFast status if a BPDU is received on it. This will force the port to participate in STP convergence. This is unlike the behavior seen with BPDU Guard where the port is put into an error-disabled mode. BPDU Filter can be enabled on the switchport using the "`spanning-tree bpdufilter enable`" command.

UplinkFast

Let's consider the network shown in Figure 3–5:

Figure 3–5: Redundant links to root bridge

Switch A is the root bridge here. Now consider the following output from SwitchB:

```
SwitchB#show spanning-tree vlan 5

VLAN0005
  Spanning tree enabled protocol ieee
  Root ID    Priority    32773
             Address     0013.c3e8.2500
             Cost        19
             Port        14 (FastEthernet0/14)
             Hello Time   2 sec  Max Age 20 sec  Forward Delay 15 sec
```

```
  Bridge ID  Priority    32773  (priority 32768 sys-id-ext 5)
             Address     0017.94bd.1680
             Hello Time   2 sec  Max Age 20 sec  Forward Delay 15 sec
             Aging Time 300

Interface           Role Sts Cost      Prio.Nbr Type
------------------- ---- --- --------- -------- --------------------------
Fa0/14              Root FWD 19        128.14   P2p
Fa0/15              Altn BLK 19        128.15   P2p

SwitchB#show spanning-tree uplinkfast
UplinkFast is disabled
```

We will use the following debug commands on the switch:

```
SwitchB#debug spanning-tree event
Spanning Tree event debugging is on
SwitchB#debug spanning-tree uplinkfast
Spanning Tree uplinkfast debugging is on
```

These debugs will show us STP events and uplink fast messages. Now, let's shut down port `fa0/14` on SwitchB, which is currently the root port as per output given above.

```
SwitchB(config-if)#shutdown
*Mar  2 22:14:30.504: STP: VLAN0005 new root port Fa0/15, cost 19
*Mar  2 22:14:30.504: STP: VLAN0005 Fa0/15 -> listening
*Mar  2 22:14:30.504: STP: UFAST: removing prev root port Fa0/14 VLAN0005
port-id 800E
*Mar  2 22:14:32.420: %LINK-5-CHANGED: Interface FastEthernet0/14, changed
state to administratively down
*Mar  2 22:14:32.504: STP: VLAN0005 sent Topology Change Notice on Fa0/15
*Mar  2 22:14:33.420: %LINEPROTO-5-UPDOWN: Line protocol on Interface
FastEthernet0/14, changed state to down
*Mar  2 22:14:45.504: STP: VLAN0005 Fa0/15 -> learning
*Mar  2 22:15:00.504: STP: VLAN0005 Fa0/15 -> forwarding
```

Note the time taken for `fa0/15` to transition to forwarding state is 30 seconds. This is faster than the expected 50 seconds because listening and learning time were short in this P2P link between switches and no other hosts / switches are connected here.

Let's enable UplinkFast on SwitchB and repeat the process:

```
SwitchB(config)#spanning-tree uplinkfast
SwitchB#show spanning-tree vlan 5

--output truncated--
```

```
Uplinkfast enabled

Interface          Role Sts Cost      Prio.Nbr Type
------------------ ---- --- --------- -------- ----------------------------
Fa0/14             Root FWD 3019      128.14   P2p
Fa0/15             Altn BLK 3019      128.15   P2p

SwitchB(config)#int fa0/14
SwitchB(config-if)#shutdown
*Mar  2 22:28:23.300: STP: VLAN0005 new root port Fa0/15, cost 3019
*Mar  2 22:28:23.300: STP FAST: UPLINKFAST: make_forwarding on VLAN0005
FastEthernet0/15 root port id new: 128.15 prev: 128.14

*Mar  2 22:28:23.300: %SPANTREE_FAST-7-PORT_FWD_UPLINK: VLAN0005
FastEthernet0/15 moved to Forwarding (UplinkFast).
*Mar  2 22:28:23.300: STP: UFAST: removing prev root port Fa0/14 VLAN0005
port-id 800E
*Mar  2 22:28:25.216: %LINK-5-CHANGED: Interface FastEthernet0/14, changed
state to administratively down
*Mar  2 22:28:25.300: STP: VLAN0005 sent Topology Change Notice on Fa0/15
*Mar  2 22:28:26.216: %LINEPROTO-5-UPDOWN: Line protocol on Interface
FastEthernet0/14, changed state to down
SwitchB(config-if)#do show spanning-tree vlan 5
-- output truncated--
  Uplinkfast enabled

Interface          Role Sts Cost      Prio.Nbr Type
------------------ ---- --- --------- -------- ---------------------------
Fa0/15             Root FWD 3019      128.15   P2p
```

Note the time taken for fa0/15 to transition to forwarding is less than a second! From 30 seconds downtime to less than a second with UplinkFast enabled. Now that you have seen the difference it makes, let's define what exactly it does.

If a switch has multiple links towards the root bridge, then UplinkFast marks the redundant link as an alternate port and brings it up quickly in case the Root Port fails. This is possible because blocked ports keep listening for BDPUs.

Cisco recommends caution when using UplinkFast. You should enable it on switches which have blocked ports.

BackboneFast

UplinkFast works by finding alternate ports for directly connected links. Similarly BackboneFast works on finding an alternate path when an indirect link to the root port goes down.

Let's consider the network given in Figure 3–6.

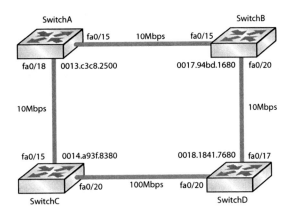

Figure 3–6: Redundant path to root bridge

SwitchA is the root bridge here. `fa0/20` on SwitchD in the root port.

Let us assume the link between SwitchA and SwitchC goes down. SwitchC will advertise itself as the root bridge to SwitchD. This BPDU is known as an inferior BPDU. SwitchB discards this new information since it knows that SwitchA is the root bridge and SwitchC is a designated switch. Eventually, SwitchC will receive a BPDU from SwitchD and mark `fa0/20` as its root port towards SwitchA. BackboneFast ensures a quick failover as soon as the inferior BPDU is received. It saves roughly 20 seconds out of the 50 seconds of convergence time.

RAPID SPANNING TREE PROTOCOL

The features discussed in the previous section—PortFast, UplinkFast, and BackboneFast were added by Cisco, and because of this they worked only on Cisco switches. IEEE added these features in a new STP protocol called Rapid Spanning Tree Protocol (RSTP) under the 802.1w standard.

> **NOTE:** People using a home lab and want to configure RSTP will need a 2950T Catalyst switch as a minimum hardware requirement.

Similar to "traditional" spanning tree, RSTP will also elect a root bridge using the same parameters as STP. All RSTP ports will be in a forwarding state (designated ports), other ports could be an alternate port, root port, backup port, or disabled.

RSTP port roles

Table 3–3: RSTP port roles

Root port	This elected port is forwarding data in the active topology.
Designated port	An elected port that is forwarding data for every switched LAN segment.
Alternate port	An alternative path to the root bridge but different from the root port path.
Backup port	This port provides a redundant path (but less desirable) to a segment to which another switch port already connects. (They can only exist when there are two ports connected between the switches.)
Disabled	This type of port does not participate in the active topology.

RSTP port states

Table 3–4: RSTP port states:

Operational status	STP port state	RSTP port state	Port in active topology
Enabled	Blocking	Discarding	No
Enabled	Listening	Discarding	No
Enabled	Learning	Learning	Yes
Enabled	Forwarding	Forwarding	Yes
Disabled	Disabled	Discarding	No

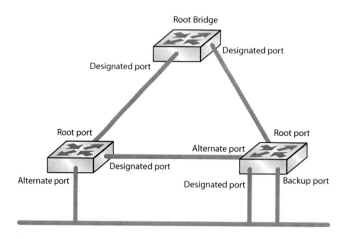

Figure 3–7: Using a root bridge

Per-VLAN STP and per-VLAN rapid STP

This will be a good time to introduce you to another very significant change which Cisco made to STP.

> **NOTE:** This section discusses VLANs. For now, remember that VLANs provide different broadcast domains at layer 2 and hence keep traffic from one subnet different from another. We will cover VLANs in more detail shortly.

When the original bridging standard (802.1d) was drafted, VLANs did not exist. Hence, one Spanning Tree instance worked across the entire switch. Eventually VLANs were introduced, and they created different networks on the same switch. This gave rise to need to have different topology for load balancing and flexible Spanning Trees. The need for per-VLAN STP can be further understood from the following network:

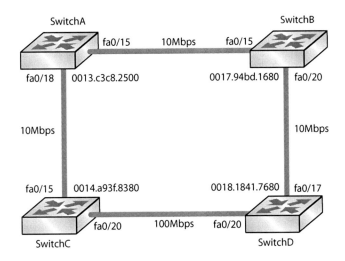

Figure 3–8: Multiple exits—multiple VLANs

Let's assume that all the switches have two VLANs configured. SwitchD has two ways to reach SwitchA. If one STP instance was running across the network, then `fa0/17` would be in the blocked state. With two STP instances running, we can have `fa0/20` blocked for one vlan and `fa0/17` blocked for another and utilize both links by loadbalancing traffic across them.

To achieve this, Cisco added the per-VLAN Spanning Tree Plus (PVST+) feature on its switches. When 802.1w (RSTP) was introduced by IEEE, it still did not accommodate multiple Spanning Tree instances on a switch. Cisco introduced the per-VLAN Rapid Spanning Tree (PVRST) to support rapid Spanning Tree instances on each VLAN on the switch. PVST+ and PVRST both provide the same functionality across both 802.1d and 802.1w standards.

PVST+ and PVRST both change the Bridge ID in the BPDU by adding the VLAN number to the configured priority.

Configuring PVRSTP+

To enable RSTP for each VLAN in our switched network, we use the following command:

```
Switch(config)#spanning-tree mode rapid-pvst
```

This is all that is needed if we need only one instance of the spanning tree protocol. Later on in this section, we will show what is needed to enable the load-sharing capabilities.

Using the "show spanning-tree vlan <vlan#>" command, we can verify which type of spanning tree is running.

```
Switch#show spanning-tree vlan 10

VLAN0010
Spanning tree enabled protocol rstp
Root ID Priority 24586
Address 0015.63f6.b700
Cost 3019
Port 107 (FastEthernet3/0/1)
Hello Time 2 sec Max Age 20 sec Forward Delay 15 sec

Bridge ID Priority 49162 (priority 49152 sys-id-ext 10)
Address 000f.f794.3d00
Hello Time 2 sec Max Age 20 sec Forward Delay 15 sec
Aging Time 300
UplinkFast enabled but inactive in rapid-pvst mode
--output truncated-
```

Two items are of interest in this output. First is the Spanning Tree Protocol—RSTP and the second is the "sys-id-ext 10". This shows that the bridge priority was configured as 41952 and VLAN id 10 was added to it.

How can load balancing be achieved in the network shown in Figure 3–8 if VLAN 1 and VLAN 5 are being used on the LAN? We can achieve it by configuring Switch A with a better priority for VLAN 1 and configuring SwitchB with a better priority for VLAN 5. This can be done using the following commands:

```
SwitchA(config)#spanning-tree vlan 1 priority 4096
SwitchB(config)#spanning-tree vlan 5 priority 4096
```

Let's see the "show spanning-tree" output for both VLANs on SwitchD to verify load balancing.

```
SwitchD#show spanning-tree
VLAN0001
  Spanning tree enabled protocol ieee
  Root ID    Priority    4097
             Address     0013.c3e8.2500
--output truncated--
```

```
Interface              Role Sts Cost       Prio.Nbr Type
-------------------    ---- --- ----------  --------  ---------------------------

Fa0/17                 Desg FWD 119         128.17    P2p
Fa0/20                 Root FWD 19          128.20    P2p


VLAN0005
  Spanning tree enabled protocol ieee
  Root ID    Priority    4101
             Address     0017.94bd.1680
--output truncated--
Interface              Role Sts Cost       Prio.Nbr Type
-------------------    ---- --- ----------  --------  ---------------------------

Fa0/17                 Root FWD 19          128.17    P2p
Fa0/20                 Desg FWD 119         128.20    P2p
```

We can see that the root bridge for VLAN1 is SwitchA, whereas the root bridge for VLAN 5 is SwitchB. Fa0/20 is the root port for VLAN 1, and Fa0/17 is the root port for VLAN 5.

TROUBLESHOOTING STP

This section touches upon common STP problems and ways to troubleshoot them. The steps given here apply to both 802.1d and 802.1w running different STP process on each VLAN.

STP is a very maintenance-free protocol and generally does not require troubleshooting. STP will mostly have the following problems:

- Incorrect root bridge
- Incorrect root port
- Incorrect designated port

Let's look at each of the problems and ways to troubleshoot them.

Incorrect root bridge

The root bridge is selected based upon the BridgeID which consists of priority and the base MAC address of the switch. The "show spanning-tree vlan <vlan#>" command will show the current root bridge. Note the MAC address and the priority of the root bridge and compare it with those of the switch which you want to make the root bridge. Decreasing the priority of the correct switch should resolve the problem. This can be done using the "spanning-tree vlan <vlan#> priority <priority>" command.

Incorrect root port

The root port is the fastest path from a switch to the root bridge. The cost is the cumulative cost of all the links in the path. So if there are two 100 Mbps links between a switch and a root bridge then the cost is 38 (19+19). "`show spanning-tree vlan (vlan #)`" will show the current root port and its cost. Compare that with the cost of the desired path. The cost of the desired path can be changed using the "`spanning-tree cost <cost>`" interface command.

Incorrect designated port

Designated port is the lowest cost port connecting a network segment to the rest of the network. The designated port cost can be seen and changed using the "`show spanning-tree vlan <vlan#>`" command and the "`spanning-tree cost <cost>`" command.

SWITCHING METHODS

Any delay in passing traffic is known as latency. Cisco switches offer three ways to switch the traffic depending upon how thoroughly you want the frame to be checked before it is passed on. The more checking you want, the more latency you will introduce to the switch.

The three switching modes to choose from are:

- Cut-through
- Store-and-forward
- Fragment-free

Cut-through

Cut-through switching is the fastest switching method meaning it has the lowest latency. The incoming frame is read up to the destination MAC address. Once it reaches the destination MAC address, the switch then checks its CAM table for the correct port to forward the frame out of and sends it on its way. There is no error checking, so this method gives you the lowest latency. The price, however, is that the switch will forward any frames containing errors.

The process of switching modes can best be described by using a metaphor.

You are the security at a club and are asked to make sure that everyone who enters has a picture ID, you are not asked to make sure the picture matches the person, only that the ID has a picture. With this method of checking, people are surely going to move quickly to enter the establishment. This is how cut-through switching works.

Store-and-forward

Here the switch reads the entire frame and copies it into its buffers. A cyclic redundancy check (CRC) takes place to check the frame for any errors. If errors are found, the frame is dropped. Otherwise the switching table is examined and the frame forwarded. Store and Forward ensures that the frame is at least 64 bytes and no larger than 1518 bytes. If smaller than 64 bytes or larger than 1518 bytes, then the switch will discard the frame.

Now imagine you are the security at the club, only this time you have to make sure that the picture matches the person, but you must write down the name and address of everyone before they can enter. Doing it this way causes a great deal of time and delay, and this is how the store-and-forward method of switching works.

Store-and-forward switching has the highest latency of all switching methods and is the default setting of the 2900 series switches.

Fragment-free (modified cut-through / runt-free)

Since cut-through can ensure that all frames are good and store-and-forward takes too long, we need a method that is both quick and reliable. Using our example of the nightclub security, imagine you are asked to make sure that everyone has an ID and that the picture matches the person. With this method you have made sure everyone is who they say they are, but you do not have to take down all the information. In switching we accomplish this by using the fragment-free method of switching.

This is the default configuration on lower-level Cisco switches. Fragment-free, or modified cut-through, is a modified variety of cut-through switching. The first 64 bytes of a frame are examined for any errors, and if none are detected, it will pass it. The reason for this is that if there is an error in the frame it is most likely to be in the first 64 bytes.

The minimum size of an Ethernet frame is 64 bytes; anything less than 64 bytes is called a "runt" frame. Since every frame must be at least 64 bytes before forwarding, this will eliminate the runts, and that is why this method is also known as "runt-free" switching.

VIRTUAL LOCAL AREA NETWORKS (VLANS)

You learned earlier that a switch breaks the collision domain and a router breaks a broadcast domain. Which means a network would look something like this:

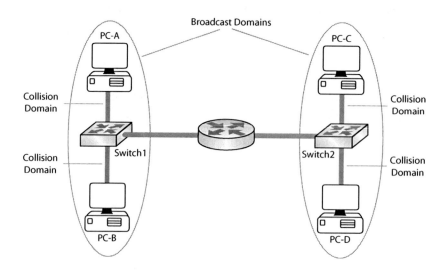

Figure 3–9: A simple flat network

Before we continue, let's discuss what a LAN really is. A LAN is essentially a broadcast domain. In the network shown in Figure 3–9, if PC-A sends a broadcast, it will be received by PC-B but not PC-C or PC-D. This is because the router breaks the broadcast domain. Now we can use virtual LANs (VLANs) to put switch ports into different broadcast domains.

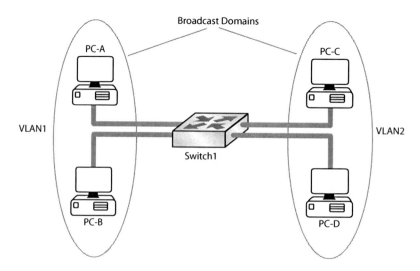

Figure 3–10: Broadcast domains with VLAN

In Figure 3–10, we have divided the layer 2 network into two broadcast domains using VLANs. Now a broadcast sent by PC-A will be received by PC-B but not PC-C and PC-D. Without VLANs PC-C and PC-D would have received the broadcasts sent by PC-A.

Let's consider some advantages of VLANs:

- Containing broadcasts within a smaller group of devices will make the network faster.
- Saves resources on devices because they process less broadcast
- Added security by keeping devices in a certain group (or function) in a separate broadcast domain.A group as implied here can mean department, security level, etc. For example, devices belonging to development or testing lab should be kept separate from the production devices.
- Flexibility in expanding a network across a geographical location of any size. For example it does not matter where in the building a PC is. It thinks it is on the same segment of the network as any other PC configured to be in the same VLAN. In Figure 3–11, all hosts in VLAN 1 can talk to each other, even though they are on different floors. The VLAN is transparent or invisible to them.

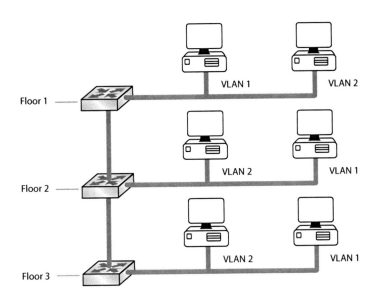

Figure 3–11: VLANs remove the physical boundaries from a LAN.

VLAN membership

There are two common ways to associate devices with VLANs, statically or dynamically:

1. With static VLANs, the ports on the switch are configured to be in different VLANs by the administrator, and the relevant device is then connected to the port. If the user needs to move

to another part of the building it will require the network administrator moving to change the configuration on the switch. **All switchports belong to VLAN 1 by default.**

2. Dynamic VLANs allow devices to join based upon MAC address. This gives the administrator the flexibility to allow users to connect to any switch or move around the building without having to change the configuration on the switch. This is achieved using a VLAN Management Policy Server (VMPS).

 IN THE REAL WORLD:

VMPS is rarely used. This is because adding the MAC address of each host is a huge task. Better and newer technology is available, but it is beyond the scope of CCNA.

Please note: Since each VLAN is a different broadcast domain, it means:

- Hosts in one VLAN cannot reach hosts in another VLAN by default
- A layer 3 device is needed for inter-VLAN communication (covered later)
- Each VLAN needs its own subnets. For example, VLAN 1—192.168.1.0/24, VLAN 2—192.168.2.0/24
- All hosts in a VLAN should belong to the same subnet.

VLAN links

We know that one switch can have hosts connected to multiple VLANs. What happens when traffic goes from one host to another? For example, in Figure 3–11 when the host in VLAN1 on Floor 1 tries to reach the host in VLAN 1 on Floor 2, how will the switch on Floor 2 know which VLAN the traffic belongs to? Switch uses a mechanism called frame tagging to keep traffic on different VLANs separate. The switch adds a header on the frame which contains the VLAN ID. In Figure 3–11, the switch on Floor 1 will tag the traffic originating from VLAN 1 and pass it to Switch2, which will see the tag and know that the traffic needs to be kept within that VLAN.

Such tagged traffic can only flow across special links called trunk links.

VLAN links can be divided into:

- Access links
- Trunk links

Access links

A switchport which is defined as an access link can only be a member of one VLAN. The device connected to the access link is not aware of the existence of any other VLANs. The switch will add a tag to a frame as it enters the access link from the host and remove the tag when a frame exits the switchport towards the host. Access links are used to connect to hosts.

Trunk links

A trunk link can carry traffic from different VLANs at a time. A trunk link is a 100 or 1000 Mbps point-to-point link between:

- Two switches
- A switch and a router
- A switch and a server

It carries the traffic from multiple VLANs at the same time.

> **NOTE:** Point-to-point links between two switches can be configured as an access link also but that will mean that traffic from a single, configured, VLAN can flow between them. If you need traffic from all or multiple VLANs to flow between switches then the link has to be configured as a trunk.
>
> When multiple switches are connected using trunks and they share information from the same VLANs, they are collectively called a Switch Fabric.

Trunking protocols define several things related to VLANs, but most importantly they define headers which carry the VLAN ID. Cisco switches support the following trunking protocols:

- ISL
- 802.1q

ISL

ISL or Inter-Switch Link, is a Cisco proprietary trunking protocol. It encapsulates the original frame in an ISL header and trailer. The original frame remains unchanged. The ISL header contains the VLAN ID. The receiving switch looks at the ISL header and then removes the ISL header and trailer. ISL can only work when both the switches across the link are Cisco switches. ISL is the default trunking protocol on Cisco switches which support it.

> **IN THE REAL WORLD:**
>
> If any untagged traffic is received by an ISL trunk link, it will be dropped.

802.1q

802.1q was created by the IEEE as a standard for tagging frames. 802.1q works by inserting a 4-byte VLAN header into the original header of the Ethernet frame. You would need to use 802.1q if you were connecting a trunk link between a Cisco switch and a non-Cisco switch. **802.1q is the only encapsulation available on the 2950 model of switch (tested in the CCNA exam).**

 IN THE REAL WORLD:

802.1q links are configured with a native VLAN.* Any untagged traffic received on the trunk link will be tagged as belonging to the native VLAN. This is a key difference between 802.1q and ISL.

*The native VLAN is nothing more than a default VLAN, given that any port in a (CISCO) switch has to assigned to one VLAN. By default all ports belong to VLAN 1 or the native VLAN.

A trunk link on a switch can be in one of five possible modes.

1. **On** — forces the port into permanent trunking mode. The port becomes a trunk even if the connected device does not agree to convert the link into a trunk link.
2. **Off** — link is not used as a trunk link, even if the connected device is set to trunk.
3. **Auto** — port is willing to become a trunk link. If the other device is set to on or desirable then the link becomes a trunk link. If both sides are left as auto then the link will never become a trunk as neither side will attempt to convert.
4. **Desirable** — the port actively tries to convert to a trunk link. If the other device is set to on, auto or desirable then the link will become a trunk link.
5. **No-negotiate** — prevents the port from negotiating a trunk connection. It will be forced into an access or trunk mode as per the configuration.

 IN THE REAL WORLD:

Switch uses Dynamic Trunking Protocol (DTP) to negotiate a trunk link and the trunking protocol to be used.

Configuring VLANs

Now that we understand VLANs and trunk links, let's configure the network as shown in Figure 3–12. We need to configure the switches such that the hosts on fa0/1 are in VLAN 5 and the link on port fa0/15 is a trunk link.

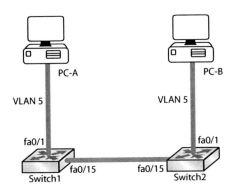

Figure 3–12: Test network

Before assigning ports to VLANs, the VLAN itself must be created. They can be created using the "vlan <vlan#>" global configuration command. This will put you into the vlan configuration mode where a descriptive name can be given to the VLANs. Here is an example:

```
Switch1(config)#vlan 5
Switch1(config-vlan)#name RnD

Switch2(config)vlan 5
Switch2(config-vlan)#name RnD
```

To see which VLANs exist on a switch, use the "show vlan" command. The output will be similar to the one below:

```
Switch1#show vlan
VLAN Name                            Status   Ports
---- -------------------------------- -------- ----------------------------
1    default                          active   fa0/1, fa0/2, fa0/3, fa0/4
                                               fa0/5, fa0/6, fa0/7, fa0/8
                                               fa0/9, fa0/10, fa0/11, fa0/12

--output truncated--

5    RnD                              active
--output truncated—
```

Let's assign port fa0/1 to VLAN 5 using the "switchport access vlan (vlan#)" interface command.

```
Switch1(config)#int fa0/1
Switch1(config-if)#switchport access vlan 5

Switch2(config)#int fa0/1
Switch2(config-if)#switchport access vlan 5
```

Let's see the output of "show vlan" now:

```
Switch1#show vlan
VLAN Name                               Status    Ports
---- --------------------------------   --------  -------------------------------
1    default                            active    fa0/2, fa0/3, fa0/4, fa0/5
                                                    fa0/6, fa0/7, fa0/8, fa0/9
                                                      fa0/10, fa0/11,
     fa0/12, fa0/13
                                                        fa0/14, fa0/16,
     fa0/17, fa0/19
     --output truncated--
5    RnD                                active    fa0/1
     --output truncated—
```

Note that Fa0/1 is now assigned to VLAN 5. Let's configure interface fa0/15 on both switches as trunk links. It should be noted here that the default mode on switchports is desirable. Hence, DTP will cause fa0/15 on both switches to become ISL trunk links. This can be verified using the "show interface trunk" command:

```
Switch1#show interface trunk

Port         Mode         Encapsulation     Status       Native vlan
Fa0/15       desirable    n-isl             trunking     1
```

Note that the mode is desirable and the encapsulation is ISL (n stands for negotiated).

Let's see how to configure the trunk to use ISL trunking:

```
Switch1(config)#interface fa0/15
Switch1(config-if)#switchport trunk encapsulation isl
Switch1(config-if)#switchport mode trunk

Switch2(config)#interface fa0/15
Switch2(config-if)#switchport trunk encapsulation isl
Switch2(config-if)#switchport mode trunk
```

The "switchport trunk encapsulation" command sets the trunking protocol on the port and the "switchport mode trunk" command sets the port to trunking. The output of "show interface trunk" will now look like:

```
Switch2#show interface trunk

Port         Mode     Encapsulation     Status       Native vlan
Fa0/15       on       isl               trunking     1
```

Note that the encapsulation is now isl instead of n-isl. This is because this time the protocol was not negotiated but configured on the interface.

Please note that this does not apply to the 2950 model of switch (which is currently used for the CCNA syllabus), which can only use dot1q encapsulation. For this reason the "switchport trunk encapsulation" command will not work on the 2950 switch.

Similarly, we can configure the switchport to use 802.1q instead of ISL:

```
Switch1(config)#interface fa0/15
Switch1(config-if)#switchport trunk encapsulation dot1q
Switch1(config-if)#switchport mode trunk

Switch2(config)#interface fa0/15
Switch2(config-if)#switchport trunk encapsulation dot1q
    Switch2(config-if)#switchport mode trunk
```

The "show interface trunk" output now looks like this:

```
Switch2#show interface trunk

Port        Mode    Encapsulation    Status       Native vlan
Fa0/15      on      802.1q           trunking     1
```

Note that the native VLAN is 1. That is, the default native vlan on a 802.1q trunk but can be changed using "switchport trunk native vlan <vlan#>" command.

Inter-VLAN Routing

Earlier, we learned that hosts in one VLAN cannot communicate with hosts in another VLAN. To facilitate this, we need a layer 3 device such as a router. The link between the router and the switch will be a trunk link. An interface on a router can be divided into logical interfaces called sub-interfaces. Each sub-interface supports a specific VLAN. The network shown in Figure 3–13 is known as a router-on-a-stick.

The concept behind router-on-a-stick is that in order to route between different subnets we would require a router. The minimum number of routers required would be one, and if it had only one available interface we would need to use it along with sub-interfaces (one per VLAN):

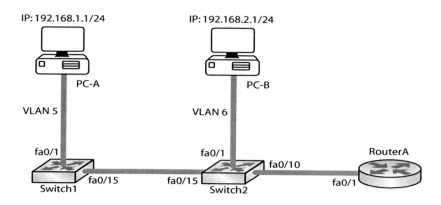

Figure 3–13: Router-on-a-stick

In such a network, RouterA's interface (fa0/1 in our case) is configured with sub-interfaces – one for each VLAN. Each sub-interface is assigned an IP address from the respective VLAN subnet. Let's configure the network and then look at how the traffic will flow from one VLAN to another:

```
Switch1(config)#interface fa0/1
Switch1(config-if)#switchport mode access
Switch1(config-if)#switchport access vlan 5
Switch1(config-if)#exit
Switch1(config)#interface fa0/15
Switch1(config-if)#switchport trunk encapsulation dot1q
Switch1(config-if)#switchport mode trunk

Switch2(config)#interface fa0/1
Switch2(config-if)#switchport mode access
Switch2(config-if)#switchport access vlan 6
Switch2(config-if)#exit
Switch2(config)#interface fa0/15
Switch2(config-if)#switchport trunk encapsulation dot1q
Switch2(config-if)#switchport mode trunk
Switch2(config-if)#exit
Switch2(config)#interface fa0/10
Switch2(config-if)#switchport trunk encapsulation dot1q
Switch2(config-if)#switchport mode trunk

RouterA(config)#interface fa0/1.5
RouterA(config-if)#encapsulation dot1q 5
RouterA(config-if)#ip address 192.168.1.10 255.255.255.0
RouterA(config-if)#exit
RouterA(config)#interface fa0/1.6
RouterA(config-if)#encapsulation dot1q 6
RouterA(config-if)#ip address 192.168.2.10 255.255.255.0
```

For the router sub-interfaces, it is common practice to number them to match the VLAN they are a member of e.g., fast Ethernet 0/1.5 for VLAN 5.

For hosts in VLAN 5, the gateway will be 192.168.1.10 and for hosts in VLAN 6 the gateway will be 192.168.2.10. Both of these IP addresses belong to sub-interfaces on RouterA. When PC-A needs to communicate with PC-B, the traffic will go from Switch1 to Switch2 through the trunk link on fa0/15. From there it will go to interface fa0/1.5 on RouterA and will then be routed out off fa0/1.6 and finally reach PC-B on VLAN 6.

Please follow the inter-VLAN routing lab for more information.

VLANs on a trunk

By default, a trunk link carries traffic for all VLANs configured on the switch. This is not always a desirable behavior. For example, you might want to restrict certain VLANs over a trunk link if you want to load balance or if you know that a certain VLAN does not exist on the other end of the trunk link. In such a situation, trunk links can be configured to not allow traffic of certain VLANs across. This can be done using the "switchport trunk allowed vlan" command. Let's consider the network shown in Figure 3–14. The trunk on port fa1/1 does not need to carry traffic belonging to VLAN 2 from SwitchA to SwitchB since there is no host from that VLAN on SwitchB.

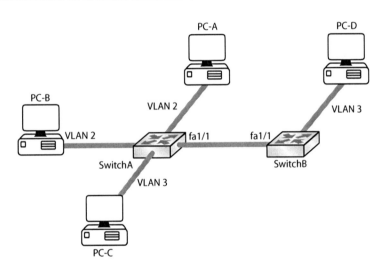

Figure 3–14: Removing VLANs from a trunk

The output of "show interface trunk" looks like this currently:

```
SwitchA#show interface trunk

Port      Mode      Encapsulation    Status       Native vlan
fa1/1     on        802.1q           trunking     1

Port      Vlans allowed on trunk
fa1/1     1-1005
```

Note that `fa1/1` currently allows traffic for VLAN 1 to 1005.

To remove VLAN 2 from the trunk's allowed VLAN list, we will use the following steps:

```
SwitchA(config)#interface fa1/1
SwitchA(config-if)#switchport trunk allowed vlan remove 2
```

The output of "`show interface trunk`" command will now look like:

```
SwitchA#show interface trunk

Port      Mode    Encapsulation   Status      Native vlan
fa1/1     on      802.1q          trunking    1

Port      Vlans allowed on trunk
fa1/1     1,3-1005
```

VLAN 2 is now not allowed across `fa1/1`.

The CCNA requires that we know all the command options available with the "`switchport trunk allowed vlan`" command. The options available are:

```
SwitchA(config-if)#switchport trunk allowed vlan ?
  WORD    VLAN IDs of the allowed VLANs when this port is in trunking mode
  add     add VLANs to the current list
  all     all VLANs
  except  all VLANs except the following
  remove  remove VLANs from the current list
```

WORD	Will clear the current allowed list and add the VLANs given in the command. **Example:** `switchport trunk allowed vlan 1 10` This command will configure the trunk link to carry traffic of VLANs 1 to 10 only.
add	Will add the specified VLAN to the current list. **Example:** `Switchport trunk allowed vlan add 10`
all	Will change the allowed list to allow all VLANs. **Example:** `Switchport trunk allowed vlan all`
except	Will change the allowed list to allow all VLANs except the specified VLAN. **Example:** `Switchport trunk allowed vlan except 2` When used with the default allowed list, it is equivalent to remove option
remove	Will remove the specified VLAN to the current list. **Example:** `Switchport trunk allowed vlan remove 2`

VLAN trunking protocol (VTP)

Imagine having 20, 50, 100 or more switches on your network. If you made a VLAN change on one of the switches, you would have to configure the others to have the same information. There is a way to make a change on one switch and have this change automatically propagate to the other switches. This method maintains consistency throughout the network and is known as VLAN trunking protocol.

Each switch has to be configured to join the same VTP domain in order to speak to each other and exchange VTP information. In order to join the domain, you simply give each switch the same VTP domain name, "Cisco" for example (see below config). Only switches in the same VTP management domain will share information. VTP information can be protected using a password. All switches in the VTP domain need to have the same password or else they will not be able to decrypt the VTP packets.

The benefits of using VTP include:

- Accurate monitoring and reporting of VLANs
- VLAN consistency across the network
- Ease of adding and removal of VLANs

Each switch using VTP advertises the management domain, revision number of the configuration and known VLANs (and their parameters) out of their trunk ports.

VTP modes

There are three possible modes a switch in a VTP domain can be in:

- client
- server
- transparent

IMPORTANT: The default VTP mode of a Cisco switch is set to server.

 IN THE REAL WORLD:

Never ever connect a switch to your network without configuring it first. If an old configuration on the switch has it set to server, the switches configuration could be passed throughout the entire network and if the domain name is same and revision number is higher, it could take the network down for hours.

Client mode

In client mode, the switch will receive VTP information and apply any changes, but it does not allow adding, removing or changing VLAN information on the switch. The client will also send out the VTP packet received out its trunk ports. Remember that you cannot add a switchport on a VTP client switch to a VLAN that does not exist on the VTP server.

Server mode

In server mode, the switch is authorized to create, modify and delete VLAN information for the entire VTP domain. Any changes you made to a server are propagated to the whole domain.

Transparent mode

In transparent mode, the switch will forward the VTP information received out of their trunk ports but will not apply the changes. A VTP transparent-mode switch can create, modify, and delete VLANs, but the changes are not propagated to other switches. VTP transparent mode also requires configuration of domain information. A VTP transparent switch is needed when a switch separating a VTP server and client needs to have a different VLAN database.

Configuring VTP

To enable VTP, you need to configure the VTP domain and VTP mode. Optionally, you can configure the VTP password. The following commands accomplish this:

```
SwitchA(config)#vtp mode server
SwitchA(config)#vtp domain Cisco
SwitchA(config)#vtp password ccna
```

The "vtp mode {server|client|transparent}" command can be used to set the desired mode.

VTP configuration can be verified using the "show vtp status" command.

```
SwitchA#show vtp status
VTP Version                       : 2
Configuration Revision            : 1
Maximum VLANs supported locally : 255
Number of existing VLANs          : 9
VTP Operating Mode                : Server
VTP Domain Name                   : test
VTP Pruning Mode                  : Disabled
VTP V2 Mode                       : Disabled
VTP Traps Generation              : Disabled
MD5 digest                        : 0x5D 0x16 0x1A 0x34 0x2C 0xAE 0xA5 0xB4
Configuration last modified by 0.0.0.0 at 3-1-02 00:37:56
Local updater ID is 0.0.0.0 (no valid interface found)
```

Now that our VTP server is configured on SwitchA, let's take a look at both SwitchA and SwitchB, which is connected to SwitchA using a 802.1q trunk on port fa1/1. The "show vlan" outputs from both the switches look like:

```
SwitchA#show vlan

VLAN Name                           Status    Ports
---- ------------------------------ --------- ----------------------------
1    default                        active    fa1/0, fa1/2, fa1/3, fa1/4
                                              fa1/5, fa1/6, fa1/7, fa1/8
                                              fa1/9, fa1/10, fa1/11, fa1/12
                                              fa1/13, fa1/14, fa1/15

2    VLAN0002                       active
3    VLAN0003                       active
4    VLAN0004                       active
5    VTPTest                        active
1002 fddi-default                   active
1003 token-ring-default             active
1004 fddinet-default                active
1005 trnet-default                  active


SwitchB#show vlan

VLAN Name                           Status    Ports
---- ------------------------------ --------- ----------------------------
1    default                        active    fa1/0, fa1/2, fa1/3, fa1/4
                                              fa1/5, fa1/6, fa1/7, fa1/8
                                              fa1/9, fa1/10, fa1/11, fa1/12
                                              fa1/13, fa1/14, fa1/15

1002 fddi-default                   active
1003 token-ring-default             active
1004 fddinet-default                active
1005 trnet-default                  active
```

Let's configure SwitchB as a VTP client to SwitchA:

```
SwitchB(config)#vtp mode client
SwitchB(config)#vtp domain Cisco
SwitchB(config)#vtp password ccna
```

The output of "show vlan" and "show vtp status" on SwitchB now looks like this:

```
SwitchB#show vlan
VLAN Name                           Status    Ports
---- ------------------------------ --------- ----------------------------
1    default                        active    fa1/0, fa1/2, fa1/3, fa1/4
                                              fa1/5, fa1/6, fa1/7, fa1/8
                                              fa1/9, fa1/10, fa1/11, fa1/12
                                              fa1/13, fa1/14, fa1/15
```

```
2     VLAN0002                        active
3     VLAN0003                        active
4     VLAN0004                        active
5     VTPTest                         active
1002  fddi-default                    active
1003  token-ring-default              active
1004  fddinet-default                 active
1005  trnet-default                   active

SwitchB#show vtp status
VTP Version                    : 2
Configuration Revision         : 2
Maximum VLANs supported locally : 256
Number of existing VLANs       : 9
VTP Operating Mode             : Client
VTP Domain Name                : Cisco
VTP Pruning Mode               : Disabled
VTP V2 Mode                    : Disabled
VTP Traps Generation           : Disabled
MD5 digest                     : 0x94 0xDE 0x28 0x9D 0x2D 0x95 0x96 0x04
Configuration last modified by 0.0.0.0 at 3-1-02 00:18:45
```

VTP pruning

VTP information can be passed around the domain and reach the same switch from several paths. To add to this, every switch that has a trunk link forwards broadcasts to every switch even if it has no ports in that VLAN. The end result is broadcasts to switches that will eventually discard the traffic.

VTP pruning prevents VLAN information, broadcasts, multicasts, and unicasts from flooding other trunk ports when there is no need. It reduces unnecessary broadcast, multicast, and flooded unicast traffic that in turn increases bandwidth. VTP pruning automatically does what we did with the "switchport trunk allowed vlan" command. To recollect when we would use this let's look at Figure 3–15. Since SwitchB does not have any clients in VLAN 2, it would be wise to ensure that traffic belonging to that VLAN never transverses the trunk link at fa1/1. If VTP pruning is enabled, then the allowed VLAN list is automatically adjusted depending on which VLAN is active on the switches. VTP pruning can only be enabled from the VTP server. Once enabled there, it will be automatically enabled on all the VTP clients.

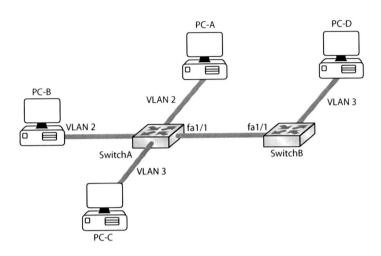

Figure 3–15: VTP pruning

VTP pruning can be enabled using the "vtp pruning" command on the VTP server.

Let's see the output of "show trunk interface" on SwitchA after VTP pruning is enabled:

```
SwitchA#show interface trunk

Port      Mode    Encapsulation    Status        Native vlan
fa1/1     on      802.1q           trunking      1

Port      Vlans allowed on trunk
fa1/1     1-1005

Port      Vlans allowed and active in management domain
fa1/1     1-5

Port      Vlans in spanning tree forwarding state and not pruned
fa1/1     1,3
```

Note that VLAN 2, 4, and 5 are pruned on interface fa1/1 since SwitchB does not have any hosts in those VLANs.

 IN THE REAL WORLD:

If there is a VTP transparent switch in between the VTP server and client, then pruning will not work.

TROUBLESHOOTING VLANS

VLANs are a fairly straightforward feature which rarely requires troubleshooting. A few of the problems that we see are mostly configuration errors. Common ones include:

1. **Inter-VLAN routing not working** — Check that the link between the switches and the routers is set up correctly and the relevant VLANs are allowed and not pruned. The "show interface trunk" command will provide the required information. Also check that the router's sub-interfaces are configured with correct encapsulation and VLAN and that the sub-interface's IP address is the default gateway for the hosts.

2. **VLANs cannot be created** — Check if the VTP mode on the switch is set to client. VLANs cannot be created if the VTP mode is client. Another important factor is number of VLANs allowed on the switch. The "show vtp status" command will provide both the information required.

3. **Hosts within the same VLAN cannot reach each other** — It is important that hosts in a VLAN have an IP address belonging to the same subnet. If the subnet is different, then they will not be able to reach each other. Another factor to consider is if the hosts are connected to the same switch or not. If they are not connected to the same switch, then ensure that the trunk link(s) between the switches is / are working correctly and that the VLAN is not excluded from the allowed list / not pruned. The "show interface trunk" command will show needed information regarding the trunk link.

TROUBLESHOOTING TRUNKS

Apart from a hardware / cable fault, most of the trunking problems originate from configuration errors. Common problems are discussed below:

1. **Trunk will not come up** — First, check if the interface status is up/up using the "show ip interface brief" or "show interface <interface>" command. The second thing to check is the mode configured on the switchport. This can be done using the "show interface <interface> switchport" command. This command will show an output similar to the one given below:

```
SwitchA#show interface fa1/1 switchport
Name: Fa1/1
Switchport: Enabled
Administrative Mode: trunk
Operational Mode: trunk
```

```
Administrative Trunking Encapsulation: dot1q
Operational Trunking Encapsulation: dot1q
Negotiation of Trunking: Disabled
Access Mode VLAN: 0 ((Inactive))
```

Important points to note are the "Administrative mode", "Negotiation of Trunking", and "Administrative Trunking Encapsulation" lines. They will tell you the mode, DTP status, and the trunking protocol on the port. Remember that ports set on Auto/Auto mode will not trunk (covered previously). A trunking protocol mismatch will not allow the trunk to come up. Also remember that the default trunking protocol is dot1q on the 2950 and usually ISL on other models of a Cisco switch.

2. **Trunk does not carry traffic from relevant VLANs** — Trunks carry the traffic for all VLANs, by default. Only two things can cause this problem: Allowed list and Pruning. The "show interface trunk" command will show which VLANs are allowed across the trunk and which VLANs are pruned.

TROUBLESHOOTING VTP

VTP problems are discussed below:

1. **VTP client does not receive or apply information from the server**—First thing to check if whether the trunk link is configured and active between the VTP server and the client. This includes trunk link between any switches between the VTP server and client if the client in consideration is not directly connected.

   Secondly ensure that the VTP domain and password are correct. Another important factor is the revision number. If the VTP client is an old switch with pre-existing configuration, then it might have a higher revision than the one being advertised by the server. In such situations change the domain of the client to something else and then revert it back to the correct domain. This will reset the revision number on the client. "show vtp status" command helps in verifying the VTP configuration. You can see plenty of examples of the show commands in the theory and labs section.

2. **New VTP client caused a change of VLAN database in the entire network**—This can only happen if the client was brought from lab or another network (using the same domain name) and had a higher revision number. This can be verified using the "show vtp status" command.

3. **VTP pruning is not working correctly**—If there is a VTP transparent switch in between the VTP server and VTP client, then VTP pruning will not work. Another reason why VTP pruning

will appear not to be working correctly is configuration of allowed VLANs on the trunk links. Some VLANs might have been removed manually. This can be verified using "show interface trunk" command.

IP HELPER-ADDRESS

Routers do not pass broadcast traffic, by default. There are instances where you may want a broadcast packet to pass through the router. An example is when a client sends a DHCP request to obtain an IP address and the DHCP server is on the other side of your router on another network.

In this instance, you can use the "ip helper-address" command, which will turn the broadcast into a multicast.

```
RouterA#config
RouterA(config)#interface fast ethernet 0
RouterA(config-if)#ip helper-address 192.168.1.1
```

The "ip helper-address" command will automatically forward eight common UDP ports that use broadcasts (we discuss port numbers in Module 7):

- Time (37)
- TACACS (49)
- DNS (53)
- BOOTP server (67)
- BOOTP client (68)
- TFTP (69)
- NetBIOS name service (137)
- NetBIOS datagram service (138)

IP FORWARD-PROTOCOL

The "ip forward-protocol" command allows you to specify a number of protocols and ports that the router will forward. The example below specifies an IP helper address and then which protocol should be forwarded.

```
RouterA#config
RouterA(config)#interface fast ethernet 0
RouterA(config-if)#ip helper-address 192.168.1.1
RouterA(config-if)#ip forward-protocol udp
```

CISCO SWITCHES

Cisco offer several varieties of switch to cater for every type of business from small offices to large corporations. Due to the fact that Cisco acquired some of their early models of switches from buying smaller companies, there are a few different varieties of switch available running different types of software.

The 1800, 1900, and 2820 models of switch came originally from a company called Grand Junction. They run a menu-driven interface configuration and a hybrid Cisco type of IOS, which features a command-line interface. The 1900, 1800, and 2820 switches are for use in smaller companies who need limited functionality. They feature mostly Ethernet and some fast Ethernet ports.

The 3000 series of switches originate from Kalpana and the 8500 and 2900XL from Cisco. The catalyst 5000 originated from a company called Crescendo.

With a couple of exceptions the two main types of switch configuration are Cisco IOS and CATOS. The CATOS-set-based command-line interface is more limited than IOS based and uses "set" commands to configure the switch. The set-based switches include the 2926, 4000, 5000, and 6000 series switches.

 IN THE EXAM:

Cisco is moving to IOS-based switching almost exclusively. The CCNA exam does not test you on CATOS.

We will now look at configuration guides for the 2950 switch that uses Cisco IOS.

CONFIGURING A 2950 SWITCH

```
Press RETURN to get started!
2950 INIT: Complete

Cisco Internetwork Operating System Software
IOS (tm) C2950 Software (C2950-I6Q4L2-M), Version 12.1(20)EA1a, RELEASE
SOFTWARE (fc1)
Copyright (c) 1986-2004 by cisco Systems, Inc.
Compiled Mon 19-Apr-04 20:58 by yenanh
Image text-base: 0x80010000, data-base: 0x805A8000
We can set the hostname of the switch:
Switch>enable
Switch#config t
Enter configuration commands, one per line.  End with CNTL/Z.
```

```
Switch(config)#hostname 2950
2950(config)#exit
And look at the version of IOS running on it:
2950#show version
Cisco Internetwork Operating System Software
IOS (tm) C2950 Software (C2950-I6Q4L2-M), Version 12.1(20)EA1a, RELEASE
SOFTWARE (fc1)
Copyright (c) 1986-2004 by cisco Systems, Inc.
Compiled Mon 19-Apr-04 20:58 by yenanh
Image text-base: 0x80010000, data-base: 0x805A8000

ROM: Bootstrap program is C2950 boot loader

Switch uptime is 11 minutes
System returned to ROM by power-on
System image file is "flash:/c2950-i6q4l2-mz.121-20.EA1a.bin"

cisco WS-C2950G-12-EI (RC32300) processor (revision E0) with 20713K bytes of
memory.
Processor board ID FHK0652X0PY
Last reset from system-reset
Running Enhanced Image
12 FastEthernet/IEEE 802.3 interface(s)
2 Gigabit Ethernet/IEEE 802.3 interface(s)

32K bytes of flash-simulated non-volatile configuration memory.
Base ethernet MAC Address: 00:0C:BE:D4:3C:40
Motherboard assembly number: 34-7410-05
Power supply part number: 34-0475-02
Motherboard serial number: FUY00LWXZ
Power supply serial number: PHI0648897W
Model revision number: E0
Motherboard revision number: A0
Model number: WS-C2950G-12-EI
System serial number: FHK0652X0PY
Configuration register is 0xF
```

Switches can be managed remotely in the same way a router can be. An IP address and default gateway can be configured on the switch. Since the switchports are layer 2 ports, they cannot be assigned an IP address. For this purpose a switch virtual interface (SVI), is created on the switch. SVI is a layer 3 interface and every VLAN can have one. SVIs are named after the VLAN ID, such as "Interface VLAN1". The SVIs can be assigned an IP address.

The default management VLAN is VLAN 1. You can, however, change this.

For a management interface to become active you must create the VLAN, add an interface to the VLAN, and configure an IP address on the relevant SVI interface and a default gateway for IP traffic.

```
2950#conf t
Enter configuration commands, one per line.  End with CNTL/Z.
2950(config)#interface vlan 2
2950(config-subif)#ip address 172.16.100.1 255.255.0.0
2950(config-subif)#exit
2950(config)#ip default-gateway 172.16.1.1
2950(config)#^Z
2950#
00:22:51: %SYS-5-CONFIG_I: Configured from console by console
2950#conf t
Enter configuration commands, one per line.  End with CNTL/Z.
2950(config)#interface fastethernet 0/1
2950(config-if)#switchport mode access
2950(config-if)#switchport access vlan 2
2950(config-if)#exit
```

Apart from this, the switch will also require line VTY configuration and enable secret / password configuration similar to a router:

```
2950(config)#enable secret cisco123
2950(config)#line vty 0 4
2950(config-line)#password cisco
2950(config-line)#login
```

Now, go through the Module 3 labs in the labs section in Part II.

SUMMARY QUESTIONS

1. What three functions do switches provide?
2. Which protocol prevents loops on the network?
3. Which switching method has the highest latency
4. How is VLAN information stored within the frame?
5. What is the default trunk encapsulation on Cisco routers?
6. What is the defaulting VTP mode on a Cisco switch?
7. Trunking can only work on what minimum port speed?
8. _____ _____ prevents VLAN information from flooding other trunk ports when there is no need.
9. Name the three VTP modes.
10. How would you make an interface a trunk link on a 2950?

RESOURCES

You can find more information at:

http://www.howtonetwork.net/public/1047.cfm

CHAPTER 4

Module 4—IP Addressing

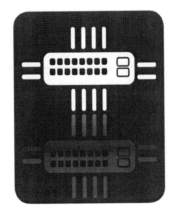

What you will learn in this module	Timings
How binary works	
How hexadecimal works	Theory: 70 minutes
IP addressing	Labs: 90 minutes
How to subnet	Review: 5 minutes
How IP subnet zero works	
VLSM and route summarization	
How NAT works	

HOW BINARY WORKS

In order to understand how IP addressing works you need to understand binary mathematics. Computers and networking equipment do not understand decimal. We use decimal because it is a numbering system using ten digits. It was invented by a caveman centuries ago when he realized we all had ten digits on our hands and they could be used for counting dinosaurs.

Computers and networking equipment can only understand electrical signals. Since an electrical signal can only be on or off, the only numbering system that will work is binary. Binary only uses two numbers, a 0 or a 1. A 0 means there is no electrical pulse on the wire, and a 1 means there is a pulse on the wire.

Any number can be made up from binary values. The more binary values we add, the larger the number can become. For every binary value we add, we double the next number i.e., 1 to 2 to 4 to 8 to 16 and so on into infinity if we wished. With two binary digits we can count up to 3. We just place a 0 or a 1 in the column to decide if we want to use that value or not.

We will start with only two binary values in the columns, 1 and 2.

2	1
0	0
0 + 0 = 0	

2	1
0	1
0 + 1 = 1	

2	1
1	0
2 + 0 = 2	

2	1
1	1
2 + 1 = 3	

If we use eight binary bit places (an octet) we can get any number from 0 up to 255.

128	64	32	16	8	4	2	1

If we add a 0 to each of these columns, we have a value of 0 in decimal.

128	64	32	16	8	4	2	1
0	0	0	0	0	0	0	0

If we add a 1 to each of these columns, we have a value of 255 in decimal.

128	64	32	16	8	4	2	1
1	1	1	1	1	1	1	1

Don't believe me?

128 + 64 + 32 + 16 + 8 + 4 + 2 + 1 = 255

So logic dictates we can actually make any number from 0 to 255 by placing an on bit or a 1 in the various columns.

128	64	32	16	8	4	2	1
0	0	1	0	1	1	0	0

32 + 8 + 4 = 44

IP addressing and subnetting are based upon the fundamentals above. We can summarize what we know so far by looking at the table below. Pay special attention to Table 4–1 because the values can be used for any subnet mask (more on that later).

Table 4–1: Binary values

Binary	Decimal
10000000	128
11000000	192
11100000	224
11110000	240
11111000	248
11111100	252
11111110	254
11111111	255

Make up some of your own binary numbers to ensure sure you understand this fully.

HOW HEXADECIMAL WORKS

Hexadecimal (or hex) is an alternative numbering system. Rather than counting in twos or tens, sixteen numbers or characters are used. Hex starts at 0 and goes all the way up to F.

0 1 2 3 4 5 6 7 8 9 A B C D E F

Each hexadecimal digit actually represents four binary digits.

Table 4–2: Binary to hex to digital conversion

Decimal	0	1	2	3	4	5	6	7
Hex	0	1	2	3	4	5	6	7
Binary	0000	0001	0010	0011	0100	0101	0110	0111

Decimal	8	9	10	11	12	13	14	15
Hex	8	9	A	B	C	D	E	F
Binary	1000	1001	1010	1011	1100	1101	1110	1111

Converting from binary to hex is fairly simple.

Decimal	13	6	2	12
Hex	D	6	2	C
Binary	1101	0110	0010	1100

Hex is a more manageable counting system for humans than binary but close enough to binary to be used by computers and networking equipment. Any number can be made using hex, as it can using binary or decimal. We just count in multiples of 16 instead. 1 then 16 then 16 multiplied by 16 (256), then 256 multiplied by 16 (4096) and so on.

			1	A
Hex	4096	256	16	1

Counting in hex therefore goes: 0 1 2 3 4 5 6 7 8 9 A B C D E F 10 11 12 13 14 15 16 17 18 19 1A 1B 1C 1D 1E 1F 20 21 22 etc. to infinity. 1A (above), for example, is an A in the 1 column and a 1 in the 16 column. A = 10 + 16 = 26.

When converting binary to hex, it makes the task easier to break the octet into two groups of four bits. So, 11110011 becomes 1111 0011. 1111 is 8 + 4 + 2 +1 = 15, and 0011 is 2 + 1 = 3. 15 is F in hex, and 3 is 3, giving us the answer F3. You can check Table 4–2 to confirm this.

Hex to binary is the same process. 7C can be split into 7, which is 0111 in binary and C is (12 in decimal or) 1100 in binary. The answer is 01111100.

Have a try

Here are some examples for you to try. If you get stuck then you can find the answers at the end of the book. A very useful thing to do would be write out the charts for working out hex and binary, i.e., for hex a 1 column, then a 16 column, then a 256, and so on.

- Convert 1111 to hex and decimal
- Convert 11010 to hex and decimal
- Convert 10000 to hex and decimal
- Convert 20 to binary and hex
- Convert 32 to binary and hex
- Convert 101 to binary and hex
- Convert A6 from hex to binary and decimal
- Convert 15 from hex to binary and decimal
- Convert B5 from hex to binary and decimal

It would be useful in the exam to write out Table 4–2 to help you work out any binary to hex to decimal conversions.

IP VERSION 4

The current version of Internet Protocol (IP) in wide deployment is version 4. Version 6 is currently in use on a number of experimental networks and will ultimately replace IPv4 on the Internet. There is, however, a lot of work yet to be done before this can happen. It is important to understand that although the exam is mostly concerned with subnetting in IPv4, you should be familiar with how to read IPv6 because at some point in the not too distant future it will soon become the standard for all networks.

IPv4 uses four groups of octets to make an IP address and each octet is made up of eight bits or 1 byte. Therefore, every IP address is 32 binary bits (4 x 8 = 32), or 4 bytes.

 IN THE EXAM:

You may see questions that ask about IP addressing in bits and bytes; pay careful attention and read the question thoroughly.

IPv4 was designed so that there would be enough IP addresses for the foreseeable future. No one predicted the huge growth in IT that was to come, so this scheme in its initial incarnation had to be amended to cater for the demand.

An example of how an IPv4 address appears in binary:

```
11000011.11110000.11001011.11111100
1st octet   2nd octet   3rd octet   4th octet
```

Each grouping of eight numbers is an octet and the four octets gives us a 32-bit IP address.

 IN THE REAL WORLD:

It is worth remembering that routers do not see an IPv4 address as four octets; they just see 32 bits. Octets just make things easier for us to see.

Powers of two

In order to really understand IP addressing you should understand the powers of two. While it may appear confusing initially, you simply start with the number 2 and keep doubling the previous number. And that is all there is to it.

$1 \times 2 = 2$

$2 \times 2 = 4$

$3 \times 2 = 8$

$4 \times 2 = 16$

The important thing is not the multiplication, it is what is happening to the answers. Each time the number doubles. If we want to work out the powers, we would write it like this:

$2\char`^1 = 2 \times 1$, which is 2

$2\char`^2 = 2 \times 2$, which is 4

$2\char`^3 = 2 \times 2 \times 2$, which is 8

$2\char`^4 = 2 \times 2 \times 2 \times 2$, which is 16

$2\char`^5 = 2 \times 2 \times 2 \times 2 \times 2$, which is 32

and so on.

The ^ character represents "to the power of".

IP addressing

So now we understand that an IP address is made up from binary numbers which are grouped into octets. The reason for this is that when IP addressing was first conceived it was determined that this amount would be more than enough for many years to come. Unfortunately, the huge growth of home and business computing was never anticipated. IPv6 has several trillion available addresses that should last a few years into the future.

IP addresses are broken into classes. Classes were used when IP addresses were first invented. Depending upon how large your organization was, dictated which class of IP address you were given.

 IN THE REAL WORLD:

IP addresses are assigned by a group called the IANA (Internet Assigned Number Authority). You can also buy one from an ISP who has in turn bought a block from the IANA.

Class A addresses

Historically, these were given to the very largest organizations that would need a tremendous number of IP addresses since they owned more computers than everyone else. Class A addresses only use the first octet to identify the network number. The remaining three octets are left for identifying the hosts on the network.

Network.Host.Host.Host

   10   .2 .5 .4

So the network is 10, and 2.5.4 is a host on that network.

In binary, it would look like:

   `nnnnnnnn.hhhhhhhh.hhhhhhhh.hhhhhhhh`

 IN THE REAL WORLD:

You would pronounce the above IP address as ten dot two dot five dot four.

Class A addresses are numbered from 1 to 126 in the first octet. Network equipment identifies a Class A address because the very first bit on the first octet has to be a 0. A Class A address cannot have a 1 in this bit position.

So, the first network number is 1.

128	64	32	16	8	4	2	1
0	0	0	0	0	0	0	1

The last possible network number is 127. (Check by adding all the values together.) Network number 127 cannot actually be used because the value 127.0.0.1 is reserved for troubleshooting (normally found on a logical interface called "loopback" on network devices). You can ping the loopback address to check if TCP/IP is working on your host.

128	64	32	16	8	4	2	1
0	1	1	1	1	1	1	1

We are not permitted to use 0 as a network number or the 127, which leaves us 126 available networks for Class A addresses.

For the hosts we can start at number one until every single possible value is used up. We will use an address starting with 10 to illustrate the example.

10.0.0.1 is the first host or in binary:

   `00001010.00000000.00000000.00000001`

   10   .0   .0   .1

(again, as a decimal)

10.0.0.2 is the second host or in binary:

```
00001010.00000000.00000000.00000010
```

10   .0   .0   .2

10.255.255.254 is the last host or in binary:

```
00001010.11111111.11111111.11111110
```

Now you can see why we use decimal. It would take a long time to write out addresses in binary and be almost impossible to remember them. You can change the router to display all addresses in binary, but there is no reason ever to do this.

Why can't we have 10.255.255.255 as a host? Because when all the binary values have a 1 on the host part of the address this tells the network that it is a broadcast packet. We will learn how this works later.

Class B addresses

Class B addresses were reserved for large organizations that needed a lot of host numbers but not as many as the largest ones. Unfortunately, when a Class B address was assigned to an organization it resulted in thousands of wasted host numbers.

Class B addresses have to have the first two binary values on the first octet reserved with a 1 and a 0 next to them.

So, the first network number is 128. We have all the available network bits on the first octet turned off.

128	64	32	16	8	4	2	1
1	0	0	0	0	0	0	0

The last available Class B network number is 191 (add the values together). Here we have turned the network bits on (on the first octet).

128	64	32	16	8	4	2	1
1	0	1	1	1	1	1	1

For Class B addresses, we use the first two octets for the network address. So for the address 130.24.5.2. 130.24 is the network number, and 5.2 is a host on that network. The rule is still that the first number you see though will always be between 128 and 191.

If we use the powers of two rule, the first two octets we will see that we can have a possible 65,536 (2^16 = 65,536) networks. We are, however, not allowed to use the first two bits of the first octet because they are reserved for showing the 10 value remember? So this leaves us with 6 + 8 digits. 2^14 gives us 16,384 networks.

We have the full two octets to use for hosts so 8 + 8 bits gives us 2^16 = 65,536 hosts per Class B network. We actually have to take two away from this value for the broadcast and subnet (more on this later) so technically it is 65,534 host addresses.

Class C addresses

These were originally reserved for any other organization that was not large enough to warrant having a Class A or Class B address. A Class C address has the first three bits reserved so the network device can recognize it as such. The first three bits must show as 110.

The first network number is 192. All the other network bits are off (0).

128	64	32	16	8	4	2	1
1	1	0	0	0	0	0	0

And the last is 223. This time all the network bits are on (on the first octet).

128	64	32	16	8	4	2	1
1	1	0	1	1	1	1	1

An example of a Class C address is 200.2.1.4. 200.2.1 is the network address and .4 is a host on that network. So, we can see that there are lots of available network numbers to assign to companies; however, we have a limited amount of numbers free to use for the hosts on our networks.

For networks we have to take the first three bits (110) from the first octet, giving us 5 + 8 + 8 = 21 (network bits).

$$2^{21} = 2,097,152$$

For the hosts we have 2^8, giving us 255 (only 254 are usable, though).

INSPIRATION:

If none of this makes any sense at the moment, this is only to be expected. I read the subnetting chapter in a very famous CCNA book for six weeks and it still made no sense to me. Eventually I worked out the easy way to subnet which I will share with you later. It is simply a case of reading through this material several (or more) times, and it will start to make more and more sense.

Class D and Class E addresses

Class D addresses are reserved for multicast traffic and cannot be used on your network. Multicast traffic is sent to multiple hosts using one IP address. A live web cast of a rock concert would be an example of multicasting.

Class E addresses are reserved for experimental use only.

Summary

So far we can condense what we know how to:

- Class A — first bit set to 0.
  Address range 1–126 (127 is reserved for testing)
  Network.Host.Host.Host
- Class B — first bits set to 10.
  Address range 128–191.
  Network.Network.Host.Host
- Class C — first bits set to 110.
  Address range 192–223.

Network.Network.Network.Host

- Class D — first bits set to 1110.
  Address range from 224–239.
- Class E — first bits set to 11110. Address range from 240–255.

We only need to look at the number in the first octet to recognize which class address we are dealing with:

- 10.1.2.1 = Class A
- 190.2.3.4 = Class B
- 220.3.4.2 = Class C

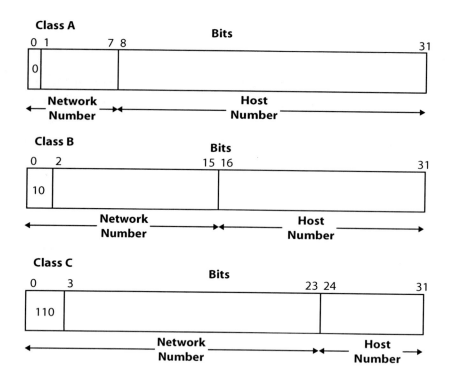

Figure 4–1: IP addressing classes summarized

To see some examples of subnetting, please watch the YouTube subnetting videos: http://www.youtube.com/user/paulwbrowning.

Reserved addresses

In order to help prevent wastage of IP addresses certain addresses were reserved for use on private networks. Any individual can use these addresses on their network providing they do not try to get out to the Internet using them. The address allocation scheme was suggested in RFC 1918 "Address Allocation for Private Internets".

 IN THE REAL WORLD:

In order to get out to the Internet a technique known as NAT (network address translation) is used to swap your private address to a public address (more on NAT later).

The reserved addresses are:

- 10.x.x.x—Any IP address beginning with 10
- 172.16.x.x–172.31.x.x—Any IP starting with 172.16 to 172.31 inclusive
- 192.168.x.x—Any IP address starting with 192.168

This idea proved to be an ideal way to avoid wasting thousands of IP addresses.

SUBNETTING

Subnetting can be one of the most difficult subjects to master for a CCNA candidate. There is a long way to subnet and a very short and easy way. It is vital you understand how the long way works first but then in real life you will use the short (easy way).

 IN THE REAL WORLD:

You would need to use the long hand way of working out subnetting when designing subnetting for a client or when troubleshooting a subnetting problem.

Address depletion

Shortly after the IPv4 addressing scheme was implemented it became apparent that there were not enough addresses to meet the demand. More and more organizations were using computers and networking equipment and the current scheme was wasting thousands of addresses.

Example

A company is given a Class A address. Class A addresses can only be given to 126 companies. The first octet is used for the network, and the other three octets are free for use on the network.

If we use every combination of numbers on the remaining 24 digits (3 x 8), then we have a maximum value of over 16 million hosts (16,777,216, in fact). We can actually work out how many networks or hosts we have by using the powers of two.

 IN THE EXAM:

You will have to be very familiar with the powers of two, hex, and binary to pass the exam.

So we have three octets free for hosts on the network, giving us 3 times 8 or 24 bits.
2 24, or 2 x 2 x 2 x 2 x 2 x 2 x 2 x 2 x 2 x 2 x 2 x 2 x 2 x 2 x 2 x 2 x 2 x 2 x 2 x 2 x 2 x 2 x 2 x 2.
So, 2 24 = 16,777,216

Historically, what happened was that a very large organization would be allocated a Class A address. They would need around 10,000 host addresses and waste the other 16 million plus. Because they owned the network number it could not be shared with other organizations so the other addresses were wasted.

For a Class B address, the story was very similar.
2 x 16 is 2 x 2 x 2 x 2 x 2 x 2 x 2 x 2 x 2 x 2 x 2 x 2 x 2 x 2 x 2 x 2 = 65,536 hosts

INSPIRATION:

Working out IP addressing and subnetting can seem like learning another language at times. Confusion comes before inspiration, not the other way around.

HOW TO SUBNET

The problem with the initial way of using IP addresses was that we were fixed with having certain parts of the address for the network and certain parts for the hosts.

Class A addresses were fixed with 8 bits for the network and 24 for the hosts. Class B addresses were fixed with 16 bits for the network and 16 for the hosts. Class C addresses were fixed with 24 bits for the network and 8 for the hosts. There had to be some way for host addresses to not be wasted. The answer came with the introduction of subnetting.

Subnetting allowed bits that were normally used for the host part to be used for the subnet part of the address. In order to let the routers or PCs know that subnetting was being used another number had to be applied to the IP address. This number is known as the subnet mask and is also in binary.

IN THE REAL WORLD:

Subnetting and many other internetworking methods and tools are introduced by Requests for Comments or RFCs. RFCs are open for anybody to comment upon before they are published (www.rfc-editor.org).

Each bit on the subnet mask is compared with the bits on the IP address to determine which parts belong to the network and which belong to the host. A default subnet mask was allocated to each class of address. If you do not want to use subnetting simply add the subnet mask to the end of the IP address. It is not possible to enter an IP address onto a PC or router without also entering the subnet mask.

Default subnet masks:
- Class A—255.0.0.0, or in binary:
  11111111.00000000.00000000.00000000
- Class B—255.255.0.0, or in binary:
  11111111.11111111.00000000.00000000
- Class C—255.255.255.0, or in binary:
  11111111.11111111.11111111.00000000

We can see that the first octet for Class A addresses is reserved for the network number. This is the default anyway, like the first two octets for Class B and the first three for Class C.

A rule for subnet masks is that the 1 and 0 network and host bits must be contiguous, i.e., connected without a break. So you can have 11111111.11111111.0000000.000000, but you cannot have 11111111.000111111.00000000.00000000. We can also see how important it is to remember that the router sees numbers in binary.

 IN THE REAL WORLD:

Whenever a network address does not look right to you, write it out in binary.

What we now have is a situation where each part of the IP address is matched with the subnet mask to determine which bits are part of the network identification and which bits are part of the host identification.

Example

```
10001100.10110011.11110000.11001000     140.179.240.200   Class B
11111111.11111111.00000000.00000000     255.255.0.0       Subnet mask
- - - - - - - - - - - - - - - - - - - - - - - - - - - - - - - - - - - - - - - - - - - - - - - -
10001100.10110011.00000000.00000000     140.179.0.0       Network Address
```

How did we get this number? The router performs something called logical ANDing. It compares the 1s and 0s to establish which numbers belong to the network and which belong to the host.

AND	0	1
0	0	0
1	0	1

So all the values are compared and anything apart from a 1 and 1 equals 0. Check the above example again to make sure you understand how it works.

 IN THE REAL WORLD:

Many network engineers do not understand subnetting. Make sure you are not one of them. Once you know it you know it forever.

Because you now know which the network addresses are and which are the hosts, you can start assigning IP addresses to hosts on your network. If all the host bits are 0 then you cannot use this to put on a network host. The all 0s represents the subnet; we shall see why and how shortly.

- 140.179.0.0 is your network address
- 140.179.0.0 in binary has all of the host bits turned off:
  10001100.10110011.00000000.00000000 ⇦ Every host bit is turned off
  Network.Network.Host.Host
- 140.179.0.1 can be used for your first host.
- 14.0179.0.2 can be used for your second host

You can keep adding hosts until both the second and third octet are (almost) full.

- 140.179.0.255 is still a valid host number
- 140.179.1.255 is still okay
- 140.179.255.254 is the last host number you can use.
  Here is the last host number in binary:
  10001100.10110011.<u>11111111.11111110</u> ⇦ Not every host bit is turned on
  Network.Network.Host.Host

Why cannot we use the last bit portion above for a host? An IP address with all 1s in the host portion is reserved to tell the network that the packet is a broadcast packet. A broadcast packet is a packet that must be examined by all hosts on the network (or more specifically, all of the hosts on this portion of the network, i.e., the subnet). The number below is a broadcast packet to every host on the 140.179 network.

- 140.179.255.255 in binary has all of the host bits turned on:
  10001100.10110011.11111111.11111111 ⇦ Every host bit is turned on
  Network.Network.Host.Host

So now we can see that we are not permitted to use all 0s for the hosts since this is the network, and we cannot use all 1s because this is reserved for a broadcast. With this information we will be able to decide how many available hosts we have per network or subnet.

IN THE EXAM:

You will be tested thoroughly in the exam on subnetting and working out how many hosts per subnet and which is the subnet and broadcast address. You must be able to do this quickly or you will run out of time.

We use the power of two formula to work out how many hosts we get on our subnet. We simply multiply two to the power of how many host bits we have and take away two—one for the network of all 0s and one for the broadcast address of all 1s.

So for our example of 140.179.0.0 255.255.0.0, we can see we that we have the last two octets free (the 0.0) to allocate to hosts on the network. That is, two lots of eight binary bits, giving us 16.

The formula for the maximum number of hosts (per subnet) is: $2^n - 2$. n = 16. Therefore, $2^{16} - 2$ = 65,534

Do you think it would be practical to have a network with over 65,000 hosts on it? We cannot break this network down into smaller units and if we have a broadcast on the network, each and every single host on the network will have to stop what they are doing to listen to the broadcast packet to see if it is the intended recipient.

Let's steal some bits from the host part of the address and make a subnet or mini-network from those bits. I will write out the network address in long hand to make it easer to understand.

```
140.179. 00000    000.00000000
[16 bits][5 bits][11 bits]
[network][subnet][host bits]
```

We have stolen five of the host bits to use to make our subnet. The advantage is that we have more than one subnet we can use and we have fewer hosts per subnet. We can use the powers-of-two formula to work out how many subnets we have and how many hosts per subnet. We do not have take two away for the subnets for reasons you will see later.

2^5 (or 2 x 2 x 2 x 2 x 2) = 32 subnets, each with
2^{11} (or 2 x 2 x 2 x 2 x 2 x 2 x 2 x 2 x 2 x 2 x 2 – 2) = 2046 hosts per subnet.

Why would we want to do this? You have fewer hosts using the bandwidth on your network segment. It is far easier to administer smaller subnets rather than one huge network. Additionally, it is desirable to limit the number of broadcasts on a given subnet because each and every host on a subnet must examine the contents of a broadcast packet, whether it is the intended recipient or not.

In an environment with an excessive number of hosts, the number of broadcasts can grow quite a bit and while not immediately measurable, this broadcast traffic will lower the overall performance of all of the networked systems. Also, you can only have one network per router interface. It is better to have a smaller number of hosts connected to a router interface rather than several thousand.

Remember: the more host bits you steal the more subnets you get but each of those subnets is capable of supporting a lesser number of hosts. Deciding how many hosts you need and how many hosts per subnet is part of the network design phase. The more host bits we steal means we have more and more subnets and less host bits available, this is the tradeoff.

Below is the table for a Class B network. Remember that for Class B addresses, we are looking at the third and fourth octets for the bit pattern. The first two octets are used for the network address and cannot be stolen.

Table 4–3: Class B subnetting summaries

Bit pattern (3rd/4th octet)	CIDR	Masked bits	Subnets	Hosts per subnet (2^x - 2)
00000000.00000000	/16 255.255.0.0	0	1 (network)	65,534
10000000.00000000	/17 255.255.128.0	1	2	32,766
11000000.00000000	/18 255.255.192.0	2	4	16,382
11100000.00000000	/19 255.255.224.0	3	8	8190
11110000.00000000	/20 255.255.240.0	4	16	4094
11111000.00000000	/21 255.255.248.0	5	32	2046
11111100.00000000	/22 255.255.252.0	6	64	1022
11111110.00000000	/23 255.255.254.0	7	128	510
11111111.00000000	/24 255.255.255.0	8	256	254
11111111.10000000	/25 255.255.255.128	9	512	126
11111111.11000000	/26 255.255.255.192	10	1024	62
11111111.11100000	/27 255.255.255.224	11	2048	30
11111111.11110000	/28 255.255.255.240	12	4096	14
11111111.11111000	/29 255.255.255.248	13	8192	6
11111111.11111100	/30 255.255.255.252	14	16,384	2
11111111.11111110	/31 255.255.255.254	15	32,768	0 (not usable)

How to write out subnet masks

We do not write out the subnet mask bits in binary, we have a way to write out subnet masks when entering them on network equipment and when writing them out by hand.

If we steal five host bits from the third octet, we have to add the binary values together.

128	64	32	16	8	4	2	1
1	1	1	1	1	0	0	0

So, we have 128 + 64 + 32 + 16 + 8 = 248.

Remember that we are using a Class B example here and so are working with the third octet. We are not allowed to alter the first two octets; they are fixed.
255.255.248.0

This tells the router we are subnetting and that we are using the first five hosts bits to carve out our subnets.

Things can get a little bit (more) complicated, and we can no longer rely upon what our eyes are telling us because the router is looking at a binary value and we are looking at a decimal value. Do not worry too much though as we will look at the quick and easy to work out subnetting later.

In order for the router to know if a host is on a certain subnet, it looks to the masked bits. If all of the masked bits match, then it follows that the host must be on the same subnet. If the subnet bits do not match, then the hosts are on different subnets.

This time we have IP address: 129.10.147.0 255.255.248.0

Again, we have a Class B address and are stealing five bits for subnetting. We know we have stolen five bits because 248 in binary is 11111000, which is five masked bits.

```
10000001.00001010.10010011.00010000  129.10.147.32
10000001.00001010.10010100.01010101  129.10.148.85
```

We can see that the subnet bits in the example above both match:

```
10000001.00001010.10011010.00000010  129.10.154.2
```

This time one of the subnet bits has changed. So, the router or PC can see it is a different subnet. Unfortunately, when we write it out in decimal, it is not very easy for us to see that this third IP address is in a different subnet.

Changing the subnet representation

Although subnet masks are displayed as dotted decimal, the format can be changed to bitcount or hex with the "ip netmask-format" command.

```
Router#show interface serial 0
Serial0 is administratively down, line protocol is down
  Hardware is HD64570
  Internet address is 192.168.1.1 255.255.255.0
```

```
RouterA#terminal ip netmask-format ?
  bit-count     Display netmask as number of significant bits
  decimal       Display netmask in dotted decimal
  hexadecimal   Display netmask in hexadecimal

RouterA#terminal ip netmask-format bit-count

Router#show interface serial 0
Serial0 is administratively down, line protocol is down
  Hardware is HD64570
  Internet address is 192.168.1.1/24
```

Bit-count shows the address with a slash value, such as `192.168.1.1/24`. Decimal displays the subnet mask in dotted decimal, such as `255.255.255.0`. Hex shows the mask in hex, such as `0XFFFFFF00`.

There are only certain values available to use as a subnet mask due to binary mathematics.

If you calculate a subnet mask and it is some other value such as 160, it is clearly wrong!

Table 4–4: Class B mask values

Binary value	Subnet value
00000000	0
10000000	128
11000000	192
11100000	224
11110000	240
11111000	248
11111100	252
11111110	254
11111111	255

Variable-length subnet masking (VLSM)

Although subnetting provides a useful mechanism to improve the IP addressing issue, network administrators were only able to use one subnet mask for an entire network. RFC 1009 addressed this issue by allowing a subnetted network to use more than one subnet mask.

Now a network administrator could have a Class B address with a 255.255.192.0 mask but further break that subnet down into smaller units with masks, such as 255.255.224.0. Instead of writing out the subnet in decimal, engineers in the real world use something called a slash address. They write out how many bits are used for subnetting. We go into VLSM in more detail starting on page 153.

Examples

255.255.0.0 can be expressed as /16 because there are 16 binary bits masked.

```
11111111.11111111.00000000.00000000 = 16 on or masked bits.
```

255.255.192.0 can be expressed as /18 because there are 18 binary bits masked.

```
11111111.11111111.11000000.00000000 = 18 on or masked bits.
```

255.255.240.0 can be expressed as /20 because there are 20 binary bits masked.

```
11111111.11111111.11110000.00000000 = 20 on or masked bits.
```

 IN THE REAL WORLD:

Cisco IOS 12.0 and later will recognize VLSM automatically. Prior to this you will need to use the "ip subnet-zero" command if you want to use VLSM.

Classless inter domain routing (CIDR)

RFC1517, 1518, 1519, and 1520 specify CIDR features. CIDR removed the need for classes of IP address and was yet another solution to the problem of depletion of IP addresses. CIDR allows for something known as route aggregation whereby a single route in a routing table can represent several network addresses saving space and routing table size.

Using CIDR, we no longer need to worry about the class system for addressing networks. Network administrators could now allocate address spaces on an as needed basis rather than having to use a Class B address and waste thousands of spare addresses.

CIDR also allows for supernetting. Supernetting enables you to advertise a summary of your network addresses providing you have a contiguous block. For example, if you owned the networks 172.16.20.0/24 up to 172.16.23.0/24. Then you could advertise a single network out to the Internet of 172.16.20.0/22. The advantage is a saving on bandwidth and greater efficiency. This is also known as route summarization.

We cover route summarization in more detail starting on page 161.

Route summarization only works if you work out the addresses in binary first.

```
11111111.11111111.11111111.00000000 = 24-bit mask
10101100.00010000.00010100.00000000 = 172.16.20.0
```

```
10101100.00010000.00010101.00000000 = 172.16.21.0
10101100.00010000.00010110.00000000 = 172.16.22.0
10101100.00010000.00010111.00000000 = 172.16.23.0
```

All of the underlined parts of the address are common and can be aggregated with one subnet mask to advertise them all. There are 22 common bits, so we can use the mask 255.255.252.0 or /22 to advertise the entire block of addresses.

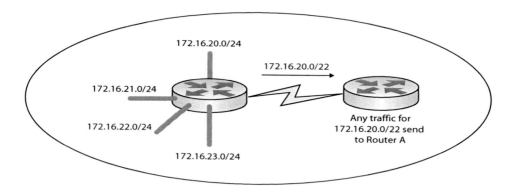

Figure 4–2: Supernetting reduces the amount of routes advertised.

CIDR allows the use of the slash system for representing subnet masks, e.g., /26 instead of 255.255.255.192. Below is a Class C subnetting chart with the CIDR representation.

Table 4–5: CIDR

Masked bits	Subnet mask	CIDR	Subnets	Hosts
0	255.255.255.0	/24	1 network	254
1	255.255.255.128	/25	2	126
2	255.255.255.192	/26	4	62
3	255.255.255.224	/27	8	30
4	255.255.255.240	/28	16	14
5	255.255.255.248	/29	32	6
6	255.255.255.252	/30	64	2

How many subnets and how many hosts?

Understanding this formula is crucial to passing the CCNA exam and also in real life networking. Many networking emergencies could have been avoided by planning for future requirements during the design stage.

IN THE REAL WORLD:

When planning a network addressing scheme, always ask the client what their expected growth for the next few years is and account for that. Never design a network addressing scheme for what they have now.

Given a network ID and subnet mask, how many subnets can we form and how many host are there per subnet?

It all boils down to the powers of two.

```
255.255.224.0
11111111.11111111.11100000.00000000
[16 bits]        [3 bits][13 bits]
[Network]        [Subnet][Host]
```

So in the Class B example above, we have three subnet bits to use and we can use every combination of three binary numbers to make up different subnets.

```
000,001,010,101,011,110,100,111
```

We used to have to disregard 000 because this is the subnet, and we could not use the 111 because this is for the broadcast. Cisco has changed this for the CCNA, and you are now permitted to use them both. The only answer is to read the question carefully. Cisco should not give you two answers to choose from one allowing subnet zero and one not.

Alternatively, we could say:
$$2^3 = (2 \times 2 \times 2) = 8$$
How many hosts?

We have 13 bits left for the host addresses.
$$2^{13} - 2 = 8190.$$

So for this subnet mask, we can see we have eight subnets and each subnet has 8190 hosts available for use.

INSPIRATION:

Do not worry if none of this makes any sense at the moment. Just keep on going. Once you learn the easy way to subnet using the Super Subnetting Chart™ you will realize that this is not difficult at all.

Another example

```
131.107.32.0 (IP address)
255.255.224.0 (subnet mask)
```

We have a Class B address and are taking three bits from the host bits (three binary bits is 11100000, which is 128 + 64 + 32 or 224). There is not room to fit in every permutation so we have had to shorten the output.

```
11111111.11111111.11100000.00000000 255.255.224.0 subnet mask
10000011.01101011.00100000.00000000 131.107.32.0* (this is the subnet)
10000011.01101011.00100000.00000001 131.107.32.1 (this is the first host)
10000011.01101011.00100000.00000010 131.107.32.2 (this is the second host)
10000011.01101011.00100000.00000011 131.107.32.3 (this is the third host)
10000011.01101011.00100001.11111111 131.107.33.255 (we keep counting up)
10000011.01101011.00100011.11111111 131.107.35.255 (keep going)
10000011.01101011.00100111.11111110 131.107.39.254 (keep going)
10000011.01101011.00111111.11111110 131.107.63.254 (this is the last host)
10000011.01101011.00111111.11111111 131.107.63.255* (the broadcast address)
```

So, our hosts are 131.107.32.1 to 131.107.63.254 (8190 in total)
   * 131.107.32.0 = subnet and 131.107.63.255 = broadcast address

Because the IP address changed from 32.1 and then 33.255 all the way up to 63.254, it is easy to look at it and mistake them for different subnets. When we write out the addresses correctly we can see that all of the hosts above are on the same subnet.

This means they will all have to be attached to one router interface. You cannot decide to put half of your addresses on one side of the router and half on the other. Many engineers have made this mistake and wasted hours trying to troubleshoot the problem.

In the above example, the first subnet would be 131.107.0.0, which is the zero subnet. We will look at this shortly.

INSPIRATION:

It may take several reviews of this chapter to understand IP addressing and subnetting. There is no need to get disheartened if it does not sink in the first or even the tenth time, just keep following the examples and re-reading.

SHORTCUT METHOD

Writing out IP addresses and subnets in binary is very time consuming. There is a quick and easy way to do it. Just follow five simple steps.

1. How many subnets?

   2 to the power of masked bits, or 2^x

2. How many hosts per subnet?

   2 to the power of unmasked bits − 2

3. What are the valid subnets?

   256 — the rightmost nonzero subnet to give us the subnet increment

4. What are number of hosts per subnet?

5. What is the broadcast address of the subnet?

Example

Which subnet is 131.107.32.1 255.255.224.0 in?

```
(255.255.224.0 is 11111111.11111111.11100000.00000000 in binary.
```

We could actually write this out with a slash mask of /19 (19 masked network bits or 1s). You can see that we are subnetting on the third octet here.

1. How many subnets?

   We have stolen three bits (128 + 64 + 32 = 224 subnet), so:

   $2^3 = 8$ subnets (or 2 x 2 x 2 = 8)

2. How many hosts per subnet?

   We have 13 bits left for hosts, so:

   $2^{13} - 2 = 8190$

3. What are the valid subnets?

   Take the right most non-zero subnet (224) away from 256.

   256 − 224 = 32

   This part is crucial. If you get it wrong, then all of your subnetting will be off. So, double check it. Some people make the mistake of doubling the numbers—i.e., 32, 64, 128, etc. We now know that we have eight valid subnets and each subnet will be an increment of 32. We can start at 0 if subnet zero is permitted 0, 32, 64, 96, 128, 160, 192, 224. (224 is also permitted if subnet zero is allowed.

4. What are the valid hosts per subnet?

    It is best to write out the subnet number and the next subnet number. From this we can work out our first and valid hosts.

    1st subnet: 131.107.0.0   ⇦ This is the zero subnet (more later)

    2nd subnet: 131.107.32.0* ⇦ 131.107.32.1 is in this subnet

    3rd subnet: 131.107.64.0

    4th subnet: 131.107.96.0

    5th subnet: 131.107.128.0

    6th subnet: 131.107.160.0

    7th subnet: 131.107.192.0

    8th subnet: 131.107.224.0

    So, now we know we can use any number including the 224 subnet if subnet zero is allowed. It is fairly clear from the list above that the host address we are looking for is on the second subnet, so we can look at the available host numbers on this.

    Subnet: 131.107.32.0

    1st host: 131.107.32.1

    2nd host: 131.107.32.2

    3rd host: 131.107.32.3 … We could keep going, but there are over 8000 hosts.

    …

    Last host: 131.107.63.254 (we take one away from the broadcast to get this value)

    Broadcast is 131.107.63.255 (we take one away from the next subnet [131.107.64.0] to get this value).

    For the third or .64 subnet, we follow the same process of writing out the subnet and broadcast address. We can work out the broadcast address by writing out the next subnet. the subnet starting 131.107.64 is the third of our eight subnets. We then take one away from that to determine the broadcast address for the previous subnet.

    Subnet: 131.107.64.0 (take one away to get the broadcast for the .32 subnet)

    1st host: 131.107.64.1

    Last host: 131.107.95.254

    Broadcast: 131.107.95.255

    We could go on, but can you see that we have gone past the IP address we are trying to find, which is 131.107.32.1?

5. What is the broadcast address?

    Broadcast address 131.107.63.255

It is pretty easy to work out if you write out the subnets first.

What just happened there?

Without being able to see the whole thing in binary, it does look a little strange. You just have to have confidence that the method works and if in doubt go back to binary. We can prove that the broadcast address is such by checking to see if it is all 1s in binary. The last host will be the last number we can use with out having all 1s (255 in decimal).

```
10000011.01101011.00111111.11111110 131.107.63.254 (One host bit not on.)
10000011.01101011.00111111.11111111 131.107.63.255 (All host bits on here.)
```

The underlined bits are the subnet bits. The .254 has all the host bits apart from one turned on. The broadcast address has all the host bits turned on. This tells the network that it is a broadcast packet to the subnet.

If we follow the process for each subnet using a subnet number of 255.255.224.0 going up in increments of 32, we will get the following host numbers:

- Subnet 1: 131.107.0.1 to 131.107.31.254
- Subnet 2: 131.107.32.1 to 131.107.63.254* (you can see host 32.1 is in this subnet)
- Subnet 3: 131.107.64.1 to 131.107.95.254
- Subnet 4: 131.107.96.1 to 131.107.127.254
- Subnet 5: 131.107.128.1 to 131.107.159.254
- Subnet 6: 131.107.160.1 to 131.107.191.254
- Subnet 7: 131.107.192.1 to 131.107.223.254
- Subnet 8: 131.107.224.1 to 131.107.255.254

 INSPIRATION:

If you still do not understand any of this be assured that this is perfectly normal. Remember your first driving lesson?

Another example

Which subnet is host 10.20.1.23 255.240.0.0 (12 bits) in?

We have taken four bits (240 in binary is 11110000 or 128 + 64 + 32 + 16) to make subnets from since Class A addresses normally have the default eight bits

(255.0.0.0 is 11111111.0000000.0000000.00000000 in binary).

1. How many subnets?

   $2^4 = 16$

2. How many hosts per subnet?

   We have 20 bits left for hosts so:

   $2^{20} - 2 = 1,048,574$ hosts per subnet

3. What are the valid subnets?

   $256 - 240 = 16$ (the increment). Our subnets go up in increments of 16.

   10.0.0.0 (the zero subnet)

   10.16.0.0

   10.32.0.0

   10.48.0.0 .... all the way up to

   10.224.0.0

   10.240.0.0

4. What are the valid hosts per subnets?

   10.0.0.0   Hosts 10.0.0.1 to 10.15.255.254

   10.16.0.0 Hosts 10.16.0.1 to 10.31.255.254 * 10.20.1.23 is in this subnet

   10.32.0.0 Hosts 10.32.0.1 to 10.47.255.254

   10.48.0.0 Hosts 10.48.0.1 to 10.63.255.254

   10.64.0.0 and so on...

   10.224.0.0 Hosts 10.224.0.1 to 10.239.255.254

   10.240.0.0 Hosts 10.240.0.1 to 10.255.255.254 (all 1s, so not accepted)

5. What are the broadcast addresses?

   This is the last address before each subnet.

   10.15.255.254 is the last host on the first subnet.

   10.15.255.255 is the broadcast address.

   10.16.0.0 is the next subnet.

   10.16.0.1 is the first host on the next subnet.

   10.31.255.254 is the last host.

   10.31.255.255 is the broadcast address.

   10.32.0.0 is the next subnet.

   10.47.255.255 broadcast address on the third subnet.

   10.48.0.0 next subnet, etc.

You will learn how to shorten this step down shortly.

Exam questions

In the exam you will have one of two types of subnetting questions. The first type you have just seen. You have been given a certain network number and subnet mask and you need to determine which subnet the IP address is in. The second type of question is to design a subnet mask to give a customer a certain number of hosts and a certain number of subnets.

We will shorten the five steps down. It does help, though, to go through them to answer any type of subnetting question.

We cover that part in "Working out how many hosts and how many subnets" on page 148.

Example

Which subnet is host 192.168.21.41 /28 in?

The first and most important task is to work out how to change the /28 mask into a full subnet mask. You already know that each octet is eight binary bits and 8 + 8 + 8 = 24 binary bits, which is 255.255.255.0. We need to add four to 24 to get 28, which is 128 + 64 + 32 + 16 binary places or 11110000, or 240. The Super Subnetting Chart™ (see later) will make this task whole task so easy you will wonder what all the fuss was about.

With four bits of masking, we know we have $2^4 = 16$ subnets. This leaves four bits for the hosts which is $2^4 - 2 = 14$ hosts per subnet.

The subnet mask is 255.255.255.240 (4 masked bits on the last octet).
256 − 240 = 16 increments

We want to go up in subnets until we find the one where host 41 is (subnet 3 below).
Subnet 1: 192.168.21.0   hosts 1–14 (broadcast = 15); this is the zero subnet
Subnet 2: 192.168.21.16 hosts 17–30 (broadcast = 31)
Subnet 3: 192.168.21.32 hosts 33–46* (broadcast = 47) * 41 is in this range
Subnet 4: 192.168.21.48 hosts 49–62 (broadcast = 63)
Subnet 5: 192.168.21.64 hosts 65–78 (broadcast = 79)
and so on ...up to
Subnet 16: 192.168.21.240 hosts 241–254 (broadcast = 255)

Example

Which subnet is host 10.65.2.5 /10 in?

Turn the /10 into a subnet mask. 255 is eight binary bits, so we need to add 2 to get to 10.
Two binary bits is 128 + 64, which is 192 or 11000000.
Two masked subnet bits = 255.192.0.0

$2^2 = 4$ subnets.

We have $2^{22} - 2 = 4,194,302$ hosts per subnet.

$256 - 192 = 64$ increment

s (for the subnets).

Subnet 1: 10.0.0.0 hosts 10.0.0.1–10.63.255.254 (broadcast = 255)

Subnet 2: 10.64.0.0 hosts 10.64.0.1–10.127.255.254 (broadcast = 255) * host 65.2.5

is in this range

Subnet 3: 10.128.0.0 hosts 10.128.0.1–10.191.255.254 (broadcast = 255)

Subnet 4: 10.192.0.0 hosts 10.192.0.1–10.255.255.254 (broadcast = 255)

Let's use the Super Subnetting Chart™ to answer the next question.

Example

Which subnet is 192.168.100.203 /27 in?

We know that three binary octets is 24 bits, and to get to 27 we need to add three. Tick down three numbers on the top subnetting part of the chart. This will give you the value of 224.

So our subnet /27 is 255.255.255.224. We can then tick three across the top to get the subnet increment, which is 32 (or just take 224 away from 256, if you prefer).

We are subnetting on the third octet, so we just add up the subnets until we get to the one with the number 203 is in. I would prefer to start with a multiple of 32 to save time (160, for example), but you may prefer to start with 0, 32, 64, etc. for now.

Just remember in the exam that time is of the essence.

Subnet 1: 192.168.100.0 hosts 1–30 (broadcast = 31)

Subnet 2: 192.168.100.32 hosts 33–62 (broadcast = 63)

Subnet 3: 192.168.100.64 hosts 65–94 (broadcast = 95)

Subnet 4: 192.168.100.96 hosts 97–126 (broadcast = 127)

Subnet 5: 192.168.100.128 hosts 129–158 (broadcast = 159)

Subnet 6: 192.168.100.160 hosts 161–190 (broadcast = 191)

Subnet 7: 192.168.100.192 hosts 193–222 (broadcast = 223) * host 203 is in this subnet

Subnet 8: 192.168.100.224 hosts 225–254 (broadcast = 255)

The host 192.168.100.203 is in the subnet 192.168.100.192.

Super Subnetting Chart™

	Bits	128	64	32	16	8	4	2	1
Subnets		✓	✓	✓					
128	✓								
192	✓								
224	✓								
240									
248									
252									
254									
255									
Powers of Two	Subnets	Hosts minus 2							
2									
4									
8									
16									
32									
64									
128									
256									
512									
1024									
2048									
4096									
8192									
16,384									

There are many more examples in Appendix A, and you can watch free subnetting videos via You-Tube at: http://www.youtube.com/user/paulwbrowning.

 IN THE REAL WORLD:

A special command called "ip subnet-zero" (more on this later) allows the use of subnets starting with 0. Cisco never used to ask about this type of subnet in the exam. It is now a valid subnet for the CCNA syllabus. Check www.cisco.com for the latest syllabus.

Working out how many hosts and how many subnets

The special chart below will get enable you to answer any question in the exam. I call it the Super Subnetting Chart™. This chart will ensure you can answer any subnetting question in the exam within 30 seconds (after practice—honest!).

Super Subnetting Chart™

	Bits	128	64	32	16	8	4	2	1
Subnets									
128									
192									
224									
240									
248									
252									
254									
255									
Powers of two	Subnets	Hosts minus 2							
2									
4									
8									
16									
32									
64									
128									
256									
512									
1024									
2048									
4096									
8192									
16,384									

 INSPIRATION:

The above chart will enable you to quickly and accurately answer any subnetting question in the exam. Students on my CCNA boot camp have saved weeks of study time and valuable exam minutes by using the Super Subnetting Chart™.

What the Super Subnetting Chart™ helps you to do is easily and quickly work out how many bits are being used for subnetting, which subnet the host is on, how many hosts per subnet, and how many subnets.

Let's look at an example.

How many subnets and hosts does the address 192.168.2.0 /26 give us?

We are taking an extra two bits from the normal 24-bit mask. Tick off two numbers down on the left hand column (128 and then 192), giving us the mask of 192. Or to be more specific 255.255.255.192.

You can work out that it is two bits being used if you remember that each octet count is eight. 255.0.0.0 is eight binary bits, 255.255.0.0 is sixteen, and 255.255.255.0 is twenty four. If we have a slash twenty-six mask, then we need to add two onto the 255.255.255.0 mask, which is twenty-four bits plus two more (or 255.255.255.192).

We have taken two bits for the subnet, so on the powers of two column on the bottom left, tick down two numbers (2 and then 4). This gives us four subnets.

Now we know we have six bits left for the hosts (8 – 2 = 6 bits remaining). So tick off six places on the hosts powers of two column to get our number of hosts. Six down gives us 64 and take two away for the subnet and broadcast gives us 62 hosts per subnet. Easy, isn't it?

Super Subnetting Chart™

	Bits	128	64	32	16	8	4	2	1
Subnets		✓	✓						
128	✓								
192	✓								
224									
240									
248									
252									
254									
255									
Powers of two	Subnets	Hosts minus 2							
2	✓	✓							

4	✓	✓							
8		✓							
16		✓							
32		✓							
64		✓							
128									
256									
512									
1024									
2048									
4096									
8192									
16,384									

Another example

You are given a network address of 192.168.5.0 255.255.255.0. You are the network administrator and need to subnet this address to make six subnets each with at least 15 hosts per subnet.

Go back to the chart and go down the powers of two until you get to a number that gives you the six subnets. Two and four will not be enough, but eight gives you six subnets with two extra (it is okay if you have to go just over). So now we know we need to steal three bits for subnetting. Count down three of the top subnet numbers starting at 128 then 192, and we get 224.

Stealing three bits leaves us five bits left for hosts per subnet. If you tick down five places on the hosts per subnet column, you will see that this gives us 30 (32 – 2) hosts per subnets, which are more than enough for our requirements.

The answer is you need subnet 255.255.255.224 (or a /27 mask) to get your six subnets. If you tick down three in the lower subnet column, you can tick down three in the upper subnets column to determine the correct subnet mask.

Super Subnetting Chart™

	Bits	128	64	32	16	8	4	2	1
Subnets		✓	✓	✓					
128	✓								
192	✓								
224	✓								
240									

	Subnets	Hosts minus 2								
248										
252										
254										
255										
Powers of two	Subnets	Hosts minus 2								
2	✓	✓								
4	✓	✓								
8	✓	✓								
16		✓								
32		✓								
64										
128										
256										
512										
1024										
2048										
4096										
8192										
16,384										

 INSPIRATION:

You will also need to work through Appendix A (The easy way to subnet) to really understand how it all works. It is like riding a bike, you will soon wonder how you ever struggled.

 IN THE EXAM:

Once the exam starts you are permitted to write anything you like on the paper provided. Write down the Super Subnetting Chart™ above and you will be able to answer any subnetting question. (This is the best tip in the whole book by the way).

IP SUBNET ZERO (AGAIN)

Since IOS version 12.0 there has been a default command known as "ip subnet-zero" turned on automatically. This command allows you to use the all 0s subnet and the all 1s subnet. This has actually been the case since RFC 1918 was released. This means that you no longer have to take away two subnets when calculating your subnetting.

```
RouterA#show run
Building configuration...

Current configuration:
!
! Last configuration change at 17:22:55 UTC Mon Mar 22 2004
! NVRAM config last updated at 17:22:55 UTC Mon Mar 22 2004
!
version 12.0
service timestamps debug datetime msec
service timestamps log datetime
no service password-encryption
!
hostname RouterA
!
enable secret 5 $1$qtEP$YykBEn/hCaQK3batxzhXc/
!
ip subnet-zero
--More—
```

Traditionally, Cisco has ignored this feature for the CCNA exam, but this has now changed. You should be aware of its existence because of its wide use in the real world of networking.

Some people do become confused about this issue. Traditionally, when calculating subnets we have always taken away two because we were not able to use the subnet and broadcast addresses. We are allowed to use them in the real world, and now for the CCNA exam we should be allowed to use it. In the very unlikely event you are not, then you know you just take two away and are not allowed to use the zero or subnet as usable subnets.

Please note however, what Cisco traditionally has to say on the subject of subnet zero:

> "Subnetting with a subnet address of zero is illegal and strongly discouraged (as stated in RFC 791) because of the confusion that can arise between a network and a subnet that have the same addresses. For example, if network 131.108.0.0 is subnetted as 255.255.255.0, subnet zero would be written as 131.108.0.0—which is identical to the network address."

Appendix A covers subnetting in more detail. It will take a few read-throughs to completely understanding subnetting and IP addressing in detail.

SECONDARY IP ADDRESS

You are not restricted to using just one IP address on an interface of a Cisco router. You can assign an unlimited number of addresses using the "ip address <ip address> <subnet mask> secondary" command.

```
Router#config t
Enter configuration commands, one per line. End with CNTL/Z.
Router(config)#interface serial 0
Router(config-if)#ip address 192.168.1.1 255.255.255.0
Router(config-if)#ip address 192.168.2.1 255.255.255.0 secondary
```

You may need to do this because you need to use one than one subnet on the same physical segment of the network. An example is an insufficient amount of host addresses available with the subnet you are using.

VLSM

VLSM is the process whereby you take a major network address and then break it down into different subnets with different subnet masks at various points. In the Cisco CCNA exam you may be faced with a scenario where you are required to design an IP addressing scheme to fit certain requirements.

IP addressing

It is best to illustrate with an example.

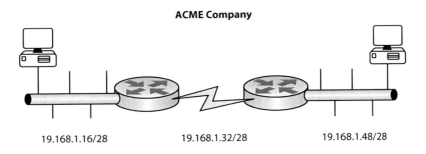

ACME Company

19.168.1.16/28   19.168.1.32/28   19.168.1.48/28

Figure 4–3: ACME Company with no VLSM

You may have spotted a few problems with the above addressing scheme. The most important issue is the breach of the conservation of IP addresses. If you are using RFC 1918 addresses (non routable such as 10.x.x.x) then perhaps you may not worry about address wastage, but this is very bad practice and, for Cisco exams, you can guarantee an expectation that you will conserve IP addresses. With a /28 mask or 255.255.255.240 you have 14 hosts per subnet. This may be fine for your LAN on either end, but for your WAN connection you only need two IP addresses. You are wasting 12! We could change the masks to /30 or 255.255.255.252, but then for our LANs we will obviously need more than two hosts.

The first workaround is to buy a separate network address for each network (two LANs and one WAN) but this would prove expensive and unnecessary. The other alternative is to break our subnet down further using VLSM which is actually what it was designed to do!

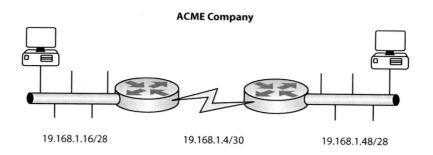

Figure 4–4: ACME Company with VLSM

In Figure 4–4, we can see that the WAN link now has a /30 mask which gives us two usable hosts. We have a tighter addressing allocation. Should ACME expand (as companies do) we can easily allocate further WAN links and LANs.

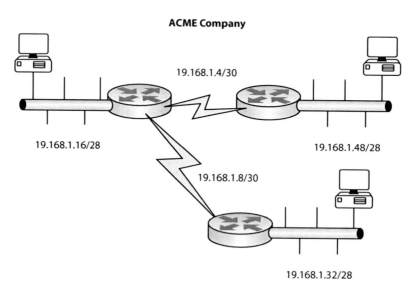

Figure 4–5: ACME with a new office

In Figure 4–5, we can see that ACME has now grown and added a remote office. Because you have taken the time to plan and allocate a carefully thought out VLSM scheme you can simply allocate the next block of IP addresses.

But will the IP addresses clash?

This is a very common question and also very valid. Let's say we have address 19.16.1.1/28 for one of our LANs. You will not, therefore, be able to use the IP address 19.16.1.1 with any other subnet mask. The IP address can only be used once, no matter which subnet mask is attached to it.

It is a bit of a head scratcher for people who are new to networking or subnetting but it does work. Feel free to think on it some more or just accept that with VLSM (RFC 950), it is not possible to reuse IP addresses.

VLSM practice for the CCNA exam

Here is a network you have been asked to design an addressing scheme for.

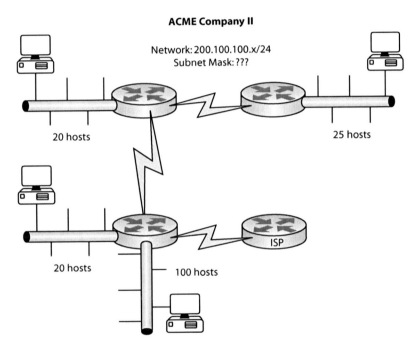

ACME Company II

Network: 200.100.100.x/24
Subnet Mask: ???

20 hosts

25 hosts

20 hosts   100 hosts

ISP

Figure 4–6: ACME II Company

In Figure 4–6, ACME II Company has been allocated the network 200.100.100.x network with a default mask of 255.255.255.0. If we keep the standard mask, we are left with one network with 254 usable hosts. If you want to check this for yourself, please use the subnetting secrets cheat sheet on www. howtonetwork.net or the direct link to download is: http://www.box.net/shared/yyx4y8y0zf.

If you use the bottom part of the subnetting secrets cheat sheet, you can tick down eight places and see that we have one subnet with 256 - 2 hosts, giving us 254. I do not want to dwell on that part of the calculations because that is covered very well, of course, in this book and on www.HowToNet-work.net.

Our challenge is this then: We have three serial connections and each only requires two usable host addresses. We have four LANs which need anything from 20 to 100 hosts. If we just design a mask to give us anything from 20 to 100 hosts we are going to be wasting a lot of addresses. To get 100 hosts (using the cheat chart), we tick down seven places giving us a mask of 255.255.255.128 (because we only have one bit left to tick down for the subnets portion). This gives us 126 hosts (128 - 2). We would then have two networks: one starting 200.100.100.0 and one starting 200.100.100.128. Not great to be honest. We need seven subnets (three WAN and four LAN), and some only require 20 hosts — so why waste 108 addresses?

What we need to do is refer to the subnetting secrets cheat chart. If we use the bottom portion, then tick down until we find a number close enough to give us the 100 hosts. The only number we can use is 128, which is seven ticks down. We are stealing seven bits from the host portion, leaving us one bit for subnetting.

Powers of 2	Subnets	Hosts - 2
2	✓	✓
4		✓
8		✓
16		✓
32		✓
64		✓
128		✓
256		
512		

If we use the upper portion of the cheat chart, then we will tick down one place to reveal the subnet mask of 128.

Subnet	
128	✓
192	
224	
248	
252	
254	
255	

When we use the 128 subnet with ACME II Company's IP address, we get subnet 200.100.100.0 and subnet 200.100.100.128 both with a mask of /25 or 255.255.255.128. We will use 200.100.100.128

subnet for the network needing 100 hosts. For the first host, we will use 200.100.100.129 and so on up to 200.100.100.229. So, now we have:

Large LAN hosts

```
200.100.100.128/25 — LAN (hosts 129-254)
200.100.100.0/25 — available for use or for VLSM
```

We need to allocate hosts to three remaining LAN networks and three WANs. The other three LANs all need anything from 20 to 30 hosts. If you tick down the hosts portion of the subnetting cheat chart, you will get to 32 if you tick down five places and take two away to give us 30 hosts. If we steal five bits from the host portion, we are left with three bits for the subnet (because there are eight bits in every octet).

Powers of two	Subnets	Hosts minus 2
2	✓	✓
4	✓	✓
8	✓	✓
16		✓
32		✓
64		
128		
256		
512		

Tick down three places on the subnets section of the cheat chart to reveal a subnet mask of 224. This mask will give us eight subnets (we only need three for the LANs) and each subnet will have up to 30 available host addresses. Can you see how this will fit ACME II's requirements?

Subnet	
128	✓
192	✓
224	✓
240	
248	
252	
254	
255	

If you tick across three places on the top row of the subnetting secrets cheat chart you will see that our subnets go up in increments of 32. Our subnets will be 0, 32, 64, and 96 and we cannot use 128 because this is used for the large LAN.

Bits	128	64	32	16	8	4	2	1
	✓	✓	✓					

So now we have:

```
LAN hosts
200.100.100.0/27 — Let's reserve this for the WAN links
200.100.100.32/27 — LAN 1 (hosts 33-62)
200.100.100.64/27 — LAN 2 (hosts 65-94)
200.100.100.96/27 — LAN 3 (hosts 96-126)
```

Next, we need IP addresses for three WAN connections. WAN IP addressing is fairly easy because we only ever need two IP addresses if it is a point-to-point link. On the hosts column, tick down two places to get 4 and we take 2 away to get two hosts. This leaves six bits for the subnet.

Powers of two	Subnets	Hosts minus 2
2	✓	✓
4	✓	✓
8	✓	
16	✓	
32	✓	
64	✓	
128		
256		
512		

Tick down six places on the subnets column to get 252 as our subnet mask.

Subnet	
128	✓
192	✓
224	✓
240	✓
248	✓
252	✓
254	
255	

Our network addresses

As a network administrator, you would keep a record of used IP addresses and subnets. So far you will have allocated the addresses as follows:

WAN links

```
200.100.100.0/30 — WAN link 1 (hosts 1-2)
200.100.100.4/30 — WAN link 2 (hosts 5-6)
200.100.100.8/30 — WAN link 3 (hosts 9-10)
```

LAN hosts

```
200.100.100.32/27 — LAN 1 (hosts 33-62)
200.100.100.64/27 — LAN 2 (hosts 65-94)
200.100.100.96/27 — LAN 3 (hosts 96-126)
```

Large LAN hosts

```
200.100.100.128/25 — LAN (hosts 129-254)
```

Chopping down

VLSM principles will let you take a network and slice it down in to smaller chunks. Those chunks can then be sliced into smaller chunks and so on. You only reach the limit when you get to the mask 255.255.255.252 or /30 because this gives you two usable hosts, which is the minimum you would need for any network.

Consider network 200.100.100.0 /24.

You change the mask from /24 to /25 and this happens:

Original mask (last octet)	00000000	1 Subnet	254 hosts
New mask (subnet 1)	00000000	200.100.100.0 - subnet 1	126 hosts
New mask (subnet 2)	10000000	200.100.100.128 - subnet 2	126 hosts

Now you have two subnets. If you take the new subnet 2 of 200.100.100.128 and break it down further by changing the mask from /25 to /26, you get this:

Original mask (last octet)	10000000	1 Subnet	126 hosts
New mask (subnet 1)	10000000	200.100.100.128 - subnet 1	62 hosts
New mask (subnet 2)	11000000	200.100.100.192 - subnet 2	62 hosts

If you take the second subnet and break it down further by changing the mask from /26 to to /28 (for example), you get this:

Original mask (last octet)	11000000	1 Subnet	62 hosts
New mask (subnet 1)	11000000	200.100.100.192 - subnet 1	14 hosts
New mask (subnet 2)	11010000	200.100.100.208 - subnet 2	14 hosts
New mask (subnet 3)	11100000	200.100.100.224 - subnet 3	14 hosts
New mask (subnet 4)	11110000	200.100.100.240 - subnet 4	14 hosts

In summary

Hopefully, this has helped you understand a bit more about VLSM. It is no mystery, really. Please take time to go over the above examples again and then have a go at the challenge below.

ACME Company II has been allocated the address, as in Figure 4–7. It requires you to design an addressing system so that hosts can be given IP addresses and the WAN links can be addressed with no wastage.

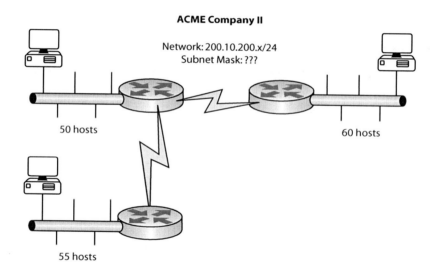

ACME Company II

Network: 200.10.200.x/24
Subnet Mask: ???

50 hosts

60 hosts

55 hosts

Figure 4–7: Address allocation

ROUTE SUMMARIZATION

There are many millions of routes on the Internet. If these routes all had to be stored individually, the Internet would have come to a stop many years ago.

Route summarization is also known as supernetting and was proposed in RFC 1338 which you can read online by visiting www.faqs.org/rfcs/rfc1338.html. If you want to read a very comprehensive guide to route summarization, then please grab a hold of Jeff Doyle's excelling Cisco book Routing TCP/IP Volume 1, which is in its second edition now.

ZIP codes

ZIP codes are used by the United States Postal Service to improve routing of letters to addresses within the USA (see Figure 4–8). The first digit represents a group of US states and then the second and third digits represent a region inside that group. The idea is that letters and parcels can be quickly routed by machine or hand into the correct state and then forwarded to that state.

When it reaches the state, it can be routed to the correct region. From there it can be routed to the correct city and so on until it is sorted into the correct mail bag for the local postman or lady.

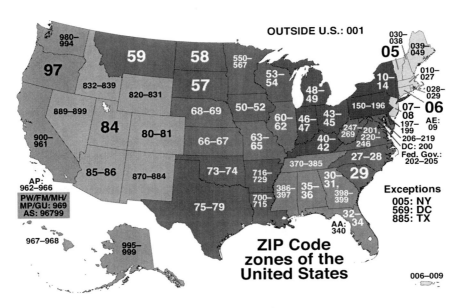

Figure 4–8: US ZIP Code system

The system was devised to make routing of mail more accurate and efficient. The sorting office in Atlanta does not need to know which street in San Francisco the packet is destined for. Having to store that information would make the sorting process unworkable.

Route summarization pre-requisites

In order to use route summarization on your network, you need to use a classless protocol such as RIPv2, EIGRP, or OSPF. You also need to design your network in a hierarchical order, which will require careful planning and design. This means that you cannot randomly assign networks to various routers or LANs within your network.

IP addresses

Let's move onto an example of a network and what the problem will look like on your network if you do not use route summarization.

Here is an example of how summarization would work with a range of IP addresses on a network.

The router has several networks attached. The first choice is to advertise all of these networks to the next hop router. The alternative is to summarize these eight networks down into one route and send that summary to the next hop router, which will cut down on bandwidth, CPU, and memory requirements (Figure 4–9).

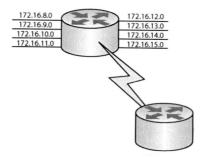

Figure 4–9: Advertise eight networks or one?

You can only really work out a summary route by converting the IP address into binary (sorry). If you do not do this, then you have no way of knowing if you are advertising the correct summary route, which will lead to problems on your network.

Firstly, write out all of the network addresses in full and then the binary versions to the right of that.

172.16.8.0	10101100.00010000.00001000.00000000
172.16.9.0	10101100.00010000.00001001.00000000
172.16.10.0	10101100.00010000.00001010.00000000
172.16.11.0	10101100.00010000.00001011.00000000
172.16.12.0	10101100.00010000.00001100.00000000
172.16.13.0	10101100.00010000.00001101.00000000
172.16.14.0	10101100.00010000.00001110.00000000
172.16.15.0	10101100.00010000.00001111.00000000
Matching Bits	10101100.00010000.00001 = 21 bits

The bits in each address that match are italicized. You can see that the first 21 bits match on every address, so your summarized route can reflect these 21 bits:

```
172.16.8.0 255.255.248.0
```

One other significant advantage of using route summarization is that if a local network on your router goes down, the summary network still be advertised out. This means that the rest of the network will not need to update its routing tables or worse still, have to deal with a flapping route (going up and down rapidly).

Exercise 1

Please write out the binary equivalents for the addresses below and then determine which bits match. The first two octets are already inserted in order for you to save time.

172.16.50.0	10101100.00010000.
172.16.60.0	10101100.00010000.
172.16.70.0	10101100.00010000.
172.16.80.0	10101100.00010000.
172.16.90.0	10101100.00010000.
172.16.100.0	10101100.00010000.
172.16.110.0	10101100.00010000.
172.16.120.0	10101100.00010000.

What summarized address would you advertise?

I make it 172.16.0.0 255.255.128.0 or /17.

Exercise 2

A company has three routers connecting to their HQ router. They need to summarize the routes advertised from London 1, London 2, and London 3 (Figure 4–10).

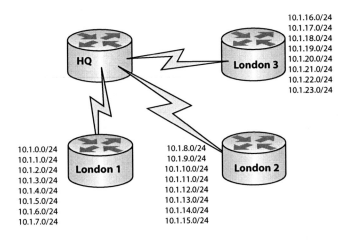

Figure 4–10: Networks for Exercise 2

Let's start with London 1.

10.1.0.0	00001010.00000001.00000000.00000000
10.1.1.0	00001010.00000001.00000001.00000000
10.1.2.0	00001010.00000001.00000010.00000000
10.1.3.0	00001010.00000001.00000011.00000000
10.1.4.0	00001010.00000001.00000100.00000000
10.1.5.0	00001010.00000001.00000101.00000000
10.1.6.0	00001010.00000001.00000110.00000000
10.1.7.0	00001010.00000001.00000111.00000000

We have 21 common bits, so London 1 can advertise 10.1.0.0 /21 to the HQ router. And for London 2.

10.1.8.0	00001010.00000001.00001000.00000000
10.1.9.0	00001010.00000001.00001001.00000000
10.1.10.0	00001010.00000001.00001010.00000000
10.1.11.0	00001010.00000001.00001011.00000000
10.1.12.0	00001010.00000001.00001100.00000000
10.1.13.0	00001010.00000001.00001101.00000000
10.1.14.0	00001010.00000001.00001110.00000000
10.1.15.0	00001010.00000001.00001111.00000000

London 2 also has 21 common bits so can advertise 10.1.8.0 /21 to the HQ router. And onto London 3.

10.1.16.0	00001010.00000001.00010000.00000000
10.1.17.0	00001010.00000001.00010001.00000000
10.1.18.0	00001010.00000001.0001010.00000000
10.1.19.0	00001010.00000001.00010011.00000000
10.1.20.0	00001010.00000001.00010100.00000000
10.1.21.0	00001010.00000001.00010101.00000000
10.1.22.0	00001010.00000001.00010110.00000000
10.1.23.0	00001010.00000001.00010111.00000000

London 3 also has 21 common bits we can advertise 10.1.16.0 /21 to the HQ router.

In conclusion

You must understand route summarization for the CCNA exam. If you can quickly work out the common bits then you should be able to answer the question quickly and accurately. If you want to learn more about route summarization, then please get yourself a copy of Jeff Doyle's book Routing TCP/IP Vol 1 2nd Edition.

Here is the answer to Exercise 1:

00110010.00000000
00111100.00000000
01000110.00000000
01010000.00000000
01011010.00000000
01100100.00000000
01101110.00000000
01111000.00000000

IP VERSION 6

Why do we need IPv6?

IPv6 is receiving a lot of attention at the moment in the IT community, even though development on it started back in 1991.

Nobody predicted the exponential explosion in the growth of the Internet when it was first developed. Who could possibly have imagined even just a few years ago that every household in the world would have a PC in it? Where possibly every person will require an IP address for their works PCs, home PCs, mobile phones, mobile IP devices and even remote IP management of such things as your home-intruder alarms, cooker, garage doors, and TV. Experts now agree that estimates of each individual requiring over 250 IP addresses is well within the bounds of possibility.

IPv4 was developed when only large companies required IP addresses. These addresses were cut into blocks from A to C with D being reserved for multicasting and E for experimental use. The original incarnation created huge wastage where for Class A addresses potentially thousands of addresses were wasted and for Class C addresses, smaller companies were forced to buy several blocks of network addresses for use in their networks. Often the addresses were non-contiguous which added to route summarization problems.

Work on IPv6 began as soon as the scale of the IPv4 problem was fully realized (1991). At this point, Internet experts argued that the current range of IPv4 addresses would become exhausted somewhere between 2005–2015.

Another issue with IPv4 is that it is a connectionless protocol. This means that there is no guarantee of data delivery and no facility to mark packets in order to correct or detect errors.

Shortfalls of IPv4

Development of IPv6 allowed some of the shortfalls of IPv4 to be addressed. Some of which include:

- **LAN latency**—when IPv4 is used on Ethernet segments there has to be a layer 3 to layer 2 mapping. IPv4 uses an ARP broadcast to perform the address resolution. This involves an ARP broadcast packet being sent to and received by all stations on an Ethernet segment. The packet is processed as an interrupt on the Ethernet port
- **Security**—IPv4 has no built-in security parameters. This function is left to PC and router firewalls.
- **Mobility**—IPv4 has no facility to allocate IP addresses to PDAs or other mobile devices.
- **Routing**—IPv4 addressing can lead to huge routing tables and vast amounts of routing update packets traversing the Internet. Changes made to DNS entries can take up to 48 hours to propagate leading to network downtime.

Anatomy of an IP packet

The design of a new IP addressing scheme has given the architects a clean slate and the ability to incorporate a wish list into the design of the IPv6 packet. The requirements were a pure design for the header with as few fields as possible.

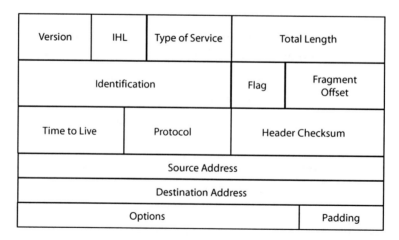

Figure 4–11: IPv4 header—20 octets

IPv6 addressing

IPv4 allows a unique network number to be allocated to every device on the Internet, but IPv6 takes this one step further.

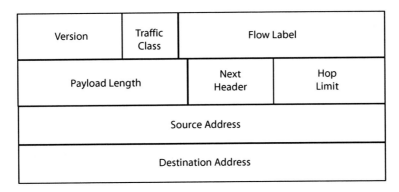

Figure 4–12: IPv6 header—40 octets

IPv6 assigns a 128-bit numerical address to each interface on a network. This, of course, will lead to extreme difficulty for network administrators to track which device is which. For this reason, IPv6 will work hand in hand with DNS. There is no requirement for a subnet mask in IPv6, and instead a prefix is used.

An IPv6 address is in two parts. The first part is the link-layer address, which identifies the host destination within the subnet. This is the layer 2 address. The second address is layer 3 and identifies the destination network the packet must reach. IPv6 uses the Neighbor Discovery Protocol and not ARP for layer 2 to layer 3 address mapping.

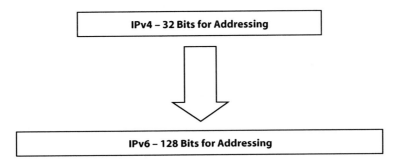

Figure 4–13: IPv6 address size

There are 2 to the power of 128 (2^{128}) addresses available with IPv6, which is exactly: 340,282,366,920,938,463,374,607,431,768,211,456 addresses. That is over 5×10^{28} addresses for every person in the world! These addresses are available without the need for private address translation or any other techniques required for address conservation.

RFC 1884 recommends that IPv6 syntax for the 128 bits is represented in eight groups of hexadecimal digits. Each group is divided by a colon so the syntax is referred to as coloned hex.
`EEDE:AC89:4323:5445:FE32:BB78:7856:2022`

The addresses can be shortened in two ways. Firstly by removing leading zeros and double colons to represent successive zeros within colons. So, using the below address as an example:
`3223:0002:3DD2:0000:0667:0000:4CC3:2002`
its second octet can be shortened to the number 2:
`3223:2:`

You may also use ONE SET of double colons to replace four consecutive zeros so 0000 becomes ::, and then our address becomes:
`3223:2:3DD2::667:0000:4CC3:2002`

The RFC states that only one pair of double colons can be used within an IPv6 address.

No broadcasting

There are three types of IPv6 address. Unicast, anycast, and multicast. Broadcasting does not exist in IPv6.

1. **Unicasts**—just the same as for IPv4, an IPv6 unicast address is applied to a single interface
2. **Anycast**—an IPv6 anycast address is an address which can be assigned to a group of interfaces. This can be used in load balancing.
3. **Multicast**—Much the same as IPv4, a packet sent to a multicast address is delivered to all the interfaces identified by that address.

In IPv6, broadcasts are replaced by multicasts and anycasts.

Migrating from IPv4 to IPv6

You will not find Internet users all over the world using IPv4 one day and then switching to IPv6 the next. The change will take place over a number of years in a phased approach. You will find that the address allocation is done in batches of addresses using a combination of DNS and DHCP or DHCPv6 auto-configuration scripts. To manually assign IPv6 addresses to nodes on a network would be an almost impossible task. DHCPv6 operation is described in RFC 3736.

There are two main methods available to phase IPv6 addressing into networks. The dual stack and tunneling.

The dual stack

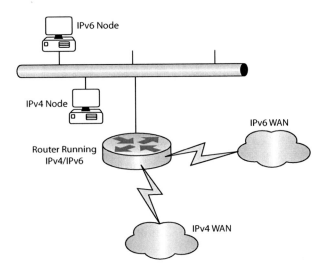

Figure 4–14: The dual stack

This is where two IP protocol stacks run on a network device—IPv4 and IPv6. The dualstack method will be the preferred migration method for networks transitioning from IPv4 to IPv6 because they can continue to run both seamlessly while the transition takes place. The dual stack can operate on the same network node interface and chooses which version of IP to use based upon the destination address.

This process has been thoroughly tested by a project team referred to as 6-Bone. The only requirement to implement IPv6 addressing on a network is connectivity to a DNS server.

Tunneling

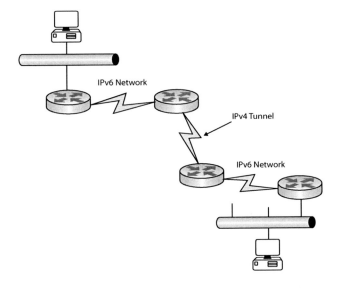

Figure 4–15: Tunneling

Tunneling in Internetworking usually refers to one type of packet being encapsulated in another type of packet. In this instance an IPv6 packet is encapsulated inside an IPv4 packet. In order for tunneling to work here, the routers must support the dual stack so both IPv4 and IPv6 are running.

IPv6 packets up to 20 bytes can be transmitted because the IPv4 header is 20 bytes in length. The IPv4 header is appended to the packet and removed at the destination router.

IPv6 tunneling will allow current IPv4 addressing to be used in conjunction with IPv6 addresses much in the same way that dual protocols can be run on a network which is transitioning from one to another.

IPv6 tunneling is defined in RFC 3056 and 2893, among others.

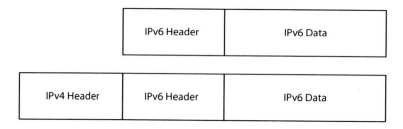

Figure 4–16: IPv4 header on an IPv6 packet

IPv6 interfaces

Each link in an IPv6 network must have a unique Interface Identifier (ID). They are the host portion of the IPv6 address and are always 64 bits long, dynamically created and based on layer 2 encapsulation. IDs are defined on interface types such as PPP, HDLC, ATM, Frame Relay, Ethernet, and so on.

For Ethernet networking, the ID is based on the MAC address, but the hex number FFFE is inserted into the 48-bit address. So,

23:80:26:F3:22:E0 would become

23:80:26:FF:FE:F3:22:E0, like this:

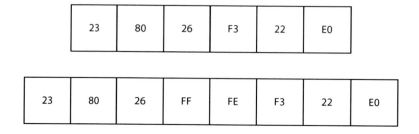

Figure 4–17: IPv6 host address

IPv6 and routing

IPv6 uses the same longest prefix match principle that IPv4 uses. IPv6 currently works with:

- Static routing
- New generation RIP
- OSPFv3
- ISIS for IPv6
- EIGRP for IPv6
- MP-BGP4

Configuring IPv6

Cisco IOS supports IPv6 commands in version 12.2(2)T or later.

To implement IPv6 on a Cisco device, simply add an IPv6 configuration to an IPv4 interface and it will run the dual stack.

```
Router#config t
Router(config)#ipv6 unicast-routing
Router(config)#interface fast ethernet 0/0
Router(config-if)#ip address 192.1681.1 255.255.255.0
Router(config-if)#ipv6 address 2eef:c001:b14:2::c12/125
Router(config-if)#exit
Router#show ipv6 interface
FastEthernet0/0 is up, line protocol is down
IPv6 is enabled, link-local address is FE80::20E:83FF:FEF5:FD4F [TENTATIVE]
Global unicast address(es):
2EEF:C001:B14:2::C12, subnet is 2EEF:C001:B14:2::C10/125 [TENTATIVE]
```

Conclusion

This has been a gentle CCNA level introduction to IPv6. It is unlikely that you would be expected to configure an IPv6 network for the CCNA or CCENT exam. Just make sure you understand how an IPv6 address is constructed and the methods of integrating IPv6 into IPv4 networks.

NETWORK ADDRESS TRANSLATION (NAT)

No discussion about IP addressing would be complete without a discussion about NAT. NAT is short for Network Address Translation and was implemented under RFC 1631. This RFC allows private internal IP addresses to be translated into addresses that are routable on the Internet. Private IP addresses allocated under RFC 1918 are not routable on the Internet.

RFC 1918 addresses the shortage of IP addresses and allocated the ranges of private addresses 10.x.x.x, 172.16.x.x–172.31.x.x, and 192.168.x.x. NAT allows private IP addresses such as 172.16.1.1 to be translated into public addresses for use on the Internet.

One of the benefits of using NAT is that it helps prevent the depletion of public IP addresses. You can immediately start to use private IP addressing on your LAN safe in the knowledge that you will still be able to connect out to the Internet.

Another benefit is that hosts inside your LAN are protected from advertising their addresses out to the Internet. Your Internet facing router will translate the private address to a public address and back again so the NATting process is invisible to the hosts even if they are on other sides of a WAN link.

A network using NAT is split into two logical halves. An inside half which (usually) uses private addresses and an outside which uses one or more public addresses. When the inside hosts attempts to contact another device on the Internet, the router swaps the private address for a public address and maintains a record of which private address was swapped for which public address.

The inside and outside parts of the network are defined with the following commands from interface configuration mode:

```
RouterA(config-if)#ip nat inside
RouterA(config-if)#ip nat outside
```

A router only needs one valid public IP address to perform NAT. This one IP address can be used many times over by assigning a port number to the inside hosts for the connection to the outside.

There are several ways to configure NAT, and your choice will depend upon different factors including how many public addresses you have and what you want to achieve with the NAT configuration. Options include:

- **Static NAT**—this maps a private to a public address on a one to one basis.
- **Dynamic NAT**—this maps the private (inside) address to a group or pool of public addresses. After a pre-determined period of time the translation times out.

- **Overloading**—this maps private addresses to one public address and is also known as port address translation (PAT).

 IN THE REAL WORLD:

NAT is used on almost every network in the world and you will be expected to configure it at some point as a Cisco engineer.

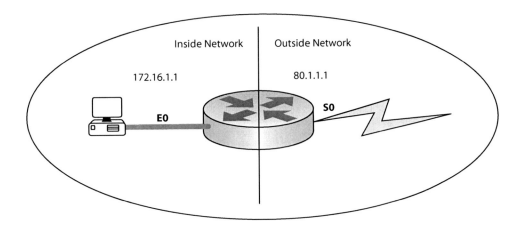

Figure 4–18: NAT connection to the Internet

Local and global addresses

The terms applied to describe the type of NATed addresses can cause some confusion but it is worth knowing which is which.

- **Inside local**—this is the address assigned to a host inside the network. It is likely to be a private address not routable (RFC 1918) on the Internet.
- **Inside global**—a routable IP address usually assigned by an ISP. This address represents one or more hosts on the LAN to the outside world.
- **Outside local**—the address of an outside host as it appears to the internal network (LAN).
- **Outside global**—an outside address assigned to a host by the administrator, this will be a public (routable) address.

A local address is an address on the inside part of the network. A global address is an address on the outside part of the network (usually the Internet). As a packet leaves the inside host it is known as an inside local address, as it is switched to the outside part of the network the source packet changes to the inside global address.

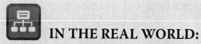

IN THE REAL WORLD:

Access lists are checked BEFORE NAT takes place.

In Figure 4–19, the static NAT configuration to have the host translated to 80.1.1.1 would be. (Some of the config has been omitted for clarity.):

```
RouterA(config)#ip nat inside source static 172.16.1.1 80.1.1.1
RouterA(config)#interface serial 0
RouterA(config-if)#ip nat outside
RouterA(config-if)#interface ethernet 0
RouterA(config-if)#ip nat inside
```

Notice in the config example that the public address of 80.1.1.1 is not applied to an interface. The public address is kept inside the router config and only used when the inside host wants to go out to the Internet. If the inside host wanted to contact another host inside the same LAN, then a NAT translation would not take place.

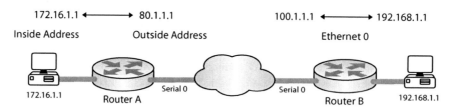

Figure 4–19: NAT example

When the host behind Router A goes out to the Internet to connect to the host behind RouterB you will see on Router A's NAT table (it may differ depending upon how you configure NAT on your router:

Inside global	Inside local	Outside global	Outside local
80.1.1.1	172.16.1.1	100.1.1.1	100.1.1.1

NOTE: The above public addresses belongs to a company somewhere on the Internet and should not be used as part of your NAT configs or for testing on your labs if you network has a connection out to the Internet.

Running a "debug ip nat" command as the host on the LAN goes through the router shows the translation taking place for a host pinging address 192.168.1.1.

```
RouterA#debug ip nat
03:38:28: NAT: s=172.16.1.1->80.1.1.1, d=192.168.1.1 [30]
03:38:29: NAT: s=192.168.1.1, d=80.1.1.1->172.16.1.1 [30]
03:38:29: NAT: s=172.16.1.1->80.1.1.1, d=192.168.1.1 [31]
03:38:29: NAT: s=192.168.1.1, d=80.1.1.1->172.16.1.1 [31]
03:38:29: NAT: s=172.16.1.1->80.1.1.1, d=192.168.1.1 [32]
03:38:29: NAT: s=192.168.1.1, d=80.1.1.1->172.16.1.1 [32]
03:38:29: NAT: s=172.16.1.1->80.1.1.1, d=192.168.1.1 [33]
03:38:29: NAT: s=192.168.1.1, d=80.1.1.1->172.16.1.1 [33]
03:38:29: NAT: s=172.16.1.1->80.1.1.1, d=192.168.1.1 [34]
03:38:29: NAT: s=192.168.1.1, d=80.1.1.1->172.16.1.1 [34]
```

The source (s=) address is the host 172.16.1.1 on the LAN which is translated to 80.1.1.1. The destination 192.168.1.1 address (d=) is another device on an outside network. The numbers in [brackets] indicates the IP identification number of the packet and is useful for debugging.

```
RouterA#show ip nat tran
Pro Inside global      Inside local      Outside local      Outside global
--- 80.1.1.1           172.16.1.1        ---                ---
```

There are several ways to configure NAT depending upon the network requirements. It is advisable to have a good working knowledge of NAT and how to configure static, dynamic and PAT. The NAT labs in the lab book will help you gain a good working knowledge of NAT.

Now go through the labs for Module 4 in Part II of this manual.

SUMMARY QUESTIONS

1. Write out 224 in binary.
2. How does a Class B address begin in binary?
3. What is the range for Class C addresses?
4. What are the reserved IP addresses?
5. Write out 255.255.255.252 as a slash address.
6. What subnet is host 192.168.2.130 /26 in?
7. Which Class C subnet will allow for only two hosts?
8. The hex value C7 is what in decimal and binary?
9. An IPv6 address consists of how many bits?
10. What are Class D addresses are used for?

CONVERSION EXERCISES

1. Convert 1111 to hex and decimal.
2. Convert 11010 to hex and decimal
3. Convert 10000 to hex and decimal
4. Convert 20 to binary and hex
5. Convert 32 to binary and hex
6. Convert 101 to binary and hex
7. Convert A6 from hex to binary and decimal
8. Convert 15 from hex to binary and decimal
9. Convert B5 from hex to binary and decimal

RESOURCES

You can find more information at:

http://www.howtonetwork.net/public/1047.cfm

CHAPTER 5

Module 5—Routing Protocols

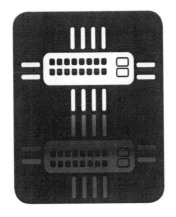

What you will learn in this module	Timings
Understand routing protocols	Theory: 90 minutes
When to use static routing	Labs: 90 minutes
Learn administrative distances	
Classful / classless protocols	
When to use dynamic routing	Review: 5 minutes
How distance vector protocols work	
How link-state protocols work	
Checking your configurations	
Routing protocols:	
RIP	
EIGRP	
ISIS	
OSPF	
BGP	

WHAT IS ROUTING?

Routing is the process of moving information across networks from point A to B. It could be down the road to a friend's house or across the world to a mail server. When we talk about routing we are talking about an OSI layer 3 process. It is the job of a router to deal with the process of routing (hence the name).

Routing involves two processes.

1. Optimal path determination — deciding the best path from A to B
2. Routing / packet switching — actually sending the information from A to B

Sending the information is the easy part, determining the best route to take is the difficult part. It is just like planning a journey across America using a map. Putting your foot on the gas and steering is the easy part. Working out the route and dealing with detours and maybe getting lost en route is the hard part.

In order to determine how to get from A to B the router has to perform a calculation to decide how many possible paths there are to get there. Just like making a phone call, a phone connection has many possible paths to choose from.

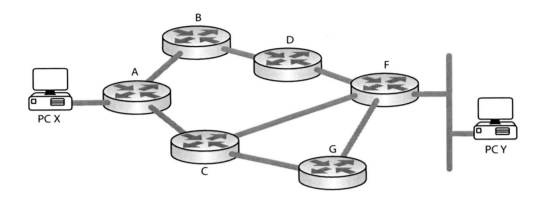

Figure 5–1: How do we find the best path from X to Y?

In Figure 5–1 above, it may appear that PC X should use the routers A, C, and then F to get to PC Y. This is the shortest path after all. What if the link between router C and F is only a 56 k link? If we take the path through A, B, D, and then F, what if the link between D and F is not very reliable? What if it keeps going up and down (flapping) every few minutes? Shall we take the slower path through A, C, and F instead?

Now we can see we have several choices to make, each has its pros and cons since the best path may not be the shortest path. Multiple factors are used to decide upon the best path.

In order for the router to decide upon the best path to take, it must know the networks it will encounter on the journey from A to B. This information can be entered manually by the network administrator or left to the router to discover this for itself.

Routing information entered by the administrator is known as static routing. If we let the router find the best path for itself, it is known as dynamic routing.

STATIC ROUTING

Static routes are very common in modern networks. The administrator tells the router that to get to a particular network either leave through a certain router interface or go to the next router (or the next "hop"). Configuring your routes in this way gives very precise control over which traffic goes where on your network.

Static routes are ideal when using something called a stub network. This is where there is only one way in and out of the network.

The disadvantage of using static routes is that if the connection to the next hop goes down the router will continue to route traffic there. It will never be aware of the fact that the path is no longer valid. Also, once you have more than a handful of static routes they can become a time consuming administrative task to change and update.

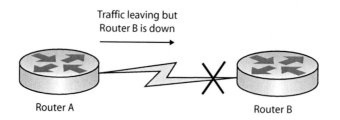

Figure 5–2: Traffic will leave an interface even if the link is down.

Configuring a static route

In order to configure a static route the router has to be in global configuration mode.

`RouterA(config)#ip route` *network prefix mask* `{address | interface} [distance]`

where:

- `network` — the destination network
- `prefix mask` — is the subnet mask for that network
- `address` — IP address of the next hop router
- `interface` — or the interface the traffic is to leave by
- `distance` — (optional) the administrative distance of the route

There are other parameters but these have been removed as they are not relevant to the CCNA exam.

Example

`ip route 10.0.0.0 255.0.0.0 131.108.3.4 110`

10.0.0.0 is the destination network. 255.0.0.0 is the subnet mask for that network and 131.108.3.4 is the next hop for the router to use. 110 is the administrative distance which we will look at later on. Static routes with an administrative distance specified by the network administrator are known as "floating static routes".

Alternatively, we could have specified the interface the traffic is to leave by.

`ip route 192.168.1.0 255.255.255.0 serial 0`

This tells the router that to get to network 192.168.1.0, leave by interface Serial 0. A static route specifying an exit interface is given an administrative distance of 0; this is the same as a connected networks AD.

We discuss administrative distances shortly.

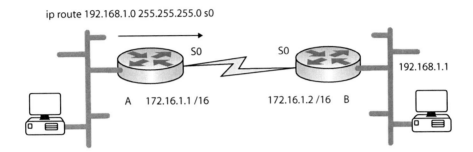

Figure 5–3: A static route to get to network B

When you give the router a static route to use, it is vital that the router knows how to get to that next hop. Normally, the next hop would be part of a directly connected network. Routers are automatically aware of directly connected networks.

One important fact to remember is that the router on the other side (destination) must have a route back to the source. If it is not aware of the source network there will never be a response. Just like if you do not put a return address on an envelope, a lost packet will not be returned to the source.

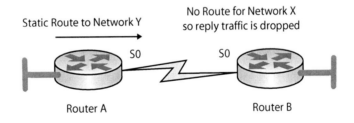

Figure 5–4: Destination routes must know how to get back to the source.

Gateway of last resort

Normally, when a router is looking for a network that is not in its routing table it will simply drop the packet (if no default network is configured). Remember, that routers never send or forward broadcasts by default. You can change this behavior but it is not advisable. Think about this, you are using routers to reduce traffic between networks so adding a broadcast option to the router defeats the purpose of using the router.

A gateway of last resort allows the router to forward traffic to a network not held in the routing table. This process can be allowed through the use of the "ip default-network" command, the "ip route 0.0.0.0 0.0.0.0" and the "ip default-gateway" command.

IP default-gateway

The "ip default-gateway" command is only used on routers without IP routing enabled. You should rarely or never need to use this command.

IP route 0.0.0.0 0.0.0.0

On the network in Figure 5–5, the stub network has only one way for the traffic to go, to reach several different networks. To configure several static routes would be a long winded way of achieving what could be done with one command.

```
Router(config)#ip route 0.0.0.0 0.0.0.0 192.168.1.2
```

The 0s indicate any network and any subnet mask. This means that any traffic to anywhere goes via the next hop 192.168.1.2.

You could have specified an exit interface instead of the next hop.

```
Router(config)#ip route 0.0.0.0 0.0.0.0 serial 0
```

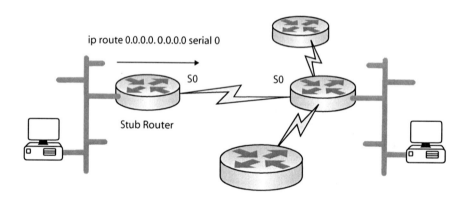

Figure 5–5: All traffic will leave the stub router through serial 0.

You could even have some static routes configured and then a default route at the end. A practical use may be that you work in a small office and any unknown traffic will be passed to a larger router at your head office that can make all the routing decisions for your router.

IP default-network

The "ip default-network" command is used on routers that have ip routing enabled. When this command is used, routes to that network are considered by the router as the gateway of last resort.

One last point. All of my network diagrams are there to illustrate a point, so please do not take them as examples of how to design your own network.

ADMINISTRATIVE DISTANCES

Administrative distances or ADs are used by the router to calculate how believable a route learned from a routing protocol is. In some instances there may be a route learned from more than one routing protocol. This situation is common when one company buys out another and they are both running different routing protocols. The most trusted routes start at 0 and go all the way up to an unknown route valued at 255 that will never be used.

Table 5–1: Administrative distances

Route source	Default distance
Connected interface	0
Static route	1
Enhanced IGRP summary route	5
External BGP	20
Internal enhanced IGRP (EIGRP)	90
IGRP	100
OSPF	110
IS-IS	115
RIP	120
EGP	140
External enhanced IGRP	170
Internal BGP	200
Unknown	255

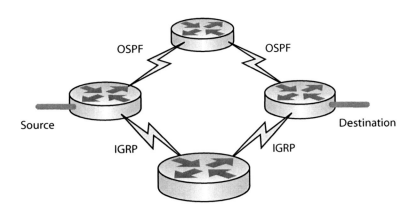

Figure 5–6: Which path will the traffic take?

IN THE EXAM:

Memorize the administrative distances! The ones most commonly referred to are in bold, but you need to know them all for the exam. These are easy marks in the exam that would be a shame to miss out on.

CLASSFUL / CLASSLESS

Remember from module 4 that we can change the subnet mask to make smaller networks or subnets from any IP address we are using? Some protocols do not understand this and presume that you are using the default subnet mask.

These types of protocols are known as classful. They do not send any subnet information with their routing updates because, as far as they are concerned, variable length subnet masking does not exist. Classful protocols do not have an option of sending the subnet mask when they advertise networks. Examples are RIP and IGRP.

Classless protocols do not make any such presumptions and always advertise the subnet mask with the routing update. For this reason, you are free to use subnet masks other than the default mask of Class A, B, or C networks. Examples of classless protocols are OSPF, EIGRP, and ISIS.

DYNAMIC ROUTING

Dynamic routing involves using a routing protocol on the router to discover which networks are present where and how best to get there. An administrator has to tell the router which networks to advertise in the chosen routing protocol. After that the routers just automatically carry on the task of finding the networks and working out how to reach them.

Dynamic routing is a far easier way to do manage a medium to large network; this is because the routing takes place automatically after the initial setup and configuration. Static routing is, however, still preferred in small networks that change very little.

Dynamic-routing protocols are divided into two types:

- distance-vector
- link-state

Both do the same job but achieve it in different ways. They all have certain roles to perform:

- Advertise connected networks
- Learn other networks
- Deal with faulty or lost routes
- Determine the best loop free path for traffic to take

DISTANCE-VECTOR PROTOCOLS

Distance-vector protocols (also known as Bellman-Ford algorithms) pass periodic copies of their entire routing tables around the network. Routers update their routing tables, allowing them to communicate changes in the network topology.

Examples of distance-vector protocols are RIP and IGRP

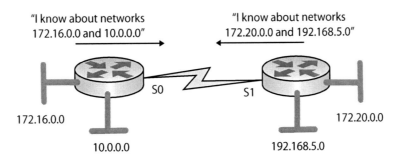

"I know about networks
172.16.0.0 and 10.0.0.0"

"I know about networks
172.20.0.0 and 192.168.5.0"

S0   S1

172.16.0.0   172.20.0.0

10.0.0.0   192.168.5.0

Figure 5–7: Routers exchange routing tables

Distance-vector routing is also known as routing by rumor. Each router is relying upon information gained from a neighbor router further downstream. This is done until each router has a complete map of the network. When all of the routers on the network agree on every route the network is said to be converged. The time it takes all of the routers to agree upon the network topology is known as the convergence time and the shorter the convergence time, the better.

Distance-vector features

Distance-vector protocols have a fairly simplistic way of viewing the network. Every router encountered on the journey from A to B is known as a hop. As the packet travels around the network a special field inside the packet is incremented by one. If the hop count limit is exceeded (such as 15 for RIP) before the packet get to its destination the packet is dropped.

Distance-vector problems

Routing loops

Routing loops can prove catastrophic for a network. They consume network bandwidth and resources, cause loss of information, and can take time to locate and troubleshoot. Perhaps, now you can see why static routes are so popular.

Routing loops are caused when network convergence is slow and routers are advertising inaccurate routing tables. A router can lose connectivity to a network, but other routers are not yet aware of the problem.

In Figure 5–8, Router D advertises network 172.20.0.x to router B. Router B tells router C, and C tells A that it knows how to get to network 172.20.0.x. Now, for some reason, network 172.20.0.x goes down. Router D informs Router B and Router B stops routing traffic for this network to Router D.

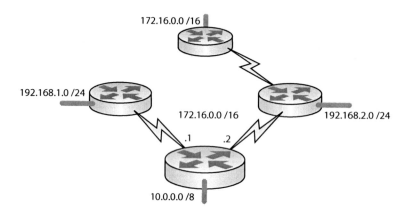

172.16.0.0 /16

192.168.1.0 /24

172.16.0.0 /16   192.168.2.0 /24

.1   .2

10.0.0.0 /8

Figure 5–8: Routing loops can happen quickly.

Eventually the message is passed to Router C but, unfortunately, during this time Router A still thinks 172.20.0.x is still up. Therefore, Router A advertises the fact it can reach 172.20.0.x to router D (via C and B) based on the previous entry it had learned before 172.20.0.x went down. Now Routers B, C, and D all believe that Router A has a path to network 172.20.0.x and route traffic to it.

When Router A receives the traffic it routes it to Router C, thinking that it is the path to take based upon the old routing entry in the routing table. When this happens the hop count keeps increasing every hop the packet takes.

Counting to infinity

Routing loops can lead to another problem known as counting to infinity. This is when a packet travels around the network looking for a particular network but never reaching its destination. This is normally because the network is down, but the sending router was not aware of this fact.

Solving distance vector problems

Maximum hop count

As the packets traverse the network the information can become out of date, or sometimes a route that was valid when the packet was sent is now invalid. Certain safety measures have been put into place to prevent this from becoming a problem.

RIP has a maximum hop count of 15 hops; at the 15th hop the packet is dropped. IGRP has a maximum hop count of 255, although the default setting is 100. This means that (for RIP) a packet can travel across a network with only 15 routers and on each router the time to live value or TTL is incremented by one. This means that RIP can only be used on a network with a maximum diameter of 15 routers.

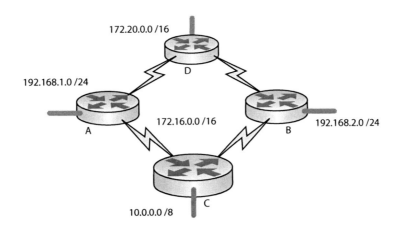

Figure 5–9: Max hop count would prevent a packet circling this network forever.

There is a field in IP packets called the TTL. The value inside this packet is incremented by one each time it passes through a router.

Figure 5–9 shows a network using RIP that uses the TTL field. If there were a routing loop, at least the looping packet would only travel 15 hops before dying and the routing loop begins all over again. Remember that maximum hop count does NOT solve routing loop problems. It only ensures that the count to infinity problem is fixed.

Split horizon

When a route is received by a router, it automatically adds this route to its routing table. The route is then advertised out of the routers interfaces so that other routers in the network hear about the route.

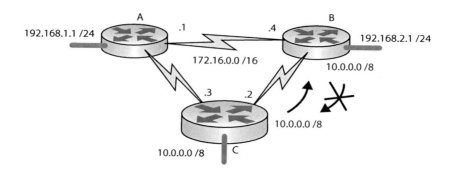

Figure 5–10: Split horizon prevents sending a network number out of the interface it was learned from.

A problem occurs when the route is advertised out of the same interface that the router learned the route from. Now there is some confusion as to where that network actually is.

In Figure 5–10, Router C tells Router B to come over the serial link if it wants to reach 10.0.0.0. Now Router B would normally send this information out of every interface. This would cause confusion to Router C where the network is directly attached. The split horizon rule prevents this from happening. Any information or route learned on an interface from a router will not be advertised back on the same interface to the same router. So in this case, Router B will not advertise network 10.0.0.0 to Router C via the serial interface (when it learns the route via Router A). Split horizon prevents the possibility of routing loops.

Hold-down timers

Hold-down timers are used to prevent route update messages being sent or received (for a period of time known as hold down time) from reinstalling a route which may actually be down. Sometimes, before an interface fails completely it goes up and down rapidly. This is known as a link flapping, and every time the interface comes up the router advertises the network as up, and when it goes down it advertises the fact it is no longer available.

When hold-down timers are in use, the router receives the message that the network is down and begins a timer. If it receives a message that the network is up before the hold-down timer expires, it will ignore the update. The theory is that by the time the timer expires the flapping interface will have stabilized.

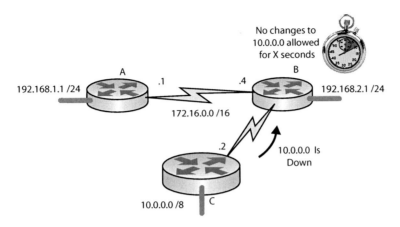

Figure 5–11: Hold-down timers prevent routing table updates for X seconds.

What can happen is that while the hold-down timer is active, an update with a better metric is received from a different router. This route will then be accepted at the end of the hold-down timer, and the hold-down timer ends. Hold-down timers can be tuned or modified but this should not be done without proper guidance and expertise. The downside of very high timer values is that network convergence takes longer while low values can lead to fast convergence but becomes ineffective in cases of links flapping.

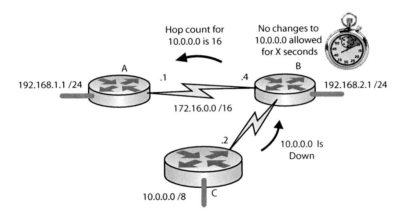

Figure 5–12: Route poisoning sets the hop count as unreachable on this RIP network.

Route poisoning

A form of split horizon uses a method known as route poisoning. Route poisoning allows a router to set the distance to a network as infinity to allow the rest of the network to converge without receiving inaccurate updates. When used with hold down timers, route poisoning can prove to be a reliable solution to prevent loops.

In Figure 5–12, RIP is the protocol in use, so Router B sends an update to Router A saying 10.0.0.0 is 16 hops away, i.e., unreachable.

Triggered updates

Distance-vector routing protocols rely upon regular updates from neighbor routers; these updates occur upon the expiration of update timers. Sometimes there are changes to the network topology, but the network will not learn about theses changes until the next routing update is due. This can cause serious problems for the network in terms of slow convergence, resulting in lost information and lost time and resources to the business.

A triggered update is an unscheduled routing update sent out due to a change in the network topology. Each router that receives the triggered update passes it on to its neighbor routers.

Using triggered updates along with hold-down timers can help prevent bad routing information from being passed around the network. Triggered updates happen along with regular updates.

 IN THE EXAM:

Be very familiar with all the methods to prevent distance-vector problems.

Distance-vector protocols are best suited for smaller networks with very few or, preferably, no redundant links.

The two most popular distance vector protocols are RIP and IGRP.

RIP (version 1)

Short for routing information protocol, RIP was very popular a few years ago, but due to its limitations, it is now only used on smaller networks.

Note: RIP version 1 is no longer tested in the CCNA exam, but understanding how it works will help you to understand RIP version 2 and other protocols. IGRP has also been removed.

RIPv1 is a classful routing protocol; this means that it does not pass subnet information in the routing update packet. RIP presumes you are using the default subnet mask for the class of IP address you are using. RIP uses UDP protocol number 520 to send routing updates.

You can see this lack of subnet mask when you execute the "debug ip rip" command.

```
Router#debug ip rip
RIP protocol debugging is on
01:26:59: RIP: sending v1 update to 255.255.255.255 via Loopback0
(192.168.1.1) ⇔ RIP sends broadcast packets (255.255.255.255)
```

```
01:26:59: RIP: build update entries
01:26:59: network 172.16.0.0 metric 1
01:26:59: network 192.168.2.0 metric 2
01:26:59: RIP: sending v1 update to 255.255.255.255 via Serial0 (172.16.1.1)
01:26:59: RIP: build update entries
01:26:59: network 192.168.1.0 metric 1
```

One of the features of RIP is that it has a maximum hop count of 15, the 16th hop is considered unreachable. This is to prevent count to infinity whereby packets forever travel the network.

By default RIP sends out its routing table every 30 seconds. If no route has been updated for 180 seconds then RIP declares that route invalid and the invalid timer begins. After 240 seconds the route is flushed from the routing table. It may take more than 240 seconds in a live network for the route to be cleared of the routing table.

You can confirm all of your routing protocol settings by issuing the command "show ip protocols".

```
RouterA#show ip protocols
Routing Protocol is "rip"
  Sending updates every 30 seconds, next due in 18 seconds
  Invalid after 180 seconds, hold down 180, flushed after 240 ⇔ timers
  Outgoing update filter list for all interfaces is not set
  Incoming update filter list for all interfaces is not set
  Redistributing: rip
  Default version control: send version 1, receive any version
    Interface          Send  Recv  Triggered RIP  Key-chain
    Loopback0           1     1 2 ⇔ default RIP updates version
    Serial0             1     1 2
  Automatic network summarization is in effect
  Maximum path: 4
  Routing for Networks:
    172.16.0.0 ⇔ The networks you are advertising
    192.168.1.0
  Routing Information Sources:
    Gateway        Distance      Last Update
    172.16.1.2         120       00:00:09
  Distance: (default is 120) ⇔ The default administrative distance of RIP
```

RIP timers

RIP has standard timers for its operation. They can be changed, but it is strongly advised to leave them at the default settings unless otherwise advised by Cisco.

- **RIP updates** — 30 seconds (routing update)
- **RIP invalid timer** — 180 seconds (expiration timer for new route or updated route)

- **RIP holddown timer** — 180 seconds (hop count set to 16 if no update received)
- **RIP flush timer** — 240 seconds (route removed)

RIP timers can be changed with the "timers basic" command, but this is not recommended.

```
Router(config)#router rip
Router(config-router)#timers basic ?
  <0-4294967295> Interval between updates

Router(config-router)#timers basic 90 ?
  <1-4294967295> Invalid

Router(config-router)#timers basic 90
% Incomplete command.

Router(config-router)#timers basic 90 ?
  <1-4294967295> Invalid

Router(config-router)#timers basic 90 180 ?
  <0-4294967295> Holddown

Router(config-router)#timers basic 90 180 180 ?
  <1-4294967295>  Flush

Router(config-router)#timers basic 90 180 180 360 ?
  <1-4294967295> Sleep time, in milliseconds
  <cr>

Router(config-router)#timers basic 90 180 180 360 360 ?
  <cr>

Router(config-router)#timers basic 90 180 180 360 360
```

If no update for a route is received for 180 seconds, it is marked as unreachable and then flushed from the routing table at 240 seconds.

```
RouterA#show ip route
Codes: C - connected, S - static, I - IGRP, R - RIP, M - mobile, B - BGP
       D - EIGRP, EX - EIGRP external, O - OSPF, IA - OSPF inter area
       N1 - OSPF NSSA external type 1, N2 - OSPF NSSA external type 2
       E1 - OSPF external type 1, E2 - OSPF external type 2, E - EGP
       i - IS-IS, L1 - IS-IS level-1, L2 - IS-IS level-2, ia - IS-IS inter
area
       * - candidate default, U - per-user static route, o - ODR
       P - periodic downloaded static route

Gateway of last resort is not set

C    172.16.0.0/16 is directly connected, Loopback0
C    172.20.0.0/16 is directly connected, Loopback1
```

```
R    172.31.0.0/16 [120/1] is possibly down
C    192.168.1.0 is directly connected, Serial0
RouterA#
```

Configuring RIP

Configuring RIP is very straightforward. Once you have an IP address on your interface you go into router configuration mode, specify RIP as the routing protocol and tell the router which network(s) you want to advertise. Both routers A and B should be using the same protocol (in this case RIP) to successfully exchange routing updates.

On Figure 5–13, we need to configure RIP on both routers. Routers A and B are connected by a serial link (we will learn more about these later). Connected to each router is a network segment with a different network address.

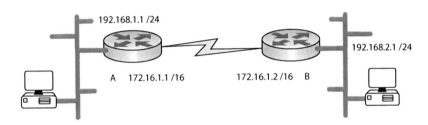

Figure 5–13: A simple network to configure using RIP

The configuration for router A would look like this:

```
RouterA#configure t
Enter configuration commands, one per line. End with CNTL/Z.
RouterA(config)#interface serial 0
RouterA(config-if)#ip address 172.16.1.1 255.255.0.0
RouterA(config-if)#clock rate 64000 ⇐ if this is the DCE interface
RouterA(config-if)#no shutdown ⇐ you have to tell the interface to open
RouterA(config-if)#interface fast ethernet 0
RouterA(config-if)#ip address 192.168.1.1 255.255.255.0
RouterA(config-if)#no shutdown
Router(config-if)#exit
RouterA(config)#
RouterA(config)#router rip ⇐ router config mode
RouterA(config-router)#network 192.168.1.0 ⇐ advertise this classful
                                                          network
RouterA(config-router)#network 172.16.0.0 ⇐ advertised attached network
RouterA(config-router)#^Z
RouterA#
```

IN THE REAL WORLD:

You may think you have to advertise every network connected to the router. Perhaps you may have a department you want to keep secret. In this instance you may not want to advertise the fact it is there. This will of course, prevent any user from reaching this network.

RIP version 2

RIPv2 was created to overcome some of the limitations of RIP. RIPv2 does send subnet mask information in the routing update, making RIPv2 a classless routing protocol. RIPv2 supports variable length subnet masking (VLSM).

RIPv2 does, however, automatically summarize subnets at major subnet boundaries. This will mean that your subnetting for a Class C address of 255.255.255.252 will be summarized to 255.255.255.0 unless you use the "no auto-summary" command. (You will learn more about this command shortly.)

```
Router#debug ip rip
RIP protocol debugging is on
01:29:15: RIP: received v2 update from 172.16.1.2 on Serial0
01:29:15:192.168.2.0/24 via 0.0.0.0 in 1 hops ⇦ sending subnet mask
01:29:40: RIP: sending v2 update to 224.0.0.9 via Loopback0 (192.168.1.1)
     ⇦ RIP v2 sends out multicast packets (224.0.0.9)
01:29:40: RIP: build update entries
01:29:40: 172.16.0.0/16 via 0.0.0.0, metric 1, tag 0
01:29:40: 192.168.2.0/24 via 0.0.0.0, metric 2, tag 0
Router#undebug all
```

All possible debugging has been turned off.

Configuring RIPv2

```
RouterA#configure t
Enter configuration commands, one per line.  End with CNTL/Z.
RouterA(config)#interface serial 0
RouterA(config-if)#ip address 172.16.1.1 255.255.0.0
RouterA(config-if)#clock rate 64000 ⇦ if this is the DCE interface
RouterA(config-if)#no shutdown ⇦ you have to tell the interface to open
RouterA(config-if)#interface fast ethernet 0
RouterA(config-if)#ip address 192.168.1.1 255.255.255.0
RouterA(config-if)#no shutdown
RouterA(config-if)#exit#
RouterA(config)#router rip ⇦ router config mode
RouterA(config-router)#version 2
RouterA(config-router)#network 192.168.1.0 ⇦ advertise these networks
```

```
RouterA(config-router)#network 172.16.0.0 ⇦ advertised attached network
RouterA(config-router)#no auto-summary ⇦ turn off automatic summarization
                                           (optional command)
RouterA(config-router)#^Z
RouterA#
```

Autonomous systems

Some protocols, such as EIGRP use autonomous system numbers or AS numbers as part of its configuration parameters. These are entered by the network administrator when configuring EIGRP routing. All routers must be in the same AS if they are to exchange routing information. Routers in different autonomous systems can also communicate but only with protocol redistribution (which is outside the scope of the CCNA).

Autonomous systems are self-contained networks normally administered by one or a single group of network administrators. They contain their own addressing scheme and normally feature just one routing protocol. Autonomous systems can be joined together by a border router, which will take care of any protocol translation and routing issues. These have to be configured manually the network administrator.

When one company buys out another company, they also acquire their network. A common method used to join the networks together is to make two autonomous systems and join them with a border router. The border router is responsible for routing between the two different ASs.

 IN THE REAL WORLD:

If your network is fairly large, you may want to split it into two autonomous systems and let another administrator look after one AS while you look after the other.

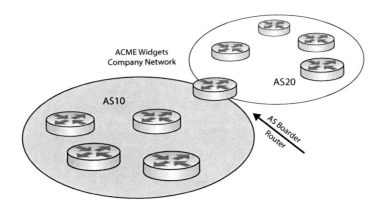

Figure 5–14: Autonomous systems joining two networks

Passive interface

When dynamic routing protocols are configured, routing updates are sent and received over a router interface configured for that protocol. You will want an interface on a router to be able to receive routing updates so that the routing table can be accurate. You may not however, want routing updates to be sent out of that interface. The "passive interface" command can be placed on the interface to prevent routing updates from being passed out.

The "passive interface" command has different effects upon different protocols such as OSPF and EIGRP. This again, is outside the scope of the CCNA syllabus.

```
RouterA#config t
RouterA(config)#router rip
RouterA(config-router)network 192.168.1.0
RouterA(config-router)passive interface ethernet0
```

If you want routing updates to be sent to a certain host that is connected to Ethernet 0, but do not want updates to be broadcast out of it, you can use the "neighbor" command. This will send a unicast packet to the neighbor.

```
RouterA#config t
RouterA(config)#router rip
RouterA(config-router)#network 192.168.1.0
RouterA(config-router)#passive interface ethernet0
RouterA(config-router)#neighbor 192.168.1.10
```

The "neighbor" command can also be used on nonbroadcast networks, such as a frame relay to allow unicast updates to pass across the media.

IP unnumbered

There is a way for you to borrow an IP address from another interface and use it on a second interface. You may want to use this to save addresses or to make sure the interface stays up. The "ip unnumbered" command is often used with loopback interfaces to increase reliability because the loopback interface cannot go down (it only exists in software).

```
RouterA#config t
RouterA(config)#interface fast ethernet 0
RouterA(config-if)ip address 192.168.1.1 255.255.255.0
RouterA(config-if)no shutdown
RouterA(config-if)#interface serial 0
RouterA(config-if)#ip unnumbered ethernet 0
RouterA(config-if)#no shutdown
```

LINK-STATE PROTOCOLS

Link state protocols use a different algorithm to calculate how to reach other networks. They are known as shortest path first (SPF) algorithms or Dijkstras algorithm after the person who created it. Routers running link state protocols hold very specific information about remote routers and how the entire network is connected.

A link can be thought of as the interface of the router. The link state looks at the relationship of this link with one or more other links on the network.

Features of link-state protocols are that updates are sent via link-state advertisements (LSAs) rather than traditional larger routing updates. A database of the entire network is built up rather then relying upon information gained from other routers. Each router runs the SPF algorithm on the data structure formed (OSPF topological database in the case of OSPF) to decide upon the best path to take from A to B.

The most popular implementation of link state protocols is open shortest path first or OSPF. The other protocol that uses link state mechanisms is ISIS which has not to date been covered by the CCNA syllabus, but please check before taking your exam.

Open shortest path first (OSPF)

OSPF is an open standards protocol which uses a link-state algorithm to calculate the best path to a particular network. It was developed in 1988 by the Internet Engineering Task Force (IETF) to meet the needs of modern networks whose purposes could no longer be served by RIP. It is a far more robust and flexible than its distance vector predecessors and ideally suited for use in modern enterprise networks.

OSPF improves on older protocols by adding features such as:
* No hop count limitation
* Rapid convergence
* Classless (allows the use of VLSM)
* Password authentication
* Advanced path selection capabilities
* Tagging of external routes
* Better use of bandwidth by using multicasts and periodic routing updates
* Allows network to be divided into smaller logical areas for efficiency
* Uses multicast addresses for efficient and reliable routing update process
* Uses equal cost load balancing over multiple paths for efficient bandwidth usage
* Supports MD5 authentication for secure route exchange

IN THE REAL WORLD:

We will barely scrape the surface of OSPF here. Implementing OSPF on your network, no matter how small requires very careful planning and design.

OSPF terminology

Table 5–2: OSPF costs per interface

Interface	Cost (10^8/Bandwidth)
ATM, fast Ethernet, Gigabit Ethernet, FDDI (> 100 Mpbs)	1
HSSI (45 Mbps)	2
16 Mbps token ring	6
10 Mbps Ethernet	10
4 Mbps token ring	25
T1 (1.544 Mbps)	64
DS-0 (64 k)	1562
56 k	1785

OSPF was traditionally considered to be a CCNP topic, and even then only a reasonable working knowledge was expected. For the CCNA you will be expected to have a basic knowledge of common OSPF features, terms, troubleshooting, and configuration commands.

- **Cost** — This is the value OSPF assigns to a link to another router. Cost is used as opposed to hops because it offers far more granularity. The cost is based upon the bandwidth of the link. (You can see the default bandwidths in Table 5–2) Cisco routers calculate cost at (10^8/Bandwidth), rounded down. The bandwidth is the configured or default bandwidth of the link.

The OSPF cost can be seen with the "show ip route" command.

- **Area** — An OSPF area is a group of routers divided into a sub-domain based upon an area ID. Every router within the same area shares the same link state information. Areas are identified by a 32-bit area ID.
- **Autonomous system** — A group of routers exchanging routing information using a common routing protocol.
- **Link** — A link is a connection to another router. The OSPF topology table is referred to as the link-state database.

- **Link state** — This is the "state" of the link to another router. The link-state database consists of a list of the status of the links between routers in the same area.

- **Link-state database** — A list of the link-state listing for other routers in the network. The link-state database is essentially the network topology. The database is built from the exchange of LSAs.

- **Link state advertisement** — LSAs are OSPF data packets that contain routing and link-state information that is shared between OSPF routers.

- **Process ID** — this is designated by the "`router ospf process id`" command such as "`router ospf 20`". The process ID is needed to identify a unique instance of an OSPF database is locally significant to the router. The process ID can be any number from 1–65,535.

- **Neighbors** — two routers which have interfaces on a common network. The neighbors are discovered and maintained using the hello protocol.

- **Designated router** — The DR is the central point for the exchange of routing information within an OSPF area. The principle is to reduce the amount of traffic passing across the area. The DR is elected via Hello packets being passed across the area. The router with the highest router ID (usually the highest IP address) wins. A backup designated router (BDR) is also elected to take over if the DR fails.

- **Internal router** — a router with all directly connected networks belonging to the same area (does not have to be area 0).

- **Area border router (ABR)** — a router with networks in more than one area.

- **Backbone router** — a router with an interface in the backbone (area 0).

- **AS boundary router (ASBR)** — a router that exchanges updates with routers in other autonomous systems.

OSPF routing table entries can either be internal to that area, represented by a "0" in the routing table or from an ABR or backbone router represented by a "0 IA". There is a third type of entry shown as "0 E2", which represents routes from an ASBR.

OSPF features

OSPF is designed to quickly locate changes in the network topology and calculate the best path available for network traffic to then take. The entire OSPF network is divided into areas. Within these areas LSAs are flooded to neighbor routers which are in the same area. This ensures that routers in other OSPF areas will not be affected by changes or problems such as links flapping.

Unlike RIP, OSPF operates within a hierarchy of areas (explained below). At the highest level is the autonomous system (AS), which is a collection of networks under a common administration. OSPF is an intra-AS (interior gateway) routing protocol. An exterior routing protocol exchanges routing information between ASs (more on this later).

An AS can be divided into a number of areas with continuous network addressing, depending on the customers requirements. Routers with multiple interfaces can participate in multiple areas if required per design. These routers are called Area Border Routers (ABRs) and maintain separate topological databases for each area.

Because OSPF uses flooding to advertise LSAs, areas are introduced to limit how far the LSAs are flooded across the network. Every router within the same area will hold the same routing database. A router with all of its interfaces in the same area is known as an internal router.

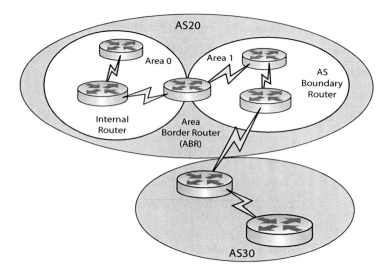

Figure 5–15: OSPF routers

OSPF will only function on a router with at least one active interface (that is an interface showing as up/up). OSPF will send out hello packets from the interface using multicast address 224.0.0.5, which is also called the AllSPFRouter address. If the OSPF link is on a Non Broadcast Multi Access link, such as a frame relay, the OSPF packet will be a unicast rather than multicast.

When the OSPF packet is verified by the other router, a neighbor relationship is formed between the two routers. Each router floods its link state database to every other OSPF router, and in this way a loop free path to every route is built.

A topological database is essentially an overall picture of the network. The topological database contains the collection of LSAs received from all routers in the same area ONLY. Because routers within the same area share the same information, they have identical topological databases.

When multiple areas are created, two different types of OSPF routes can be seen, depending on whether the source and the destination are in the same or different areas. Intra-area routing occurs when the source and destination networks (or subnets) are in the same area and inter-area routing occurs when they are in different areas.

An OSPF backbone (also known as area 0) is responsible for distributing routing information between other non area 0 areas. All routers with at least one interface in area 0 are known as backbone routers.

 IN THE REAL WORLD:

It is recommended to have all non-backbone (Area 0) areas connect to Area 0. Virtual links can be used to join areas not connected to Area 0 but this subject is outside the scope of the CCNA.

Any router with all of its interfaces within the same area are known as an internal routers or IR. Any router acting as a connection between routers running other routing protocols or instances of OSPF are known as autonomous system boundary routers or ASBRs.

 IN THE EXAM:

Cisco are giving more and more emphasis to OSPF, so make sure you are familiar with this protocol and how to configure it.

Designated router (DR) and backup designated router (BDR)

On networks such as ethernet or token ring (known as multi-access) it would not be efficient for OSPF to flood the links with advertisements to its neighbors. Neither would it be efficient for every router to become adjacent. In this instance OSPF will elect one router which is known as the designated router or DR. The DR will listen to link state advertisements on address 224.0.0.6 and flood them on 224.0.0.5.

In addition to the DR a backup designated router is elected. The BDR will take over the role of the DR should the DR fail for any reason. Any new OSPF routers will only form an adjacency with the DR and the BDR.

The DR and BDR are elected when then OSPF process starts. Once they have been elected, even if a router with a higher priority joins the network, a replacement will not be selected. They will only be replaced in the event that the router fails.

DR and BDR routers are selected based upon the routers ID (see below).

OSPF router ID

Every router running OSPF has to have a separate identity to the other routers. The router will select its own ID based upon the routers interface. The router will choose the router ID from the highest IP address on the router or the routers loopback address if it has one. The loopback will be chosen above any other IP address.

Please note that when the router boots, OSPF will only consider an address for the router ID if it is active (that is up up). Once the router ID is set it cannot be changed unless the router is reloaded.

```
Router#show ip interface brief
Interface       IP-Address   OK? Method Status                 Protocol
Ethernet0       unassigned   YES unset  administratively down  down
Loopback0       172.16.1.1   YES manual up                     up
Serial0         192.168.1.1  YES manual up                     up
Serial1         unassigned   YES unset  administratively down  down
Router#

Router#show ip ospf 20
 Routing Process "ospf 20" with ID 172.16.1.1  ⇦ OSPF router ID
 Supports only single TOS(TOS0) routes
 Supports opaque LSA
 SPF schedule delay 5 secs, Hold time between two SPFs 10 secs
 Minimum LSA interval 5 secs, Minimum LSA arrival 1 secs
 Number of external LSA 0. Checksum Sum 0x0
 Number of opaque AS LSA 0. Checksum Sum 0x0
```

You can force a particular router to become the DR or BDR by configuring it with a high loopback address (such as 192.168.100.x) or by using the "router-id" command.

```
Router#config t
Router(config)#router ospf 20
Router(config-router)#router-id 192.168.100.100
```

OSPF timers

OSPF uses several timers to control broadcasts, link state propagation, and several other operational factors. The default timers are different, depending upon the type of network OSPF is configured on—point-to-point and non-broadcast are two examples.

OSPF timers can be seen with the "show ip ospf interface x" command, where x is the relevant interface.

```
Router#show ip ospf interface serial 0
Serial0 is down, line protocol is down
  Internet Address 192.168.1.2/24, Area 0
  Process ID 20, Router ID 192.168.1.2, Network Type POINT_TO_POINT, Cost: 64
```

```
    Transmit Delay is 1 sec, State DOWN,
    Timer intervals configured, Hello 10, Dead 40, Wait 40, Retransmit 5

  Router#show ip ospf int s0
  Serial0 is up, line protocol is up
    Internet Address 192.168.1.2/24, Area 0
    Process ID 20, Router ID 192.168.1.2, Network Type NON_BROADCAST, Cost: 64
    Transmit Delay is 1 sec, State DOWN, Priority 1
    No designated router on this network
    No backup designated router on this network
    Timer intervals configured, Hello 30, Dead 120, Wait 120, Retransmit 5
```

Hello interval — The default parameter for this timer depends entirely upon what type of interface OSPF is operating on. For broadcast interfaces (such as Ethernet), the timer value is 10 seconds, and for Non-Broadcast Multi Access (such as frame relay), it is 30 seconds. OSPF timers on the same area should have the same timers if they are to exchange updates.

```
  RouterA(config-if)#ip ospf hello-interval 40
```

This command will change the hello timer to 40 seconds. The dead and wait timers will automatically be changed when you change this timer.

Dead interval — The dead interval is the time it takes to declare the neighbor dead if there is no hello. The dead interval is four times the hello interval.

```
  RouterA(config-if)#ip ospf dead-interval 240
```

This command would change the dead interval to 240 seconds.

Retransmit interval — changes the retransmission interval between neighbors. When OSPF sends an update to a neighbor router, it expects to receive an acknowledgment. If no acknowledgment is heard, a retransmit takes place. The default is 5 seconds.

```
  RouterA(config-if)#ip ospf retransmit-interval 10
```

The wait timer is the interval that breaks the wait period and causes the designated router to be selected on the router. This timer is always the same as the dead timer.

Configuring OSPF

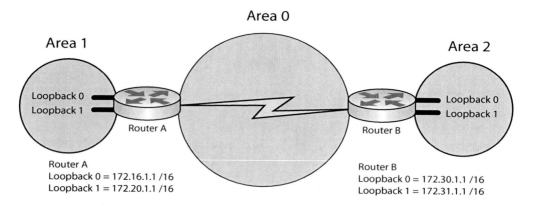

Figure 5–16: OSPF areas

Configuring OSPF can be a fairly complicated process due to issues with the protocol and also the type of interface you are configuring the protocol on. In order to configure the protocol on the interface, you have to specify a process identifier and an IP address with a wildcard mask and then choose which area the OSPF network is to be a part of. Wildcard masks can specify networks or subnets.

The OSPF process ID is locally significant and need not be the same on all routers within an area or entire network. In real world networks, many times the OSPF process IDs are kept unique to make troubleshooting an easier task.

The OSPF can be configured in two steps for a very simple network (usually with only one area).

1. Define OSPF on the router.
   `Router(config)#router ospf` *process-id*
   The process ID is an internal number and is used to identify multiple instance of OSPF running on one router.

2. Assign networks to the relevant OSPF area.
   `Router(config-router)#`*network address wildcard-mask area area ID*
   `Address` — is the network address.
   `Wildcard mask` — is discussed in detail in Module 7.
   `Area/area ID`—the OSPF area you wish the interface / network to be in. If you are using only one area, it must be area 0.

Example (refer to fig 5-16)

```
RouterA(config)#router ospf 130 ⇦ 130 is the process ID
RouterA(config-router)#network 192.168.1.0 0.0.0.3 area 0 ⇦ wildcard mask
RouterA(config-router)#network 172.16.0.0 0.0.255.255 area 1 ⇦ area 1
RouterA(config-router)#network 172.20.0.0 0.0.255.255 area 1
RouterB(config)#router ospf 131
RouterB(config-router)#network 192.168.1.0 0.0.0.3 area 0
RouterB(config-router)#network 172.30.0.0 0.0.255.255 area 2
RouterB(config-router)#network 172.31.0.0 0.0.255.255 area 2
```

Troubleshooting OSPF

There are several commands you can use to verify and troubleshoot OSPF.

- `show ip protocols` — shows all routing protocol information on the router
- `show ip route` — shows the routing table
- `show ip ospf interface` — shows which interfaces are in which OSPF areas
- `show ip ospf` — shows the link state update interval and SPF details
- `show ip ospf neighbor detail` — shows a list of OSPF neighbors in detail
- `show ip ospf database` — shows the OSPF topological database

You can test these commands when you configure the OSPF labs from the labs section.

This has been a brief introduction to OSPF, and many of the features and capabilities of the protocol have not been discussed. www.cisco.com contains a lot of information about OSPF. I would recommend studying it further after you have passed your CCNA. For now you have enough information to reach CCNA level.

If you want to learn more about OSPF then please read the CCNP OSPF chapter on www.HowToNetwork.net.

ISIS

ISIS stands for intermediate system to intermediate system. It is a (classless) link state protocol, which is in popular use with ISPs.

ISIS follows the same principles as other link-state protocols in that it divides the network into areas, and these areas form part of the backbone or non backbone. ISIS routers exchange hello packets and form adjacency with neighbor routers.

Configuring and troubleshooting ISIS is outside the scope of this book, but it is worth knowing of its existence and the fact it is link state.

Link-state problems

When you are deciding which routing protocol is best for your network you will have to make a choice based upon certain advantages and disadvantages of the protocols you are considering. Link state protocols are no different. There are pros and cons to using them. Whether you do use a link state protocol will depend upon the benefits outweighing the costs for your particular network and requirements.

The two main drawbacks with using OSPF are:

1. High CPU utilization
2. Bandwidth utilization

INSPIRATION:

Your employer or clients will really appreciate you being able to give them all of the pros and cons of the various routing protocols so they can make an informed decision.

CPU and memory requirements

In order to run the SPF protocol, a large number of CPU cycles will be consumed. While this is happening, other processes on the router will slow down due to the fact they have limited CPU time available to them. A router running a link-state protocol will require more memory and CPU power than a distance vector algorithm.

Link state in action

Link-state protocols are extremely popular in modern networks. Although they use more CPU cycles and bandwidth, they can have faster convergence and they offer more power and granularity when configuring various parameters so they make a very attractive choice.

IN THE REAL WORLD:

You can check on the CPU load on a router with the "show process cpu" command.

```
RouterA#show process cpu
CPU utilization for five seconds:4%/0%; one minute: 2%;five minutes: 1%
 PID Runtime(ms)Invoked uSecs  5Sec 1Min 5Min TTY Process
   1 820        898       913 0.00% 0.03% 0.05%   0 Load Meter
   2 16236      1672      9710 4.33% 1.18% 0.61%  0 Exec
```

There will be many more processes than the shortened example above.

The solution to the high-CPU issue is to spend more money on a higher-end router capable of running the protocol. Although low end routers can run OSPF, it is not recommended to run OSPF on them in real world environment. Users should check Cisco documentation to confirm the CPU load to see it the router is suitable to run OSPF on.

Bandwidth utilization

Link-state protocols do not require a lot of bandwidth after the network is converged. When the protocol is first enabled, the network is flooded with LSA packets that last until convergence is complete. If you have limited bandwidth, it can be completely consumed for some time severely impacting upon your network.

HYBRID PROTOCOLS

There is a protocol that uses features from both distance vector and link-state protocols. It is known as the Enhanced Interior Gateway Routing Protocol or EIGRP and uses distance vector measurements along with triggered updates.

Enhanced interior gateway routing protocol (EIGRP)

EIGRP is a Cisco proprietary protocol, so you cannot use it on non-Cisco equipment. It was developed to allow Cisco customers to address the shortcomings of IGRP. Once the network is converged only changes are propagated (partial updates). EIGRP offers faster convergence, VLSM support, and support for multiple routed protocols (IP, IPX, Appletalk). It is the only protocol that supports multiple routed protocols, there are separate tables maintained for each routed protocol.

EIGRP is a classless routing protocol and uses Diffusing Update Algorithm (DUAL) to calculate loop free routes based upon information collected. DUAL tracks routes advertised by neighbor routers and selects the best path based upon composite metrics consisting of bandwidth, delay, reliability, and load. DUAL allows for rapid convergence, making it a good choice of routing protocol for many networks.

EIGRP automatically summarizes networks at major network boundaries. This is default behavior for the protocol. If you are using VLSM on your network, you may need to turn this feature off using the "no auto-summary" command (see the EIGRP lab for an example of this).

```
RouterA#config terminal
RouterA(config)#router eigrp 20
RouterA(config-router)#no auto-summary
```

EIGRP does not send periodic updates. Instead, when a metric for a route changes, a partial update is sent out. Periodic hello packets are sent out at predetermined intervals. These hello packets inform neighbor routers that the router is alive and available to receive and send routing updates.

EIGRP terminology

Metric — EIGRP uses the IGRP algorithm for metric calculation. EIGRP multiplies the IGRP metric by 256 to determine the metric. Available metrics are bandwidth, delay (of the line), reliability, and load. EIGRP uses bandwidth and delay by default (metric = [bw + delay] x 256).

Topology table — each EIGRP router maintains a topology table for every configured protocol, such as IP, IPX, etc. All routes learned via EIGRP are held in this table. The topology table holds the metrics and feasible distances associated with the routes.

Neighbor table — the neighbor table is a list of adjacent routers running EIGRP. Because EIGRP does not advertise its routes, it must form adjacencies with other routers. The "show ip eigrp neighbors" command shows the neighbors.

Successor / feasible successor — When EIGRP runs the DUAL algorithm, it forms a loop-free topology of the network. Part of this process is to determine a successor and feasible successor to every route in the EIGRP routing table. The successor is the primary path to the route, and the feasible successor is the next best route if the successor is not available. The feasible successor is a backup route based upon the topology table.

Internal route — routes which originate from within an EIGRP AS are known as internal routes. This route is propagated within the entire AS.

External route — these routes are learned from another routing protocol, AS, or show in the routing table as static routes.

Configuring EIGRP

Configuring EIGRP is very straightforward. You need to specify the network number and the autonomous system number. All routers sharing the same AS number will share routing information. Using this method you can split your network into smaller parts, each part only speaking to neighbors in the same administrative domain or AS.

To configure EIGRP you need to follow at least two steps.

```
Enable EIGRP and the AS number.
Router(config)#router eigrp AS number
```

Configure the relevant networks into the EIGRP AS.

```
Router(config-router)#network 192.168.1.0
```

Example

```
RouterA#config t
Enter configuration commands, one per line.  End with CNTL/Z.
RouterA(config)#interface serial 0
RouterA(config-if)#ip address 192.168.1.1 255.255.255.0
RouterA(config-if)#router eigrp 20   ⇦ Specify the AS
RouterA(config-router)#network 192.168.1.0  ⇦ You do not need the subnet
RouterA(config-router)#^Z
RouterA#
```

Troubleshooting EIGRP

You can try the following commands when you configure the EIGRP lab in the lab book.

- `show ip eigrp neighbors`—shows EIGRP neighbors discovered via the protocol.
- `show ip route eigrp`—displays the EIGRP topology table.
- `show ip protocols`—shows only the EIGRP routes in the routing table.
- `show ip eigrp traffic`—shows details of EIGRP packets received and sent.
- `show ip eigrp topology`—shows EIGRP entries in topology table.

 IN THE REAL WORLD:

EIGRP has a huge amount of features and possibilities and so it is well worth researching further after you pass the CCNA.

DISTANCE VECTOR OR LINK STATE?

Choosing which protocol to use will depend upon may factors. Available budget, capabilities of the equipment on site, expertise of IT staff, bandwidth, size of network, and many other things.

Specialist advice can be obtained from Cisco if you have a support contract or from a network design specialist.

ROUTING TABLE

At the core of any discussion about routing is the routing table. The routing table is a display of what information the router holds about the topology of the network and the connections to other networks. The routing table is displayed with the "show ip route" command.

The "show ip route" output displays seven columns, each of which gives different information about the connection.

```
RouterA#show ip route
Codes: C - connected, S - static, I - IGRP, R - RIP, M - mobile, B - BGP
       D - EIGRP, EX - EIGRP external, O - OSPF, IA - OSPF inter area
       N1 - OSPF NSSA external type 1, N2 - OSPF NSSA external type 2
       E1 - OSPF external type 1, E2 - OSPF external type 2, E - EGP
       i - IS-IS, L1 - IS-IS level-1, L2 - IS-IS level-2, ia - IS-IS inter
area
       * - candidate default, U - per-user static route, o - ODR
       P - periodic downloaded static route

Gateway of last resort is not set
1   2
C 172.16.0.0/16 is directly connected,Serial0 ⇦ directly connected
C 192.168.1.0/24 is directly connected,Ethernet0
              3 4    5       6     7
R 192.168.2.0/24 [120/1] via 172.16.1.2,00:00,Serial0 ⇦ RIP learned
```

- 1 is the source of the routing table entry, i.e., connected, RIP, IGRP, etc.
- 2 is the destination network along with the subnet mask information.
- 3 is the administrative distance for the network.
- 4 is the metric.
- 5 is the next hop address or source of the routing table entry.
- 6 is the age of the routing table entry.
- 7 is the local interface via which traffic to that network will be sent.

You can either examine the entire routing table with the "show ip route" command or look at a particular network or host routing entry with the "show ip route 172.16.0.0" command (for example).

CHECKING YOUR CONFIGURATIONS
Once you have configured routing, you need to know how to check if everything is working.

show ip interface brief — this command gives you a summary of the state of your interfaces. They need to be showing line status as up and protocol up.

down/down — means the interface is physically down and no protocol is active (probably because the line is down) `administratively down/down` — means that you have not issued the "no shut" command on the interface. Generally the interface is put into administratively shut state (with the "shut" command) when an administrator needs to perform administrative or maintenance work.

`up/down` — means that the interface is physically connected but it is not seeing data link layer keepalives from the other side of the link.

`up/up` — means everything at layers 1 and 2 is working correctly.

```
RouterA#show ip interface brief
Interface       IP-Address    OK? Method Status              Protocol
BRIO            unassigned    YES unset  administratively down down
BRIO:1          unassigned    YES unset  administratively down down
BRIO:2          unassigned    YES unset  administratively down down
Ethernet0       172.20.1.1    YES manual up                  up
Serial0         192.168.1.1   YES manual up                  up
```

In order to examine your routing table on your router type the "show ip route" command. The output below is from Router A on Figure 5–17.

192.168.1.1 /24

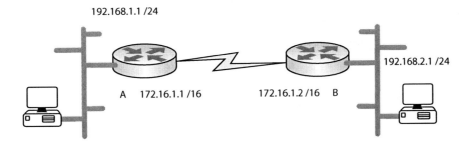

A   172.16.1.1 /16   172.16.1.2 /16   B

192.168.2.1 /24

Figure 5–17: The above RIP network has been configured

```
RouterA#show ip route
Codes: C - connected, S - static, I - IGRP, R - RIP, M - mobile, B - BGP
       D - EIGRP, EX - EIGRP external, O - OSPF, IA - OSPF inter area
       N1 - OSPF NSSA external type 1, N2 - OSPF NSSA external type 2
       E1 - OSPF external type 1, E2 - OSPF external type 2, E - EGP
       i - IS-IS, L1 - IS-IS level-1, L2 - IS-IS level-2, ia - IS-IS inter
area
       * - candidate default, U - per-user static route, o - ODR
       P - periodic downloaded static route

Gateway of last resort is not set

C 172.16.0.0/16 is directly connected,Serial0 ⇦ directly connected
C 192.168.1.0/24 is directly connected,Ethernet0
R 192.168.2.0/24 [120/1] via 172.16.1.2,00:00,Serial0 ⇦ RIP learned
```

You can check which networks are being received and advertised by running a debug depending upon which protocol you are using.

```
debug ip rip
RouterA#debug ip rip
RIP protocol debugging is on
02:27:17: RIP: sending v1 update to 255.255.255.255 via Ethernet0
(192.168.1.1) ⇦ This is a broadcast packet
02:27:17: RIP: build update entries
02:27:17:network 172.16.0.0 metric 1 ⇦ This network is one hop away
02:27:17:network 192.168.2.0 metric 2 ⇦ This network is two hops away
02:27:17:RIP:sending v1 update to 255.255.255.255 via Serial0 (172.16.1.1)
02:27:17:RIP: build update entries
02:27:17:network 192.168.1.0 metric 1
02:27:27:RIP: received v1 update from 172.16.1.2 on Serial0
02:27:27:192.168.2.0 in 1 hops

RouterA#undebug all
All possible debugging has been turned off
```

The same result can be achieved by using the "un all" command, which is the shortened version.

 IN THE REAL WORLD:

The "clear ip route *" command is very useful. It clears the routing table and forces the routing protocol to exchange route tables.

In the next example, we add a default route so that any traffic for a network not in the routers routing table, rather than being dropped, is sent out of the routers serial 0 interface.

```
RouterA>enable
RouterA#config t
Enter configuration commands, one per line.  End with CNTL/Z.
RouterA(config)#ip route 0.0.0.0 0.0.0.0 s0
RouterA(config)#exit
RouterA#show ip route
Codes: C - connected, S - static, I - IGRP, R - RIP, M - mobile, B - BGP D -
EIGRP, EX - EIGRP external, O - OSPF, IA - OSPF inter area
N1 - OSPF NSSA external type 1, N2 - OSPF NSSA external type 2
E1 - OSPF external type 1, E2 - OSPF external type 2, E - EGP
i - IS-IS, L1 - IS-IS level-1, L2 - IS-IS level-2, ia - IS-IS inter area * -
candidate default, U - per-user static route, o - ODR
P - periodic downloaded static route

Gateway of last resort is 0.0.0.0 to network 0.0.0.0 ⇦ Default gateway

C 172.16.0.0/16 is directly connected, Serial0
C 192.168.1.0/24 is directly connected, Ethernet0
R 192.168.2.0/24 [120/1] via 172.16.1.2, Serial0 ⇦ AD for RIP is 120
S* 0.0.0.0/0 is directly connected, Serial0 ⇦ Static route
```

You will use more debug commands in the lab part of this book. The commands make far more sense when you can see them working on a real network.

 IN THE REAL WORLD:

It is hugely beneficial to start your configurations by putting an IP address on either side of a point-to-point link and then pinging across it. If you add static routes and access lists it then becomes more problematic to troubleshoot.

INTERIOR GATEWAY AND EXTERIOR GATEWAY PROTOCOLS

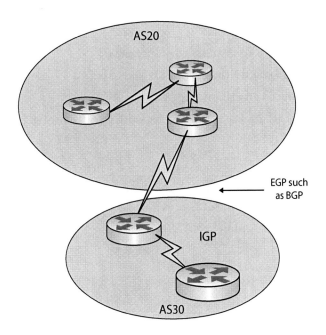

Figure 5–18: An EGP is needed to connect different ASs

All of the routing protocols discussed so far serve a certain purpose. They are there to connect devices within a certain network or autonomous system together. These protocols are known as interior gateway protocols or IGPs. Having just one routing protocol to connect network from all over the world together is not feasible. Instead, an exterior gateway protocol (EGP) is needed.

An EGP is used to connect ASs from all over the world together. An AS is usually under the administrative control of a single or group of network administrators. They are used by ISPs and very large networks. The most popular EGP is border gateway protocol, which is always referred to as BGP.

In Figure 5–18, we have two autonomous systems. Internally they will be using an IGP, such as OSPF or RIP. And to connect to another AS, the Internet facing router will use an EGP, such as BGP.

Now go through the Module 5 lab exercises in the labs section.

SUMMARY QUESTIONS

1. Routing involves which two processes?
2. What is the administrative distance for RIP?
3. Is RIP classful or classless?
4. What is the maximum hop count for RIPv2?
5. Link state sends out what to inform of route changes?
6. How do you see your routing table?
7. Which protocol has an administrative distance of 90?
8. When all routing tables agree the network is said to be?
9. Static routes can specify an exit interface or?
10. "D - 172.16.0.0/16" indicates that the network was discovered by?

RESOURCES

You can find more information at:

http://www.howtonetwork.net/public/1047.cfm

CHAPTER 6

Module 6—Network Management and TCP/IP

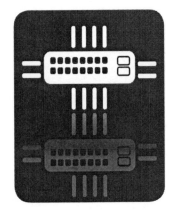

What you will learn in this module	Timings
How TCP and UDP work	Theory: 45 minutes
How TCP/IP services operate	Review: 5 minutes
File transfer methods	Labs: 60 minutes
Using ICMP as a troubleshooting tool	
Understand how ARP works	
How CDP discovers neighbors	
DNS Configuration	
DHCP Configuration	

TRANSMISSION CONTROL PROTOCOL / INTERNET PROTOCOL (TCP / IP)

We have already briefly looked at some TCP/IP services.

TCP/IP is a suite of protocols rather than just one or two. TCP/IP is just an abbreviation for the entire suite. TCP/IP, or any protocol in fact, can be thought of as a set of standards used for communication. Put together, it is possible to run many services over a LAN or WAN using some of the services from the protocol suite.

If you want to connect over the Internet, then you have to use TCP/IP. It is the accepted standard. This is because TCP/IP does not belong to any one company. It is maintained and developed by people submitting suggestions for protocols and improvements—called Requests for Comment or RFCs.

Go to RFC Editor for more information: www.rfc-editor.org.

INTERNET PROTOCOL (IP)

IP is a protocol which operates at the network layer of the OSI. It is connectionless and responsible for transporting data over the network. IP addressing is a function of IP. IP examines the network layer address of every packet and determines the best path for that packet to take to reach the destination. IP is discussed in detail in RFC 791.

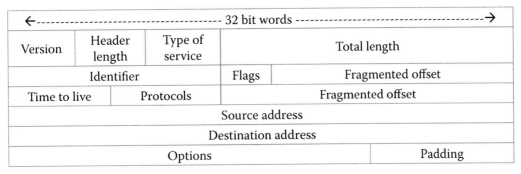

Figure 6–1: IP header

The IP header is 20 bytes long.

- **Version** — refers to the version of IP the packet is using. This is usually set to 0100 in binary or IPv4.
- **Header length** — describes the length of the IP header.
- **Type of service** — used for special handing of the packet.
- **Total length** — specifies the total length of the packet, including the header in octets.
- **Identifier** — used for unique identification of the packet.
- **Flags** — used to specify whether fragmenting occurs.
- **Fragment offset** — specifies the beginning of the fragment and used to reassemble a fragmented packet.
- **Time to live** — this field is decremented by one for each router the packet passes through. When the field reaches zero, the packet is discarded.
- **Protocol** — indicates the type of packet, such as TCP (protocol 6) or UDP (protocol 17).
- **Header checksum** — this is the error-checking field. It performs a cyclic redundancy check (CRC) on the header only.
- **Source / destination address** — 32-bit IP address of source and destination.
- **Options** — used for testing, etc.

You can debug IP packets with the "debug ip packet" command (but it is not recommended to ever use this command on a live network).

TRANSMISSION CONTROL PROTOCOL (TCP)

TCP operates at the transport layer of the OSI model. It provides a connection oriented service for reliable transfer of data between network devices. TCP provides flow control, sequencing, windowing, and error detection.

TCP is described in RFC 793. It attaches a 32-bit header to the application layer data, which is in turn encapsulated in an IP header. The TCP header format can be seen below:

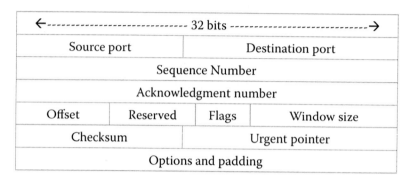

Figure 6–2: TCP header

The TCP header is 20 bytes long.

- **Source/destination port** — specifies which applications the encapsulated data is accessing. A port number along with the target IP address is called a socket.
- **Sequence number** — this is a 32-bit value that is used to identify which packets have been received and which have not.
- **Acknowledgment number** — identifies the sequence number sent by the remote host.
- **Header length/ data offset** — identified the length of the header.
- **Reserved** — all bits set to zero.
  - **Flags** — can be urgent, push, acknowledge, reset, synchronize and final bits. Used for data flow and connection.
  - **Window size** — specifies how many bits can be received at the receiving end before an acknowledgment is required.
  - **Checksum** — covers the header and data parts of the packet and is used to confirm the integrity of the information. Allows for error detection.
  - **Urgent pointer** — used when the urgent flag is set.
  - **Options and padding** — seldom used

TCP offers several features in order to ensure reliable delivery. These include checksums, flow control, and acknowledgments.

Common TCP ports include:

- **FTP data** — 20
- **FTP Control** — 21

- **SSH** — 22
- **Telnet** — 23
- **SMTP** — 25
- **DNS** — 53 (uses UDP also)
- **HTTP** — 80
- **POP3** — 110
- **NNTP** — 119
- **NTP** — 123
- **SNMP** — 161/162
- **SSL** — 443

You can debug TCP with the "debug ip tcp" command.

USER DATAGRAM PROTOCOL (UDP)

UDP also operates at the transport layer of the OSI model. It transports information between network devices but unlike TCP, no connection is established first. UDP is connectionless, gives best effort delivery and gives no guarantee the data will reach the destination. UDP is much like sending a letter with no return address. You know it was sent, but you never know if the letter got there.

UDP is described in RFC 768. It consumes less bandwidth than TCP and is suitable for applications which do not need the reliability or guarantee. Both TCP and UDP are carried over IP.

←----------------------- 32 bits ----------------→	
Source port	Destination port
UDP length	Checksum

Figure 6–3: UDP header

The UDP header is 8 bytes long and, therefore, considerably shorter than a TCP header. Common UDP port numbers include:

- **DNS** — 53
- **TFTP** — 69

You can debug UDP traffic by using the "debug ip udp" command.

TCP/IP SERVICES

File transfer protocol (FTP)

FTP operates at the application layer and is responsible for reliably transporting data across a remote link. Because it has to be reliable, FTP uses TCP for data transfer.

You can debug FTP traffic with the "debug ip ftp" command.

FTP uses both ports 20 and 21. Usually a first connection is made to the FTP server from the client on port 21. A second "data" connection is then made either leaving the FTP server on port 20 or from a random port on the client to port 20 on the FTP server.

Trivial file transfer protocol (TFTP)

For less reliable transfer of data, TFTP provides a good alternative. TFTP provides a connectionless transfer by using UDP. TFTP can be difficult to use because you have to specify exactly the directory where the file is.

To use TFTP you need to have a client (the router in our case) and a TFTP server. The TFTP server could be a router or a PC or server on the network (preferably on the same subnet). You need to have TFTP software on the server so the files can be pulled off it and onto the client.

 IN THE REAL WORLD:

Having a laptop or PC as a TFTP server containing backup copies of the start-up config, and IOS is a very good idea indeed.

TFTP is used extensively on Cisco routers to backup configurations, upgrade the router. The command to do this is:

```
RouterA#copy tftp flash
```

You will be prompted to enter the IP address of the other host where the new flash file is.

```
Address or name of remote host []? 10.10.10.1
```

You will then have to enter the name of the flash image on the other router:

```
Source filename []? / c2500-js-1.121-17.bin
Destination filename [c2500-js-1.121-17.bin]?
```

You will be prompted to erase the flash on your router before copying and then the file is transferred. When the router reloads your new flash image should be present.

Other options are to "copy flash tftp" if you want to store a backup copy or "copy running-config tftp" if you want to back up your running configuration file.

You can run a debug on tftp traffic with the "debug tftp" command.

Simple mail transfer protocol (SMTP)

SMTP defines how e-mails are sent to the email server from the client. It uses TCP to give a reliable connection. SMTP e-mails are pulled off the SMTP server in different ways depending upon your e-mail client. POP3 is one of the most popular ways to do this. POP3 is the protocol that transfers the email from the server to the client.

Hyper text transfer protocol (HTTP)

HTTP uses TCP to send text, graphics and other multimedia files from a web server to clients. It is the protocol that allows you to view web pages. It sits at the application layer of the OSI. HTTPS is a secure version of HTTP that uses something known a Secure Sockets Layer (SSL) to encrypt the data before it is sent.

You can debug HTTP traffic with the "debug ip http" command.

Telnet

Telnet uses TCP to allow remote connection to network devices. We will be looking at telnet in the labs. Telnet is not secure so many administrators are now using Secure Shell (SSH) to give a secure connection. Telnet is the only utility to check all seven layers of the OSI model, so if you can telnet to a site then all seven layers are working properly.

In order to telnet to a Cisco router there must be a VTY password configured on the router. If you are trying to telnet to another device but cannot connect, you can enter Ctrl+Shift+6 together and then enter x to quit. To quit an active telnet session, you can simply enter "exit" or "disconnect".

You can debug telnet with the "debug telnet" command.

We cover a secure version of Telnet called SSH in the next module.

Internet control message protocol (ICMP)

ICMP is a protocol used to report on problems or issues with IP packets (or datagrams) on a network. ICMP is a requirement for any vendor who wishes to use IP on their network. When a problem is experienced with an IP packet, the IP packet is destroyed and an ICMP message is generated and sent to the host that originated the packet.

ICMP delivers messages inside IP packets. It was defined in RFC 792. The most popular use of ICMP is to send ping packets to test network connectivity of remote hosts. A ping command issued from a network device generates an echo request packet that is sent to the destination device. Upon receiving the echo request the destination device generates an echo reply.

Because pings also have a time to live (TTL) field, they give a good indicator of network latency (delay). The ping output below is from a desktop PC.

```
C:\>ping cisco.com

Pinging cisco.com [198.133.219.25] with 32 bytes of data:

Reply from 198.133.219.25: bytes=32 time=460ms TTL=237
Reply from 198.133.219.25: bytes=32 time=160ms TTL=237
Reply from 198.133.219.25: bytes=32 time=160ms TTL=237
Reply from 198.133.219.25: bytes=32 time=180ms TTL=237

Ping statistics for 198.133.219.25:
    Packets: Sent = 4, Received = 4, Lost = 0 (0% loss),
Approximate round trip times in milli-seconds:
    Minimum = 160ms, Maximum =  460ms, Average =  240ms
```

The ping packet is 32 bytes long, the time field reports on how many milliseconds the response took, and the TTL is the time-to-live field.

The ping command on a Cisco router has an verbose facility that provides more granularity where you can specify the source you are pinging from, how many pings and what size you send along with other parameters. This feature is very useful for testing and is used several times in the accompanying lab scenarios.

```
Router#ping ⇐ press Enter here
Protocol [ip]:
Target IP address: 172.16.1.5
Repeat count [5]:
Datagram size [100]: 1200
Timeout in seconds [2]:
Extended commands [n]: yes
Source address:
Type of service [0]:
```

```
Set DF bit in IP header? [no]: yes
Data pattern [0xABCD]:
Loose, Strict, Record, Timestamp, Verbose[none]:
Type escape sequence to abort.
Sending 5, 1000-byte ICMP Echos to 131.108.2.27, timeout is 2 seconds:
U U U U U
Success rate is 0% percent, round-trip min/avg/max = 4/6/12 ms
```

There are several notations to represent the response the ping packet receives.

- ! — One exclamation mark per response
- . — One full stop for each time out
- U — Destination unreachable
- N — Network unreachable
- P — Protocol unreachable
- Q — Source quench message
- M — Could not fragment
- ? — Unknown packet type

You can terminate a ping session by holding down the Ctrl-Shift-6 keys (all together) and then the x key (on its own).

ICMP packet types are defined in RFC 1700. Learning all of the code numbers and names is outside the scope of the CCNA syllabus (check before you take your exam though) but they include:

Table 6–1: ICMP packet types

Type	Code	Name
0	0	Echo reply (ping reply)
3		Destination unreachable
	0	Network unreachable
	1	Host unreachable
	2	Protocol unreachable
	3	Port unreachable
	4	Fragmentation needed but bit not set
	5	Source route failed
	6	Destination network unknown
	7	Destination host unknown
4	0	Source quench
8	0	Echo request
30	-	Traceroute

You can debug ICMP traffic with the "debug ip icmp" command.

Traceroute

Traceroute is a very widely used facility which can test network connectivity and is a handy tool for measurement and management. Traceroute follows the destination IP packets take by sending UDP packets with a small maximum TTL field and then listens for an ICMP time exceeded response.

As the traceroute packet progresses, the records are displayed for you hop by hop. Each hop is measured three times. An asterisk "*" indicates a hop has exceeded its time limit.

Cisco routers use the "traceroute" command, whereas Windows PCs use "tracert".

```
C:\Documents and Settings\pc>tracert hello.com

Tracing route to hello.com [63.146.123.17]
over a maximum of 30 hops:

 1  81 ms  70 ms  80 ms  imsnet-cl10-hg2-berks.ba.net [213.140.212.45]
 2  70 ms  80 ms  70 ms  192.168.254.61
 3  70 ms  70 ms  80 ms  172.16.93.29
 4  60 ms  81 ms  70 ms  213.120.62.177
 5  70 ms  70 ms  80 ms  core1-pos4-2.berks.ukore.ba.net [65.6.197.133]
 6  70 ms  80 ms  80 ms  core1-pos13-0.ealng.core.ba.net [65.6.196.245]
 7  70 ms  70 ms  80 ms  transit2-pos3-0.eang.ore.ba.net [194.72.17.82]
 8  70 ms  80 ms  70 ms  t2c2-p8-0.uk-eal.eu.ba.net [165.49.168.33]
 9  151 ms  150 ms  150 ms  t2c2-p5-0.us-ash.ba.net [165.49.164.22]
10  151 ms  150 ms  150 ms  dcp-brdr-01.inet.qwest.net [205.171.1.37]
11  140 ms  140 ms  150 ms  205.171.251.25
12  150 ms  160 m   150 ms  dca-core-02.inet.qwest.net [205.171.8.221]
13  190 ms  191 ms  190 ms  atl-core-02.inet.qwest.net [205.171.8.153]
14  191 ms  180 ms  200 ms  atl-core-01.inet.net [205.171.21.149]
15  220 ms  230 ms  231 ms  iah-core-03.inet.net [205.171.8.145]
16  210 ms  211 ms  210 ms  iah-core-02.inet.net [205.171.31.41]
17  261 ms  250 ms  261 ms  bur-core-01.inet.net [205.171.205.25]
18  230 ms  231 m  230 ms  bur-core-02.inet.net [205.171.13.2]
19  211 ms  220 ms  220 ms  buc-cntr-01.inet.net [205.171.13.158]
20  220 ms  221 ms  220 ms  msfc-24.buc.qwest.net [66.77.125.66]
21  221 ms  230 ms  220 ms  www.hello.com [63.146.123.17]

Trace complete.
```

The fields in the traceroute output are:

- ... — timeout
- U — port unreachable message
- H — host unreachable message

- **P** — protocol unreachable message
- **N** — network unreachable message
- **?** — unknown packet type
- **Q** — source quench received

Address resolution protocol (ARP)

There are two types of addressing used to identify network hosts. The IP or layer 3 address and the local or data link address. The data link address is also commonly referred to as the MAC address. Address resolution was defined in RFC 826 and is the process of the IOS determining the data link address from the network layer (or IP) address.

ARP resolves a known IP address to a MAC address. When a host needs to transfer data across the network it needs to know the other hosts MAC address. The host checks its ARP cache and if the MAC address is not there it sends out an ARP broadcast message to find the host.

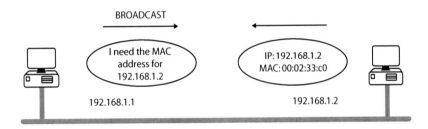

Figure 6–4: Hosts broadcasts for another host's MAC address

You can debug ARP with the "debug arp" command.

Proxy ARP

Proxy ARP (Figure 6–5) is defined in RFC 1027. Proxy ARP enables hosts on an Ethernet network to communicate with hosts on other subnets or networks even though they have no knowledge of routing.

If an ARP broadcast reaches a router it will not forward it (by default). Routers do not forward broadcasts but if they do know how to find the host (i.e., they have a route to it) they will send their own MAC address to the host. This process is called proxy ARP and it allows the host to send off the data thinking it is going straight to the remote host. The router swaps the MAC address and then forwards the packet to the correct next hop.

The command "ip proxy-arp" is enabled on Cisco routers by default.

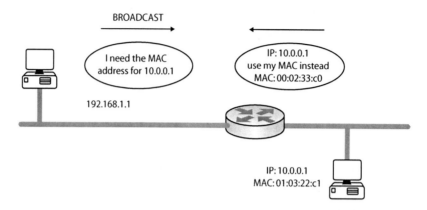

Figure 6–5: Router uses proxy ARP to allow the hosts to connect.

Reverse address resolution protocol (RARP)

Reverse ARP maps a known MAC address to an IP address. Hosts such as diskless workstations (also known as thin clients) know their MAC address when they boot. They use RARP to discover their IP address from a server on the network.

Simple network management protocol (SNMP)

SNMP is used for network management services. An SNMP management system allows network devices to send messages called traps to a management station. This informs the network administrator of any faults on the network such as faulty interfaces, high CPU utilization on servers, etc.

You can debug SNMP traffic with the "debug snmp" command.

Domain name system (DNS)

DNS resolves hostnames to IP addresses. This allows us to enter www.cisco.com in a Web browser rather than 198.133.219.25. Every ISP will have its own DNS servers that list the most common IP addresses. If the address of the server you want is not there, then the ISP will pass the request onto a DNS root server.

> "Either TCP or UDP can be used to transport DNS protocol messages, connecting to server port 53 for either. Ordinary DNS requests can be made with TCP, though convention dictates the use of UDP for normal operation. TCP must be used for zone transfers, however, because of the danger of dropping records with an unreliable delivery protocol such as UDP."

Reproduced from www.freesoft.org/CIE/Topics/77.htm—a wonderful resource for CCNAs (www.freesoft.org).

You can configure a host name to an IP address mapping with the command "ip host {*name*} {*ip address*}":

```
RouterA(config)#ip host RouterB 192.168.1.2
You can then ping the hostname:
RouterA#ping routerb ⇦ Not case sensitive

Type escape sequence to abort.
Sending 5, 100-byte ICMP Echos to 192.168.1.2, timeout is 2 seconds:
!!!!!
Success rate is 100 percent (5/5), round-trip min/avg/max = 32/32/32 ms
RouterA#
```

You can specify one or more hosts to act as name servers (DNS) to resolve IP addresses to host names. To do this you need to use the "ip name-server <*server-address 1*> <*server-address 2*> (etc)" command.

```
RouterA(config)#ip name-server 192.168.1.1
```

Routers automatically try to resolve an entry to a hostname if it is not an IOS command. If it does not know who the hostname is, it tries to translate it:

```
RouterA#tggt
Translating "tggt"...domain server (255.255.255.255) ⇦ broadcast packet
 (255.255.255.255)
Translating "tggt"...domain server (255.255.255.255)
% Unknown command or computer name, or unable to find computer address
RouterA#
```

This can be very frustrating because you have to wait for several seconds while the router tries to resolve the hostname. You can turn this feature off by using the "no ip domain-lookup" command:

```
RouterA#config terminal
Enter configuration commands, one per line. End with CNTL/Z.
RouterA(config)#no ip domain-lookup
RouterA(config)#^z
RouterA#tggt

Translating "tggt"
% Unknown command or computer name, or unable to find computer address
RouteA#'
```

You can debug DNS traffic with the "debug domain" command.

DNS on the management plane

From IOS you can enter DNS name servers and use fully qualified domain names (FQDN). Note that you can not use FQDN in access-lists! Let's add a public DNS server to IOS and ping a website by name.

```
Router(config)#ip name-server 4.2.2.2

Router#ping www.cisco.com
Translating "www.cisco.com";
% Unrecognized host or address, or protocol not running
```

What we have to do is tell the router to use DNS. We do that by enabling domain-lookup.

```
Router(config)#ip domain-lookup
Router#ping www.cisco.com

Translating "www.cisco.com";...domain server (4.2.2.2) [OK]

Type escape sequence to abort.
Sending 5, 100-byte ICMP Echos to 198.133.219.25, timeout is 2 seconds:
!!!!!
Success rate is 100 percent (5/5)
```

If we look closer at the output above we can see the router queried the DNS server at 4.2.2.2 and it responded back with the IP address of 198.133.219.25. You could of course, enter your private DNS servers and you would be able to ping your internal names from your network equipment. This is for the management plane only and in the next section we'll look at using IOS for hosting DNS solutions.

DNS proxy

There are occasions where your router provides DHCP and it would make life easier if that same router could forward DNS too. Well it can! Let's take a look at how we do that. Just like above, We have to tell the router where to find a name server (DNS) and enable the router to provide a DNS service. You will understand this better once you have completed the DNS and DHCP lab.

```
Router(config)#ip name-server 4.2.2.2
Router#ping www.howtonetwork.com
Translating "www.howtonetwork.com"
% Unrecognized host or address, or protocol not running.

Router(config)#ip domain-lookup
```

Next, we enable DNS on the router with the following commands:

```
Router(config)#ip dns server
```

That is it! Now clients can use the router as a DNS server. Figure 6–6 helps explain the process. But what if you need the router to resolve an internal address? We can now add DNS records directly on the router.

```
Router(config)#ip host server1.mydomain.com 10.10.10.5
```

From a host let's set the DNS server to the router and lookup the server1 DNS name.

```
F:\>nslookup
Default Server: dns-p1.mydomain.com
Address: 10.10.10.11

> server 10.10.10.254  ⇦ set the system to use the DNS server
Default Server: [10.10.10.254]
Address: 10.10.10.254

> server1.mydomain.com  ⇦ query for the name server1.mydomain.com
Server: 10.10.10.254  ⇦ the FQDN for the DNS server

Address: 10.10.10.254

Name: server1.mydomain.com  ⇦ the response from the router running DNS
Address: 10.10.10.5  ⇦ the IP address of server1.mydomain.com
```

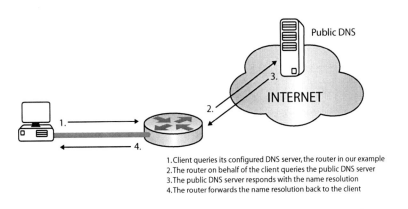

1. Client queries its configured DNS server, the router in our example
2. The router on behalf of the client queries the public DNS server
3. The public DNS server responds with the name resolution
4. The router forwards the name resolution back to the client

Figure 6–6: Router used as a DNS server

It is recommended that you do not use a router as a DNS server. A router was meant to route packets and that is what it does best. This previous scenario was for demonstration purposes and should be avoided when possible.

Dynamic host discovery protocol (DHCP)

DHCP is based upon the older bootstrap protocol (BOOTP), it utilizes UDP and is used on local area networks in a client server model. Servers at a central point on the LAN are configured with TCP/IP information that is relayed to clients in response to a request from the client.

When a LAN client (usually a PC) boots up, it sends a DHCP DISCOVER message onto the LAN requesting information from the DHCP server. This information will include the IP address to be used by the host. The DHCP discover message takes the form of a broadcast `255.255.255.255` (or in hex `FF:FF:FF:FF:FF:FF`) as the destination address and `0.0.0.0` as the host address.

The DHCP DISCOVER message is responded to by the server with a DHCP OFFER. The client will then respond with a DHCP REQUEST and then the server with either a DHCP ACK or DHCP NACK.

First, let's review the network diagram in Figure 6–7. This will help with the configuration that follows. This particular router has three interfaces, `E0/0`, `E0/1`, and `S0/0`. Interface `S0/0` connects to our ISP, so DHCP should not be used there. The other two interfaces do require DHCP.

Let's start configuring DHCP. First, we create an IP DHCP pool and assign it a name.

```
Router(config)#ip dhcp pool E01_DHCP_Pool
```

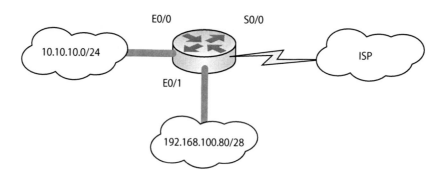

Figure 6–7: Router using the DHCP protocol

Next, we designate the Network ID and subnet mask of the pool. It is important to note here that the network ID determines which interface DHCP will be listening on and handing out addresses to. In our example it will be interface `E0/1`.

```
Router(dhcp-config)#network 192.168.100.80 255.255.255.240
```

Now we can start to add DHCP scope features. Here we add some DNS servers, the local domain name, the default gateway and the lease time.

```
Router(dhcp-config)#dns-server 24.196.64.39 24.196.64.40 ⇦ DNS servers
Router(dhcp-config)#domain-name mydomain.com ⇦ local domain name
Router(dhcp-config)#default-router 192.168.100.94 ⇦ default gateway
Router(dhcp-config)#lease 3 ⇦ lease time in days
```

We do not have to apply the configuration to an interface. The network statement does that for us. DHCP will now start handing out address on the E0/1 interface. Now, we will configure DHCP for the E0/0 interface.

```
Router(config)#ip dhcp pool E00_DHCP_Pool
Router(dhcp-config)#network 10.10.10.0 255.255.255.0
Router(dhcp-config)#dns-server 24.196.64.39 24.196.64.40
Router(dhcp-config)#domain-name mydomain.com
Router(dhcp-config)#default-router 10.10.10.254
Router(dhcp-config)#lease 1
```

Now, the router will start to hand out 10.10.10.0 addresses on the E0/0 interface. The router will hand out all addresses in the network assignment. Since our local interface is also in that block, we need to make some exceptions to the DHCP pool. We can either restrict a single IP or a range of IPs.

```
Router(config)#ip dhcp excluded-address 10.10.10.254
Router(config)#ip dhcp excluded-address 10.10.10.250 10.10.10.254
```

We can also set reservations. This is useful for devices such as printers. Here we configure the router to always hand out IP 10.10.10.50 to the device with MAC address of 01-00-15-00-2c-1b-ae. Note that the MAC address is 2 bytes too long. For a reservation, you need to prepend 01 to the actual MAC address. Only one reservation is allowed per DHCP pool.

```
Router(config)#ip dhcp pool E00_DHCP_Pool
Router(dhcp-config)#host 10.10.10.50 255.255.255.0
Router(dhcp-config)#client-identifier 0100.1500.2c1b.ae
```

There are quite a few options that you can set for DHCP. We showed the most common. If you have a specific setting, consult the configuration guide on www.cisco.com. Here are some of the options currently available.

```
Router(dhcp-config)#?
DHCP pool configuration commands:
  accounting              Send Accounting Start/Stop messages
  bootfile                Boot file name
  class                   Specify a DHCP class
  client-identifier       Client identifier
  client-name             Client name
  default-router          Default routers
  dns-server              DNS servers
  domain-name             Domain name
  exit                    Exit from DHCP pool configuration mode
  hardware-address        Client hardware address
  host                    Client IP address and mask
  import                  Programmatically importing DHCP option
```

```
parameters
lease                        Address lease time
netbios-name-server          NetBIOS (WINS) name servers
netbios-node-type            NetBIOS node type
network                      Network number and mask
next-server                  Next server in boot process
no                           Negate a command or set its defaults
option                       Raw DHCP options
origin                       Configure the origin of the pool
relay                        Function as a DHCP relay
subnet                       Subnet allocation commands
update                       Dynamic updates
utilization                  Configure various utilization parameters
vrf                          Associate this pool with a VRF
```

Next let's look at how we manage DHCP. Really the only thing we should ever need to look at outside the configuration is who is assigned what address. In IOS it is easy.

```
Router(config)#show ip dhcp binding

IP address      Client-ID/              Lease expiration        Type
                Hardware address/
                User name
10.10.10.5      0100.c09f.9456.2f       Oct 12 2007 08:55 AM    Automatic
10.10.10.6      0100.15c5.198b.f8       Oct 12 2007 10:10 AM    Automatic
10.10.10.12     0100.032d.0aed.aa       Oct 11 2007 03:06 PM    Automatic
10.10.10.103    0100.1111.058f.c8       Oct 11 2007 12:15 PM    Automatic
10.10.10.104    0100.1111.058d.b3       Oct 12 2007 08:58 AM    Automatic
```

Cisco discovery protocol (CDP)

CDP is a Cisco proprietary protocol designed to collect information about neighboring network devices. CDP is on by default on Cisco devices.

You can view the CDP settings on a router by typing "show cdp":

```
RouterA#show cdp
Global CDP information:
        Sending CDP packets every 60 seconds
        Sending a holdtime value of 180 seconds
        Sending CDPv2 advertisements is enabled
```

You can view which neighbor devices are connected by typing "show cdp neighbor" (US spelling):

```
RouterA#show cdp neighbor
Capability Codes: R - Router, T - Trans Bridge, B - Source Route Bridge
                  S - Switch, H - Host, I - IGMP, r - Repeater
```

```
Device ID    Local Intrfce    Holdtme    Capability  Platform  Port ID
RouterB      Ser 0            175        R           2522      Ser 0
RouterA#
```

Here, we can see that the device is a router and is a 2522 model, and we are connected to its serial 0 interface.

"show cdp neighbor detail" gives a lot more information:

```
RouterA#show cdp neighbor detail
-----------------------
Device ID: RouterB
Entry address(es):
  IP address: 192.168.1.2
Platform: cisco 2522,  Capabilities: Router
Interface: Serial0,  Port ID (outgoing port): Serial0
Holdtime : 173 sec

Version :
Cisco Internetwork Operating System Software
IOS (tm) 2500 Software (C2500-IS-L), Version 12.2(4)T1,  RELEASE SOFTWARE
(fc1)
TAC Support: http://www.cisco.com/tac
Copyright (c) 1986-2001 by cisco Systems, Inc.
Compiled Thu 25-Oct-01 16:33 by ccai

advertisement version: 2
```

The command "show cdp traffic" gives interface traffic statistics:

```
RouterA#show cdp traffic
CDP counters :
        Total packets output: 174, Input: 174
        Hdr syntax: 0, Chksum error: 0, Encaps failed: 0
        No memory: 0, Invalid packet: 0, Fragmented: 0
        CDP version 1 advertisements output: 0, Input: 0
        CDP version 2 advertisements output: 174, Input: 174
```

You can debug CDP traffic with the "debug cdp" command.

 IN THE REAL WORLD:

CDP should be disabled on the routers at the edge of your network to prevent CDP information from being propagated to unknown networks. This is a security risk.

Now go through the Module 6 labs in the labs section.

SUMMARY QUESTIONS

1. Is UDP connection oriented or connectionless?
2. Which protocol allows remote access to the router for management?
3. What protocol does ping use?
4. Which command traces IP traffic over multiple hops?
5. Which protocol maps a MAC address to a known IP address?
6. Which command backs up your startup configuration file to another router?
7. Which command shows what Cisco devices you are connected to?
8. Which protocol maps hostnames to IP addresses?
9. You want to be able to ping Router B by its name, what command will you use?
10. Which protocol tests all seven OSI layers?

RESOURCES

You can find more information at:

http://www.howtonetwork.net/public/1047.cfm

FURTHER READING

- Novell's Guide to Troubleshooting TCP/IP — Silvia Hagen & Stephanie Lewis
  IDG Books Worldwide; ISBN 0-7645-4562-0
  A superb book and on everything TCP/IP (out of print, I believe)

- Routing TCP/IP Vol 1, 2nd Edition — Jeff Doyle
  Cisco Press; ISBN 978-1587052026
  Required reading for any serious Cisco student

CHAPTER 7

Module 7—Security and Access Lists

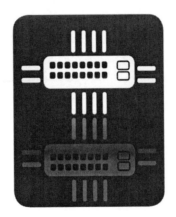

What you will learn this module	Timings
How to secure the router	
Securing the switch	Theory: 90 minutes
Using access lists	Labs: 90 minutes
Applying wildcard masks	Review: 5 minutes
Learn port numbers	
Applying access lists	
Troubleshooting access lists	
Network security threats	

SECURING THE ROUTER

Network security is the number one topic in the world of Internetworking and will remain so as long as the threat of intrusion, espionage, theft or hacking exists. There are literally thousands of hackers operating all over the world constantly scanning IP addresses and ports trying to gain access to your PC or network equipment.

As a CCNA technician, you should be able to configure a router to only allow certain people to access it and only allow certain traffic to pass through from your network to the Internet or vice versa. You should also be able to restrict access to certain applications and services within the network.

 IN THE EXAM:

You may not be specifically questioned about security issues in the CCNA exam but you will be expected to be able to carry out some simple measures to make it more difficult for people to access your router. You may also have to configure or troubleshoot an access list.

PASSWORDS AND LOGGING

Do you want just anybody to access your router? Perhaps you want only a handful of people to be able to log onto the router and a few others to be able to remotely connect to the router and administer it. Logical router access needs to be protected from internal staff and external intruders.

Passwords on Cisco routers must contain from 1 to 25 uppercase and lowercase alphanumeric characters. Passwords are case sensitive; spaces can be used but not as the first character.

Cisco recommends that the best way to handle passwords is to maintain them on a TACACS+ or RADIUS authentication server. Most routers, however, will have a locally stored (in the routers config) privileged level password.

Enable password

Protecting privileged mode (or enable mode) on your router is very important, and the process is very simple. When any person attempts to enter privileged mode from user exec mode they will be prompted for a password.

```
Router>enable
Router#config t
Enter configuration commands, one per line. End with CNTL/Z.
Router(config)#enable password cisco ⇦ Passwords ARE case sensitive
Router(config)#disable
Router>enable
Password:         ⇦ the password will not show as you type it
Router#
```

By default, the enable password can be seen when any user looks at the running or startup configuration of the router. You probably do not want this to happen (see the "service password-encryption" command below).

```
Router#show run
01:34:42: %SYS-5-CONFIG_I: Configured from console by console
Building configuration...

Current configuration : 813 bytes
!
version 12.2
service timestamps debug uptime
service timestamps log uptime
no service password-encryption
!
hostname Router
!
enable password cisco
```

You can take off the enable password by entering a "no" in front of the command again.

```
Router(config)#no enable password
```

You do not need to enter the password again.

IN THE REAL WORLD:

Most commands on a router can be shortened to save time and effort. In the exam unfortunately, a lot of the shortened commands will not work because you will be working on a router simulator. Practice the long versions for the exam, but then in the real world always use the shortened commands to save time. You can also use the TAB key to finish off a command you have started to type if the characters you have typed are unique to that command.

Enable secret password

```
Router#conf t ⇔ Short for configure terminal
Enter configuration commands, one per line. End with CNTL/Z.
Router(config)#no enable password ⇔ Take off the enable password
Router(config)#enable secret cisco
Router(config)#exit
Router#disable
01:32:39: %SYS-5-CONFIG_I: Configured from console by console
Router>enable
Password:          ⇔ the password will not show as you type it
Router#
```

You can see that when a "show running-configuration" command is issued the enable secret password is encrypted. Only the relevant part of the configuration is shown.

```
Router#show run ⇔ Short for show running-configuration
Building configuration...

Current configuration : 838 bytes
!
version 12.2
service timestamps debug uptime
service timestamps log uptime
no service password-encryption
!
hostname Router
!
enable secret 5 $1$F3Dy$wOmwxVmJ79Ug9pK/snpRe/ ⇔ Hashed using the MD5
                                                   algorithm
```

The number 5 after the enable secret stands for level 5 encryption. This uses a hashed value of the MD5 algorithm, it is harder to crack than level 7, which uses a weaker algorithm.

IN THE REAL WORLD:

Cisco advise you to use the enable secret method of securing their routers. The "ser-vice password-encryption" method is less secure, and non-Cisco sources have released cracker programs on the Internet to break these.

 IN THE REAL WORLD:

Do not presume that a having a level 5 password means it still cannot be guessed. Never use an obvious word for your passwords. You could be subject to a dictionary attack, which will crack your password in minutes.

Service password encryption

You can actually encrypt all of the passwords on the router with the "service password-encryption" command.

```
Router(config)#enable password cisco
Router(config)#service password-encryption
Router(config)#exit
Router#show run
Building configuration...

Current configuration : 819 bytes
!
version 12.2
service timestamps debug uptime
service timestamps log uptime
service password-encryption
!
hostname Router
!
enable password 7 070724404206 ⇔ Weaker "reversible" algorithm
```

 IN THE REAL WORLD:

The "service password-encryption" command does not provide a high level of security. Use this command with additional security measures.

Auxiliary password

In order to protect connections through your aux port you will need to assign a password to it. Note that when you configure a port, the router drops into something called "config-line" mode, as show below.

```
Router#config t
Enter configuration commands, one per line. End with CNTL/Z.
Router(config)#line aux ?
  <0-0>  First Line number

Router(config)#line aux 0
RouterA(config-line)#password cisco ⇐ Config-line mode
Router(config-line)#login
Router(config-line)#^Z
Router#
```

The "login" command is very important, it tells the router to ask the user for a password. The command "login local" (see "Configuring user-specific passwords" on page 225) tells the router to check a username and password you have configured on the router itself (the local database). You can instead, put a server on the network which does the job of authenticating all the users. These servers are known as TACACS or RADIUS servers but are outside the scope of the CCNA.

The "login" and "login local" commands are covered comprehensively in the lab book.

Telnet password

In order to connect to your router over the Internet or remotely you may want to telnet to it. In order to allow telnet sessions you need to have a password set on the telnet port. Telnet ports are logical and so not physically attached to the router, you will normally telnet via the serial port or Ethernet port and a virtual terminal (known as VTY) will be opened. The number of available ports depends upon your model of router.

```
RouterA#config t
Enter configuration commands, one per line. End with CNTL/Z.
RouterA(config)#line vty ?
  <0-4> First Line number

RouterA(config)#line vty 0 4 ⇐ The 5 VTY ports are 0-4 inclusive
RouterA(config-line)#password cisco
RouterA(config-line)#login
RouterA(config-line)#^Z
```

Now I can telnet to Router A from Router B:

```
RouterB#telnet 192.168.1.1
Trying 192.168.1.1 ... Open
User Access Verification

Password:
RouterA>enable
Password:
```

```
RouterA#  ⇦ I am now connected to Router A from Router B
RouterA#exit ⇦ you can use Ctrl+Shift+6 and x to exit

[Connection to 192.168.1.1 closed by foreign host]
RouterB#
```

Configuring the router for telnet access alone is not sufficient. The enable or enable secret password must also be configured to allow for privileged access once telnet access has been allowed. If there is no VTY password on the remote router, you will see:

```
RouterB#telnet 192.168.1.1
Trying 192.168.1.1 ... Open

Password required, but none set

[Connection to 192.168.1.1 closed by foreign host]
RouterB#
```

If a VTY password is set but there is no enable password, you will see:

```
RouterB#telnet 192.168.1.1
Trying 192.168.1.1 ... Open

User Access Verification

Password:         ⇦ The password will not show as you type it

RouterA>enable
% No password set
RouterA>
```

If you are connected to Router A, you can see other connections to the router with the "show line" command. The asterisk indicates an active connection.

```
RouterA#show line
   Tty Typ  Tx/Rx     A Modem  Roty AccO AccI  Uses  Noise  Overruns Int
*    0 CTY             -    -      -    -    -     0     0    0/0      -
     1 AUX 9600/9600   -    -      -    -    -     0     0    0/0      -
*    2 VTY             -    -      -    -    -     2     0    0/0      -
     3 VTY             -    -      -    -    -     0     0    0/0      -
     4 VTY             -    -      -    -    -     0     0    0/0      -
     5 VTY             -    -      -    -    -     0     0    0/0      -
     6 VTY             -    -      -    -    -     0     0    0/0      -
```

The * indicates that there is an active connection on that line. The CTY is the console port, you can see there is a console connection active. The AUX is for connections to the auxiliary port. The VTY are the virtual terminal lines and are used for inbound telnet connections.

There is a fourth type of connection knows as a TTY. These are asynchronous lines used for modem and terminal connections.

You may want to clear a telnet session coming into your router either to throw the user off or to free up a VTY line that should have cleared but has not. You would use the "clear line #" command.

```
RouterA#clear line 2
[confirm]
 [OK]
```

Console password

It is very important to protect your console port on the router. If not, any person who can get physical access to the router will be able to reconfigure it and reboot it.

```
RouterA#config t
Enter configuration commands, one per line. End with CNTL/Z.
RouterA(config)#line console ?
  <0-0>  First Line number

RouterA(config)#line console 0
RouterA(config-line)#password hello
RouterA(config-line)#login
RouterA(config-line)#exit
RouterA(config)#exit
```

For added security you can specify a timeout value to lock the console connection if there is no activity for a specified amount of minutes. This will also work on the VTY and AUX ports.

```
RouterB(config)#line console 0
RouterB(config-line)#exec-timeout 5 ⇐ sets timeout for 5 minutes
```

Timeout values can be set on AUX, console, and VTY lines. If you wish to set it to never timeout then the values must be 0 0. This does represent a security issue though as the lines will remain open.

Configuring user-specific passwords

You may not wish to have a generic password on your connections to the router. You can configure specific username and password combinations on a per user basis.

```
RouterA#config term
Enter configuration commands, one per line. End with CNTL/Z.
RouterA(config)#username paul password cisco
RouterA(config)#username stuart password hello
```

```
RouterA(config)#username davie password football
RouterA(config)#line vty 0 4
RouterA(config-line)#login local
RouterA(config-line)#exit
RouterA(config)#exit
```

I can now telnet from Router B to Router A providing I know my username and password.

```
RouterB#telnet 192.168.1.1
Trying 192.168.1.1 ... Open

User Access Verification

Username: paul
Password:           ⇐ Does not show as it is typed in
```

Privilege levels

You can specify access levels for user accounts on the router. You may, for example, only want junior network team members to be able to use some basic troubleshooting commands. It is also worth remembering that Cisco routers have two modes of password security, user mode (exec) and privileged mode (enable).

Cisco routers have 16 different (0–15) privilege levels available to configure, 15 is full access.

```
RouterA#conf t
Enter configuration commands, one per line. End with CNTL/Z.
RouterA(config)#username support privilege 4 password soccer

  LINE  Initial keywords of the command to modify

RouterA(config)#privilege exec level 4 ping
RouterA(config)#privilege exec level 4 traceroute
RouterA(config)#privilege exec level 4 show ip interface brief
RouterA(config)#line console 0
RouterA(config-line)#password basketball
RouterA(config-line)#login local ⇐ password is needed
RouterA(config-line)#^z
```

The support person logs in to the router and tries to go into config mode, but this command and any other command not available are not valid and cannot be seen.

```
RouterA con0 is now available

Press RETURN to get started.

User Access Verification
```

```
Username: support
Password:
RouterA#config t ⇔ not allowed to use this command
              ^
% Invalid input detected at '^' marker.
```

Login

The login local password on the console, AUX, or VTY line overrides the console, AUX, or VTY password so any person who telnets into Router A will be asked for their username and password from the local database.

You can use the "enable secret {*level*} *password*" to define a password for a specific level of access and then only give the password to those who you wish to have that level of access. You would then use the "privilege mode level command" command to specify the commands available at the various access levels.

Banner messages

You can configure the router to show a warning message when a user logs or telnets into the router. The banner motd message is displayed before the router login prompt. Administrators normally enter some sort of legal notice. You have to enter the command "banner motd =". The = is known as a delimiting character and could be any character you choose (including symbols or letters) but when you type that character it tells the router that you have finished typing the banner, so do not choose a letter from the alphabet.

```
RouterA(config)#banner motd =
Enter TEXT message. End with the character '='.
Unauthorised access to this network will result in prosecution

=
RouterA(config)#
```

Now I telnet to Router A from Router B.

```
RouterB>enable
RouterB#telnet 192.168.1.1
Trying 192.168.1.1 ... Open
Unauthorised access to this network will result in prosecution

User Access Verification

Password:
```

You can also use the "banner login" command which displays a banner message for the username and password login prompts.

There are several other banner options including:

- `banner exec` — displayed as the user logs into the router
- `banner incoming` — used for reverse telnet sessions (console connection)
- `banner login` — displayed after the motd and before the login prompt

 INSPIRATION:

A good working knowledge of router and network security will ensure you are never short of work in the IT industry.

TACACS+, RADIUS, and AAA

Whilst these subjects are outside the scope of the CCNA exam it is worth at least acknowledging the existence of TACACS and RADIUS and what it is they do.

TACACS+ stands for Terminal Access Controller Access Control System Plus. It is a protocol that uses TCP. TACACS+ provides access control for network devices including routers, network access servers via one or more centralized servers.

RADIUS stands for Remote Authentication Dial-In User Service. It is a protocol that uses UDP. It is a system of distributed network security that secures remote access to the network.

If you have TACACS+ or RADIUS, you may wish to enable Authentication, Authorization and Accounting or AAA. AAA is installed on a server and monitors a database of user accounts for the network. Users access, protocols, connections and disconnect reasons as well as many other features can be monitored.

Note: Cisco security features are covered in great detail in the CCNA Security exam which we host on www.HowToNetwork.net. We highly recommend you take that exam after your CCNA.

Logging router access

As a network administrator, it is highly likely that you will want to be aware of who is attempting to log into your network and to also be aware of any other network events.

Local logging

There are several features included in Cisco IOS to monitor events locally on the router:

- `logging console [level]` — monitors connections via the console port. Levels can be from 0–7. You can use the "`no logging console`" to turn off console output if you do not want it appearing on your screen constantly.

Table 7–1: Logging levels

Level	Logging Message
0	Emergencies
1	Alerts
2	Critical
3	Errors
4	Warnings
5	Notifications
6	Informational
7	Debugging

- `terminal monitor` — will allow debug and system messages to appear on your terminal connection to a router. If you are telnetted into a remote router you will need to use this command if you want to see the debug commands.
- `logging buffered [size in bytes | level]` — will allow log messages to be kept in the routers memory.
- `access list [specify action] log` — enables logging of packets that match the NAT configuration line criteria, e.g., access list 10 permit 192.168.1.1 log
- `service timestamps` — allows the router to timestamp logging or debug messages.
- `logging host address` — will send logging messages to a syslog server.

```
Router(config)#logging 172.16.1.5
```

You can view the current logging levels with the "`show logging`" command.

```
RouterB#show logging
Syslog logging: enabled (0 messages dropped, 0 flushes, 0 overruns)
    Console logging: level debugging, 20 messages logged
    Monitor logging: level debugging, 0 messages logged
    Buffer logging: level debugging, 20 messages logged
    Trap logging: level informational, 24 message lines logged
Log Buffer (4096 bytes):
```

```
00:00:09: %LINK-3-UPDOWN: Interface Serial0, changed state to down
00:00:09: %LINK-3-UPDOWN: Interface Serial1, changed state to down
00:01:43: %LINK-5-CHANGED: Interface BRIO, changed state to administratively
down
```

In summary, logging options include:

- `logging buffered` — logs messages to the router buffer
- `logging host` — logs messages to a syslog server
- `terminal monitor` — logs messages to a non console session
- `logging console` — logs messages to the console port

You can have logging (debug) messages time stamped with the "`service timestamps debug datetime msce localtime`" command.

SNMP

Simple Network Management Protocol is a hugely popular protocol. It is used to monitor network events and report back to a central device called the network management station (see module 6).

SECURING THE SWITCH

Implementing switch security is now part of the exam objectives for the CCNA and CCENT. You should be able to perform basic security measures for the CCENT and slightly more advanced security for the CCNA. Also, if you are responsible for maintaining the switches on your network, there are some very simple steps you should take NOW to secure your switches.

Commands and configuration are based on a Cisco 3560 running IOS 12.2(35)SE1. Depending on the platform and IOS version, some commands may be different.

Update IOS

One of the best ways to ensure your switch is secure is to maintain the software on your Cisco switch. I repeat, one of the best ways to ensure your switch is secure is to maintain the software on your Cisco switch. IOS updates will not only fix bugs, but they also provide feature enhancements. Most of Cisco's stackable switches offer lifetime warranties (which includes software updates) so there are no excuses!

Enable password versus enable secret

```
Switch(config)#enable password HoWtOnEtWoRk
Switch(config)#enable secret hOwToNeTwOrK
```

Next, let's do a show run to see the passwords:

```
enable secret 5 $1$NpDl$AjSKrDlyLKK6NyBVBb5fN1
enable password HoWtOnEtWoRk
```

We can see that the enable password is shown in clear text. We certainly do not want that. To encrypt the password, we use the command "service password-encryption" from global configuration mode.

Another show run and we can see that the enable password is now encrypted. If you look closely, you will see that the enable secret has a 5 prepended and the enable password has a 7 prepended. A level of 5 means the password has been hashed using the stronger MD5 algorithm. A level of 7 means the password has been encrypted with a weak algorithm.

```
enable secret 5 $1$NpDl$AjSKrDlyLKK6NyBVBb5fN1
enable password 7 052309383563402C0D32182000
```

By looking at the hash of each password you can see that enable secret is more secure. It is derived from an MD5 hash. The enable password is a simple encryption algorithm that was never intended for complete password security. In short, you should always use the enable secret command and remove the enable password, if it exists. There are multiple free programs on the Internet that can reverse the level7 enable passwords.

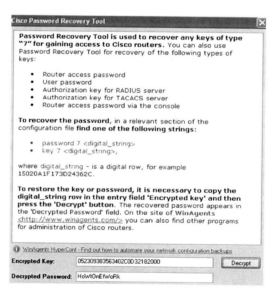

Figure 7–1: Example of enable password weakness

Local usernames

Local usernames provide another level of security to your switch. Instead of having to enter just the VTY password to get access, you now have to enter both a username and a password. You can create multiple user accounts as well. In this section we will cover creation of user accounts. In the next section (Management Ports) we will cover applying the local user accounts to the Management ports for access.

```
username MMessier password 7 097E4F271E000501
```

If we do a show run and take a look at the user we just created, we see that the password is encrypted at level 7. That is because of the previous command we entered service password-encryption. If we entered the command "no service password-encryption", we would see the username and the clear text password.

```
username MMessier password 0 RaNgers
```

If you need to create usernames with irreversible passwords try the following:

```
username MRichter secret ImAgOaLiE
```

Again we do a show run to view the users, and you can see that the MRichter username is now using the MD5 hash.

```
username MRichter secret 5 $1$1IHy$.5phAQQD2Gg/7I9mvvU7c.
```

Management ports

When we discuss management ports, we are referring to direct Console access and VTY lines. We must secure these ports because they provide access to our switches. In the previous section we discussed using local usernames and passwords. Now that we have them set up, let's look at applying them to the management ports. First we must enable AAA, second we configure AAA to assign the local usernames to the default AAA group.

AAA stands for Authentication, Authorization, and Accounting. Authentication is proving who you are with access via a username/password, a token or a certificate. Authorization defines what you can or can not do. This is typically deployed as security levels or ACLs. Accounting is the auditing of what you do. For example, you can configure the switch to allow you to login in using your Windows domain username and password combination (Authentication), give you full access to the switch (Authorization), and log all the commands you type into the switch (Accounting). Each mode of AAA is completely independent of each other so you can implement one, two, or all three of them.

```
Switch(config)#aaa new-model ⇦ This enables AAA on the switch.
Switch(config)#aaa authentication login default local ⇦ Here we define the
        login group named default to use the local username database
```

Finally, we go to the management interfaces and set the login authentication to use the default group.

```
Switch(config)line# vty 0 15
Switch(config-line)#login authentication default
Switch(config-line)#line con 0
Switch(config-line)#login authentication default
```

Note that we do not have to use the `login` or `password` <password> commands.

Next, let's configure a time out for our connection. This will disconnect our telnet/SSH/Console session if idle for 5 minutes and 0 seconds.

```
Switch(config-line)#exec-timeout 5 0
```

Now we'll set the transport. This determines which protocols are allowed in/out of the VTY lines. For example if you have SSH configured and you do not want to allow telnet access to your switches, set the transport input for SSH only.

```
Switch(config-line)#transport input ssh
```

Let's add to that. We can only SSH into the switch, but we want to allow both telnet and SSH out to other devices from the VTY lines. Remember this for the management plane only; you are not permitting/blocking traffic flowing through the switch!

```
Switch(config-line)#transport output telnet ssh
```

Let's block telnet sessions from leaving our switch and see what happens when we try to establish a telnet connection. First, we will block telnet.

```
Switch(config)#line vty 0 15
Switch(config-line)#trans output ssh
Switch(config-line)#end
```

Now, let's try and establish a session to 192.168.100.254.

```
Switch#telnet 192.168.100.254
% telnet connections not permitted from this terminal
Switch#
```

As you can see we are not allowed to telnet out.

One last thing to lock down. We can use an access-list to determine who can access the VTY lines. First, we create the access-list, and then we assign it to the VTY lines.

```
Switch(config)#access-list 11 permit 10.10.9.23
Switch(config)#access-list 11 permit 10.10.10.7
```

```
Switch(config)#line vty 0 15
Switch(config-line)#access-class 11 in
```

Let's do a show run and take a look at the configuration.

```
line vty 0 15
 access-class 11 in
 exec-timeout 5 0
 login authentication default
 transport input ssh
 transport output telnet ssh
```

With that configuration only 10.10.9.23 and 10.10.10.7 are allowed to connect, they must use a local defined username and password, and they have to connect using SSH. If any one of those conditions fails, they will not be able to establish a session with the switch.

Banners

A banner is text presented to the user connecting or that is logging to the switch. Banners can provide a variety of information to the user and the most common is an acceptable use policy. A banner gives notice to anyone who connects to a switch that it is for authorized use only and any use of it will be monitored. Courts have dismissed cases against those who have attacked systems without banners. Thus, no banner on a switch may lead to legal or liability problems.

Below is an example.

NOTICE TO USERS

This is an official computer system and is the property of the ORGANIZATION. It is for authorized users only. Unauthorized users are prohibited. Users (authorized or unauthorized) have no explicit or implicit expectation of privacy. Any or all uses of this system may be subject to one or more of the following actions: interception, monitoring, recording, auditing, inspection and disclosing to security personnel and law enforcement personnel, as well as authorized officials of other agencies, both domestic and foreign. By using this system, the user consents to these actions. Unauthorized or improper use of this system may result in administrative disciplinary action and civil and criminal penalties. By accessing this system you indicate your awareness of and consent to these terms and conditions of use. Discontinue access immediately if you do not agree to the conditions stated in this notice.

There are three types of banners we will cover; MOTD, login, and exec. MOTD is short for Message of the Day and is similar to the one used in Unix. This banner is displayed at connection. If we want to create a banner that states "Authorized users Only!" the command would be:

```
Switch(config)#banner motd $
Enter TEXT message. End with the character '$'.
Authorized Users Only!
$
Switch(config)#
```

Let's dissect the commands above to see what we are doing. The first line of `banner motd $` simply states that we want to create an MOTD banner. The `$` is a delimiting character or in other words it is the character to let the switch know that we are done with the banner text. The delimiting character is set in the command and can be anything you like. However, it makes sense to use a character that will not be used in your banner. If you do use a character that is in your banner text, it will end prematurely. Here is an example.

Let's create a banner that states, "I will make lots of $ if I get my CCNA".

Let's see what happens if we use a $ as a delimiting character.

```
Switch(config)#banner motd $
Enter TEXT message. End with the character '$'.
I will make lots of $ if I get my CCNA
```

It looks like the switch took the command, but let's do a show run just to make sure.

```
!
banner motd ^C
I will make lots of ^C
!
```

You can see the switch was looking for the $ and stopped accepting banner text when it encountered it. Simply change the delimiting character. In the configuration you see the delimiting character is ^C, this is the Cisco default in the configuration file.

The next banner we want to take a look at is the login banner. The login banner is displayed after connection (and after MOTD) but before login.

```
Switch(config)#banner login $
Enter TEXT message. End with the character '$'.
This is the login banner
$
```

Finally, the EXEC banner is displayed once a user establishes an EXEC process (i.e., successful login).

```
Switch(config)#banner exec $
Enter TEXT message. End with the character '$'.
Authorized engineers only!
$
```

Services

You should always disable the services you are not going to use. Cisco has done a good job by not enabling insecure or rarely use services/protocols, however you might want to disable them just to make sure. There are some services that are helpful as well. The majority of services are found under the command "service" in global configuration mode.

```
Switch(config)# service ?
compress-config         Compress the configuration file
config                  TFTP load config files
counters                Control aging of interface counters
dhcp                    Enable DHCP server and relay agent
disable-ip-fast-frag    Disable IP particle-based fast fragmentation
exec-callback           Enable exec callback
exec-wait               Delay EXEC startup on noisy lines
finger                  Allow responses to finger requests
hide-telnet-addresses   Hide destination addresses in telnet command
                        linenumber enable line number banner for each exec
nagle                   Enable Nagle's congestion control algorithm
old-slip-prompts        Allow old scripts to operate with slip/ppp
pad                     Enable PAD commands
password-encryption     Encrypt system passwords
password-recovery       Disable password recovery
prompt                  Enable mode specific prompt
pt-vty-logging          Log significant VTY-Async events
sequence-numbers        Stamp logger messages with a sequence number
slave-log               Enable log capability of slave IPs
tcp-keepalives-in       Generate keepalives on idle incoming network
                        connections
tcp-keepalives-out      Generate keepalives on idle outgoing network
                        connections
tcp-small-servers       Enable small TCP servers (e.g., ECHO)
telnet-zeroidle         Set TCP window 0 when connection is idle
timestamps              Timestamp debug/log messages
udp-small-servers       Enable small UDP servers (e.g., ECHO)
```

Generally speaking, the most common services to enable/disable are listed below. The description of the service is in the [bracket].

- no service pad [packet assembler/disassemble, used in asynchronous networking, rarely used]
- no service config [prevents the switch from getting its config file from the network]
- no service finger [disable the finger server, rarely used]

- `no ip icmp redirect` [prevents ICMP redirects which can be used for router poisoning]
- `no ip finger` [another way to disable the finger service]
- `no ip gratuitous-arps` [disable to prevent man-in-the-middle attacks]
- `no ip source-route` [disable user provided hop by hop routing to destination]
- `service sequence-numbers` [in each log entry give it an number and increase sequentially]
- `service tcp-keepalives-in` [prevent the router from keeping hung management sessions open]
- `service tcp-keepalives-out` [same as service tcp-keepalives-in]
- `no service udp-small-servers` [disables echo, chargen, discard, daytime, rarely used]
- `no service tcp-small-servers` [disables echo, chargen, discard, rarely used]
- `service timestamps debug datetime localtime show-timezone` [timestamp each logged packet (in debug mode) with the date and time, using local time, and show the timezone]
- `service timestamps log datetime localtime show-timezone` [timestamp each logged packet (not in debug mode) with the date and time, using local time, and show the timezone]

SSH

When possible you should always use SSH instead of telnet and SNMP for accessing your switches. SSH stands for secure shell and allows a secure exchange of information between two devices on a network. SSH uses public-key cryptography to authenticate the connecting device. Telnet and SNMP are unencrypted and susceptible to packet sniffing. SSH on the other hand is encrypted. To enable SSH you must have a version of IOS that supports encryption. A quick way to find out is the "`show version`" command. Look for k9 in the file name and/or the security statement of Cisco Systems.

```
Switch#sh version
Cisco IOS Software, C3560 Software (C3560-ADVIPSERVICESK9-M), Version
12.2(35)SE1, RELEASE SOFTWARE (fc1)
Copyright (c) 1986-2006 by Cisco Systems, Inc.
Compiled Tue 19-Dec-06 10:54 by antonino
Image text-base: 0x00003000, data-base: 0x01362CA0
ROM: Bootstrap program is C3560 boot loader
BOOTLDR: C3560 Boot Loader (C3560-HBOOT-M) Version 12.2(25r)SEC, RELEASE
SOFTWARE (fc4)
Switch uptime is 1 hour, 8 minutes
System returned to ROM by power-on
System image file is "flash:/c3560-advipservicesk9-mz.122-35.SE1.bin"
This product contains cryptographic features and is subject to United
States and local country laws governing import, export, transfer and
```

```
use. Delivery of Cisco cryptographic products does not imply
third-party authority to import, export, distribute or use encryption.
Importers, exporters, distributors and users are responsible for
compliance with U.S. and local country laws. By using this product you
agree to comply with applicable laws and regulations. If you are unable to
comply with U.S. and local laws, return this product immediately.
A summary of U.S. laws governing Cisco cryptographic products may be found
at:
http://www.cisco.com/wwl/export/crypto/tool/stqrg.html
If you require further assistance please contact us by sending email to
export@cisco.com.
--More--
```

*If you do not have a security version of IOS, you must purchase a license for it.

In order for our connection to encrypt, we need to create a private/public key on the switch (see below). When we connect, we use the public key to encrypt the data and the switch uses its private key to decrypt the data. For authentication, we use a username/password combination. We set the switch hostname name and domain because the private/public keys will be created using the hostname.domainname nomenclature. Obviously, it makes sense for the key to be named something representing the system.

Configuring SSH on the switch

Firstly we have to make sure we have a hostname other than the default of Switch. Next, we want to add our domain name (this typically matches your FQDN in Windows Active Directory). Then, we create the crypto key that is used for encryption. The modulus is the length of the keys we want to use. The range is from 360 to 2048, with the latter being the most secure. 1024 and above is considered secure. At this point, SSH is enabled on the switch. There are a few maintenance commands we should enter as well. The ip ssh time-out 60 will time out any SSH connection that has been idle for 60 seconds. The ip ssh authentication-retries 2 will reset the initial SSH connection if authentication fails two times. This will not prevent the user from establishing a new connection and retrying authentication.

```
Switch(config)#hostname SwitchOne
SwitchOne(config)#ip domain-name mydomain.com
SwitchOne(config)#crypto key generate rsa
Enter modulus: 1024
SwitchOne(config)#ip ssh time-out 60
SwitchOne(config)#ip ssh authentication-retries 2
```

Let's take a look at one of our keys. In this example, the key was generated for HTTPS. This key was automatically generated when enabling HTTPS, so the name is also auto generated.

```
firewall#show crypto key mypubkey rsa
Key name: HTTPS_SS_CERT_KEYPAIR.server
Temporary key
Usage: Encryption Key
Key is not exportable.
Key Data:
306C300D 06092A86 4886F70D 01010105 00035B00 30580251 00C41B63 8EF294A1
DC0F7378 7EF410F6 6254750F 475DAD71 4E1CD15E 1D9086A8 BD175433 1302F403
2FD22F82 C311769F 9C75B7D2 1E50D315 EFA0E940 DF44AD5A F717BF17 A3CEDBE1
A6A2D601 45F313B6 6B020301 0001
```

To verify SSH is enabled on the switch, enter the following command:

```
Switch#show ip ssh
SSH Enabled - version 1.99
Authentication timeout: 120 secs; Authentication retries: 2
Switch#
```

To enable SSH on the VTY lines, please see the Management Ports section. If you have SSH enabled you should probably disable telnet and HTTP. Disabling telnet is under the Management Ports section; however, here it is once again. When you enter the "transport input" command, any protocol entered after is allowed. Any protocol not entered is not allowed. In our example below, we can see that we are only allowing SSH. The second example shows that we will allow both SSH and telnet.

```
line vty 0 15
transport input ssh
```

Example

```
line vty 0 15
transport input ssh telnet
```

You can disable HTTP access with one simple command:

```
Switch(config)#no ip http server
To view the status of the HTTP server on the switch:
Switch#show ip http server status
HTTP server status: Disabled
HTTP server port: 80
HTTP server authentication method: enable
HTTP server access class: 0
HTTP server base path: flash:html
Maximum number of concurrent server connections allowed: 16
Server idle time-out: 180 seconds
Server life time-out: 180 seconds
Maximum number of requests allowed on a connection: 25
```

```
HTTP server active session modules: ALL
HTTP secure server capability: Present
HTTP secure server status: Enabled
HTTP secure server port: 443
HTTP secure server ciphersuite: 3des-ede-cbc-sha des-cbc-sha rc4-128-md5 rc4-12
HTTP secure server client authentication: Disabled
HTTP secure server trustpoint:
HTTP secure server active session modules: ALL
```

CDP

CDP stands for Cisco Discovery Protocol. It is a very useful troubleshooting tool that runs on nearly all Cisco equipment (and some HP). It is a layer 2 protocol that discovers other Cisco devices that are directly connected and provides some very useful information about the device. Here is an example:

```
Switch#show cdp neighbor
Capability Codes: R - Router, T - Trans Bridge, B - Source Route Bridge
S - Switch, H - Host, I - IGMP, r - Repeater, P - Phone
Device ID Local Intrfce Holdtme Capability Platform Port ID
abc2.testlink.com
Fas 0/41 169 R 2611XM Fas 0/0
abc1.testlink.com
Fas 0/40 167 R 2611XM Fas 0/0
```

You should be very careful when disabling CDP. Some Cisco services, such as VoIP, depend on it. You can enable/disable CDP either globally or per interface.

```
Switch(config)#no cdp run
Switch#show cdp
% CDP is not enabled
Switch#
```

Disabling on an interface (note the slight change in the command):

```
Switch(config)#interface FastEthernet0/1
Switch(config-if)#no cdp enable
```

Port security

You can use the port security feature to restrict input to an interface by limiting and identifying MAC addresses of the workstations that are allowed to access the port. When you assign secure MAC addresses to a secure port, the port does not forward packets with source addresses outside the group of defined addresses. If you limit the number of secure MAC addresses to one and assign a single secure MAC address, the workstation attached to that port is assured the full bandwidth of the port.

If a port is configured as a secure port and the maximum number of secure MAC addresses is reached, when the MAC address of a workstation attempting to access the port is different from any of the identified secure MAC addresses a security violation occurs.

A security violation can generate one of two actions; an SNMP trap notification or port shutdown. With SNMP trap notification an SNMP trap is sent to the SNMP manager. The port shutdown feature will shut the port down, disabling all network access. It can be re-enabled manually or after a specified amount of time.

Let's take a look at a port before any configuration.

```
Switch#show port-security interface fastethernet 0/48
Port Security              : Disabled
Port Status                : Secure-down
Violation Mode             : Shutdown
Aging Time                 : 0 mins
Aging Type                 : Absolute
SecureStatic Address Aging : Disabled
Maximum MAC Addresses      : 1
Total MAC Addresses        : 0
Configured MAC Addresses   : 0
Sticky MAC Addresses       : 0
Last Source Address:Vlan   : 0000.0000.0000:0
Security Violation Count   : 0
```

Now, let's configure the port to allow only one MAC address that we assign manually.

```
Switch(config)#interface FastEthernet0/48
Switch(config-if)#switchport mode access
Switch(config-if)#switchport port-security
Switch(config-if)#switchport port-security mac-address sticky
Switch(config-if)#switchport port-security mac-address 0005.1b00.5b58
```

The only allowed device on the port must have the MAC address of 00051b005b58. If a device with a different MAC address tries to connect, the port will shutdown. Let's look at the port again. We can see that port security has been enabled and what attributes are set for the port.

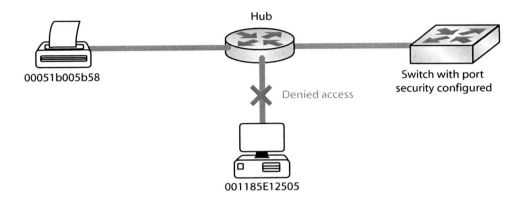

Figure 7–2: Port security via MAC addressing

```
Switch#show port-security interface fastethernet 0/48
Port Security              : Enabled
Port Status                : Secure-down
Violation Mode             : Shutdown
Aging Time                 : 0 mins
Aging Type                 : Absolute
SecureStatic Address Aging : Disabled
Maximum MAC Addresses      : 1
Total MAC Addresses        : 1
Configured MAC Addresses   : 1
Sticky MAC Addresses       : 0
Last Source Address:Vlan   : 0000.0000.0000:0
Security Violation Count   : 0
```

You can also set the port to learn MAC addresses, allow multiple MAC addresses, etc. There is a myriad of options and knobs to turn so please follow the port security lab to learn more about this important subject.

Logging

Logging is crucial to security on a switch. Thankfully, logging is very easy to configure and is probably the most useful troubleshooting tools on any Cisco device. Let's take a look at some configuration options.

The switch itself has a logging buffer where it can store logging messages. This buffer has a limited amount of memory space on the switch, although that area is configurable. This buffer area is called buffered.

```
Switch(config)#logging buffered ?
<4096-2147483647> Logging buffer size
```

The default size is 4096 and is usually adequate for a stable switch. You might want to make it a little bigger if you have to log for security reasons or debugs.

```
Switch(config)#logging buffered 16000
```

Next we want to configure the error level that buffer should log.

```
logging buffered ?
<0-7>Logging severity level
alerts – Immediate action needed (severity=1)
critical – Critical conditions (severity=2)
debugging – Debugging messages (severity=7)
emergencies – System is unusable (severity=0)
errors – Error conditions (severity=3)
informational – Informational messages (severity=6)
notifications – Normal but significant conditions (severity=5)
warnings – Warning conditions (severity=4)
```

As you can see we can use either the name of the severity level or the number associated with it. There are also some basic descriptions set to each level. Error messages about software or hardware malfunctions, displayed at levels "warnings" through "emergencies". These types of messages mean that the functionality of the switch is affected.

Output from the debug commands are displayed at the debugging level. Interface up or down transitions and system restart messages, displayed at the notifications level. This message is only for information; switch functionality is not affected.

Your logging level will depend on your security policy. A safe starting point would be informational. Both of the commands below accomplish the same thing.

```
Switch(config)#logging buffered 6
Switch(config)#logging buffered informational
```

Now let's see what our logging settings are set to (note there is no mention in the configuration file). The level for buffering is informational and the size is 16,000 bytes, just like we set.

```
Switch#show log
Syslog logging: enabled (0 messages dropped, 1 messages rate-limited, 0
flushes, 0 overruns, xml disabled, filtering disabled)
Console logging: level debugging, 94 messages logged, xml disabled,
filtering disabled
Monitor logging: level debugging, 0 messages logged, xml disabled,
filtering disabled
Buffer logging: level informational, 1 messages logged, xml disabled,
filtering disabled
Exception Logging: size (4096 bytes)
```

```
Count and timestamp logging messages: disabled
File logging: disabled
Trap logging: level informational, 97 message lines logged

Log Buffer (16000 bytes):
```

You can also log to a couple of other places; the Console (when you console directly to the switch), the Monitor (the VTY lines), and to Syslog (Syslog is both a protocol and a function. With Syslog, you can configure your switches to send its system messages to another server. This is useful because your switch has limited capacity for message storage whereas the Syslog server will store the messages as plain text on the local hard drive). Each place you log to can be set to different levels which is very convenient not only for security, but also for troubleshooting.

Finally, you must turn logging on.

```
Switch(config)#logging on
```

If you want to log messages to the console (meaning you will see them only when you are directly consoled into the switch) enter the following:

```
Switch(config)#logging console
```

If you want to log messages to the VTY lines (meaning you want to see messages if you are telnet/ SSH into the switch) enter the following:

```
Switch(config)#logging monitor
```

If you would like to also send log messages to a SYSLOG server, enter the following:

```
Switch(config)#logging host <IP Address of SYSLOG Server>
```

Time

The time on a switch is often overlooked, however it is very important. When you encounter security violations, SNMP traps, or logging of events it uses a timestamp (see the "service timestamps" command on page 233). If the time on your switch is incorrect, it will be difficult figuring out when the event happened. For example, let's take a look at our switch and check the time.

```
Switch#show clock
*23:09:45.773 UTC Tue Mar 2 1993
```

The time is not accurate, so let's change it. But first, let's set some attributes.

```
clock timezone CST -6
clock summer-time CDT recurring
clock summer-time CST recurring 2 Sun Mar 2:00 1 Sun Nov 2:00
```

The first thing we want to do is set the time zone. I'm in the Central time zone, and I'm 6 off of GMT. Next, we tell the switch that summertime (the time change) is recurring. Finally, we set what the summertime time really is. Now, let's set the time and date.

```
Switch#clock set 14:55:05 June 19 2007
Switch#
1d23h: %SYS-6-CLOCKUPDATE: System clock has been updated from 17:26:01 CST
Tue Mar 2 1993 to 14:55:05 CST Tue Jun 19 2007, configured from console by
console.
Switch#show clock
14:55:13.858 CST Tue Jun 19 2007
```

Notice we set the clock in enable mode, not configuration mode. Alternatively, you can use NTP. NTP stands for Network Time Protocol. It allows you to synchronize your switches clock to an atomic clock, ensuring very accurate time.

```
Switch(config)#ntp server 134.84.84.84 prefer
Switch(config)#ntp server 209.184.112.199
```

You can see if your clock has synchronized with your NTP sources with the following two commands:

```
Switch(config)#show ntp associations
Switch(config)#show ntp status
```

Port configuration

You can configure the port to be either an access port or a trunk port. We will take a look at the access port first.

```
Switch(config-if)#switchport mode access
Switch(config-if)#switchport access vlan 5
```

The first command tells the port to be an access port. This port will not try and establish a connection as a trunk. The second "switchport" command tells the port what VLAN it belongs to, in this case VLAN 5.

Now, let's configure a port for trunking.

```
Switch(config-if)#switchport mode trunk
Command rejected: An interface whose trunk encapsulation is "Auto" can not be
configured to "trunk" mode.
```

We received an error that translated into layman terms means that you must set the trunking protocol before setting the port to trunk. Let's do that next and we will use dot1q.

```
Switch(config-if)#switchport trunk encapsulation dot1q
```

Now the rest of the trunk configuration. For security reasons we only want VLANs 5 & 6 on the trunk, so we'll set that as well.

```
Switch(config-if)#switchport mode trunk
Switch(config-if)#switchport trunk allowed vlan 5-6
```

VTP

If you use VTP in your network, you will certainly want to configure a password. This will ensure only authorized switches are installed into your VTP domain.

```
Switch#show vtp password
The VTP password is not configured.
```

Let's configure the password.

```
Switch(config)#vtp password IwAnTmYcCnA
Setting device VLAN database password to IwAnTmYcCnA
Switch(config)#end
Switch#show vtp password
VTP Password: IwAnTmYcCnA
```

You will have to configure the password on each switch in your VTP domain. If a switch does not have the password, it will not participate in VTP.

SNMP

SNMP allows for management of your network via one or more network management stations. Simple Network Management Protocol uses a system of trap messages to notify the SNMP management station about events on the network. It can also be used to remotely manage your network devices. SNMP is disabled by default. However, you can verify that with the following command:

```
Switch#show snmp
%SNMP agent not enabled
```

Let's configure SNMP for read-only access (only use write access if it is absolutely necessary) and with an access-list.

```
Switch(config)#snmp-server community HoWtOnEtWoRk ro 15
Switch(config)#access-list 15 permit 10.10.10.15
Switch(config)#access-list 15 permit 10.10.10.16
```

In the first line we configured SNMP and we are using the community string of HoWtOnEtWoRk, it only has read access (that us the ro), and only the two address in access-list 15 are permitted. It is pretty easy to secure SNMP. You just need to map out what you want to do. SNMPv3 is coming soon, and it will offer authentication and encryption for additional security.

Conclusion

You can see that with a few simple steps you can secure the switches on your network from the most common security threats. This knowledge will be crucial for your CCNA and CCNET exam success but also for when you come to apply your knowledge to a live network.

ACCESS LISTS

The most fundamental way to protect your network is to decide which traffic can enter and leave your router. Access lists are a set of filters that the traffic is checked against. When the traffic matches the access list it can either be permitted or denied depending upon what you have configured.

Although access lists are relatively straightforward to configure they can cause problems for many network engineers. This is due to the fact that there are some commands at the bottom of any access list that exist but which cannot be seen (they are known as implicit commands). Also, access lists operate by a certain set of special rules and if you are not aware of these rules your access list will not work or will only work part of the time.

 IN THE REAL WORLD:

If you suspect your access list is causing problems, just remove it. If the problem goes away you can be sure your access list needs to be reconfigured.

Traffic comes into the router interface, is checked against the access list and if it is permitted it is routed and then sent to the outbound interface.

Figure 7–3: Access lists in action

Rule 1: You are only permitted certain number of access lists on the router. One ingoing and one outgoing per interface per protocol. The idea is that you should be able to be specific enough to configure all of your settings in one access list in any given direction. The skill comes in doing it with the minimum amount of commands.

Rule 2: The router starts at the top of the access list and works its way down. As soon as it finds a match it permits or denies the traffic and looks no further. Processing of access list statements after this is not done.

IP access lists come in two varieties—standard and extended. Standard access lists are very simple to configure but do not allow any granularity. Extended access lists are far more flexible but they are more complex to configure.

Access list numbers

There are many ranges of access list based upon protocol type, in order for the router to understand which one you want to configure you have to use the correct range. For example, to configure IP standard access lists, use any number from 1 to 99.

Table 7–2: Access list ranges

Protocol	Range
Standard IP	1 to 99
Standard IP (Expanded range)	1300 to 1999
Extended IP	100 to 199
Extended IP (Expanded range)	2000 to 2699
Ethernet type code	200 to 299
Ethernet address	700 to 799
Transparent bridging (protocol type)	200 to 299
Transparent bridging (vendor code)	700 to 799
Extended transparent bridging	1100 to 1199
DECnet and extended DECnet	300 to 399
XNS	400 to 499
Extended XNS	500 to 599
AppleTalk	600 to 699
Source-route bridging (protocol type)	200 to 299
Source-route bridging (vendor code)	700 to 799
IPX	800 to 899
Extended IPX	900 to 999
IPX SAP	1000 to 1099
Standard VINES	1 to 100
Extended VINES	101 to 200
Simple VINES	201 to 300

Standard IP access lists

Standard IP access lists filter traffic based upon the IP source address of the traffic only. They do not filter web, e-mail or any other variety of traffic or filter based upon destination.

The access list is given a number to identify the type of list it is (see Table 7–2), configured to permit or deny traffic and then configured with the parameters of which traffic to permit or deny. Many people then think this is all they need to do. You actually have to apply this access list to an interface. Otherwise, the access list will just sit there doing nothing in particular and all traffic will be allowed through the router.

Rule 3: All traffic not included in the access list is denied. Even if you do not enter a "deny any" command at the end of the list, it will do this automatically (unless you configure it to permit everything). The rationale is if you are permitting certain traffic, surely you want to deny everything else! This is known as the Implicit Deny Rule, and you need to remember this ALWAYS!

The command syntax for a standard access list is:

```
access-list number {deny | permit} source source-wildcard log
```

Wildcard masks

The wildcard mask can cause confusion amongst anybody new to access lists. Just remember that the router is looking in binary instead of decimal. The wildcard mask is there to tell the access list which parts of the address to look at. A 1 in binary means that part of the address can be ignored, and a 0 means it must match.

Example

If I want to match all traffic from 172.16.2.x, then I would add the wildcard mask 0.0.0.255 or in binary:

```
10101100.00010000.00000010.00000000 = 172.16.2.0
00000000.00000000.00000000.11111111 = 0.0.0.255
Match     Match     Match     Ignore
```

In action, this would mean any host from the network starting with 172.16.2.x would match the access list. 172.16.3.x would not match the access list.

Example

Here we have an access list permitting any traffic from the 10.x.x.x network:

```
access-list 9 permit 10.0.0.0 0.255.255.255
```

Remember that there is an implicit "deny any" at the end of the access list. When you apply this to an interface the only permitted network will be 10.x.x.x.

```
access-list 9 permit 10.0.0.0 0.255.255.255
(access-list 9 deny 0.0.0.0 255.255.255.255) ⇦ This is present, but you
                          will not see it. It is the implicit "deny any".
```

Example
```
access-list 12 permit 172.16.2.0 0.0.0.255   ⇦ 172.16.2.x allowed
access-list 12 permit 192.168.1.0 0.0.0.255  ⇦ 192.168.1.x allowed
access-list 12 permit 10.4.0.0 0.0.255.255   ⇦ 10.4.x.x allowed
```

This access list permits three networks and denies traffic from any other network.

Example
```
access-list 15 deny 172.16.0.0 0.0.255.255
access-list 15 deny 192.168.2.1 ⇦ You can specify a host address.
access-list permit any
```

When you want to deny a few networks, subnets or hosts and permit the rest, use the logic shown above. We are denying anything from 172.16.x.x network but we can also specify a single host without using a wildcard mask. Just enter the host number and the router will add an automatic 0.0.0.0 to it.

Lastly, we have added "permit any" to the end of the list. This is to prevent the implicit "deny any" from denying any other traffic anyway. If you forget this line all traffic will be denied anyway.

You can break wildcard masks down from the default subnet boundaries just as you can use VLSM to change the default subnet mask for an IP address.

Example
If you wanted to deny the 192.168.100.96 255.255.255.224 subnet, you would use the wildcard mask:
```
0.0.0.31
```

It would make more sense if we write this out in binary:

```
1.1.1.1.1.1.1.1 1.1.1.1.1.1.1.1  1.1.1.1.1.1.1.1  1.1.1.0.0.0.0.0 =
255.255.255.224
0.0.0.0.0.0.0.0  0.0.0.0.0.0.0.0  0.0.0.0.0.0.0.0  0.0.0.1.1.1.1.1 =
0.0.0.31
```

So, the access list is matching the first 27 bits, and the last 5 can be any. The simplest way to look at it is to swap each on bit to an off bit when you are writing out the wildcard mask.

Example

    10.1.64.0 255.255.192.0

If you wanted to permit or deny this subnet you would need to create a specific wildcard mask to match that subnet. The wildcard mask needs to be the reverse of the subnet mask to permit or deny this subnet.

    1.1.1.1.1.1.1.1 1.1.1.1.1.1.1.1 1.1.0.0.0.0.0.0 0.0.0.0.0.0.0.0 =
    255.255.192.0
    0.0.0.0.0.0.0.0 0.0.0.0.0.0.0.0 0.0.1.1.1.1.1.1 1.1.1.1.1.1.1.1 =
    0.0.63.255

So long as when you add the two columns together you get 255, you know the wildcard mask is correct. This is shown in the example above.

Subnet mask	255	255	192	0
Wildcard mask	0	0	63	255
Equals	255	255	255	255

Example

What wildcard mask would deny the subnet 172.16.32.0 255.255.240.0?

Subnet mask	255	255	240	0
Wildcard mask	0	0	15	255
Equals	255	255	255	255

The access list would read permit/deny 172.16.32.0 0.0.15.255.

Wildcard masks are commonly used with OSPF to advertise specific subnets.

 IN THE EXAM:

It would be time well spent to practise your wildcard masks for various subnets such at 192, 224, 240, etc.

Access list logging

There is an optional "log" command you can add to the end of an access list. This allows any matches to the access list to be logged to the console session or router memory in case you want to check for hacking attacks or configuration problems.

```
access-list 15 deny 172.16.0.0 0.0.255.255 log
```

If you added the "logging buffered" command to the config, the output would be added to the routers memory buffer. This could be interrogated later to investigate access list violations.

 IN THE REAL WORLD:

Logging access lists consumes CPU cycles so use the command with caution.

Rule 4: Access lists only filter traffic going through the router. They do NOT filter traffic originating from the router.

Extended IP access lists

Many administrators find they need a lot more flexibility when locking down their networks. Just being able to filter based upon traffic source address only is very limited. Extended access lists can filter based upon source address, destination address, protocol, port number and other features (see explanation of port numbers below).

Here is the syntax for a TCP access list. As we will see, there are also IP, UDP, and ICMP access lists. The syntax is slightly different for each.

access-list *access-list-number* <dynamic *dynamic-name* <timeout *minutes*>>
{deny | permit} tcp *source source-wildcard* <operator <port>> *destination destination-wildcard* <operator <port>> <established>
<precedence *precedence*> <tos *tos*> <log | log-input>

- number — extended access lists can be from 100–199
- dynamic — creates temporary entries in the access list
- timeout — how long the dynamic list is activated for
- deny/permit — is the list allowing or denying the traffic
- tcp — you could deny a tcp port or all tcp traffic
- source — source host or network
- destination — destination host or network

- `operator` — can be greater than, less than, equal to
- `port` — port number
- `established` — only permit traffic instigated from the inside of your network
- `precedence` — filters based on the precedence level 0–7
- `tos` — filters based on service level 0–5 or by name
- `log` — log the access list violations

It is worth briefly mentioning the "`established`" command in more detail. Perhaps you want to allow certain types of traffic into your network but only if your internal users have started the session or requested the service. The established keyword checks for the ACK or acknowledge bit in the packet. If the ACK or RST (reset) bit is set then this indicates that the packet is a response packet to a TCP request made from your network and is safe.

The access list looks at source address to destination, i.e., the first address is from and the second is to.

 IN THE REAL WORLD:

You need not be too concerned with all of the available syntax, generally you will only use about half of the available commands.

Your list of operators may be shorter or longer than this depending upon your IOS release. Most of them you will probably never use. It would probably help to have some examples now.

Example
```
access-list 101 permit tcp any any
```
permits TCP traffic from any network to any network.

Example
```
access-list 102 permit udp host 20.0.2.1 any eq 53 ⇔ permits UDP traffic
     from host 20.0.2.1 to anywhere provided the port is equal to 53 (DNS).
access-list 101 permit tcp host 11.1.2.1 host 172.16.1.1 eq telnet
access-list 101 permit tcp host 11.1.1.2 host 172.16.1.1
access-list 101 permit udp host 15.2.1.5 host 172.16.1.1
access-list 101 permit ip 15.1.1.0 0.0.0.255 172.16.1.0 0.0.0.255
```

Permits telnet traffic from host 11.1.2.1 to 172.16.1.1, you could have put 23 at the end instead of the word telnet. Any TCP traffic is allowed from host 11.1.1.2 to host 172.16.1.1. Any UDP traffic is permitted from host 15.2.1.5 to host 172.16.1.1 and then any IP traffic from network 15.1.1.x to network 172.16.1.x. The specific deny any at the end of the access list will deny any other traffic.

DISCLAIMER: The access lists here are for demonstration purposes only. Do not take them as examples to use on live networks.

Port numbers

Traffic flowing from network to network does use IP addressing but the traffic is going there for a reason; to access some information, a certain service or to carry out a certain task. In order for the network to understand what type of traffic is contained within the packet a port number is used.

A port number identifies whether the traffic is web, e-mail, telnet, name resolution, etc. There are literally thousands of port numbers available. The port numbers from 0–1023 are called well known numbers and are reserved. There are 65,535 available port numbers in total.

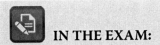 **IN THE EXAM:**

You will need to remember a few port numbers.

Table 7–3: Common port numbers

Port number	Service	Protocol
20	File transfer protocol - Data (FTP)	TCP
21	File transfer protocol (FTP)	TCP
22	Secure shell (SSH)	TCP
23	Telnet	TCP
25	Simple mail transfer protocol (SMTP)	TCP
53	Domain name system (DNS)	UDP
69	Trivial file transfer protocol (TFTP)	UDP
80	Hypertext transfer protocol (HTTP)	TCP/UDP
110	Post office protocol (POP3)	TCP
119	Network news transfer protocol (NNTP)	TCP
123	Network time protocol (NTP)	UDP
161, 162	Simple network management protocol (SNMP)	UDP
443	HTTP secure (HTTPS)	TCP

You need to be aware that some ports are exclusive to TCP, some to UDP and some are shared (such as DNS). You can either type in the port number or (depending upon your IOS release) use the service name.

```
Router(config)#access-list 100 permit tcp any any eq ?
  <0-65535>     Port number
  bgp           Border Gateway Protocol (179)
  chargen       Character generator (19)
  cmd           Remote commands (rcmd, 514)
  daytime       Daytime (13)
  discard       Discard (9)
  domain        Domain Name Service (53)
  echo          Echo (7)
  exec          Exec (rsh, 512)
  finger        Finger (79)
  ftp           File Transfer Protocol (21)
  ftp-data      FTP data connections (used infrequently, 20)
  gopher        Gopher (70)
  hostname      NIC hostname server (101)
  ident         Ident Protocol (113)
  irc           Internet Relay Chat (194)
  klogin        Kerberos login (543)
  kshell        Kerberos shell (544)
  login         Login (rlogin, 513)
  lpd           Printer service (515)
  nntp          Network News Transport Protocol (119)
  pim-auto-rp   PIM Auto-RP (496)
  pop2          Post Office Protocol v2 (109)
  pop3          Post Office Protocol v3 (110)
  smtp          Simple Mail Transport Protocol (25)
  sunrpc        Sun Remote Procedure Call (111)
  syslog        Syslog (514)
  tacacs        TAC Access Control System (49)
  talk          Talk (517)
  telnet        Telnet (23)
  time          Time (37)
  uucp          Unix-to-Unix Copy Program (540)
  whois         Nicname (43)
  www           World Wide Web (HTTP, 80)
Router(config)#access-list 100 permit udp any any eq ?
  <0-65535>     Port number
  biff          Biff (mail notification, comsat, 512)
  bootpc        Bootstrap Protocol (BOOTP) client (68)
  bootps        Bootstrap Protocol (BOOTP) server (67)
  discard       Discard (9)
  dnsix         DNSIX security protocol auditing (195)
  domain        Domain Name Service (DNS, 53)
  echo          Echo (7)
  isakmp        Internet Security Association and Key Management Protocol (500)
  mobile-ip     Mobile IP registration (434)
  nameserver    IEN116 name service (obsolete, 42)
```

```
netbios-dgm    NetBios datagram service (138)
netbios-ns     NetBios name service (137)
netbios-ss     NetBios session service (139)
ntp            Network Time Protocol (123)
pim-auto-rp    PIM Auto-RP (496)
rip            Routing Information Protocol (router, in.routed, 520)
snmp           Simple Network Management Protocol (161)
snmptrap       SNMP Traps (162)
sunrpc         Sun Remote Procedure Call (111)
syslog         System Logger (514)
tacacs         TAC Access Control System (49)
talk           Talk (517)
tftp           Trivial File Transfer Protocol (69)
time           Time (37)
who            Who service (rwho, 513)
xdmcp          X Display Manager Control Protocol (177)
```

You can find all port numbers listed at:

http://www.iana.org/assignments/port-numbers

Access lists can also filter ICMP traffic (see Module 6 for more info on ICMP).

```
Router(config)#access-list 100 permit icmp any any ?
  <0-255>                        ICMP message type
  administratively-prohibited    Administratively prohibited
  alternate-address              Alternate address
  conversion-error               Datagram conversion
  dod-host-prohibited            Host prohibited
  dod-net-prohibited             Net prohibited
  echo                           Echo (ping)
  echo-reply                     Echo reply
  general-parameter-problem      Parameter problem
  host-isolated                  Host isolated
  host-precedence-unreachable    Host unreachable for precedence
  host-redirect                  Host redirect
  host-tos-redirect              Host redirect for TOS
  host-tos-unreachable           Host unreachable for TOS
  host-unknown                   Host unknown
  host-unreachable               Host unreachable
  information-reply              Information replies
  information-request            Information requests
  log                            Log matches against this entry
  log-input                      Log matches against this entry, including
                                 input interface
  mask-reply                     Mask replies
  mask-request                   Mask requests
  mobile-redirect                Mobile host redirect
  net-redirect                   Network redirect
  net-tos-redirect               Net redirect for TOS
  net-tos-unreachable            Network unreachable for TOS
  net-unreachable                Net unreachable
```

```
network-unknown              Network unknown
no-room-for-option           Parameter required but no room
option-missing               Parameter required but not present
packet-too-big               Fragmentation needed and DF set
parameter-problem            All parameter problems
port-unreachable             Port unreachable
precedence                   Match packets with given precedence value
precedence-unreachable       Precedence cutoff
protocol-unreachable         Protocol unreachable
reassembly-timeout           Reassembly timeout
redirect                     All redirects
router-advertisement         Router discovery advertisements
router-solicitation          Router discovery solicitations
source-quench                Source quenches
source-route-failed          Source route failed
time-exceeded                All time exceededs
time-range                   Specify a time-range
timestamp-reply              Timestamp replies
timestamp-request            Timestamp requests
tos                          Match packets with given TOS value
traceroute                   Traceroute
ttl-exceeded                 TTL exceeded
unreachable                  All unreachables
```

 IN THE REAL WORLD:

You will usually only need to use "echo" and "echo-reply".

Access list rules

When using access lists on Cisco routers, certain rules and exceptions can cause confusion. There are very few references to the exceptions in books or websites. You usually have to find the information on newsgroups or by trial and error.

Without knowing how access list rules work, it is very easy to make it completely ineffective or not operate how you intended it to.

Rule 5: You cannot edit an access list on the router. You have to cut and paste it into a text editor, make your changes, and then apply it to the router again. This rule does not apply to named access lists (see later).

The exact steps are to:

1. Cut and paste the complete access list into a text editor and then make your changes.
2. Apply a "no access-list #" (add the access list number at the # point) to the router.
3. You can then go back into config mode and paste the new access list in.

Rule 6: If you want to make an access-list inactive, you can either remove the access list completely or simply go to interface configuration mode and remove it from the interface with the "no ip access-group 101 in/out" command (see "Removing access lists" on page 254).

Rule 7: You can use the same access list more than once. You could, for example, configure access list 100 and apply it to your aux port and your serial interface.

Rule 8: Do not remove one line of an access list with the "no" command. The whole access list will be removed.

Rule 9: Start with the most specific entries at the top of the access list and move to the more general nearer to the bottom.

Access lists and routing protocols

Access lists will permit the traffic you specify. It is vital to remember that if you are using routing protocols and access lists on your router that you permit the routing protocol as well.

To permit IGRP specify:
```
access-list 101 permit igrp any any
```

To permit RIP specify:
```
access-list 101 permit udp any any eq rip
```

To permit OSPF specify:
```
access-list 101 permit ospf any any
```

To permit EIGRP specify:
```
access-list 101 permit eigrp any any
```

Applying access lists

Access lists need to be placed on an interface if they are to do their job. You will need to decide which interface is best. Look at the network below.

Figure 7–4: Access lists need to be applied to an interface

If you want to block traffic coming in from the source network, would you want to place it on the serial or Ethernet interface? If you place it on the Ethernet then the traffic will come into the serial interface, be routed and then passed to the Ethernet interface and then dropped.

If you want to block some traffic leaving your network, is it best to place the list on the serial or Ethernet interface?

The syntax for placing an access list changes depending upon where you are using it, an interface or a port on the router and the type of access list. **Cisco recommends that you place standard access lists as close to the destination as possible and extended access lists as close to the source as possible.** The final decision will be up to you.

In order to place an access list on an interface you use the following syntax:

```
ip access-group <number|name> <in|out>
```

Example

```
Router#config t
Enter configuration commands, one per line. End with CNTL/Z.
Router(config)#access-list 10 permit 10.0.0.0 0.0.0.255
Router(config)#interface s0
Router(config-if)#ip access-group 10 in
Router(config-if)#^Z
Router#
```

To apply an access list to a port the syntax is slightly different:

```
access-class <number|name> <in|out>

Router#conf t
Enter configuration commands, one per line. End with CNTL/Z.
Router(config)#line console 0
Router(config-line)#access-class 10 in
```

or to the virtual terminal ports (telnet):

```
Router#config t
Enter configuration commands, one per line. End with CNTL/Z.
Router(config)#line vty 0 4
Router(config-line)#access-class 10 in
Router(config-line)#exit
Router(config)#exit
```

You can check that the correct access list is applied to the telnet ports by issuing a "show line" command. The VTY lines should show access list 20 applied to them for inbound connections (AccI) in the output below.

```
Router#config t
Router(config)#access-list 20 permit 10.0.0.1
Router(config)#line vty 0 4
Router(config-line)#access-class 20 in
Router(config-line)#^Z
Router#
Router#show line
    Tty Typ     Tx/Rx      A Modem  Roty AccO AccI   Uses   Noise  Overruns
Int
*    0 CTY                 -   -      -    -    -      0      0      0/0
    33 TTY     9600/9600   -   -      -    -    -      0      0      0/0
    34 TTY     9600/9600   -   -      -    -    -      0      0      0/0
    35 TTY     9600/9600   -   -      -    -    -      0      0      0/0
    36 TTY     9600/9600   -   -      -    -    -      0      0      0/0
    37 TTY     9600/9600   -   -      -    -    -      0      0      0/0
    38 TTY     9600/9600   -   -      -    -    -      0      0      0/0
    39 TTY     9600/9600   -   -      -    -    -      0      0      0/0
    40 TTY     9600/9600   -   -      -    -    -      0      0      0/0
    41 TTY     9600/9600   -   -      -    -    -      0      0      0/0
    42 TTY     9600/9600   -   -      -    -    -      0      0      0/0
    43 TTY     9600/9600   -   -      -    -    -      0      0      0/0
    44 TTY     9600/9600   -   -      -    -    -      0      0      0/0
    45 TTY     9600/9600   -   -      -    -    -      0      0      0/0
    46 TTY     9600/9600   -   -      -    -    -      0      0      0/0
    47 TTY     9600/9600   -   -      -    -    -      0      0      0/0
    48 TTY     9600/9600   -   -      -    -    -      0      0      0/0
    65 AUX     9600/9600   -   -      -    -    -      0      0      0/0
    66 VTY                 -   -      -    -   20      0      0      0/0
    67 VTY                 -   -      -    -   20      0      0      0/0
    68 VTY                 -   -      -    -   20      0      0      0/0
    69 VTY                 -   -      -    -   20      0      0      0/0
    70 VTY                 -   -      -    -   20      0      0      0/0

Line(s) not in async mode -or- with no hardware support:
1-32, 49-64
```

Removing access lists

You will either want to stop an access list from working for a short time or remove the whole access list. Remember that you cannot make changes to individual lines on the standard access list. You have to copy the entire list to a text editor such as notepad, remove the access list from the router and then paste the new access list with the changes made in notepad into the configuration file at the Router(config)# prompt.

Removing an access list from an interface:

```
Router(config)#interface serial 0
Router(config-if)#no ip access-group 10 out ⇦ specify the direction
Router(config-if)#^Z
```

Deleting an access list:

```
Router(config)#no access-list 10 ⇦ specify the access list #
```

Troubleshooting access lists

You can check which access lists are configured on your router with the "show ip access-lists" command.

```
Router#show ip access-lists
Standard IP access list 10
    permit 10.1.1.2
Extended IP access list 100
    permit tcp any any eq domain
    permit udp any any eq 25
    permit tcp any any eq www
Router#
```

You can see an access list on an interface by using the command "show ip interface <interface type/number>".

```
Router#show ip interface serial 0
Serial0 is up, line protocol is up
  Internet address is 192.168.1.1/24
  Broadcast address is 255.255.255.255
  Address determined by setup command
  MTU is 1500 bytes
  Helper address is not set
  Directed broadcast forwarding is disabled
  Outgoing access list is not set
  Inbound  access list is 10
```

Or by typing "show run interface x".

Note that this command may not be available on your router, depending upon the IOS release you are using.

```
Router#show run interface serial 0
Building configuration...

Current configuration : 86 bytes
```

```
!
interface Serial0
 ip address 192.168.1.1 255.255.255.0
 ip access-group 10 in
end
```

It is possible to run a debug on access lists. This is outside the scope of the CCNA syllabus (please check the latest syllabus). You would specify the traffic you wish to monitor with an access list and then enter the below command in global config mode.

```
Router(config)#debug ip packet 101 [detail] [dump]  ⇦ where 101 is your
                                                            access list
```

detail — gives more detailed information in the debug.

dump — is a hidden command (you cannot see it when you type ?) and should only be used at the request of Cisco TAC engineers.

You can clear the counters on an access list with the "clear access-list counters" command.

```
Router# show access-lists 100
Extended IP access list 100
    permit tcp host 192.168.1.1 any established (308 matches)
    permit udp host 192.168.1.2 any eq domain (12 matches)
    permit icmp host 192.168.1.3 any
    permit tcp host 192.168.4.5 host 10.0.0.1 gt 1023
    permit tcp host 192.168.4.8 host 10.0.0.2 eq smtp (4 matches)

Router#clear access-list counters ?
  <0-199>  Access list number
  WORD     Access list name
  <cr>

Router#clear access-list counters 100
Router# show access-lists 100
Extended IP access list 100
    permit tcp host 192.168.1.1 any established
    permit udp host 192.168.1.2 any eq domain
    permit icmp host 192.168.1.3 any
    permit tcp host 192.168.4.5 host 10.0.0.1 gt 1023
    permit tcp host 192.168.4.8 host 10.0.0.2 eq smtp
```

Make sure you try all of the above commands on the access lists you configure in the lab book.

Named access lists

As well as using numbers for access lists, you can also use names. Named access lists were available from IOS release 11.2. Using a name instead of a number makes the access list easier to identify when looking at the config.

Because you are using names, you have to specify if the access list is standard or extended.

```
ip access-list {standard | extended} name
```

The following syntax will depend upon whether you are configuring a standard or extended access list. The access list below has been named "inbound_access".

```
Router(config)#ip access-list extended inbound_access
Router(config-ext-nacl)#permit tcp any 172.16.0.0 0.0.255.255 eq 80
Router(config-ext-nacl)#exit
Router(config)#int s0
Router(config-if)#ip access-group inbound_access in
Router(config-if)#exit
Router(config)#
```

Named access lists operate in a slightly different way to standard or extended access lists. For a named access list you are able to delete a specific entry, for standard or extended access lists you have to delete the old access list and create a new one.

```
Router#conf t
Enter configuration commands, one per line. End with CNTL/Z.
Router(config)#ip access-list standard lan_traffic
Router(config-std-nacl)#permit 172.16.0.0
Router(config-std-nacl)#permit 172.30.0.0
Router(config-std-nacl)#permit 192.168.2.0
Router(config-std-nacl)#permit 10.0.0.0
Router(config-std-nacl)#exit
Router(config)#int fast 0
Router(config-if)#ip access-group lan_traffic in
Router(config-if)#ip access-list standard lan_traffic
Router(config-std-nacl)#no permit 10.0.0.0
Router(config-std-nacl)#exit
Router(config)#exit
Router#
Router#show ip access-lists
Standard IP access list lan_traffic
    permit 192.168.2.0
    permit 172.30.0.0
    permit 172.16.0.0 ⇐ the 10.0.0.0 entry has been deleted
Extended IP access list inbound_access
    permit tcp any 172.16.0.0 0.0.255.255 eq www
Router#
```

An alternative to access lists

An alternative to using access lists, which can become complicated and take up valuable CPU cycles is to install a route to a null interface. A null interface, much like a loopback interface exists in software only. Any traffic routed to the null interface is automatically dropped by the router.

Example

We wish to prevent any traffic leaving our router destined for network 10.2.4.x 255.255.255.0. We install a static route and send traffic destined for that network to the null 0 interface.

```
Router(config)#ip route 10.2.4.0 255.255.255.0 null 0
```

There many other types of access list such as turbo, time based, lock and key, reflexive and a few others. It is well worth having a very good working knowledge of access lists for the CCNA exam and as a Cisco engineer.

NETWORK SECURITY THREATS

In this lesson you will learn about threats facing a modern data network and common counter measures you can implement.

What type of threats?

Network threats have always been prevalent but the motivation of the hacker might have changed. In the beginning it was more to prove themselves by accessing a network now it can be more malicious, DoS attacks, identity theft, terrorism, etc.

Denial of Service (DOS) attacks. Here we can have three types:

- Destroyers — this is intended to destroy data
- Crashers — here the object is to disconnect the attacked host from the network
- Flooders — with this type the object of the attack is the network and makes it unusable.

Reconnaissance attacks — this type of attack is not about getting data, destroying data, but more about finding a way in. Can we obtain an IP Address? Which TCP/UDP ports are open?

Access attacks — here the object is to steal data, get financial information, industrial espionage.

As an example at this stage, a virus can be used to execute all the above attacks. So, updating your personal anti-virus software with the latest signatures/virus definitions is a must.

Besides viruses, the following tools can be used to perform an attack on your network:

- **Port Scanners** — these are used to discover open TCP/UDP ports, e.g., nmap
- **Spy Ware** — a piece of software that is installed on the user's PC without him knowing and looks and partially takes control over the user's interaction with the PC
- **Worm** — a self-replicating program that sends copies of itself to other computers without the user's intervention and usually used for DoS attacks
- **Keystroke logger** — a piece of software that captures the user's key strokes
- **Phishing** — a technique in which the attacker sets up, e.g., a website that is similar to an existing site in order to get sensitive information like usernames and passwords
- **Malware** — a general term for hostile, annoying and intrusive software.

Using the diagram below, let's look at a few common security issues on an enterprise network.

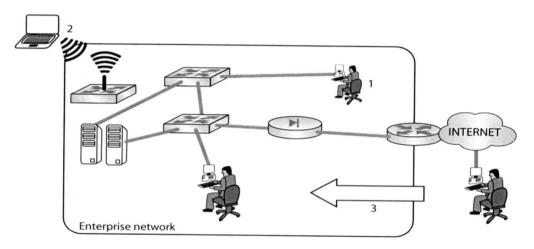

Figure 7–5: Common security issues

1. Disgruntled employees, the user can copy sensitive data from the corporate servers and use that information at his/her new company.
2. Wireless access from outside the enterprise. The signal travels over quite a distance and an attacker might be sitting on the other side of the street accessing your network and stealing important information.
3. An infected laptop, this can happen when a user brings his/her own laptop in the enterprise with no anti-virus software on or the user's enterprise laptop has outdated virus definitions.

These are just some examples of methods that your network can be vulnerable for network threats. Having NAC (Network Access Control), the last two attacks would not be possible due to credentials to be checked (username/password), scan of the computer (virus definitions up-to-date and enabled), but this would not prevent a disgruntled employee.

Countermeasures

The firewall or, when using the Cisco product line, a PIX or ASA (Adaptive Security Appliance) is a piece of software or hardware that allows or denies packets to enter the network. It divides the network into trusted, semi-trusted, and untrusted zones.

When we look at Figure 7–6, we see the three zones:

1. trusted zone or LAN
2. semi-trusted zone or DMZ (Demilitarized Zone)
3. untrusted zone, usually the Internet

For example if we want to allow external users access our Web page, we would create a rule on the firewall that allows TCP traffic on port 80—the standard http port. Following this principle of allowing and denying UDP/TCP ports, we build our rule base.

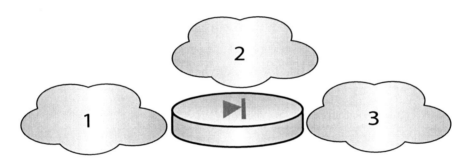

Figure 7–6: A firewall offers network security.

The ASA goes a step further so as well as being a firewall a lot more functionality has been built into the appliance or in Cisco's terminology anti-x.

The ASA can do the following:

- Anti-virus
- Anti-spyware
- Anti-spam
- Anti-phishing
- URL filtering
- Email filtering

Some forms of attack can be easily detected by the ASA, e.g., virus attached to an email, but other attacks use more sophisticated means of attack. For these attacks we use IPS, Intrusion Prevention System or IDS, Intrusion Detection System.

These systems look at certain patterns in the packet stream to detect the attack. One of those attacks was the Slammer worm.

IPS works in real-time to react to such threats by blocking or preventing them. An IDS will send a warning to the administrator warning about an attack taking place.

VPN

Now what if we want to send traffic to our branch offices or telecommuters. We could buy leased lines, but those are expensive or use the Internet. But is the Internet secure?
Here is where a VPN (virtual private network) comes in. A VPN allows us to send secure data via an unsecure medium (the Internet).

VPNs can provide:

1. Authentication — to prove the identity of both endpoints
2. Confidentiality — to provide protection against packet sniffing
3. Message integrity — to prove that the message has not been tampered with.

As we can see in Figure 7–7, there are two types of VPNs:

- Site-to-site VPN — the upper line
- Access VPN — the lower line

Figure 7–7: Virtual private network (VPN)

The upper and the lower lines symbolize the VPN. This is the encrypted tunnel that secures the data between the endpoints. There is huge amount of detail about network security in our CCNA Security section on www.howtonetwork.net.

IN THE EXAM:

You will be expected to know how to configure standard and extended access lists for the exam. Please check the latest syllabus for any additions to this.

Now go through the Module 7 labs in the labs section.

SUMMARY QUESTIONS

1. What command will allow a message to appear when a user connects to your router?
2. What is the number range for extended access lists?
3. What is the wildcard mask for network 172.16.0.0?
4. Which port number does telnet'se?
5. Which port number does web traffic use?
6. How do you apply an access list to an interface?
7. Port 53 refers to which protocol?
8. Which command would produce "enable password 7 070724404206"?
9. Which access list command allows traffic in only when it has originated from inside your network?
10. Which command applies an access list to the aux port?

RESOURCES

You can find more information at:

http://www.howtonetwork.net/public/1047.cfm

CHAPTER 8

Module 8—Wide Area Networking

What you will learn in this module	Timings
Understand WAN topologies	Theory: 90 minutes
Learn about HDLC	Labs: 90 minutes
Configure PPP	Review: 5 minutes
How frame relay works	
WAN troubleshooting	

WAN TOPOLOGIES

WANs are used to connect LANs together. Because of the long distances involved, we will normally have to use a third-party company known as a service provider, a telephone company (telco) to provide us with this service.

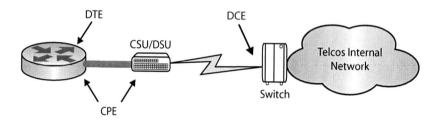

Figure 8–1: WAN equipment

The type of equipment used between the customer and the service provider is usually the same. The main difference is in the local configuration. The customer's Internet facing router has to receive a clock from the telco to synchronize the speed of the interfaces and to ensure the customer equipment is sending data out at a speed that matches the speed the provider is to receive the data at.

The interface we use to connect to the service provider with is known as Data Terminal Equipment or DTE. The service provider uses a different interface type that is used to provide the clock, known as Data Communication Equipment or DCE.

DCE equipment also includes a utility referred to as a channel service unit / data service unit. This device provides conversion from your LAN data format to one compatible with your telco's requirements.

In any WAN diagram, we normally use a cloud to refer to the public switched network. We are not normally able to draw every switch and router inside there, and it is usually beyond the scope of an engineer outside the service provider's network

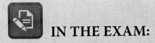

IN THE EXAM:

You should be familiar with how WANs work, what equipment is necessary to connect over a WAN, and which protocols are used, as well as OSI layers.

OTHER WAN NETWORKING TERMS

There are many other terms you will hear when discussing WAN technologies.

Customer premise equipment (CPE)

CPE is any equipment owned and maintained internally and located on your premises. If the CPE breaks, it will be your responsibility to resolve the problem as the network engineer.

Data terminal equipment (DTE)

This is normally the interface on your side of the WAN link that connects to the telcos network. The DTE interface uses clocking signals generated by the DCE interface to synchronize traffic.

Data communications equipment (DCE)

DCE interfaces provide connection to the service providers network. Here traffic is forwarded, data is synchronized, and clocking signals provided. When practicing networking with routers at home, you will have to configure your own DCE interface because one end of the cable will be DTE and one end DCE. On the DCE end of the cable, you simply add the clock rate command and give a clocking number.

You can normally tell which end of the cable is DCE because it will have the letters "DCE" stamped on it. A DCE interface is normally defined by the cable and not the actual interface. You can check which type of cable you have attached with the "show controllers serial x" command, where x is the number of the interface. If you have a DCE cable attached to the interface, you need to add the "clock rate #" command.

```
RouterA#config t
RouterA(config)#interface serial 0
RouterA(config-interface)#clock rate 56000 ⇔ sets the speed to 56,000 bps
```

Demarcation point (demarc)

Normally inside a switching closet in the communications room is where the CPE meets the local loop. This is usually installed by the service provider as the termination of a digital service line, such as T1, T3, E1, E3, etc.

Local loop

This is the cabling and connectivity that extends from the demarcation point to the nearest local telco switch or exchange. It can sometimes cause confusion that the local loop includes only the interface/trunk/or line card of the telco device connecting to the other end of the circuit.

Central office (CO)

This is the main point of presence for the telco's WAN service to the end user.

Modems

A modem converts digital signals to analog and back again. It MODulates data over frequencies outbound and DEModulates the received signal.

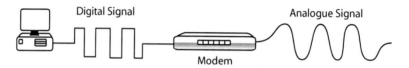

Figure 8–2: A modem converts digital signals to analog.

The correct name for a modem is modulator / demodulator. The purpose of a modem is to convert a digital signal to an analog signal for use across Plain Old Telephone Service, or POTS lines. It is used for small bandwidth requirements or more commonly as a backup solution.

Figure 8–3: An end-to-end modem connection

WAN CONNECTION TYPES

There are three main connection types for WANs:

1. Leased lines
2. Circuit switching
3. Packet switching

Leased line

A leased line is a dedicated connection between your site and another site. It can also be referred to as a point-to-point link. The link is not shared with any other company and is available 24 hours a day. Leased lines can be very expensive, depending upon bandwidth and distance but do eliminate some of the security and traffic engineering problems associated with connections to your remote site over the Internet or with shared connections.

Leased Line (point-to-point)

Figure 8–4: A point-to-point leased line

Circuit switching

Just like a telephone call, for a circuit-switched connection to take place, a dedicated temporary connection has to be made between the end devices. Once the session is no longer required between the two end devices the connection is normally torn down.

All packets travel along the WAN taking the same path for a circuit-switched connection. Integrated services digital network (ISDN) is an example of a circuit-switched network.

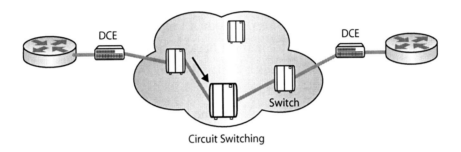

Circuit Switching

Figure 8–5: A circuit-switched network

Packet switching

In packet-switched connections, users may share a connection with other networks. The cost is generally less for users since the telco can make more efficient use of their bandwidth. End-to-end connectivity in packet-switched networks is known as having virtual circuits or VCs. Common examples of packet-switched networks are frame relay, ATM, and X.25

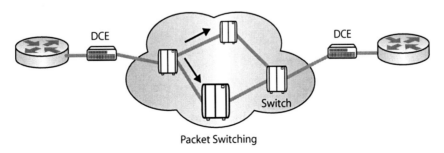

Packet Switching

Figure 8–6: A packet-switched network

You have no choice over which path your data takes over a packet-switched connection. Typically, the policy of the service provider will allow for an optimal path. The telco will decide depending upon how much traffic is saturating their connections. When your data arrives at the other end, it is reassembled and put into the correct order.

POINT-TO-POINT PROTOCOLS

There are several protocols you can use when connecting over a WAN. Some are compulsory when you use a certain service and some you can choose from. When you pay for a leased line on your point-to-point connection, you will normally choose from HDLC or PPP.

High-level data-link control (HDLC)

HDLC is a layer 2 protocol used for WAN connectivity. It is based primarily on IBM's Synchronous Data Link Control (SDLC) protocol. HDLC uses keepalives to monitor connectivity with the remote end device.

The DCE side of the connection sends the DTE side a keepalive packet containing a sequence number. The DTE side echos this sequence number back to the DCE proving connectivity. If three consecutive packets are not received, the link is declared down.

You can monitor the keepalives on a HDLC link with the "debug serial interface" command. You can test this command on the accompanying WAN labs.

Although HDLC is a widely used protocol Cisco has created their own proprietary version of the protocol, if you are connecting a Cisco device to a non-Cisco device you may not be able to use it. Configuring it on an interface is very straightforward. Remember though, it is on by default on Cisco serial interfaces.

```
Router#config t
Enter configuration commands, one per line. End with CNTL/Z.
Router(config)#interface serial 0
Router(config-if)#encapsulation hdlc ⇦ Set the encapsulation type
Router(config-if)#ip address 192.168.1.1 255.255.255.0
Router(config-if)#no shutdown
Router(config-if)#^Z
Router#
```

You can check your interface protocol settings (and many other interface settings) by typing "show interface serial 0". You would never normally need to set the encapsulation type to HDLC on a Cisco router since it is the default.

```
Router#show interface serial 0
Serial0 is up, line protocol is up
  Hardware is HD64570
  Internet address is 192.168.1.1/24
  MTU 1500 bytes, BW 1544 Kbit, DLY 20000 usec,
      reliability 255/255, txload 1/255, rxload 1/255
  Encapsulation HDLC, loopback not set ⇐ Encapsulation setting
  Keepalive set (10 sec)
```

Encapsulation HDLC or PPP

Figure 8–7: There must be the same encapsulation type on each side of the connection.

Point-to-point protocol (PPP)

PPP is very popular for use over dedicated and circuit-switched links and also when you are connecting to non-Cisco equipment.

PPP's popularity is due to the fact it can work over many different connection types, including synchronous (clocks on both sides agree), asynchronous (clocks differ), ISDN, Digital Subscriber Line (DSL), and High Speed Serial Interface (HSSI) links.

PPP is made up of two main components, NCPs and LCP:

- **Network Control Protocol (NCPs)** — a family of independent protocols that encapsulate network layer protocols, such as TCP/IP.
- **Link Control Protocol (LCP)** — negotiates, sets up, and tears down control options for the data-link connection to the WAN.

PPP authentication

PPP offers optional authentication and has two ways of authenticating the calling router — PAP and CHAP.

Password authentication protocol (PAP) uses something called a two way handshake allowing the remote host to authenticate itself. The password is sent in clear text so it can easily be captured and read.

Challenge handshake authentication protocol (CHAP) uses a three-way handshake and never sends the password over the link in clear text. Instead a hashed value made from the password is sent. This hashed value can only be read by a host with the appropriate key to the MD5 algorithm, which is a very strong level of encryption.

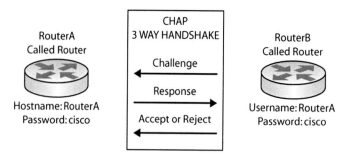

Figure 8–8: CHAP uses a three-way handshake.

On the calling router, a hostname and username / password must be added. Of course encapsulation must be set to PPP and authentication type to CHAP.

On the called or authenticating router, a hostname and username / password of which routers will be calling has to be configured.

LCP configuration options

Cisco routers offer several configuration options to use some of the features LCP offers.

Table 8–1: LCP options

Feature	Operation	Protocol	Command
Authentication	Requires a password, Performs challenge handshake	PAP, CHAP	`ppp authentication pap` `ppp authentication chap`
Compression	Compresses data at the source and decompresses at destination	Stacker, Predictor	`ppp compress stacker` `ppp compress predictor`
Error Detection	Monitors dropped data, avoids frame looping	Quality, Magic number	`ppp quality <number 1-100>`
Multilink	Performs multiple link load balancing	Multilink protocol	`ppp multilink`

Configuring PPP

Configuring PPP on a synchronous serial line is fairly straightforward. First, you need to configure the router interface to use PPP encapsulation; next add a username and password in order to be authenticated (if you wish to use authentication). Lastly, you need to tell the router which type of authentication to use. Only the first step is compulsory.

CHAP will make more sense after you have read this section and then configured the PPP lab in the labs section (Part II).

Figure 8–9: Each router using CHAP must have a username and password.

PPP using CHAP
Router A:

```
Router#config t
Enter configuration commands, one per line. End with CNTL/Z.
Router(config)#hostname RouterA
RouterA(config)#username RouterB password cisco ⇦ the calling router
RouterA(config)#interface serial 0
RouterA(config-if)#encapsulation ppp ⇦ encapsulation from HDLC to PPP
RouterA(config-if)#ppp authentication chap ⇦ authenticate other router
                                                using CHAP
RouterA(config-if)#ip address 192.168.1.1 255.255.255.0
RouterA(config-if)#clock rate 64000 ⇦ this is a DCE interface
RouterA(config-if)#no shutdown
RouterA(config)#exit
```

Router B:

```
Router#config t
Enter configuration commands, one per line. End with CNTL/Z.
Router(config)#hostname RouterB ⇦ you will declare this hostname when
                                     calling
RouterB(config)#username RouterA password cisco
RouterB(config)#interface s0
RouterB(config-if)#ip address 192.168.1.2 255.255.255.0
RouterB(config-if)#encapsulation ppp
RouterB(config-if)#ppp authentication chap
RouterB(config-if)#no shutdown
RouterB(config-if)#^Z
```

PPP in action
Please follow the PPP lab to see how PPP works.

Serial line Internet protocol (SLIP)

Also known as serial line interface protocol, SLIP is a popular WAN protocol that operates at the data link layer. It has been overtaken in popularity by PPP for use in dial-up connections due to the fact that, although it is connection oriented, it is unreliable. SLIP is limited to use with IP only, whereas PPP can be used for other protocols.

Frame relay

Frame relay is a very popular packet-switched layer 2 WAN protocol that is used internationally. It is becoming less popular due to the increase of the availability of broadband. Frame relay can provide connection speeds from 56 kbps up to 2 Mbps. The nature of frame relay is that your connection is normally shared with other companies, which brings down the cost.

Your frame relay service provider guarantees you a minimum amount of bandwidth. If the line is quiet, you may be able to use bandwidth belonging to other users, providing they are not using it. Frame relay is based upon an older standard called X.25. Based upon the fact that service provider lines were advancing in quality, the error correction and subsequent overhead related to X.25 was no longer needed. Changes were made and all windowing and retransmission systems were taken out, leaving the upper OSI layers to control this. This made it a lot more efficient than its predecessor, with a higher payload and less overhead per packet.

The default encapsulation type on cisco frame relay interfaces is cisco. The alternative is IETF.

- **Cisco** — this is to be used when connecting to other Cisco devices
- **IETF** — this is to be used when connecting to non-Cisco devices.

Virtual circuits

A feature of frame relay is the establishment of virtual circuits (VCs). This is a logical connection made between two DTE devices. Frame relay virtual circuits come in two varieties, permanent virtual circuits (PVCs) and switched virtual circuits (SVCs). SVCs are less common; they are temporary connections between two devices used for occasional communications. PVCs are permanent connections used when regular data transmission is taking place.

Forward explicit congestion notification (FECN)

Part of the frame relay header consists of the FECN field. When the DTE device sends frames onto the network, if the DCE end detects congestion on the network it sets the FECN bit value to 1. The receiving DTE device, upon receiving the frame, can then see that the packets received from the sending device experienced congestion on the path there.

Backwards explicit congestion notification (BECN)

DCE devices will set the BECN bit to 1 for returning frames that have had their FECN bit set. This will inform the original sender that congestion was experienced on the path between the devices. The "show frame-relay pvc" command will show any FECN or BECN bits.

Data link connection identifier (DLCI)

DLCIs are used in frame relay networks for addressing between the DTE and the DCE device belonging to the frame relay provider. Your router at one end of the connection could have a different DLCI from the router at the other end. They are only significant to your local connection to the frame relay switch belonging to the provider.

When you apply for a frame relay connection, you will be given your DLCI number by your frame relay provider. So, if you are given DLCI number 300, you will configure this on your interface. Your traffic will go into the frame relay switch at the provider's end and then be directed to the destination (see Figure 8–10).

You have two choices for using a DLCI with an IP address, dynamically or statically. With dynamic mapping, frame relay uses ARP to get the remote interfaces IP address and then maps this to the DLCI used to connect to the local frame relay switch. Frame relay ARP is normally referred to as Inverse ARP. Static mapping means you have to configure the IP details yourself. We will look at both under the configuring frame relay section.

Frame relay inverse ARP

Frame relay inverse ARP is a mechanism that allows the remote layer 3 addresses to be associated with the local layer 2 DLCI. When the frame relay circuit is initialized, the interface sends an inverse ARP request out on each local DLCI defined. The remote router replies to the request with its IP address.

Frame relay inverse ARP is known as dynamic-address mapping. It is enabled by default on a physical interface.

Frame relay address mapping

There are two ways for frame relay to discover the IP address for the other end of the connection. Using the "frame-relay map" command, the "frame-relay interface-dlci" commands or none at all if frame relay inverse ARP is in operation. You would use static mapping if the other end of the circuit does not support inverse ARP or does not support inverse ARP for a specific protocol you want to use across the frame relay link.

Which commands you use for the configuration depend entirely upon how you have the frame relay set up and which remote devices you are connecting to and whether they support frame relay inverse ARP.

Putting frame relay on an interface will allow it to use frame relay inverse ARP to discover the IP address of the remote end. If you use frame relay sub-interfaces, you will have to choose one of the below commands.

On a multipoint interface, you would use the "frame-relay map" command.

On a point-to-point interface, you would use the "frame-relay interface dlci" command. Frame relay mapping is covered in great detail in our Cisco CCNP Routing Exam guide at www. HowToNetwork.net. See "Frame relay sub-interfaces" on page 299.

Discard eligibility

The DE bit is marked on frames that have a lower importance than other frames. The DE bit is part of the frame relay address header. If the DE bit is set to 1, the DCE device can discard those frames as opposed to frames without the DE bit set.

Cyclic redundancy check (CRC)

The CRC mechanism is a 2bit check that compares two values in the frame to determine if an error occurred on the frame during transit from source to destination. This process is known as error detection; error correction is taken care of by higher levels of the OSI in the case of frame relay.

Local management interface (LMI)

LMI is a standard used for signaling between the DTE and the frame relay switch. The connection is continually monitored in the same fashion that a keepalive is used on serial or Ethernet connections.

There are three types of LMI connection type to choose from, but on Cisco routers the default is left at "cisco". You would only change it if your frame relay provider tells you to or if you are connecting to non-Cisco equipment. The three LMI types are cisco, q933a, and ansi. The LMI frame encompasses a frame check sequence (FCS), which verifies the integrity of the data transmitted.

You can monitor the passing of the frame relay LMIs between the router and the frame switch. If you experience problems with your frame relay connection, the first thing you would look at are the LMI statistics.

LMI exchange between the router and the frame relay switch can be monitored with the "debug frame-relay lmi" command.

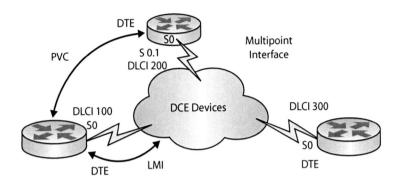

Figure 8–10: Frame relay PVC and LMI

Frame relay sub-interfaces

There are many situations where you have one router at the core of your network but three or four remote sites who wish to connect to the core. In this circumstance, you would have to purchase a router with an interface for every connection it needs to reach.

An alternative to this is to use a topology known as hub-and-spoke. In this topology you will use one physical interface but create something known as a sub-interface on that one physical interface. Sub-interfaces can either be:

- point-to-point or
- multipoint.

Point-to-point sub-interfaces are purely used when you have one-to-one connections from one router to another. Point-to-point sub-interfaces can use inverse ARP to discover the remote address after you configure the DLCI value. Alternatively, you can statically configure the mapping.

Different point-to-point sub-interfaces have to be in different subnets. This is the whole reason for using them. This will allow several routers to connect to your hub router when you only have one physical interface.

Multipoint interfaces are used when you have two or more other sites connecting to this one physical interface. All multipoint addresses on the same interface have to be in the same subnet. For multipoint sub-interfaces, you have to statically map the remote IP address to the DLCI value (see Figure 8–10).

Using sub-interfaces allows you to overcome the split-horizon issue where an interface cannot advertise a route out of the same interface it was received on. Split horizon is on by default for IGRP, RIP, and EIGRP networks and prevents routing updates from being passed on multipoint interfaces (see Module 5).

To turn off split horizon for networks using RIP or IGRP, use the "no ip split-horizon" command. To turn it off for EIGRP networks, use the "no ip split-horizon eigrp 20", where 20 is the AS number.

If you are using point-to-point interfaces, each sub-interface will be in a different network so you will not need to address any split horizon issues.

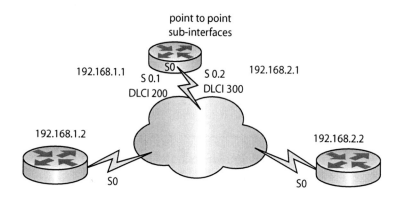

Figure 8–11: Frame relay networks point-to-point sub-interfaces

When using sub-interfaces, you leave the IP address off the physical interface and add the configuration values to the sub-interface.

```
RouterA#config t
RouterA(config)#interface serial 0
RouterA(config-if)#encapsulation frame-relay
RouterA(config-if)#exit
RouterA(config)#interface serial 0.1 point-to-point ⇔ sub-interface
RouterA(config-subif)#ip address 192.168.1.1 255.255.255.0
RouterAconfig-subif)#frame-relay interface-dlci 200 ⇔ dynamic mapping
RouterA(config-fr-dlci)#^Z ⇔ your command line may look different
RouterA#config t
RouterA(config)#interface serial 0.2 point-to-point ⇔ sub-interface
RouterA(config-subif)#ip address 192.168.2.1 255.255.255.0
RouterA(config-subif)#frame-relay interface-dlci 300
RouterA(config-fr-dlci)#^Z
```

Note that on point-to-point sub-interfaces, each address has to be in a different subnet or network.

```
RouterA#config t
RouterA(config)#interface serial 0
RouterA(config-if)#encapsulation frame-relay
RouterA(config-if)#exit
RouterA(config)#interface s0.1 multipoint ⇦ Static Mapping
RouterA(config-subif)#ip address 192.168.1.1 255.255.255.0
RouterA(config-subif)#frame-relay map ip 192.168.1.2 200 broadcast
RouterA(config-subif)#frame-relay map ip 192.168.1.3 300 broadcast
RouterA(config-if)#no ip split-horizon ⇦ turns off split horizon (optional)
RouterA(config-subif)#^Z
```

The "`frame-relay map ip`" statement tells the router which DLCI to use to get to a particular network address. The "`broadcast`" parameter allows protocols such as OSPF and RIPv2 to multicast across the DLCI.

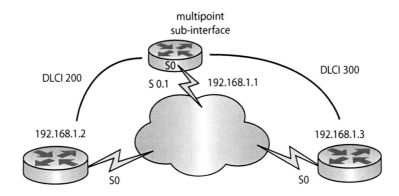

Figure 8–12: Frame relay networks multipoint sub-interfaces

Configuring frame relay

```
RouterA(config)#interface serial 0
RouterA(config-if)#encapsulation frame-relay ? ⇦ just press Enter here
  ietf  Use RFC1490/RFC2427 encapsulation ⇦ add ietf if connecting to
                                              non-Cisco devices
RouterA(config-if)#encapsulation frame-relay
RouterA(config-if)#frame-relay lmi-type ? ⇦ leave this out if both are
                                             Cisco routers
  cisco
  ansi
  q933a


RouterA(config-if)#frame-relay lmi-type ansi
RouterA(config-if)#frame-relay map ip 192.168.1.2 200 broadcast ⇦ static
                                                                   map
RouterA(config-if)#^Z
```

Troubleshooting frame relay

If your network users report problems with the frame relay connection, there are several commands that will give you a lot of information.

First check that your interface is up.

```
RouterA#show interface serial 0 ⇐ or "sh int s0" for short
Serial0 is up, line protocol is up
  Hardware is HD64570
  MTU 1500 bytes, BW 1544 Kbit, DLY 20000 usec,
     reliability 255/255, txload 1/255, rxload 1/255
  Encapsulation FRAME-RELAY, loopback not set
  Keepalive set (10 sec)
  LMI enq sent  1133, LMI stat recvd 1133, LMI upd recvd 0, DTE LMI down
  LMI enq recvd 0, LMI stat sent  0, LMI upd sent  0
  LMI DLCI 1023  LMI type is CISCO  frame relay DTE
  Broadcast queue 0/64, broadcasts sent/dropped 0/0, interface broadcasts 0
```

You can check that the router is seeing LMIs coming from the frame switch or sending them.

```
RouterA#debug frame-relay lmi
Frame Relay LMI debugging is on
Displaying all Frame Relay LMI data
00:46:38: Serial0(out): StEnq, myseq 53, yourseen 54, DTE up
00:46:38: datagramstart = 0xE3EEA4, datagramsize = 13
00:46:38: FR encap = 0xFCF10309
00:46:38: 00 75 01 01 01 03 02 35 34
00:46:38:
00:46:38: Serial0(in): Status, myseq 53
00:46:38: RT IE 1, length 1, type 1
00:46:38: KA IE 3, length 2, yourseq 53, myseq 53
00:46:48: Serial0(out): StEnq, myseq 54, yourseen 53, DTE up
00:46:48: datagramstart = 0xE3EEA4, datagramsize = 13
00:46:48: FR encap = 0xFCF10309
00:46:48: 00 75 01 01 01 03 02 36 35
00:46:48:
00:46:48: Serial0(in): Status, myseq 54
00:46:48: RT IE 1, length 1, type 1
00:46:48: KA IE 3, length 2, yourseq 54, myseq 54
00:46:58: Serial0(out): StEnq, myseq 55, yourseen 54, DTE up
00:46:58: datagramstart = 0xE3EEA4, datagramsize = 13
00:46:58: FR encap = 0xFCF10309
00:46:58: 00 75 01 01 00 03 02 37 36
00:46:58:
00:46:58: Serial0(in): Status, myseq 55
00:46:58: RT IE 1, length 1, type 0
00:46:58: KA IE 3, length 2, yourseq 55, myseq 55
00:46:58: PVC IE 0x7 , length 0x6 , dlci 100, status 0x2 , bw 0
RouterA#un all
All possible debugging has been turned off
```

Watch the myseq and yourseq incrementing "status 0x2" means that the PVC is operational. Have a look at the PVC statistics. Does it show as active or inactive?

```
RouterA#show frame PVC

PVC Statistics for interface Serial0 (Frame Relay DTE)
                Active      Inactive     Deleted      Static
    Local         1            0            0           0
    Switched      0            0            0           0
    Unused        0            0            0           0

DLCI = 200, DLCI USAGE = LOCAL, PVC STATUS = ACTIVE, INTERFACE = Serial0

    input pkts 0            output pkts 0         in bytes 0
    out bytes 0             dropped pkts 0        in FECN pkts 0
    in BECN pkts 0          out FECN pkts 0       out BECN pkts 0
    in DE pkts 0            out DE pkts 0
    out bcast pkts 0        out bcast bytes 0
    5 minute input rate 0 bits/sec, 0 packets/sec
    5 minute output rate 0 bits/sec, 0 packets/sec
    pvc create time 00:00:10, last time pvc status changed 00:00:10
```

See how many LMI packets have been sent and replied to. If you are sending more packets than you have received a reply to, then you may have a problem.

```
RouterA#show frame lmi
LMI Statistics for interface Serial0 (Frame Relay DTE) LMI TYPE = CISCO
    Invalid Unnumbered info 0           Invalid Prot Disc 0
    Invalid dummy Call Ref 0            Invalid Msg Type 0
    Invalid Status Message 0            Invalid Lock Shift 0
    Invalid Information ID 0            Invalid Report IE Len 0
    Invalid Report Request 0           Invalid Keep IE Len 0
    Num Status Enq. Sent 1133          Num Status msgs Rcvd 1133 ⬛ LMIs
    Num Update Status Rcvd 0           Num Status Timeouts 0
Have you mapped the correct dlci and is it active?
RouterA#show frame-relay map
Serial0 (administratively down): ip 192.168.1.2
            dlci 200(0xC8,0x3080), static, ⇦ address mapped statically
               broadcast,
               CISCO, status defined, active
```

If you want to configure a frame relay lab, you will need to add a third router and configure that to be a frame relay switch. Configuring a frame relay switch is outside the CCNA syllabus, but you can find out how to do it by doing the frame relay labs in the labs section.

WAN TROUBLESHOOTING

When investigating any reported problems over the WAN, there are several commands you can use to locate the source of the problem. You will not be able to call your service provider to report a problem unless you can actually show that it is not your equipment that is at fault rather than theirs.

The first command used by most network engineers is "ping" or ICMP echo. Try to ping the faulty host and ping the default gateway from the network segment. This will tell you if you have IP connectivity. Traceroute can also be used to identify where the packet may be failing.

"show ip interface brief"

This command gives a snapshot of all of your interfaces and whether they are up or down. A quick and easy way of seeing what is happening.

```
RouterB#show ip interface brief
Interface        IP-Address    OK? Method Status                Protocol
Ethernet0        unassigned    YES unset  administratively down down
Ethernet1        unassigned    YES unset  administratively down down
Serial0          192.168.1.2   YES manual up                    up
Serial1          unassigned    YES unset  administratively down down
RouterB#
```

"show interface X"

Gives a lot of statistics—shows the configuration. The default bandwidth on serial interfaces is 1544 kbits or 1.544 Mbps. This is purely for routing protocols to decide which path to take. It does not affect the speed of the interface at all.

```
RouterB#show interface serial 0
Serial0 is up, line protocol is up
  Hardware is HD64570
  Internet address is 192.168.1.2/24
  MTU 1500 bytes, BW 1544 Kbit, DLY 20000 usec,
     reliability 255/255, txload 1/255, rxload 1/255 ⇔ transmission and
                                                        receive load
  Encapsulation HDLC, loop back not set ⇔ encapsulation settings
  Keepalive set (10 sec)
  Last input 00:00:07, output 00:00:00, output hang never
  Last clearing of "show interface" counters never
  Input queue: 0/75/0/0 (size/max/drops/flushes); Total output drops: 0
  Queueing strategy: weighted fair
  Output queue: 0/1000/64/0 (size/max total/threshold/drops)
     Conversations   0/1/256 (active/max active/max total)
     Reserved Conversations 0/0 (allocated/max allocated)
  5 minute input rate 0 bits/sec, 0 packets/sec
  5 minute output rate 0 bits/sec, 0 packets/sec
     18 packets input, 2813 bytes, 0 no buffer ⇔ traffic statistics
```

```
Received 18 broadcasts, 0 runts, 0 giants, 0 throttles
0 input errors, 0 CRC, 0 frame, 0 overrun, 0 ignored, 0 abort
19 packets output, 1728 bytes, 0 underruns
0 output errors, 0 collisions, 4 interface resets ⇔ errors on the
                                                        interface
0 output buffer failures, 0 output buffers swapped out
2 carrier transitions
DCD=up  DSR=up  DTR=up  RTS=up  CTS=up
```

You should always issue a "clear counters" command when troubleshooting interface problems. Interface counters are cumulative, so you may be looking at errors that occurred some time ago.

```
RouterA#clear counters
Clear "show interface" counters on all interfaces [confirm]
```

Another useful command is:

"debug serial interface".

 IN THE REAL WORLD:

Be very cautious when using debug commands on a live network. "debug serial interface" will detect whether your interface is sending and receiving keepalives.

```
RouterB#debug serial interface
Serial network interface debugging is on
RouterB#
02:33:41: Serial0: HDLC myseq 39, mineseen 39*, yourseen 39, line up
02:33:51: Serial0: HDLC myseq 40, mineseen 40*, yourseen 40, line up
02:34:01: Serial0: HDLC myseq 41, mineseen 41*, yourseen 41, line up
```

"show controllers serial x"

This is a very useful command. It tells you if there is a cable attached to the interface and what type of cable it is. If there is no cable detected, it could mean the cable has come loose or is faulty. You have to have a space after the word "serial" when issuing the "show controllers serial" command. You do NOT need a space when issuing the "show interface serial0" command, though. The "show interface serial0" will work with or without the space.

```
RouterB#show controllers serial 0
HD unit 0, idb = 0x162890, driver structure at 0x168C18
buffer size 1524  HD unit 0, V.35 DCE cable, clockrate 64000
cpb = 0xE2, eda = 0x2904, cda = 0x2918
```

There are literally hundreds of resources to be found on troubleshooting at www.cisco.com. Now go through the Module 8 labs in the labs section.

SUMMARY QUESTIONS

1. Networking equipment inside the demarc for which you are responsible is known as what?
2. What part of PPP negotiates and sets up and tears down control options over the WAN link?
3. Which PPP authentication protocol sends an encrypted hash value of the password?
4. Which command tells you if you have a DTC or DCE cable attached?
5. What is the frame relay keepalive known as?
6. Which command gives you a snapshot of all your interfaces?
7. How often are frame relay lmi packets sent?
8. The point where your telco takes responsibility for your network is known as?
9. Frame relay provides connection speeds up to?
10. What is the default serial encapsulation type on Cisco routers?

RESOURCES

You can find more information at:

http://www.howtonetwork.net/public/1047.cfm

CHAPTER 9

Module 9—Troubleshooting the Network

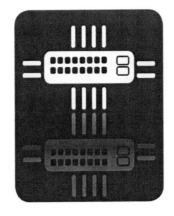

What you will learn in this module	Timings
How to troubleshoot	Theory: 30 minutes
Using the OSI to troubleshoot	
Resolving layer 1, 2, 3, and 4 issues	

HOW TO TROUBLESHOOT

Troubleshooting the network is not some mysterious skill that can only be carried out by the select few. With a methodical plan and by using a step-by-step process you should quickly be able to troubleshoot, diagnose and resolve most of the problems you encounter on a computer network.

For the CCNA exam you will be expected to be able to troubleshoot some problems on a simulated network. You must be able to look at network topologies and identify the cause of the problem and quickly resolve it. This module is primarily focused on showing you the kind of problem you could come across in the CCNA exam. It is the troubleshooting system that is important here and not the specific problems we will look at.

There are many books written about troubleshooting in a Cisco networking environment and as you progress through your career you should plan to read several of them. Before starting our review of the kind of problem you will see on the CCNA exam let's first discuss some general background about troubleshooting.

A structured approach to troubleshooting is generally the best method to use when troubleshooting networking issues. In a larger organization this includes how problems are reported to the networking team, the troubleshooting procedures followed by the team and the processes used to include other departments for problems that span organizational units. In smaller organizations the formal structure may not be as well defined as much of the approach will reside in a single person, namely you.

The initial steps in troubleshooting involve isolating the source of the problem. During this step (if it were a live network) you will want to discuss the symptoms seen by the people reporting the problem. Users on the network may mislead you with the wrong information, either due to lack of knowledge on their part that they are reporting symptoms and not the root cause of the problem. Sometimes users think they know what the problem is and present the facts that support their conclusion. The best advice during this step is to determine how widespread the problem is.

Attempt to isolate the issue to a single location, building, floor and finally a specific network segment or node. One method often used is termed "divide and conquer" and if you parse the network into progressively smaller sections to isolate the problem. You continue doing so until you isolate the location of the problem.

Once you have isolated the problem in the network topology then continue to apply structured, critical thinking to isolate the root cause of the problem. You may use the OSI model as a reference to help you organize the troubleshooting commands and tools that you have at your disposal. In order to solve many network problems you will need to be familiar with Cisco troubleshooting tools as well as those provided by other vendors for use on their products, such as Microsoft for Windows operating systems, and the Open Source Foundation for Linux operating systems.

OSI layer 1 (physical) problems

- Faulty or broken cables
- Broken or faulty pins/connectors
- No power
- No cable connected or wrong interface
- Failing or damaged interface
- Incorrect cable for the interface

Layer 2 (data link) problems

- Incorrect configuration on the interface
- Clock rate missing or incorrect
- Incorrect layer 2 protocol settings
- Faulty network card
- Interface shut down

Layer 3 (network) problems

- Misconfigured routing protocol
- Incorrect IP/network addressing
- Incorrect subnet masking

In the CCNA exam you will be presented with a "live" network that is not working correctly. If you use a systematic approach to troubleshoot the problem you should quickly be able to identify and resolve the issues.

Example 1

Here we have a very simple network running RIP version 2 (Figure 9–1). The network numbers are 10.0.0.0, 11.0.0.0, 12.0.0.0, and 13.0.0.0.

We know that each router should be able to see all of the networks. For Router A, we know that networks 10.0.0.0 and 11.0.0.0 are directly connected to the router. Networks 12.0.0.0, and 13.0.0.0 should be in the routing table as a RIP route. In order for this to happen all of the interfaces connected to the other routers should be up/up and the correct routes should be in the routing table.

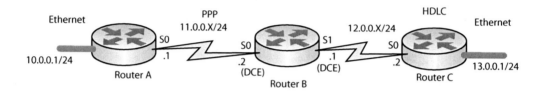

Figure 9–1: Simple network running RIP version 2

Rather than checking to see if the cables are attached first check to see if the router can see the other networks.

 IN THE REAL WORLD:

The simulator will have a slight lag so be patient. Also please note that the simulator in the exam may not recognise shortened commands such as "sh ip int brie" so you may need to type the full command in.

```
RouterA#show ip route
Codes: C - connected, S - static, I - IGRP, R - RIP, M - mobile, B - BGP
       D - EIGRP, EX - EIGRP external, O - OSPF, IA - OSPF inter area
       E1 - OSPF external type 1, E2 - OSPF external type 2, E - EGP
       i - IS-IS, L1 - IS-IS level-1, L2 - IS-IS level-2, * - candidate
default
       U - per-user static route

Gateway of last resort is not set
C       10.0.0.0/24 is directly connected, 10.0.0.1
```

We can see that only the directly connected Ethernet network can be seen. The WAN network is not there. Start at layer 1 and check that the router can see the cable.

```
RouterA#show controllers serial 0
HD unit 0, idb = 0x1AE828, driver structure at 0x1B4BA0
buffer size 1524  HD unit 0, V.35 DTE cable
```

So we can see that the cable is attached. It is a DTE cable, so we know we do not need to use the "clock rate" command on this interface. If the cable on the other end was DCE then it should have the "clock rate" command configured on it.

Next we need to check layer 2. The interface has a cable attached but is it showing up/up?

```
RouterA#show ip interface brief
Interface        IP-Address     OK? Method Status          Protocol
Serial0          11.0.0.1       YES unset  administratively down down
Ethernet0        10.0.0.1       YES unset  up                   up
```

Somebody has neglected to open or "no shutdown" the serial interface. This can easily be corrected with the "no shut" command.

```
RouterA#config t
RouterA(config)#interface serial 0
RouterA(config-if)#no shutdown
%LINK-3-UPDOWN: Interface Serial0, changed state to up
RouterA(config-if)#z
RouterA#
%LINK-3-UPDOWN: Interface Serial0, changed state to down
%LINEPROTO-5-UPDOWN: Line protocol on Interface Serial0, changed state to
down
```

We should now look at the interfaces to see if there is a difference.

```
RouterA#show ip interface brief
Interface        IP-Address     OK? Method Status          Protocol
Serial0          11.0.0.1       YES unset  up               down
Ethernet0        10.0.0.1       YES unset  up               up
```

Okay, so now the interface is administratively up; however, it is showing as up/down. If the serial interface cannot see keepalives from the other interface then it will remain up/down.

We need to examine the configuration on our serial interface and compare it with its neighbor on Router B.

```
RouterA#show run interface serial 0 ⇐ Use "show run" on a simulator
interface Serial0
 ip address 11.0.0.1 255.255.255.0
 no ip directed-broadcast
 encapsulation ppp
```

The encapsulation type is set to PPP that is not the default HDLC. The diagram indicates that this side should be using PPP.

On Router B, we would also check to make sure the interfaces are up/up.

```
RouterB#show ip interface brief
Interface      IP-Address     OK? Method Status                    Protocol
Serial0        11.0.0.2       YES unset  up                        down
Serial1        12.0.0.1       YES unset  down                      down
Ethernet0      unassigned     YES unset  administratively down down
Ethernet1      unassigned     YES unset  administratively down down
Bri0           unassigned     YES unset  administratively down down
Bri0:1         unassigned     YES unset  administratively down down
Bri0:2         unassigned     YES unset  administratively down down
```

We can see that the interface connected to Router A is down down. We can check the configuration on the interface to see what could be wrong.

```
RouterB#show run interface serial 0  ⇦ (note: you may have to use
                                            "show run" in the exam).
interface Serial0
 ip address 11.0.0.2 255.255.255.0
 no ip directed-broadcast
clock rate 1000000  ⇦ clockrate present
```

We can immediately see a difference between the configurations on Router A and Router B. Router A's serial interface shows that the encapsulation is set to PPP. Router B does not show an encapsulation type because it is left at the default for Cisco which is HDLC.

```
RouterB#show interface serial 0
Serial1 is down, line protocol is down
   Hardware is HD64570
   Internet address is 12.0.0.1/24
   MTU 1500 bytes, BW 1544 Kbit, DLY 1000 usec, rely 255/255, load 1/255
   Encapsulation HDLC, loopback not set, keepalive set (10 sec)
```

We can now change the encapsulation type (layer 2) to PPP on RouterB.
```
RouterB#config t
RouterB(config)#interface serial 0
RouterB(config-if)#encapsulation ppp
%LINK-3-UPDOWN: Interface Serial0, changed state to up
%LINEPROTO-5-UPDOWN: Line protocol on Interface Serial0, changed state to up
RouterB(config-if)#^Z
%SYS-5-CONFIG_I: Configured from console by console

RouterB(config-if)#^Z
%SYS-5-CONFIG_I: Configured from console by console
```

```
RouterA#show ip interface brief
Interface      IP-Address     OK? Method Status          Protocol
Serial0        11.0.0.1       YES unset  up              up
Ethernet0      10.0.0.1       YES unset  up              up
```

So now we are satisfied that layers 1 and 2 are now operational. To confirm, we ping Router A from Router B.

```
RouterA#ping 11.0.0.2
Type escape sequence to abort.
Sending 5, 100-byte ICMP Echos to 11.0.0.2, timeout is 2 seconds:
!!!!!
Success rate is 100 percent (5/5), round-trip min/avg/max = 1/2/4 ms
```

We can now check the routing table for Router A to see if it can see the rest of the network.

```
RouterA#show ip route
Codes: C - connected, S - static, I - IGRP, R - RIP, M - mobile, B - BGP
       D - EIGRP, EX - EIGRP external, O - OSPF, IA - OSPF inter area
       E1 - OSPF external type 1, E2 - OSPF external type 2, E - EGP
       i - IS-IS, L1 - IS-IS level-1, L2 - IS-IS level-2, * - candidate
default
       U - per-user static route

Gateway of last resort is not set
C       10.0.0.0/24 is directly connected, 10.0.0.1
C       11.0.0.0/24 is directly connected, 11.0.0.1
R       12.0.0.0/24 [120/1] via 11.0.0.2, 00:01:33, Serial0
```

This is better than before; however, we still can only see as far as network 12.0.0.0. We could check on Router B, but since network 13.0.0.0 is connected to Router C, we can start there.

```
RouterC#show ip interface brief
Interface      IP-Address     OK? Method Status          Protocol
Serial0        12.0.0.2       YES unset  up              up
Ethernet0      13.0.0.1       YES unset  up              up
```

Both interfaces are up/up, so we know that the Ethernet interface can see its own network (13.0.0.0) and that the serial interface is capable of advertising the route. Layers 1 and 2 appear fine, so we can check layer 3.

We could type in the "show run" command; however, we could be more specific than that.

```
RouterC#show ip protocols
Routing Protocol is "rip"
  Sending updates every 30 seconds, next due in 19 seconds
  Invalid after 180 seconds, hold down 180, flushed after 240
```

```
Outgoing update filter list for all interfaces is not set
Incoming update filter list for all interfaces is not set
Redistributing: rip
Default version control: send version 2, receive version 2
  Interface              Send  Recv  Triggered RIP  Key-chain
  Ethernet0              2     2
  Serial0               2     2
Automatic network summarization is not in effect
Maximum path: 4
Routing for Networks:
  12.0.0.0
  14.0.0.0
Routing Information Sources:
  Gateway         Distance       Last Update
  12.0.0.1            120        00:00:17
Distance: (default is 120)
```

The problem appears to be that although network 13.0.0.0 is attached to ethernet 0, the router has been configured to advertise network 14.0.0.0. We can easily correct this problem.

```
RouterC#configure terminal
RouterC(config)#router rip
RouterC(config)#version 2
RouterC(config-router)#no network 14.0.0.0
RouterC(config-router)#network 13.0.0.0
RouterC(config-router)#^Z
%SYS-5-CONFIG_I: Configured from console by console

RouterC#show ip protocols
Routing Protocol is "rip"
  Sending updates every 30 seconds, next due in 19 seconds
  Invalid after 180 seconds, hold down 180, flushed after 240
  Outgoing update filter list for all interfaces is not set
  Incoming update filter list for all interfaces is not set
  Redistributing: rip
  Default version control: send version 2, receive version 2
    Interface              Send  Recv  Triggered RIP  Key-chain
    Ethernet0              2     2
    Serial0               2     2
  Automatic network summarization is in effect
  Maximum path: 4
  Routing for Networks:
    12.0.0.0
    13.0.0.0
  Routing Information Sources:
    Gateway         Distance       Last Update
    12.0.0.1            120        00:00:17
Distance: (default is 120)
```

We are now advertising the correct networks. We should check that Router C can see all of the networks before we move on.

```
RouterC#show ip route
Codes: C - connected, S - static, I - IGRP, R - RIP, M - mobile, B - BGP
       D - EIGRP, EX - EIGRP external, O - OSPF, IA - OSPF inter area
       E1 - OSPF external type 1, E2 - OSPF external type 2, E - EGP
       i - IS-IS, L1 - IS-IS level-1, L2 - IS-IS level-2, * - candidate
default
       U - per-user static route

Gateway of last resort is not set
C       12.0.0.0/24 is directly connected, 12.0.0.2
C       13.0.0.0/24 is directly connected, 13.0.0.1
R       11.0.0.0/24 [120/1] via 12.0.0.1, 00:07:13, Serial0
R       10.0.0.0/24 [120/2] via 12.0.0.1, 00:06:37, Serial0
```

We can go back to Router A to see if it can see all of the networks.

```
RouterA#show ip route
Codes: C - connected, S - static, I - IGRP, R - RIP, M - mobile, B - BGP
       D - EIGRP, EX - EIGRP external, O - OSPF, IA - OSPF inter area
       E1 - OSPF external type 1, E2 - OSPF external type 2, E - EGP
       i - IS-IS, L1 - IS-IS level-1, L2 - IS-IS level-2, * - candidate
default
       U - per-user static route

Gateway of last resort is not set
C       10.0.0.0/24 is directly connected, 10.0.0.1
C       11.0.0.0/24 is directly connected, 11.0.0.1
R       12.0.0.0/24 [120/1] via 11.0.0.2, 00:04:17, Serial0
R       13.0.0.0/24 [120/2] via 11.0.0.2, 00:04:34, Serial0
```

All the routes are now visible.

Example 2

Next, we have a network running EIGRP with an access list on Routers A and C, preventing FTP traffic.

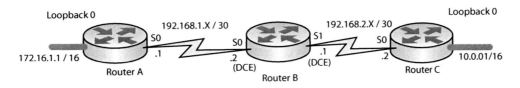

Figure 9–2: Network running EIGRP

Looking at the network above, we can see that every router should have a route for every network on every router. Each router will have an entry for directly attached networks and routes learned by EIGRP.

You should be able to ping end-to-end, each router should have a routing entry for every network with the correct subnet mask value (/30 and /16).

In the exam, there will be a few faults inserted into the network. You may feel confused and not know where to begin. Just remember the simple layer 1-2-3 strategy for troubleshooting, and you will quickly be able to identify and resolve any issues.

The quickest way to make an initial check for connectivity issues is with the "show ip interface brief" command.

```
RouterA#show ip interface brief
Interface      IP-Address      OK? Method Status                     Protocol
Ethernet0      unassigned      YES unset  administratively down      down
Loopback0      172.16.1.1      YES manual up                         up
Serial0        192.168.1.1     YES manual up                         up
Serial1        unassigned      YES unset  administratively down      down
```

This is good news, all of our interfaces are up up meaning there are no protocol issues, missing clockrates or faulty cables. We need to see if there is a route for all the networks.

```
RouterA#show ip route
Codes: C - connected, S - static, I - IGRP, R - RIP, M - mobile, B - BGP
       D - EIGRP, EX - EIGRP external, O - OSPF, IA - OSPF inter area
       N1 - OSPF NSSA external type 1, N2 - OSPF NSSA external type 2
       E1 - OSPF external type 1, E2 - OSPF external type 2, E - EGP
       i - IS-IS, L1 - IS-IS level-1, L2 - IS-IS level-2, ia - IS-IS inter
area
       * - candidate default, U - per-user static route, o - ODR
       P - periodic downloaded static route

Gateway of last resort is not set

C    172.16.0.0/16 is directly connected, Loopback0
     192.168.1.0/24 is variably subnetted, 2 subnets, 2 masks
D       192.168.1.0/24 is a summary, 00:16:44, Null0
C       192.168.1.0/30 is directly connected, Serial0
```

There is only a route for the attached network. It has been summarized as /24 but we can see from the diagram and from either of the "show run interface serial 0" or "show run" or "show interface serial 0" that there is a /30 mask configured on it.

```
RouterA#show run interface serial 0
Building configuration...

Current configuration : 89 bytes
!
interface Serial0
  ip address 192.168.1.1 255.255.255.252
  ip access-group 101 in
end

RouterA#show interface serial 0
Serial0 is up, line protocol is up
  Hardware is HD64570
  Internet address is 192.168.1.1/30
  MTU 1500 bytes, BW 1544 Kbit, DLY 20000 usec,
      reliability 255/255, txload 1/255, rxload 1/255
  Encapsulation HDLC, loopback not set
  Keepalive set (10 sec)
```

Some output omitted (as well as the "show run").

We can fix the incorrect subnet mask issues right away or make a note of it and fix it after we look at the other side of the network. The answer should be in how the routing has been set up and can be resolved by using the "no auto-summary" command.

```
RouterA#show ip protocols
Routing Protocol is "eigrp 30"
  Outgoing update filter list for all interfaces is not set
  Incoming update filter list for all interfaces is not set
  Default networks flagged in outgoing updates
  Default networks accepted from incoming updates
  EIGRP metric weight K1=1, K2=0, K3=1, K4=0, K5=0
  EIGRP maximum hopcount 100
  EIGRP maximum metric variance 1
  Redistributing: eigrp 30
  Automatic network summarization is in effect ⇐ EIGRP is summarizing
  Automatic address summarization:
    192.168.1.0/24 for Loopback0
      Summarizing with metric 2169856
    172.16.0.0/16 for Serial0
  Maximum path: 4
  Routing for Networks:
    172.16.0.0
    192.168.1.0
  Routing Information Sources:
    Gateway        Distance      Last Update
    (this router)        90      00:22:26
    192.168.1.2          90      00:25:53
  Distance: internal 90 external 170
```

```
RouterA#config t
Enter configuration commands, one per line.  End with CNTL/Z.
RouterA(config)#router eigrp 30
RouterA(config-router)#no auto-summary ⇐ Turn off auto summarization
RouterA(config-router)#^Z
RouterA#show ip protocol
Routing Protocol is "eigrp 30"
  Outgoing update filter list for all interfaces is not set
  Incoming update filter list for all interfaces is not set
  Default networks flagged in outgoing updates
  Default networks accepted from incoming updates
  EIGRP metric weight K1=1, K2=0, K3=1, K4=0, K5=0
  EIGRP maximum hopcount 100
  EIGRP maximum metric variance 1
  Redistributing: eigrp 30
  Automatic network summarization is not in effect ⇐ no auto summarization
                                                           now
  Maximum path: 4
  Routing for Networks:
    172.16.0.0
    192.168.1.0
  Routing Information Sources:
    Gateway          Distance      Last Update
    (this router)          90      00:22:55
    192.168.1.2            90      00:26:21
  Distance: internal 90 external 170
```

Do you understand what just happened there? If you go back to module 5, you will see that EIGRP automatically summarizes networks at major boundaries. The 255.255.255.252 mask was summarized back to its usual 255.255.255.0 mask when it left the router. To prevent this happening, we need to add the "no auto-summary" command under the routing protocol configuration.

Let's look at Router B.

```
RouterB#show ip interface brief
Interface     IP-Address    OK? Method Status                 Protocol
Ethernet0     unassigned    YES unset  administratively down  down
Serial0       192.168.1.2   YES manual up                     up
Serial1       192.168.2.1   YES manual down                   down
RouterB#
```

The Serial 1 interface is down down, meaning there is a physical issue or no keepalives are being seen from the other side.

```
RouterB#show run interface serial 1 ⇐ or "show run" if this
                                         command is not recognized
Building configuration...
```

```
Current configuration : 82 bytes
!
interface Serial1
 ip address 192.168.2.1 255.255.255.252
 clockrate 64000
end
```

The configuration appears fairly standard; the IP address is correct. We can look at Router C to get a better idea of what is wrong.

```
RouterC#show run ⇦ or "show run interface serial 0" if this works
Building configuration...
Current configuration : 695 bytes
!
version 12.1
service timestamps debug uptime
service timestamps log uptime
no service password-encryption
!
hostname RouterC
!
ip subnet-zero
!
interface Loopback0
 ip address 10.0.0.1 255.255.0.0
!
interface Ethernet0
 no ip address
 shutdown
!
interface Serial0
 ip address 192.168.2.2 255.255.255.252
 ip access-group 101 in
 shutdown
```

Interface serial 0 is shutdown and needs to be "no shut"ed.

```
RouterC#config t
Enter configuration commands, one per line. End with CNTL/Z.
RouterC(config)#interface serial 0
RouterC(config-if)#no shut
RouterC(config-if)#exit
RouterC(config)#exit
RouterC#
01:22:54: %SYS-5-CONFIG_I: Configured from console by console
01:22:54: %LINK-3-UPDOWN: Interface Serial0, changed state to up
01:22:55: %LINEPROTO-5-UPDOWN: Line protocol on Interface Serial0, changed
state to up ⇦ the interface is now up
RouterC#
```

We can now make sure the routing is working.

```
RouterC#show ip route (some output omitted)

Gateway of last resort is not set

     10.0.0.0/8 is variably subnetted, 2 subnets, 2 masks
D       10.0.0.0/8 is a summary, 00:02:39, Null0
C       10.0.0.0/16 is directly connected, Loopback0
     192.168.2.0/24 is variably subnetted, 2 subnets, 2 masks
D       192.168.2.0/24 is a summary, 00:02:39, Null0
C       192.168.2.0/30 is directly connected, Serial0
RouterC#
```

The routing is working; however, we need to correct the /24 mask to show /30 on every router that is missing the "no auto-summary command". Use the "show run", "show run interface serial X", or better still, the "show ip protocols" command on Routers B and C and add the command if it is missing.

```
RouterC#config t
Enter configuration commands, one per line. End with CNTL/Z.
RouterC(config)#router eigrp 30
RouterC(config-router)#no auto-summary
RouterC(config-router)#

RouterB#config t
Enter configuration commands, one per line. End with CNTL/Z.
RouterB(config)#router eigrp 30
RouterB(config-router)#no auto-summary
RouterB(config-router)#exit
RouterB(config)#exit
RouterB#
```

We can now check the routing tables again.

```
RouterA#show ip route (some output omitted)
Gateway of last resort is not set

C    172.16.0.0/16 is directly connected, Loopback0
     192.168.1.0/30 is subnetted, 1 subnets
C       192.168.1.0 is directly connected, Serial0
```

Something is amiss here. All of the EIGRP routes have gone! We know that the interfaces are up up, so layers 1 and 2 are okay. We are advertising the correct networks and the IP addressing on the interfaces is correct, so layer 3 is fine.

The only thing left is the acccess list, but what could be wrong with that?

```
RouterA#show ip access-lists
Extended IP access list 101
    deny tcp any any eq ftp
```

Do you remember what the invisible entry at the end of the access list is? "Deny any". We need to write the access list from scratch to permit IP traffic so the EIGRP routing updates can be permitted.

Let's remove the access list altogether and see what happens. We can turn on EIGRP debugging to see if there are any updates passing. The debug may not work in the exam.

```
RouterA#debug ip eigrp
IP-EIGRP Route Events debugging is on
Nothing passes for a while.
RouterA(config)#no access-list 101
Turning off all possible debugging on ACL 101
RouterA(config)#
```

As soon as the access list is removed EIGRP updates begin to pass.

```
01:40:12: IP-EIGRP: 172.16.0.0/16 - do advertise out Serial0
01:40:12: IP-EIGRP: Int 172.16.0.0/16 metric 128256 - 256 128000
01:40:12: IP-EIGRP: 192.168.1.0/30 - do advertise out Serial0
RouterA(config)#
```

Write out the access list again, this time permitting all IP traffic.

```
RouterA#config t
Enter configuration commands, one per line. End with CNTL/Z.
RouterA(config)#no access-list 101 ⇔ wipe the old access list off
RouterA(config)#access-list 101 deny tcp any any eq ftp
RouterA(config)#access-list 101 permit ip any any
RouterA(config)#exit
01:42:59: %SYS-5-CONFIG_I: Configured from console by console
RouterA#clear ip route * ⇔ clear the routing table
RouterA#debug ip eigrp
IP-EIGRP Route Events debugging is on

RouterA#show ip route (some output omitted)
Gateway of last resort is not set

C    172.16.0.0/16 is directly connected, Loopback0
     192.168.1.0/30 is subnetted, 1 subnets
C       192.168.1.0 is directly connected, Serial0
     192.168.2.0/30 is subnetted, 1 subnets
D       192.168.2.0 [90/2681856] via 192.168.1.2, 00:00:14, Serial0
```

Now do the same on Router C.

```
RouterC#config t
Enter configuration commands, one per line. End with CNTL/Z.
RouterC(config)#no access-list 101 ⇔ wipe off the old access list
RouterC(config)#access-list 101 deny tcp any any eq 21
RouterC(config)#access-list 101 permit ip any any
RouterC(config)#exit
RouterC#
01:46:27: %SYS-5-CONFIG_I: Configured from console by console

RouterC#show ip route (some output omitted)

Gateway of last resort is not set

D    172.16.0.0/16 [90/2809856] via 192.168.2.1, 00:00:39, Serial0
     10.0.0.0/16 is subnetted, 1 subnets
C       10.0.0.0 is directly connected, Loopback0
     192.168.1.0/30 is subnetted, 1 subnets
D       192.168.1.0 [90/2681856] via 192.168.2.1, 00:00:39, Serial0
     192.168.2.0/30 is subnetted, 1 subnets
C       192.168.2.0 is directly connected, Serial0
RouterC#
```

Now that the "permit ip any any" is working, EIGRP updates can pass. We can see that the correct subnet mask of /30 is being advertised. We can see the loopback address on Router A so the only thing left is to ping it.

```
RouterC#ping 172.16.1.1

Type escape sequence to abort.
Sending 5, 100-byte ICMP Echos to 172.16.1.1, timeout is 2 seconds:
!!!!!
Success rate is 100 percent (5/5), round-trip min/avg/max = 60/60/64 ms
RouterC#
```

If, on the above network, FTP was to be denied and only EIGRP routing updates were to be permitted; you would have configured the access list on Routers A and C, as below.

```
RouterA#show ip access-lists
Extended IP access list 101
    deny tcp any any eq ftp
    permit eigrp any any (30 matches)
```

We can still see the routes because EIGRP updates are permitted.

```
RouterA#show ip route (some output omitted)

Gateway of last resort is not set
```

```
C     172.16.0.0/16 is directly connected, Loopback0
      10.0.0.0/16 is subnetted, 1 subnets
D        10.0.0.0 [90/2809856] via 192.168.1.2, 00:00:03, Serial0
      192.168.1.0/30 is subnetted, 1 subnets
C        192.168.1.0 is directly connected, Serial0
      192.168.2.0/30 is subnetted, 1 subnets
D        192.168.2.0 [90/2681856] via 192.168.1.2, 00:00:03, Serial0
```

But we cannot ping across because all other IP traffic including ICMP is denied.

```
RouterA#ping 10.0.0.1

Type escape sequence to abort.
Sending 5, 100-byte ICMP Echos to 10.0.0.1, timeout is 2 seconds:
.....
Success rate is 0 percent (0/5)
```

 INSPIRATION:

If most of what we have just done here did not make much sense then you are in good company. Almost everyone struggles to start with. Learning the material and techniques is a gradual process. Be patient with yourself and you will do just great.

A WORD ON DEBUGGING

The debug facility is a very useful addition to a network engineers toolkit. Depending upon what type of debug you are running though, you can force the routers CPU to dangerously high levels and even cause a reload. Debugs such as "debug ip packet" have been known to cause this on a busy network.

To reduce the dangers associated with using the debug command enter the "no logging console" command. You can then issue the "terminal monitor" command. This will send the output of the debugs to the display you are using for your terminal session (i.e., your screen when you are telnetted in).

The "logging synchronous" command is very useful if you want to prevent logging information from appearing whilst you are entering commands on the router from a console connection. If this command is not on and a console message appears half way through your typing a command, you can simply hold down the Ctrl+L or Ctrl+R keys to redisplay the line you were typing.

If you are consoled into the router, issuing a debug can be dangerous due to the high amount of debugs sent to the console session.

```
RouterA(config)#line console 0
RouterA(config-line)#logging synchronous
```

A FINAL WORD ON TROUBLESHOOTING

There are many good books available on network and Cisco troubleshooting. It would be a futile task to attempt to cover every eventuality in these pages. I do however, firmly believe that the above guide will get you though almost any troubleshooting issues you will come across in the exam. When you get out in the real world you should expect anything and everything.

A great book to help you with real life troubleshooting is:
Internetworking Troubleshooting Handbook published by Cisco Press.

ISBN: 1587050056
If I had to carry only one book in my briefcase when out in the field it would be:
Cisco Field Manual: Router Configuration (Cisco Press).
ISBN: 1587050242
(It is an absolute cracker.)

With a methodical approach you should be able to quickly and effectively troubleshoot and resolve any problem you encounter in the exam and on a live network in fact.

Now go through the advanced lab exercises in the labs section.

CHAPTER 10

Module 10—Wireless Networking

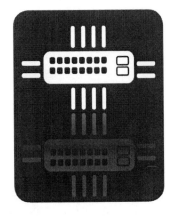

What you will learn in this module	Timings
How wireless works	Theory: 45 minutes
Wireless standards	
Wireless security	
Wireless troubleshooting	

WLANS OR WIRELESS LOCAL AREA NETWORKS

We all know that networks need a medium to connect the client to the resources and usually requires running a lot of cables in the building(s). In the last few years wireless LANs have increased in popularity with improved performance and security.

Figure 10–1 demonstrates a simple wireless network setup.

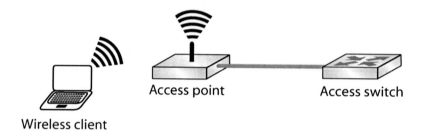

Figure 10–1: Simple wireless network

We see in the figure that our wireless client connects to an access point. The access point then connects via a cable to an access switch. This setup allows the client to access resources on the local area network. The wireless client can be a built-in wireless network card or a PCMCIA/PCI Cisco Aironet card.

Figure 10–2: Cisco Aironet PCI Card

Figure 10–3: Cisco Aironet PCMCIA Card

And looking at Figure 10–4, we see a couple of access points.

Figure 10–4: Wireless access points

HOW DOES WIRELESS WORK?

A radio transmits the signal on a specified frequency (2.4 Ghz or 5 Ghz band, depending on the standard) and this is received by a receiver (antenna). Looking at the diagram above, the wireless client radio sends the signal to the receiver (antenna) of the access point. The access point converts the wireless signal or radio signal into Ethernet to send it on to the wired network. This way the client can access the resources on the local area network. The strength of the radio, the transmitting power is defined in the US by the Federal Communications Commission (FCC). These limitations are called EIRP, Equivalent Isotropically Radiated Power. EIRP represents the total effective transmit power of the radio, including the gain that the antenna provides and the loss of the antenna cable.

The gain of the antenna represents how well it increases the effective power signal in decibels, dB. We can have a directional antenna or omnidirectional antenna. Below you can see some examples of both antenna's and their radiation patterns and you can see why they are named that way.

As you can see from the radiation patterns the signal travels in all directions. This results in signal loss that can be caused by:

- Reflection — the signal bounces of a smooth non-absorbing surface
- Scattering — the signal bounces on an uneven surface
- Absorption — the signal gets absorbed when hitting water, wood and even people
- Attenuation — the signal loses its amplitude.

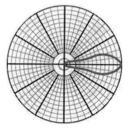

Figure 10–5: Directional antennas and their radiation pattern.

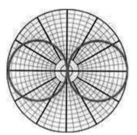

Figure 10–6: Omnidirectional antenna and its radiation pattern

TWO MODES OF WIRELESS NETWORKS

Ad-hoc mode

With this mode, you can compare with a peer-to-peer network, the nodes / devices are in close proximity to each other.

Client A   Client B

Figure 10–7: Peer-to-peer network

It is important to note that in ad-hoc mode client A and client B use the same channel / frequency and SSID (Service Set Identifier). The SSID or network name is a 32-bit alphanumeric (letters and numbers) character case-sensitive variable. Clients that want to communicate with each other must have the same SSID.

Benefits of ad-hoc mode are that it is easy and quick to set up and there is no need to buy access points. But it has also drawbacks, the performance is better with access points, network management (e.g., monitoring) is much harder, and there is limited network access.

Infrastructure mode

In this mode, we use an access point that you can consider as a wireless hub.

Figure 10–8 shows a BSS (basic service set). A BSS consist of an access point, which is wired to the local resources (not shown), and multiple clients. An ESS (extended service set) consists of two or more BSSs from the same subnetwork.

In infrastructure mode the clients need to be configured with the same SSID to be able to communicate with each other.

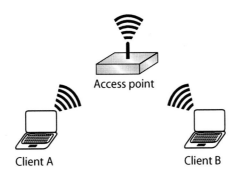

Access point

Client A   Client B

Figure 10–8: Wireless hub

Benefits of infrastructure mode are centralized security management, scalable and increased reach. The extra cost of the access points is the only drawback of this type of wireless network.

Let's now have a look at how to configure an access point and wireless client to establish a wireless connection. We will use the Cisco Wireless client software in these examples. If you want to use Windows or any other clients, the configuration steps differ but in principle remain the same.

In the examples, you will see different screenshots from access points. The images with a white background are from access points running Cisco IOS; the others are running VxWorks. The principles, though, remain the same — just the location of the fields differs.

When you connect to the access point using the default IP address and you click on express setup, you see a screen similar to Figure 10–8 (please note that your outputs may differ slightly to mine). Here you can change the hostname, the IP address for management, default gateway, and change the SNMP community. Changing the IP address will result in you losing connection to the access point and you need to change the IP address on the computer to be in the same subnet again if directly connected.

The role in the radio network is usually root for the first access point in the network. We press the apply button to save the changes. Now that the basic setup has been completed, we can complete the configuration of the access point to accept connections.

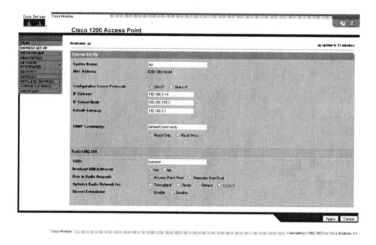

Figure 10–9: Express set-up screen

When clicking on the express security tab, we see the following screen.

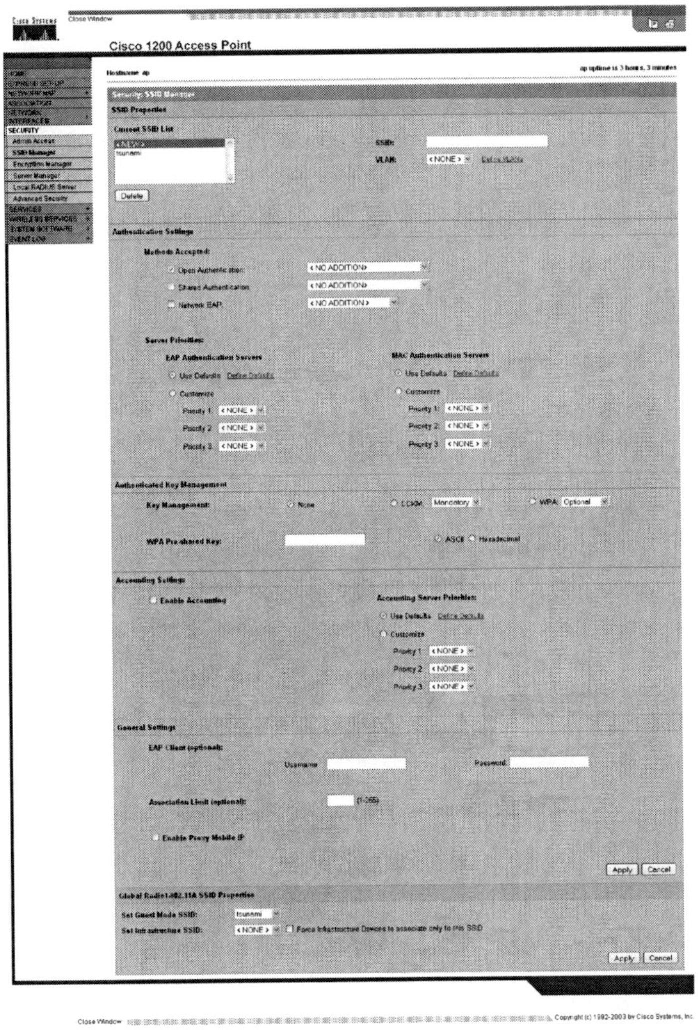

Figure 10–10: Express Security screen

As you can see here, we fill in the SSID and what type of security we will be using in our wireless network. All these parameters have to be consistent in the wireless network. A very important field is that when using multiple VLANs on the access point (maximum 16) a native VLAN has to be configured. This is because the access points use 802.1Q as its trunking protocol. This native VLAN also needs to be consistent in the entire network to ensure operability.

For the purpose of this lesson, we are not going to elaborate on the security settings. We will cover that in depth in a later lesson. And this is how it looks on a VxWorks access point.

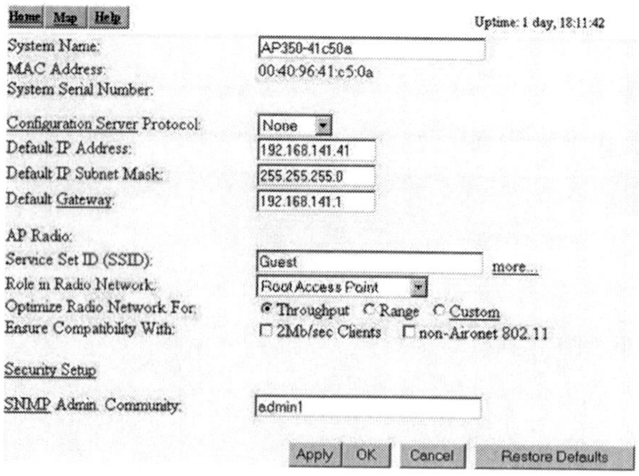

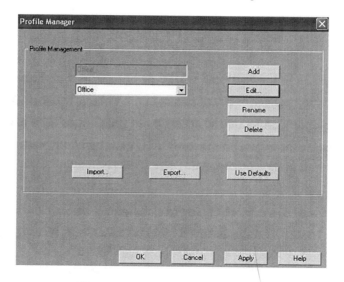

Figure 10–11: VxWorks access point

And if you have an IOS-based access point and using the CLI:

```
AP#configure terminal
AP(config)#hostname name
AP(config)#interface dot11radio 0
AP(config-if)#ssid ssid-string
AP(config-if)#station role root
AP(config-if)#exit
AP(config)#interface bvi 1
AP(config-if)#ip address address mask
AP(config-if)#exit
AP(config)#ip default-gateway address
AP(config)#exit
AP#copy running-config startup-config
```

Now that the access point is configured, we will configure the client. When you installed the wireless client software and drivers, we need to create a new profile (Figure 10–12).

Figure 10–12: Creating a new profile

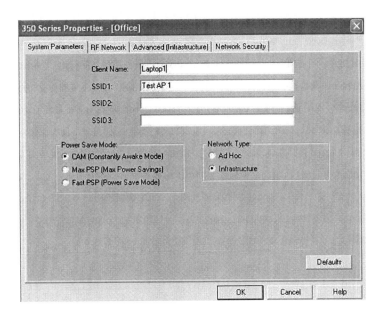

Figure 10–13: Setting basic settings for the client

When a profile is created, we can then set the basic settings for our client (Figure 10–13).

The SSID used here is the same as the one we have configured on the access point. We select infrastructure mode because we are using an access point.

When clicking OK, we have configured the client for a basic network. By checking the association table on the access point we can see if our client is associated.

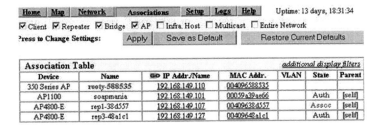

Figure 10–14: Checking the association table on the access point

Or using the CLI,

```
AP#show dot11 associations client
```

OVERVIEW OF COMMON WIRELESS STANDARDS

In 1997, the 802.11 standard (or Wi-Fi standard) was created by the IEEE and had a maximum bandwidth of 2 Mbit/sec. This bandwidth was used in the 2.4–2.5 Ghz frequency spectrum. In that standard the speeds and frequency are defined and also carrier sense multiple access with collision avoidance (CSMA/CA) to be used as protocol. This was used because on Wireless LAN a node cannot listen while it is sending data, and therefore collision detection is not possible. In CSMA/CA, a node will send a signal to the other nodes not to transmit, it will then wait for a little while longer and checks if the channel is still free. If it is free it, will transmit the data and wait for an acknowledgment that the data has been received. Modulation is done either using Frequency hopping or DSSS Direct-Sequence Spread Spectrum. The range is approximately 20 meters indoors and 100 meters outdoors (in good conditions, line of sight, walls, etc.).

802.11b became a standard in 1999, and the bandwidth increased to 11 Mbit/sec (Actual throughput we are looking at 7.1 Mbit/sec UDP and 5.9 Mbit/sec TCP. This is because of the CSMA/CA overhead.) Another change was the modulation used by 802.11b. It still uses DSSS, but technically it uses CCK (Complementary Code Keying). When the signal is degrading, the speed can drop to 5.5 Mbit/sec, 2 Mbit/sec and 1 Mbit/sec. This is called adaptive-rate selection. With this adaptive-rate selection, the range for 802.11b indoors at 11 Mbit/sec is 38 meters and 90 meters at 1 Mbit/sec, outdoors about 140 meters.

Because 802.11b operates in the 2.4 GHz band, interference arises from microwave ovens, cordless phones, and baby monitors. Another interference source is the channel overlap that exists in the 2.4 GHz band. There are 14 available channels, frequencies, but only channel 1, 6, and 11 are not overlapping. Each channel had a width of 22 MHz.

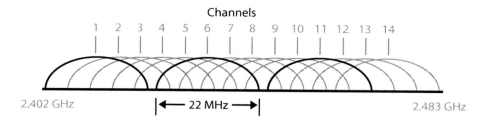

Figure 10–15: Frequency distribution of the 2.4 GHz band

In June 2003, 802.11g was ratified and has a maximum bandwidth of 54 Mbit/sec, using the 2.4 Ghz band. This means that 802.11g has the same interference issues as 802.11b. The increase in speed is achieved using OFDM (Orthogonal Frequency-Division Multiplexing) and data rates of 54, 48, 36, 24, 18, 12, 9, and 6 Mbit/sec. CCK is used for data rates of 5.5 and 11 Mbit/sec and DBPSK/DQPSK+DSSS for 2 Mbit/sec and 1 Mbit/sec (Differential Binary Phase Key Shifting/Differential Quaternary Phase Key Shifting).

The range of 802.11g is indoors 38 meters and 140 meters outdoors — just like 802.11b.

In 1999, not only was 802.11b ratified, but also 802.11a, using the 5 GHz frequency spectrum. Using OFDM (Orthogonal Frequency-Division Multiplexing) on 52 subcarriers, it achieves a maximum bandwidth of 54 Mbit/sec. This maximum bandwidth is achieved using OFDM (Orthogonal Frequency-Division Multiplexing) and data rates of 54, 48, 36, 24, 18, 12, 9, and 6 Mbit/sec. This OFDM type modulation was later used in 802.11g, as you saw in the previous paragraph.

802.11a has twelve non-overlapping channels, as you can see in Figure 10–16. The first eight channels are intended for indoor use, the last four for outdoor use (point-to-point links). The benefit of 802.11a is that it does not have the interference issues of 802.11b/g, so it is more reliable, but the range of 802.11a is not as great as 802.11b/g, 35 meters indoors, and 120 meters outdoors.

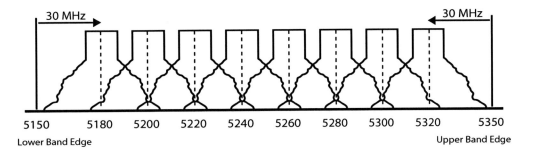

Upper U-NII Bands: 4 Carriers in 100MHz / 20MHz Spacing

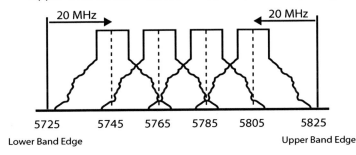

Figure 10–16: 802.11a frequency allocation

The future... 802.11n

802.11n has recently been approved. 802.11n adds MIMO (Multiple-Input Multiple-Output) to improve system performace—increased bandwidth and range. This is done by using multiple transmitters (radios) and receivers (antennas). Features of 802.1n include an operating frequency of 5Ghz and or 2.4 Ghz, 144 Mbit/sec, indoor range around 300 ft (91 metres, outdoor range around 600ft (182 meters).

The above standards were all defined by the IEEE (Institute of Electrical and Electronic Engineers), an international non-profit professional organization for the advancement of technology related to electricity. Besides IEEE, there is also the FCC (Federal Communication Commission), and its European counterpart — ETSI (European Telecommunications Standards Institute). Both organizations are responsible for the use of the frequency spectrum (2.4 GHz and 5 GHz unlicensed frequencies used for WLAN).

The Wi-Fi alliance is there to improve the interoperability between vendor's products based on the 802.11 standard. Some of its members are Cisco, Nokia, Apple, Microsoft, Pioneer, etc. When products have been tested and verified by the Wi-Fi alliance, it will receive the following logo:

WIRELESS SECURITY

Let's go a bit deeper into how a station / node connects to an access point. We already know that the SSID has to be the same on the client and access point. But how is a connection built?

Before a station can send data, it must authenticate and associate with an access point. Two methods for authentication exist:

1. Open-system authentication
2. Shared-key authentication.

Open-system authentication

In this method, the client sends an association request to the access point. The latter will respond with a success or failure message. A failure can occur when the MAC address of the client is denied in the configuration of the access point.

Shared-key authentication

Here a shared key or passphrase is configured on both the client and access point. The client sends an association request, the access point sends a challenge based on the shared key, the clients sends a response and if this response is correct then the authentication is a success.

There are three types of shared key authentication WEP, WPA, and WPA2. Once authentication is a success, then the client will associate with the access point.

Now, let's look closer at the three types of shared-key authentication.

WEP

WEP—Wired Equivalent Privacy — is an encryption algorithm built into the 802.11 standard. It uses RC4 40bit or 104-bit keys and a 24-bit initialization vector. It is also a symmetric algorithm because the encryption and decryption uses the same key.

Let's have a look at how we configure WEP on the access point.

On a VxWorks access point:

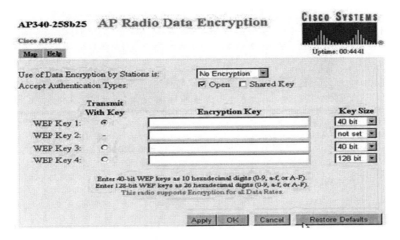

Figure 10–17: Configuring WEP on a VxWorks access point

On an IOS-based access point:

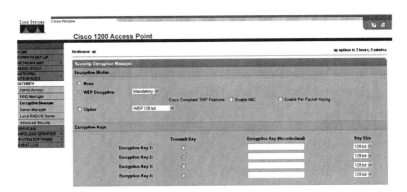

Figure 10–18: Configuring WEP on an IOS-based access point

It is important to note that when you use key 1 on the access point, you have to use key 1 on the client as well (Figure 10–19). This includes the key and key size.

Because WEP only has a 24-bit Initialization Vector, there are only +/- 16.7 million variations available, which isn't many in the encryption world and, therefore, is a weakness in the algorithm and, hence, the security level is decreased.

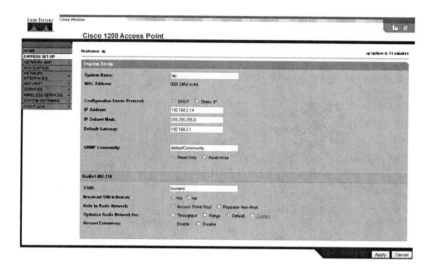

Figure 10–19: Configuring the client

WPA

WPA (Wi-Fi protected access) was created by the Wi-Fi alliance in order to make wireless networks more secure than using weak WEP security. This method uses dynamic-key management, adds a stronger encryption cipher and is built on the EAP/802.1X mechanism.

One of the enhancements of WPA is the use of TKIP (Temporal Key Integrity Protocol), and the Initialization Vector is increased to 48 bit (more then 500 trillion key combinations).

WPA is mainly used in the enterprise environment in combination with a RADIUS server, WPA-PSK (WPA pre-shared key) is what we would find in SoHo and home users that want improved security compared to WEP.

To configure WPA-PSK on an IOS-based access point:

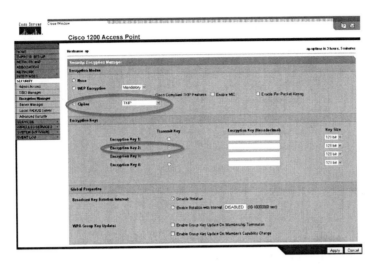

Figure 10–20: Configuring WPA-PSK on an IOS-based access point (a)

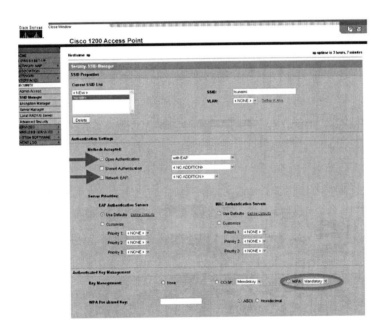

Figure 10–21: Configuring WPA-PSK on an IOS-based access point (b)

As you can see, WPA is configured into two different places. We enter our pre-shared key and then state for that particular SSID we use WPA.

On the client, we do the following:

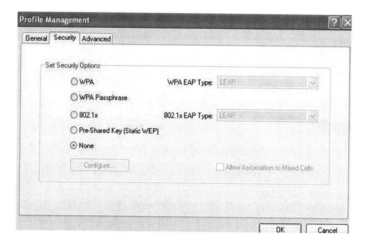

Figure 10–22: Setting the security options for the client

Select the WPA passphrase option and enter the same passphrase (key) as on the access point.

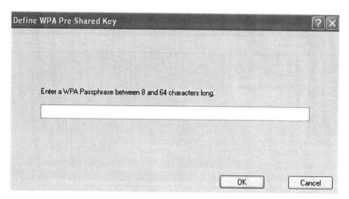

Figure 10–23: Enter the WPA pre-shared key

As you can see the configuration looks very similar to WEP, but your wireless network is more secure.

WPA2

WPA2 (Wi-Fi protected access 2) is the next generation in wireless security. It is the Wi-Fi Alliance interoperable implementation of the IEEE 802.11n ratified standard.

Even stronger encryption than WPA is achieved by using AES (advanced encryption standard). Also, WPA2 creates a new key for every new association. This has a benefit over WPA that the client's keys are unique and specific to that client.

Same as WPA, WPA2 has a personal and enterprise mode.

Let's configure the access point for WPA2-PSK:

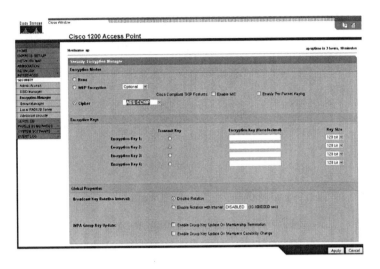

Figure 10–24: Configure WPA2-PSK access point. (a) Select the AES cipher.

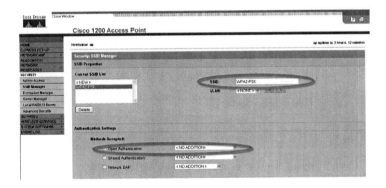

Figure 10–25: Configure WPA2-PSK access point. (b) Check for Open Authentication.

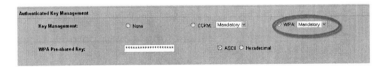

Figure 10–26: Configure WPA2-PSK access point. (c) Enter Authenticated Key Management.

As you noticed, three steps are needed:

1. Select the AES cipher.
2. Make sure it is Open Authentication.
3. Fill in the Authenticated Key Management with the pre-shared key.

On the client, the following has to be configured:

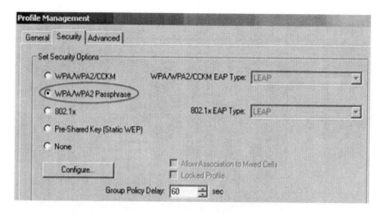

Figure 10–27: Configure the client security options.

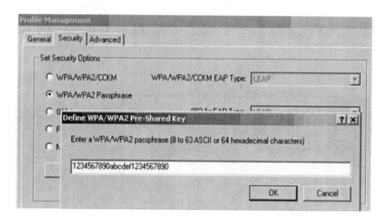

Figure 10–28: Enter the WPA2 pre-shared key.

WIRELESS TROUBLESHOOTING

When troubleshooting wireless networks, documentation is an important means of helping. It can contain the placement of the access points, the channels used, and the pre-shared keys used (if the latter should be in the documentation, make sure it is kept in a very safe place).

If you are using WEP, WPA, or WPA2, you have to make sure that when entering the pre-shared key that no typos are entered. You can see this behavior when the wireless client will associate with the access point, but there is no authentication. In general, a user would not have an IP Address, access to resources, etc.

When we have an user complaining about bad performance of the wireless network, we need to look at interference, as there could be overlapping channels. These overlapping channels are not necessarily coming from your network, but a neighboring wireless network could be using the same channel as you or it could be a cordless phone or microwave oven.

Slow performance of a wireless network is not always related to the wireless network itself. It could be that the wired network is not functioning correctly or cannot cope with an increase of wireless users (switch port 10 Mbit/sec instead of 100 Mbit/sec).

Another reason could be that the wireless client is not having the optimal LOS (Line of Sight). This is especially crucial in outdoor implementation of wireless networks because distances are far greater than indoor.

Because a direct LOS is not always possible and the signal bounces off objects in its path, an access point can receive the signal more than once. This is called multi-path and has a degrading effect on the wireless network. While this is a negative point in the a/b/g networks in the 802.11n draft (as time of writing), this behavior is used in the MIMO technology.

This concludes the chapter on wireless networks. You have learned the wireless standards in use, how connections are made, how to secure wireless networks, and what to look for when troubleshooting wireless networks.

SUMMARY QUESTIONS
1. Which three components are required to connect hosts to the network?
2. Which four ways can the wireless signal be lost?
3. Name the two wireless network modes.
4. A BSS consits of what?
5. An ESS consists of what?
6. Name two benefits of infrastructure mode.
7. Which 802 standard refers to wireless networking?
8. Name the two methods of wireless authentication.
9. Name the three types of shared-key authentication
10. WPA2 achieves stronger encryption by the use of _____.

CHAPTER 11

Module 11—Security Device Manager

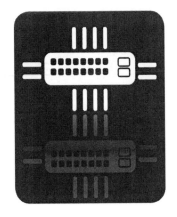

What you will learn in this module	Timings
SDM introduction	Theory: 45 minutes
SDM basics	
Installing SDM	

SDM—AN INTRODUCTION

Security Device Manager is one of the most exciting products to be released by Cisco Systems for some time. SDM is a graphical router configuration and network management tool. You can now use this Java network management tool, which uses a web browser graphical user interface (GUI) to configure and troubleshoot your routers. You can use SDM to configure your LAN, WAN, firewall, and VPN.

The hardest task facing most network engineers is having to create a mental picture of the network in their minds after examining the router configuration looking at the command line interface.

This skill can often take years to master and even then, it makes configuring, verifying and troubleshooting networks a difficult task. Now, the task can be carried out using a graphical model of the network. You no longer need any command line skills to configure your routers.

SDM—IN THE CCNA AND CCNET EXAMS

You will be expected to be familiar with SDM if you want to pass the above exams. Check the latest syllabus requirements for your specific exam at www.cisco.com/go/ccent.

For the CCNA you will be expected to be familiar with the SDM environment and be able to configure:

- NAT*
- DHCP*
- DNS*
- Basic configuration including IP addressing
- Access lists

The above will also include using SDM to troubleshoot problems using SDM troubleshooting utilities. The items marked with the asterisk (*) are tested on the CCENT but again, please check Cisco's website for up-to-date information.

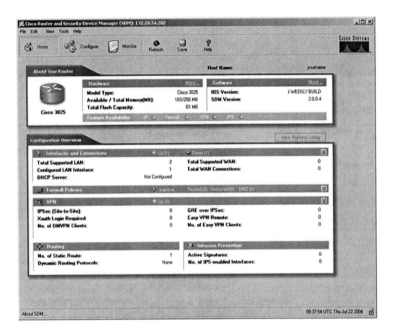

Figure 11–1: Security Device Manager

SDM BASICS

SDM is currently supported on the devices listed in Table 11–1, but to see an up-to-date list, please visit www.cisco.com/go/sdm.

To view the current version of IOS on your router, you need to issue the "show version" command.

```
R2#show version
Operating System Software
IOS (tm) C1700 Software (C1700-K9O3SY7-M), Version 12.3(22), RELEASE SOFTWARE
(f
c2)
Technical Support: http://www.cisco.com/techsupport
Copyright (c) 1986-2007 by cisco Systems, Inc.
Compiled Wed 24-Jan-07 15:39 by ccai
Image text-base: 0x8000816C, data-base: 0x811068E0

ROM: System Bootstrap, Version 12.2(7r)XM2, RELEASE SOFTWARE (fc1)
ROM: C1700 Software (C1700-K9O3SY7-M), Version 12.3(22), RELEASE SOFTWARE
(fc2)

R2 uptime is 10 minutes
System returned to ROM by power-on
System restarted at 21:01:40 UTC Wed Dec 6 2006
System image file is "flash:c1700-k9o3sy7-mz.123-22.bin"
```

Table 11–1: Minimum IOS software requirements

Router model	Minimum IOS release
831,836,837	12.2(13)ZH, 12.3.2XA, 12.3(2)T
1701,1711,1712,1710,1721,1751,1751-v,1760,1760-v	12.2(15)ZL, 12.3.2XA 12.2(13)ZH, 12.2(13)T3
1801, 1802, 1803, 1811, 1812 and 1841	12.3(8)YI,12.3(8)T4
Cisco 2610XM, 2611XM, 2620XM, 2621XM, 2650XM, 2651XM, and 2691	12.2(11)T6 , 12.3(1)M, 12.3(2)T
2801, 2811, 2821 and ,2851	12.3(8)T4
3620, 3640A,3640, 3661, and 3662	12.2(11)T6, 12.3(1)M, 12.3(2)T
3725 and 3745	12.2(11)T6, 12.3(1)M, 12.3(2)T
3825 and 3845	12.3(11)T
7204VXR,7206VXR and 7301	12.3(2)T, 12.3(3)M

SDM comes pre-installed with all 850, 870, 1800, 2800, and 3800 routers and is free of charge to download and install on all routers from 830 to 7300. SDM also supports English, Simplified Chinese, Spanish, German, Italian, and French.

There are built in TAC-approved configuration files you can apply to your routers and also wizards to help you install and configure VPN, QoS, IPS (Intrusion Prevention System), firewall features, and even wireless.

FAQ

Can I still use Cisco IOS?

Yes, the graphical interface actually configures command line entries for you. You can go into the command line to check your configs or add lines of code if you wish.

Do I install SDM on my router or PC?

You can do both or one of the above. If you want to install it on your router you will need to ensure you have the minimum version of IOS installed and room on your flash to fit the SDM files.

INSTALLING SDM

Part I

You can install SDM software or on your router if there is enough memory on your flash. You need 6 MB free memory on your router for SDM software or 5.5 MB free memory on your PC. SDM will work on any Pentium III or higher PC running Windows 98SE or later. You will need IE 5.5 or higher for the web interface, and SDM requires Sun Java Runtime Environment (JRE) version 1.4.2_05 or later, or Java Virtual Machine (JVM) 5.0.0.3810.

When you first come to install SDM, you will need to ascertain if it is installed on your router already:

```
Router#show flash:
System flash directory:
File Length Name/status
1 5238536 c1700-k9o3sy7-mz.123-22.bin
2 14617 sdm.shtml
3 669 sdmconfig-83x.cfg
4 2290688 sdm.tar
5 14617 sdm.shtml.hide
```

If you want to install SDM onto your router and it is not currently running a version of IOS which supports SDM then you will need to upgrade the IOS (or install the software on your PC).

Before you install SDM you must enable certain parameters on your router. SDM can be installed on a router that is already in service on your network. You will need to add the below config onto your router even if you are installing SDM on your PC only.

Step 1: Enable HTTP and HTTPS on your router (HTTPS optional)

```
Router#configure terminal
Enter configuration commands, one per line. End with CNTL/Z.
Router(config)#ip http server
Router(config)#ip http secure-server
Router(config)#ip http authentication local
Router(config)#ip http timeout-policy idle 600 life 86400 requests 10000
```

Step 2: Enable level 15 privilege access to the router:

```
Router(config)#username howtonetwork privilege 15 secret 0 chopsuey
```

Step 3: Enable ssh and telnet access for privilege level 15.

```
Router(config)#line vty 0 4
Router(config-line)#privilege level 15
Router(config-line)#login local
Router(config-line)#transport input telnet ssh
Router(config-line)#exit
Router(config)#end
Router#
```

Part II

Next, you need to download the SDM software from Cisco's website.
(http://www.cisco.com/pcgi-bin/tablebuild.pl/sdm).

You can use the username — anonymous — and your e-mail as the password. The files will be zipped, so you can use WinZip to unzip them.

Please set yourself up with a free Cisco CCO account (via Cisco's home page) before you attempt to download SDM. You will need to use the e-mail address associated with your CCO account to download SDM.

Step 1: Access the above Web page. Make sure you install the latest version available and in the correct language.

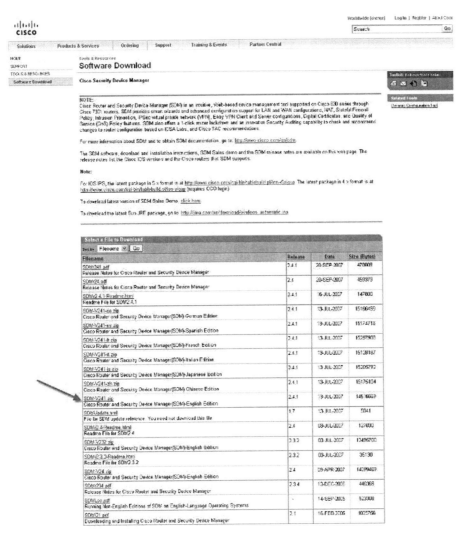

Figure 11–2: Step 1

Step 2: Click on the file and then confirm you have the correct image by clicking "Next".

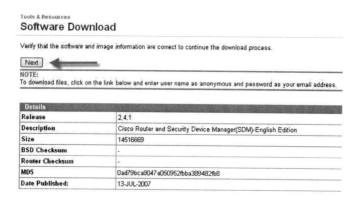

Figure 11–3: Step 2

Step 3: Accept the license agreement.

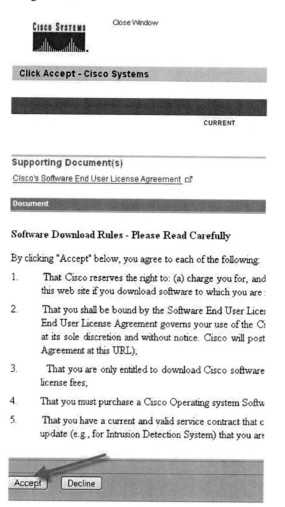

Figure 11–4: Step 3

Step 4: Enter the User Name "anonymous" and password.

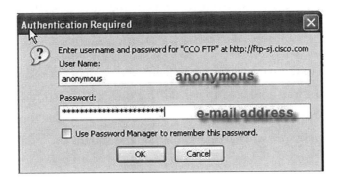

Figure 11–5: Step 4

Step 5: Download the zipped file.

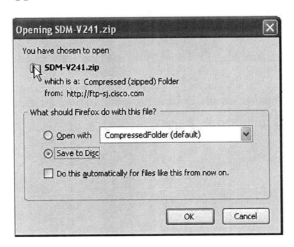

Figure 11–6: Step 5

Because SDM is a graphical tool, it is better for you to download it and use it yourself rather than look at endless screenshots. The video section of www.HowToNetwork.net has SDM videos or, if you have access to YouTube, you can subscribe to my videos there. Here is the URL for the SDM tour video: http://www.youtube.com/watch?v=7BeYUMw3Q8M.

THE END?

Congratulations on getting this far. Studying for and passing the CCNA is a hard process for all but the few gifted engineers who seem to pick things up effortlessly with hardly any study at all.

If you follow the advice in these pages, on the website, and in Appendix A, you will pass the exam. Aim for at least two to three hours study per day for one to two months. Unlike may other IT certifications, you have to actually know stuff to pass the CCNA. Be glad though because when you get the certificate you know you will have earned it fair and square.

If I can do anything to help you please drop me a line. Please let me know when you pass so I can pass the good news on to help inspire other students.

Look at your CCNA as another notch on your belt. I sincerely hope that you go onto take other exams whether they be Cisco CCNP, security, or anything else you choose. Help others in need when you hear that they are studying. Please recommend my website and books to them.

If you can see any way to improve on what I have done so far, then let me know. I'm far from perfect and so is this book, but I'm aiming to get it there.

Best wishes,

Paul Browning — October 2009

help@howtonetwork.net

SUMMARY QUESTIONS

1. Will SDM run on your 2950 switch?
2. Where can SDM software run?
3. Which commands will enable http and https on your router?
4. Which router privilege level needs to be enabled in order to run SDM?
5. Can you view the routers' show run from SDM?
6. Your router has 5 Mb free memory. Can you install SDM onto it?
7. What software needs to be present on your PC to run SDM?

PART 2

Labs

CHAPTER 12

Module 2 Labs

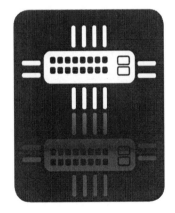

LAB 1: CHANGING THE CONFIG-REGISTER

Purpose

Knowing how to change a router's configuration register is a vital skill for any Cisco engineer. If you want to perform a password recovery or reset the router to factory defaults, then you will need to know how to change the config-register (from memory). Leave your router at 0x2142 so you have to practice a config from start to finish every time.

This lab was performed on a Cisco 2500. If you are using a different model, you may need to follow slightly different steps. Search Google for "Cisco changing config register" to check for your model.

"^Z" indicates that you should hold down the Ctrl and Z keys at the same time.

Lab objectives

1. Connect to the console port.
2. Enter privileged mode (enable mode).
3. Enter global configuration mode.
4. Change the config-register setting.
5. Exit to privileged mode.
6. Check the config-register setting with the "show version" command.
7. Reload the router.

Lab walk-through

1. From user exec mode go into privileged exec mode:

```
Router>enable
Router#
```

2. Check the config-register settings (your output will be slightly different from the one below due to there being different models of router and IOS). You will need to press the spacebar once to get to the bottom of the "show version" output:

```
Router#show version

Cisco Internetwork Operating System Software
IOS (tm) 2500 Software (C2500-JS-L), Version 12.1(17), RELEASE SOFTWARE
(fc1)
Copyright (c) 1986-2002 by cisco Systems, Inc.
Compiled Wed 04-Sep-02 03:08 by kellythw
```

```
Image text-base: 0x03073F40, data-base: 0x00001000

ROM: System Bootstrap, Version 11.0(10c)XB2, PLATFORM SPECIFIC RELEASE
SOFTWARE (fc1)
BOOTLDR: 3000 Bootstrap Software (IGS-BOOT-R), Version 11.0(10c)XB2,
PLATFORM SPECIFIC RELEASE SOFTWARE (fc1)

Router uptime is 12 minutes
System returned to ROM by reload
System image file is "flash:c2500-js-l.121-17.bin"

cisco 2500 (68030) processor (revision L) with 14336K/2048K bytes of
memory.
Processor board ID 01760497, with hardware revision 00000000
Bridging software.
X.25 software, Version 3.0.0.
SuperLAT software (copyright 1990 by Meridian Technology Corp).
TN3270 Emulation software.
2 Ethernet/IEEE 802.3 interface(s)
2 Serial network interface(s)
32K bytes of non-volatile configuration memory.
16384K bytes of processor board System flash (Read ONLY)

Configuration register is 0x2102
```

3. Enter config mode:

```
Router#configure terminal ⇦ Or "config t" for short
Router(config)#
```

4. Change the config-register setting:

```
Router(config)#config-register 0x2142 ⇦ Tells router to ignore
                                           the startup config
Router(config)#exit
```

5. Check the config-register setting:

```
Router#show version

Cisco Internetwork Operating System Software
IOS (tm) 2500 Software (C2500-JS-L), Version 12.1(17), RELEASE SOFTWARE
(fc1)
Copyright (c) 1986-2002 by cisco Systems, Inc.
Compiled Wed 04-Sep-02 03:08 by kellythw
Image text-base: 0x03073F40, data-base: 0x00001000

ROM: System Bootstrap, Version 11.0(10c)XB2, PLATFORM SPECIFIC RELEASE
SOFTWARE (fc1)
BOOTLDR: 3000 Bootstrap Software (IGS-BOOT-R), Version 11.0(10c)XB2,
PLATFORM SPECIFIC RELEASE SOFTWARE (fc1)
```

```
RouterA uptime is 12 minutes
System returned to ROM by reload
System image file is "flash:c2500-js-l.121-17.bin"

cisco 2500 (68030) processor (revision L) with 14336K/2048K bytes of
memory.
Processor board ID 01760497, with hardware revision 00000000
Bridging software.
X.25 software, Version 3.0.0.
SuperLAT software (copyright 1990 by Meridian Technology Corp).
TN3270 Emulation software.
2 Ethernet/IEEE 802.3 interface(s)
2 Serial network interface(s)
32K bytes of non-volatile configuration memory.
16384K bytes of processor board System flash (Read ONLY)

Configuration register is 0x2102 (will be 0x2142 at next reload)
```

6. Reload the router:

```
Router#
Router#reload

System configuration has been modified. Save? [yes/no]: n  ⇐ Put "no"
                                                    or "n" here
Proceed with reload? [confirm]  ⇐ Press Enter here

00:14:47: %SYS-5-RELOAD: Reload requested
System Bootstrap, Version 11.0(10c)XB2, PLATFORM SPECIFIC RELEASE SOFTWARE
(fc1)
```

The reload may take a few minutes so be patient. Press Enter every few seconds to see if you have a prompt.

7. You will be asked if you want to enter config dialog. Enter "n" for "no".

```
--- System Configuration Dialog ---

Would you like to enter the initial configuration dialog? [yes/no]: n
```

*Note: A CCNA will never use initial configuration mode. It is far too time consuming and is unlikely to produce the configuration you need.

8. The router has no config; hence the "Router>" prompt. Check the config-register setting now (you will need to use the spacebar again):

```
Router>enable
Router#show version
Cisco Internetwork Operating System Software
IOS (tm) 2500 Software (C2500-JS-L), Version 12.1(17), RELEASE SOFTWARE
(fc1)
Copyright (c) 1986-2002 by cisco Systems, Inc.
```

```
Compiled Wed 04-Sep-02 03:08 by kellythw
Image text-base: 0x03073F40, data-base: 0x00001000

ROM: System Bootstrap, Version 11.0(10c)XB2, PLATFORM SPECIFIC RELEASE
SOFTWARE (fc1)
BOOTLDR: 3000 Bootstrap Software (IGS-BOOT-R), Version 11.0(10c)XB2,
PLATFORM SPECIFIC RELEASE SOFTWARE (fc1)

Router uptime is 3 minutes
System returned to ROM by reload
System image file is "flash:c2500-js-1.121-17.bin"

cisco 2500 (68030) processor (revision L) with 14336K/2048K bytes of
memory.
Processor board ID 01760497, with hardware revision 00000000
Bridging software.
X.25 software, Version 3.0.0.
SuperLAT software (copyright 1990 by Meridian Technology Corp).
TN3270 Emulation software.
2 Ethernet/IEEE 802.3 interface(s)
2 Serial network interface(s)
32K bytes of non-volatile configuration memory.
16384K bytes of processor board System flash (Read ONLY)
Configuration register is 0x2142
```

If you reload the router now it will continue to skip the start up config file until you reset the config-register back to 0x2102.

LAB 2: BASIC LAB — ROUTER MODES AND COMMANDS

The physical topology is as shown in Figure 12–1.

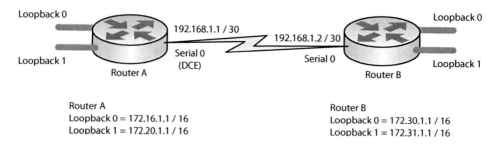

Figure 12–1: Physical topology

Purpose

Any person new to configuring Cisco routers needs to feel comfortable navigating around the various router features and modes. This lab will be a great icebreaker for a budding CCNA.

Lab objectives

1. Connect to the console port.
2. Enter privileged mode (enable mode).
3. Enter global configuration mode (config mode).
4. Enter the interface configuration mode.
5. Enter the routing configuration mode (router mode).
6. Exit to privileged mode.
7. Execute some useful commands.
8. Exit to user exec mode.
9. Interface statistics.
10. Change router hostname.

Lab walk-through

When connecting to the console of the router, you will typically see the following message:

```
Router con0 is now available

Press RETURN to get started.
```

As instructed, you simply need to press the Enter key and you will enter the first mode of the router, user exec mode:

```
Router>
```

11. Now you are in user exec mode. You will next need to enter privileged mode, or enable mode as it is more commonly known. To do this type:

```
Router>enable
```

You will now be presented with a new prompt that has a hash (#) sign instead of the greater than (>) sign:

```
Router>enable
Router#
```

Enable mode is used to perform all the show and debug commands: these will be explained further later in the lab.

12. The next mode to enter is global configuration mode, or config mode as it is also known. To enter config mode type:

```
Router#config terminal
```

As you will soon learn, all the commands in the Cisco IOS (operating system) can be abbreviated, e.g., you could have entered:

```
Router#config t
```

If you just type "config" and press Enter you will receive the following:

```
Router#config
Configuring from terminal, memory, or network [terminal]?
```

As you will see terminal is the default (indicated by the square brackets, [ ]), so you can simply press Enter to go into config or privileged mode.

13. Once in config mode you will be prompted with the following message:

```
Router#config terminal
```

Enter configuration commands, one per line. End with Ctrl+Z.

```
Router(config)#
```

This is telling you that when you have finished in config mode, type Ctrl+Z to exit (while holding the Ctrl key down, press the Z key).

Once in config mode, you will have noticed the prompt changed again, this time from "Router#" to "Router(config)#" indicating that you are in config mode. There are sub-layers to config mode, but we are only interested in two of them, the first being interface config mode:

```
Router(config)#interface fast ethernet 0 ⇐ Or loopback 0 if your
                               router does not have an Ethernet interface
Router(config-if)#
```

If you are not sure which interfaces you have on your router, you can look at the back or use the "show ip interface brief" command at the "Router#" prompt. If you do not have an Ethernet interface, replace the above with "interface loopback 0".

You will see that the prompt has changed again: the "-if" tells you that you are now in interface configuration mode:

```
Router(config)#interface fast ethernet 0
Router(config-if)#
```

14. The second sublayer to config mode we will be concerned with is the router configuration mode:

```
Router(config)#interface fastethernet 0 ⇐ Use loopback 0 if your
                               router does not have an Ethernet 0
Router(config-if)#exit
Router(config)#router rip
Router(config-router)#
```

You will see that when you exit from interface configuration mode and type "router rip", you enter router config mode. You can see that the prompt has changed again to reflect this.

15. To exit config mode and go back to privileged (enable) mode you simply need to type:

```
Router(config-if)#^Z ⇐ Hold down the "Ctrl" and "Z" keys (together)
Router#
```

When you do this, you will get the following message displayed after a few seconds:

```
Router(config-if)#^Z
Router#
%SYS-5-CONFIG_I: Configured from console by console
Router#
```

16. Now that we are back in enable mode, we can use some useful show commands. The common ones to use are:

```
Router#show ip interface brief
RouterA#show ip int brief
Interface  IP-Address   OK?   Method Status            Protocol

Loopback0 172.16.1.1    YES   manual up                up

Serial0 192.168.1.1     YES   manual up                up

Serial1 unassigned      YES   unset  administratively down down
```

The benefit of this command is that it shows the status and IP addresses of all interfaces in a table. Do not worry if your output is different from the one above.

The next command that is useful is "show running-configuration", which will display the current configuration (yours may look different from the one below). The output will be cut short so you can see it all on your monitor. You can press the Enter key to go through it line by line or press the spacebar to scroll up a page at a time:

```
Router#show running-config
or
Router#show run  ⇔ Abbreviated command

Router#
Router#show run
Building configuration...

Current configuration:
!
version 12.0
service log backtrace
service timestamps debug uptime
service timestamps log uptime
no service password-encryption
!
hostname Router
!
ip subnet-zero
!
interface Ethernet0
 no ip address
 shutdown
!
interface Serial0
 no ip address
 shutdown
!
interface Serial1
 no ip address
```

```
 no ip directed-broadcast
 shutdown
!
line con 0
!
line aux 0
!
line vty 0 4
!
end

Router#
```

Type "show version".

```
Router#show version
Cisco Internetwork Operating System Software
IOS (tm) 2500 Software (C2500-IK8OS-L), Version 12.2(7a), RELEASE SOFTWARE
(fc2)
Copyright (c) 1986-2002 by cisco Systems, Inc.
Compiled Wed 20-Feb-02 23:44 by pwade
Image text-base: 0x0306C4A8, data-base: 0x00001000
ROM: System Bootstrap, Version 11.0(10c)XB2, PLATFORM SPECIFIC RELEASE
SOFTWARE (fc1)
BOOTLDR: 3000 Bootstrap Software (IGS-BOOT-R), Version 11.0(10c)XB2,
PLATFORM SPECIFIC RELEASE SOFTWARE (fc1)

Router uptime is 1 week, 2 days, 40 minutes
System returned to ROM by power-on
System image file is "flash:c2500-js.bin"
cisco 2500 (68030) processor (revision L) with 14336K/2048K bytes of
memory.
Processor board ID 15743551, with hardware revision 00000000
Bridging software.
X.25 software, Version 3.0.0.
2 Ethernet/IEEE 802.3 interface(s)
2 Serial network interface(s)
32K bytes of non-volatile configuration memory.
16384K bytes of processor board System flash (Read ONLY)
Configuration register is 0x2102
```

17. To exit to the user exec mode, you simply need to type "disable" (opposite of "enable"):

```
Router#disable
Router>enable
Router#
```

18. You can also examine the interface statistics. The most relevant statistics are in bold.

```
Router#show interface serial 0
Serial0 is administratively down, line protocol is down
```

```
Hardware is HD64570
MTU 1500 bytes, BW 1544 Kbit, DLY 20000 usec,
    reliability 255/255, txload 1/255, rxload 1/255
Encapsulation HDLC, loopback not set
Keepalive set (10 sec)
Last input never, output never, output hang never
Last clearing of "show interface" counters never
Input queue: 0/75/0/0 (size/max/drops/flushes); Total output drops: 0
Queueing strategy: weighted fair
Output queue: 0/1000/64/0 (size/max total/threshold/drops)
    Conversations  0/0/256 (active/max active/max total)
    Reserved Conversations 0/0 (allocated/max allocated)
    Available Bandwidth 1158 kilobits/sec
5 minute input rate 0 bits/sec, 0 packets/sec
5 minute output rate 0 bits/sec, 0 packets/sec
    0 packets input, 0 bytes, 0 no buffer
    Received 0 broadcasts, 0 runts, 0 giants, 0 throttles
    0 input errors, 0 CRC, 0 frame, 0 overrun, 0 ignored, 0 abort
    0 packets output, 0 bytes, 0 underruns
    0 output errors, 0 collisions, 1 interface resets
    0 output buffer failures, 0 output buffers swapped out
    0 carrier transitions
    DCD=down  DSR=down  DTR=down  RTS=down  CTS=down
```

19. You can change the hostname of the router:

```
Router#config
Configuring from terminal, memory, or network [terminal]? ⇐ Press
                                                            Enter
Enter configuration commands, one per line. End with CNTL/Z.
Router(config)#hostname RouterA
RouterA(config)#
```

20. Now reload the router: do not save any changes.
```
Router#reload
```

CHAPTER 13

Module 3 Labs

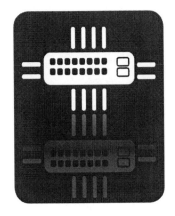

LAB 1: VLANS ON AN IOS (2950) SWITCH

The physical topology is as shown in Figure 13–1.

192.168.1.1 / 24

192.168.1.2 / 24

Router A

Router B

Fast
Ethernet

Fast
Ethernet

Ethernet 0

Ethernet 0

Figure 13–1: IOS VLANs

Lab exercise

Your task is to configure the network in Figure Figure 13–1. All the router interfaces on the switch and router are in VLAN 2. If you use 2500 series routers, you will need to attach a transceiver to the AUI interface in order to attach the Ethernet cable. If you do not wish to use routers, you can use PCs and configure the IP address on the Ethernet card instead. Any switch running IOS will do for this lab.

Purpose

Creating VLANs on an IOS switch is one of the core competencies of a Cisco engineer. Make sure you are very familiar with doing this.

Lab objectives

1. Configure the switch to use VLAN 2 name "Cisco".
2. Place two interfaces on the switch in VLAN 2.
3. Configure the routers' interfaces.
4. Ping across the LAN on VLAN 2.

Lab walk-through

1. To configure the IP address on the routers do the following:

```
Router>enable
Router#
Router#configure terminal
Router(config)#hostname RouterA
RouterA(config)#interface fast ethernet 0
RouterA(config)#ip address 192.168.1.1 255.255.255.0
RouterA(config-if)#no shut
RouterA(config-if)#^Z
RouterA#
Router B:
```

```
Router>enable
Router#config t
Router#hostname RouterB
RouterB(config)#interface fast ethernet 0
RouterB(config)#ip address 192.168.1.2 255.255.255.0
RouterB(config-if)#no shut
RouterB(config-if)#^Z
RouterB#
```

If you have plugged directly into the switch, you will be able to ping from router to router or switch to switch. This is because the switch will use VLAN 1 by default.

```
RouterA#ping 192.168.1.2
Type escape sequence to abort.
Sending 5, 100-byte ICMP Echos to 192.168.1.2, timeout is 2 seconds:
!!!!!
Success rate is 100 percent (5/5), round-trip min/avg/max = 4/4/4 ms
RouterA#
```

2. To configure both the routers to connect to VLAN 2 on the switch, enter the following commands:

```
Switch#config t
Switch(config)#vlan 2 ⇐ Create VLAN 2
Switch(config-vlan)#name Cisco
Switch(config-vlan)#^z
Switch#
```

3. To configure the interfaces on the switch to use VLAN 2, use the following commands.

```
Switch#config t
Enter configuration commands, one per line. End with CNTL/Z.
Switch(config)#interface fastethernet 0/1
Switch(config-if)#

Switch(config-if)#description ToRouterA ⇐ Set the description.
Switch(config-if)#switchport mode access ⇐ On, by default
Switch(config-if)#switchport access vlan 2 ⇐ Add to VLAN 2.
Switch(config-if)#^Z
```

4. We can try to ping from router B to router A now. Since we have only put one interface into VLAN 2 (router A), the second (router B) remains in VLAN 1 (by default).

```
RouterB#ping 192.168.1.1

Type escape sequence to abort.
Sending 5, 100-byte ICMP Echos to 192.168.1.1, timeout is 2 seconds:
.....
Success rate is 0 percent (0/5)
```

5. We now put the Ethernet interface connecting to router B into VLAN 2.

```
Switch#config t
Enter configuration commands, one per line. End with CNTL/Z.
Switch(config)#interface fastethernet 0/3
Switch(config-if)#description ToRouterB
Switch(config-if)#switchport mode access ⇐ You can omit this.
Switch(config-if)#switchport access vlan 2
Switch(config-if)#^Z
```

6. We can now ping across the LAN from router A to router B. The first one or two pings will fail until the switch has built up a database of which MAC addresses are connected to which ports.

```
RouterA#ping 192.168.1.2

Type escape sequence to abort.
Sending 5, 100-byte ICMP Echos to 192.168.1.2, timeout is 2 seconds:
.....
Success rate is 0 percent (0/5)
RouterA#ping 192.168.1.2

Type escape sequence to abort.
Sending 5, 100-byte ICMP Echos to 192.168.1.2, timeout is 2 seconds:
.!!!!
Success rate is 80 percent (4/5), round-trip min/avg/max = 4/4/4 ms
RouterA#ping 192.168.1.2

Type escape sequence to abort.
Sending 5, 100-byte ICMP Echos to 192.168.1.2, timeout is 2 seconds:
!!!!!
Success rate is 100 percent (5/5), round-trip min/avg/max = 4/4/4 ms
RouterA#
```

7. Reload the switch.

```
Switch#erase ?
  flash:           Filesystem to be erased
  nvram:           Filesystem to be erased
  startup-config   Erase contents of configuration memory

Switch#erase start
Erasing the nvram filesystem will remove all files! Continue? [confirm]
[OK]
Erase of nvram: complete
Switch#reload

System configuration has been modified. Save? [yes/no]: n
Proceed with reload? [confirm]
```

Show runs

```
RouterA#
RouterA#show run
Building configuration...

Current configuration : 428 bytes
!
version 12.1
no service single-slot-reload-enable
service timestamps debug uptime
service timestamps log uptime
no service password-encryption
!
hostname RouterA
!
ip subnet-zero
!
interface fastethernet 0
  ip address 192.168.1.1 255.255.255.0
!
interface Serial0
 no ip address
 shutdown
!
interface Serial1
 no ip address
 shutdown
!
ip classless
no ip http server
!
line con 0
line aux 0
line vty 0 4
!
end

 - - -

RouterB#show run
Building configuration...

Current configuration : 428 bytes
!
version 12.1
no service single-slot-reload-enable
service timestamps debug uptime
service timestamps log uptime
no service password-encryption
!
hostname RouterB
```

```
!
ip subnet-zero
!
interface fastethernet 0
 ip address 192.168.1.2 255.255.255.0
!
interface Serial0
 no ip address
 shutdown
!
interface Serial1
 no ip address
 shutdown
!
ip classless
no ip http server
!
line con 0
line aux 0
line vty 0 4
!
end

RouterB#


- - -


Switch

Switch#
Switch#show run
Building configuration...

Current configuration:
!
version 12.0
no service pad
service timestamps debug uptime
service timestamps log uptime
no service password-encryption
!
hostname Switch
!
ip subnet-zero
!
interface FastEthernet0/1
 description ToRouterA
 switchport access vlan 2
!
interface FastEthernet0/2
!
interface FastEthernet0/3
```

```
 description ToRouterB
 switchport access vlan 2
!
interface FastEthernet0/4
!
!
interface GigabitEthernet0/1
!
interface GigabitEthernet0/2
!
interface VLAN1
 no ip directed-broadcast
 no ip route-cache
!
!
line con 0
 transport input none
 stopbits 1
line vty 5 15
!
end
```

LAB 2: TRUNKING ACROSS IOS SWITCHES

Lab exercise

Your task is to configure the network in Figure 13–2. All the router interfaces on the switch and router are in VLAN 2. You will need two switches running Cisco IOS; we have used two 2950 switches.

If you do not want to keep swapping between switches, then follow the entire config for one 2950 switch. We have broken it down into smaller chunks to make the various stages more understandable.

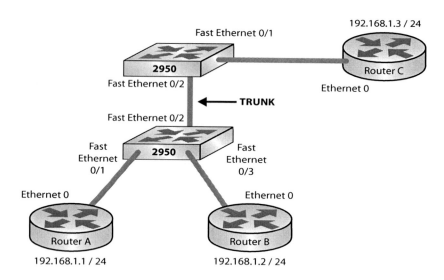

Figure 13–2: Trunking across switches

Purpose

Being able to trunk between switches is a necessary skill for a Cisco engineer.

Note: Do a "show run" on the switches to check which interfaces they have and which one you are plugged into. You can also go through the entire switch config in one go rather than in phases (as below) to save time.

Lab objectives

1. Configure the switch to use VLAN 2, name "Cisco".
2. Place two interfaces on the switch in VLAN 2 on the 2950 switch and one interface in VLAN 2 on the other 2950 switch.
3. Configure the routers' interfaces with the IP addresses as in Figure 13–2.
4. Ping across the LAN on VLAN 2.

Lab walk-through

1. To configure the IP address on the routers, do the following:

```
Router>enable
Router#
Router#configure terminal
Router(config)#hostname RouterA
RouterA(config)#interface fastethernet 0
RouterA(config-if)#ip address 192.168.1.1 255.255.255.0
RouterA(config-if)#no shut
RouterA(config-if)#^Z
RouterA#
Router B:
Router>enable
Router#config t
Router(config)#hostname RouterB
RouterB(config)#interface fastethernet 0
RouterB(config-if)#ip address 192.168.1.2 255.255.255.0
RouterB(config-if)#no shut
RouterB(config-if)#^Z
RouterB#
Router C:
Router>enable
Router#config t
Router(config)#hostname RouterC
RouterC(config)#interface fastethernet 0
RouterC(config-if)#ip address 192.168.1.3 255.255.255.0
RouterC(config-if)#no shut
RouterC(config-if)#^Z
RouterC#
```

If you have plugged directly into the switch, you will be able to ping from router A to router B and router C. This is because they are all in VLAN 1, by default. If you have just booted up the switch, it may take a few moments for the database to be built.

```
RouterB#ping 192.168.1.1

Type escape sequence to abort.
Sending 5, 100-byte ICMP Echos to 192.168.1.1, timeout is 2 seconds:
.....
Success rate is 0 percent (0/5)
RouterB#ping 192.168.1.1

Type escape sequence to abort.
Sending 5, 100-byte ICMP Echos to 192.168.1.1, timeout is 2 seconds:
..!!!
Success rate is 60 percent (3/5), round-trip min/avg/max = 4/4/4 ms
RouterB#ping 192.168.1.1

Type escape sequence to abort.
```

```
Sending 5, 100-byte ICMP Echos to 192.168.1.1, timeout is 2 seconds:
!!!!!
Success rate is 100 percent (5/5), round-trip min/avg/max = 4/4/4 ms
RouterB#
```

2. Configure VLAN 2 on the IOS switches.

```
Switch>
Switch>enable
Switch#config t
Enter configuration commands, one per line. End with CNTL/Z.
Switch(config)#hostname Top2950
Top2950(config)#^Z
Top2950(config)#vlan 2
Top2950(config-vlan)#name Cisco
Top2950(config-vlan)#^z
Now configure VLAN 2 on the bottom 2950:
Switch>
Switch>enable
Switch#config t
Enter configuration commands, one per line. End with CNTL/Z.
Switch(config)#hostname Bottom2950
Bottom2950(config)#vlan 2
Bottom2950(config-vlan)#name Cisco
Bottom2950(config-vlan)#^z
```

3. Put the relevant ports in VLAN 2 on each switch.

```
Top2950#config t
Top2950(config)#interface fast 0/1
Top2950(config-if)#switchport access vlan 2
Top2950(config-vlan)#^z
Top2950#
```

```
===
```

```
Bottom2950#config t
Bottom2950(config)#interface fast 0/1
Bottom2950(config-if)#switchport access vlan 2
Bottom2950(config-vlan)#int fast 0/3
Bottom2950(config-if)#switchport access vlan 2
Bottom2950(config-if)#^z
Bottom2950#
```

4. Turn trunking on—on the interfaces between the switches.

```
Bottom2950(config-if)#interface fastethernet 0/2
Bottom2950(config-if)#switchport mode trunk
Bottom2950(config)#exit
Bottom2950#
```

```
---
Top2950(config-if)#interface fastethernet 0/2
Top2950(config-if)#switchport mode trunk
Top2950(config)#exit
Top2950#
```

5. Ping from router C to router A.

```
RouterC#ping 192.168.1.1

Type escape sequence to abort.
Sending 5, 100-byte ICMP Echos to 192.168.1.1, timeout is 2 seconds:
.!!!! ⇐ one ping fails due to the ARP lookup
Success rate is 80 percent (4/5), round-trip min/avg/max = 4/4/4 ms
RouterC#ping 192.168.1.1

Type escape sequence to abort.
Sending 5, 100-byte ICMP Echos to 192.168.1.1, timeout is 2 seconds:
!!!!!
Success rate is 100 percent (5/5), round-trip min/avg/max = 4/6/8 ms
RouterC#
```

Show runs

```
RouterA#show run
Building configuration...

Current configuration : 428 bytes
!
version 12.1
no service single-slot-reload-enable
service timestamps debug uptime
service timestamps log uptime
no service password-encryption
!
hostname RouterA
!
ip subnet-zero
!
interface fastethernet
ip address 192.168.1.1 255.255.255.0
!
interface Serial0
no ip address
shutdown
!
interface Serial1
no ip address
shutdown
!
```

```
ip classless
no ip http server
!
line con 0
line aux 0
line vty 0 4
!
end

---


RouterB#show run
Building configuration...

Current configuration : 428 bytes
!
version 12.1
no service single-slot-reload-enable
service timestamps debug uptime
service timestamps log uptime
no service password-encryption
!
hostname RouterB
!
ip subnet-zero
!
interface fastethernet
ip address 192.168.1.2 255.255.255.0
!
interface Serial0
no ip address
shutdown
!
interface Serial1
no ip address
shutdown
!
ip classless
no ip http server
!
line con 0
line aux 0
line vty 0 4
!
end

---



RouterC#show run
Building configuration...
```

```
Current configuration:
!
version 12.0
no service pad
service timestamps debug uptime
service timestamps log uptime
no service password-encryption
!
hostname RouterC
!
ip subnet-zero
!
process-max-time 200
!
interface fastethernet0
ip address 192.168.1.3 255.255.255.0
no ip directed-broadcast
!
interface BRI0
no ip address
no ip directed-broadcast
shutdown
isdn guard-timer 0 on-expiry accept
!
no ip http server
ip classless
!
!
line con 0
transport input none
stopbits 1
line vty 0 4
!
end

RouterC#
```

Switch show runs (truncated)

```
Top 2950


2950#show run
Building configuration...

Current configuration:
!
version 12.0
no service pad
service timestamps debug uptime
service timestamps log uptime
no service password-encryption
```

```
!
hostname Top2950
!
ip subnet-zero
!
interface FastEthernet0/1
switchport access vlan 2
!
interface FastEthernet0/2
switchport mode trunk
!
interface FastEthernet0/3


====


2950#show run


Building configuration...

Current configuration:
!
version 12.0
no service pad
service timestamps debug uptime
service timestamps log uptime
no service password-encryption
!
hostname Bottom2950
!
ip subnet-zero
!
interface FastEthernet0/1
switchport access vlan 2
!
interface FastEthernet0/2
switchport mode trunk
!
interface FastEthernet0/3
switchport access vlan 2
```

LAB 3: PORT SECURITY

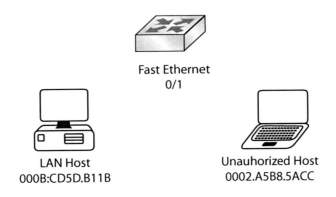

Fast Ethernet
0/1

LAN Host
000B:CD5D.B11B

Unauhorized Host
0002.A5B8.5ACC

Figure 13–3: Port Security

Lab exercise

A PC is connected directly to the fast Ethernet 0/1 interface of your switch. You apply port security permitting only the LAN Host to connect through the port and a static MAC address. If a violation is detected, then the port should be shut down. You plug in the unauthorized host to check the configuration is working correctly.

Purpose

Security is very crucial for any network. Layer 2 security will ensure that no one can compromise the security from inside the network. You will be expected to know how to configure port security for the CCNA exam.

Lab objectives

1. Enable Port Security on fa0/1 on the switch.
2. Configure a static MAC address for port security on fa0/1.
3. Configure violation action on switchport.
4. Test the port by connecting a different device.

Lab walk-through

1. Enable Port Security on `fa0/1` on the switch.

```
Switch#configure terminal
Switch(config)#interface fa0/1
Switch(config-if)#switchport port-security
```

(Note — the port you apply this command to must be an access and not trunk. If the interface is connected to another switch the switch may convert to trunk. The "`show interfaces trunk`" command will display your trunk interfaces:

```
Switch#show interfaces trunk

Port        Mode          Encapsulation   Status      Native vlan
Fa0/1       desirable     802.1q          trunking    1
```

If you attempt to apply the command to a non-access port you will see the below output.

```
Switch(config-if)#switchport port-security
Command rejected: Not eligible for secure port.
```

To set an interface into access mode please apply the command:

```
Switch#conf t
Enter configuration commands, one per line.  End with CNTL/Z.
Switch(config)#int fast 0/1
Switch(config-if)#switchport mode access
```

2. Configure a static MAC address for port security on `fa0/1`. This will be the MAC address we want to permit to pass traffic through the switch port. You will need to alter the MAC address for your own.

```
Switch(config-if)#switchport port-security mac-address 000b.cd5d.b11b
```

(Note — you have several other options here. You can set the maximum number of mac addresses permitted through the switch port, hard set the mac address and the action upon violation of your settings (see step 3):

```
Switch(config-if)#switchport port-security ?
  mac-address   Secure mac address
  maximum       Max secure addrs
  violation     Security Violation Mode
  <cr>
```

3. Configure violation action on switchport. You may choose from restrict (inform the network admin of the violation), shutdown or protect (only permit frames from the permitted devices.

```
Switch(config-if)#switchport port-security violation ?
  protect   Security violation protect mode
  restrict  Security violation restrict mode
  shutdown  Security violation shutdown mode
```

We are going to have the port shutdown when it detects a restriction.

```
Switch(config-if)#switchport port-security violation shutdown
```

4. Now plug the authorized host (LAN host) into your switchport fast ethernet 0/1. After about 30 seconds the switchport light will go from amber to green and show as up. You can then check the port security status with the "show port-security" command.

```
Switch#
00:40:32: %LINK-3-UPDOWN: Interface FastEthernet0/1, changed state to up
00:40:33: %LINEPROTO-5-UPDOWN: Line protocol on Interface FastEthernet0/1,
changed state to up
Switch#

Switch#show port-security int fast 0/1
Port Security               : Enabled
Port Status                 : Secure-up
Violation Mode              : Shutdown
Aging Time                  : 0 mins
Aging Type                  : Absolute
SecureStatic Address Aging  : Disabled
Maximum MAC Addresses       : 1
Total MAC Addresses         : 1
Configured MAC Addresses    : 1
Sticky MAC Addresses        : 0
Last Source Address         : 000b.cd5d.b11b
Security Violation Count    : 0
```

5. Unplug the authorized host and plug in the unauthorized host. Once frames reach the switch port it will be closed down.

```
Switch#
00:40:32: %LINK-3-UPDOWN: Interface FastEthernet0/1, changed state to up
00:40:33: %LINEPROTO-5-UPDOWN: Line protocol on Interface FastEthernet0/1,
changed state to up
Switch#
00:41:04: %PM-4-ERR_DISABLE: psecure-violation error detected on Fa0/1,
putting Fa0/1 in err-disable state
00:41:04: %PORT_SECURITY-2-PSECURE_VIOLATION: Security violation occurred,
caused by MAC address 0002.a5b8.5acc on port FastEthernet0/1.
00:41:05: %LINEPROTO-5-UPDOWN: Line protocol on Interface FastEthernet0/1,
changed state to down
```

6. The interface has been shutdown. You can now check the port security status.

```
Switch#show port-security int fast 0/1
Port Security              : Enabled
Port Status                : Secure-shutdown
Violation Mode             : Shutdown
Aging Time                 : 0 mins
Aging Type                 : Absolute
SecureStatic Address Aging : Disabled
Maximum MAC Addresses      : 1
Total MAC Addresses        : 1
Configured MAC Addresses   : 1
Sticky MAC Addresses       : 0
Last Source Address        : 0002.a5b8.5acc
Security Violation Count    : 1
```

7. To re-enable the interface plug the authorized host back in and then "shut" and "no shut" the fast Ethernet interface.

One last point. Please take some time to use the other port security commands. You can for example, permit a maximum number of MAC addresses through the port or choose a specific range of allowed addresses.

Running configuration

```
Switch1#sh run
Building configuration...
--output truncated--
hostname Switch
!
interface FastEthernet0/1
 switchport mode access
 switchport port-security
 switchport port-security violation shutdown
 switchport port-security mac-address 000b.cd5d.b11b
!
```

LAB 4: INTER-VLAN ROUTING

Lab exercise

Your task is to configure the network such that PC-A in VLAN 2 can ping PC-B in VLAN 3 across the switches. In the topology shown in Figure 13–4, you can always swap the PCs for routers and use the fast Ethernet interfaces to connect to the switches.

Purpose

This topology is known as a router on a stick. When you have VLANs on your network, they must each reside in their own subnet (please refer to the theory notes for more on that). In order for subnets to be able to communicate, you must have a router (higher-level switches can usually perform routing functions, but this is outside the scope of the CCNA).

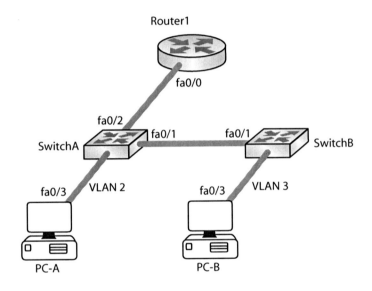

Figure 13–4: Inter VLAN Routing

Vlan 2 – 192.168.2.0/24, PC-A 192.168.2.2/24

Vlan 3 – 192.168.3.0/24, PC-B 192.168.3.2/24

Because you may have only one available fast Ethernet interface on your router, you will need to divide the physical interface into logical sub-interfaces. For example, if your router interface is fast Ethernet 0/0, then the sub-interface would be 0/0.1. It is common practice to name your sub-interface to match your VLANs. So, you would name the sub-interface for VLAN 2 — fast Ethernet 0/0.2.

In order to use the router Ethernet interface as a trunk connection to the switches the encapsulation type must be set to dot1q. Depending upon your model of switch, this may be your only encapsulation choice so the encapsulation command may not work (this applies to 2950 model switches).

One last note, in the above lab you may swap PCs for fast Ethernet interfaces on routers. You will need to add static routes on the routers though (see below).

Lab objectives

1. Configure SwitchA to trunk with SwitchB and Router1 using 802.1q
2. Configure SwitchB to trunk to SwitchA using 802.1q
3. Configure port `fa0/3` to be in the correct VLANs on both switches
4. Configure Router1's `fa0/0` interface with two sub-interfaces in the correct VLANs and with correct IP addresses (`.1` in respective subnets)
5. Configure the PCs with respective Gateway addresses (address of the sub-interface on Router1)
6. Ping from PC-A to PC-B.

Lab walk-through

1. To configure SwitchA for trunking on relevant ports. We need trunking ports because they can carry multiple VLAN information. Do the following:

```
Switch#configure terminal
Switch#(config)#hostname SwitchA
SwitchA(config)#interface range fa0/1 - 2
SwitchA(config-if-range)#switchport trunk encapsulation dot1q
SwitchA(config-if-range)#switchport mode trunk
```

Please note — you need a space between the interface numbers if you are using the range command and the command may not work if your IOS version does not support it. If you are using different model switches, your interfaces may show as 1/1, etc. Also, the encapsulation dot1q will not work if you are using a 2950 model switch because it can only use dot1q.

You can check encapsulation type with the "show interface trunk" command.

```
Switch#show interface trunk

Port      Mode        Encapsulation  Status      Native vlan
Fa1/2     on          802.1q         trunking    1
```

2. To configure SwitchB for trunking, do the following:

```
Switch#config t
Switch#(config)#hostname SwitchB
SwitchB(config)#int fa0/1
SwitchB(config-if)#switchport trunk encapsulation dot1q
SwitchB(config-if)#switchport mode trunk
```

(Please note — you should not need the encapsulation command on 2950 switches because this is the default).

3. Access ports are used to connect hosts to the switch. They should actually be access ports by default, but it is useful to know the command. To configure the access ports, do the following.

```
SwitchA(config)#interface fa0/3
SwitchA(config-if)#switchport mode access
SwitchA(config-if)#switchport access vlan 2

SwitchB(config)#interface fa0/3
SwitchB(config-if)#switchport mode access
SwitchB(config-if)#switchport access vlan 3
```

Please note — we have put the interfaces into the respective VLANs 2 and 3 with the above commands. Also, if VLAN 2 or 3 is not already created on the switch you may see:

```
SwitchB(config-if)#switchport access vlan 2
% Access VLAN does not exist. Creating vlan 2
```

You can see from earlier labs that we create vlans with the: "Switch(config)#vlan 2" command.

4. To configure the router port, we need to add sub-interfaces and configure dot1q encapsulation so the interface can trunk the VLANs. Do the following:

```
Router#config t
Router(config)#hostname Router1
Router1(config)#interface fa0/0
Router1(config-if)#no shut
Router1(config-if)#interface fa0/0.2
Router1(config-subif)#encapsulation dot1q 2
Router1(config-subif)#ip address 192.168.2.1 255.255.255.0
Router1(config-subif)#interface fa0/0.3
Router1(config-subif)#encapsulation dot1q 3
Router1(config-subif)#ip address 192.168.3.1 255.255.255.0
```

(Please note — interface fa0/0.2 is used for VLAN 2. We have also added the correct VLAN number after the "dot1q" command. You can see the output the router expects below.)

```
Router1(config-subif)#encap dot1q ?
  <1-4095>  IEEE 802.1Q VLAN ID required, range 1 - 0xFFF.
```

5. (Optional) Depending on the Operating System of the PCs, configure their gateway to be 192.168.2.1 and 192.168.3.1, respectively.

In this example, I have used the switching rack at http://racks.howtonetwork.net and used two routers (connected to switches A and B) fast ethernet interfaces instead of PCs. They are only required to prove that the VLANs can communicate. Fast Ethernet 0/0 on RouterA is given an IP address within VLAN 2 and RouterB in VLAN 3. If you do use routers, please remember to add a static route, e.g., on the Router with IP add 192.168.3.2 add static route 0.0.0.0 0.0.0.0 192.168.3.1.

```
Router(config)#hostname RouterA
RouterA(config)#int fast 0/0
RouterA(config-if)#ip add 192.168.2.2 255.255.255.0
RouterA(config-if)#no shut
RouterA(config-if)#^Z
RouterA#
```

```
Router(config)#hostname RouterB
RouterB(config)#int fast 0/0
RouterB(config-if)#ip add 192.168.3.2 255.255.255.0
RouterB(config-if)#no shut
RouterB(config-if)#^Z
RouterB#
```

6. Now ping 192.168.3.2 from PC-A (or RouterA if you are using routers):

```
RouterA#ping 192.168.3.2

Type escape sequence to abort.
Sending 5, 100-byte ICMP Echos to 192.168.3.2, timeout is 2 seconds:
!!!!!
```

Success rate is 100 percent (5/5), round-trip min/avg/max = 1/2/4 ms

```
Router#
```

(Please note — I do not know which model of switch you will use for this lab, so it may work slightly differently for you. For mine, I had to set both my switches to VTP server, erase the vlan.dat file, and set up a VTP domain between the switches with the commands:

```
SwitchB#vlan database
SwitchB(vlan)#vtp domain howtonetwork

Running Configuration
Router1#sh run
Building configuration...
```

```
--output truncated--
hostname Router1
!
interface FastEthernet0/0
 no ip address
 duplex auto
 speed auto
!
interface FastEthernet0/0.2
 encapsulation dot1Q 2
 ip address 192.168.2.1 255.255.255.0
!
interface FastEthernet0/0.3
 encapsulation dot1Q 3
 ip address 192.168.3.1 255.255.255.0
!

SwitchA#sh run
Building configuration...

--output truncated--
hostname SwitchA
!
interface FastEthernet1/0
!
interface FastEthernet1/1
 switchport mode trunk
!
interface FastEthernet1/2
 switchport mode trunk
!
interface FastEthernet1/3
switchport mode access
switchport access vlan 2
!

SwitchB#sh run
Building configuration...

--output truncated--
hostname SwitchB
!
interface FastEthernet1/0
!
interface FastEthernet1/1
 switchport mode trunk
!
interface FastEthernet1/2
!
interface FastEthernet1/3
switchport mode access
switchport access vlan 3
!
```

LAB 5: STP ELECTION

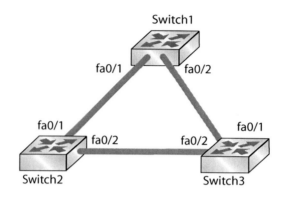

Figure 13–5: STP election
VLAN 2 and 3 exist on all switches.

Lab exercise

Your task is to configure the above network so that Switch2 is always the Root Bridge for VLAN 2 and Switch3 is the Root Bridge for VLAN 3. You will need to connect the three switches together with crossover cables.

Purpose

STP is a very important topic for the CCNA exam and you can expect to be tested on both your theoretical knowledge and hands on ability. For this lab you will configure the switches to ensure that the correct switch in the Root Bridge. In the real world, if the incorrect Switch becomes the Root Bridge, the network will experience delays.

Lab objectives

1. Configure Ports `fa0/1` and `fa0/2` on all switches as 802.1q trunks (default on 2950 switches).
2. Create VLAN 2 and VLAN 3 on all the switches.
3. Configure Bridge Priority on Switch2 and Switch3 for VLAN 2 and VLAN 3, respectively.

Lab walk-through

1. Let's first check the status of the switches. The VTP domain name should match. We will also want to check if any interfaces are already trunking. We will check the outputs on Switch1. You can do the same on Switch2 and Switch3.

```
Switch1#sh vtp status
VTP Version                 : 2
Configuration Revision      : 1
```

```
Maximum VLANs supported locally : 250
Number of existing VLANs         : 10
VTP Operating Mode               : Server
VTP Domain Name                  : howtonetwork
VTP Pruning Mode                 : Disabled
VTP V2 Mode                      : Enabled
VTP Traps Generation             : Disabled
MD5 digest                       : 0xB7 0xE3 0x3A 0x57 0x1D 0x41 0x42 0x40
Configuration last modified by 0.0.0.0 at 3-1-93 01:11:38
Local updater ID is 0.0.0.0 (no valid interface found)

Switch1#show interface trunk

Port       Mode        Encapsulation Status      Native vlan
Fa0/1      desirable   802.1q        trunking    1

Port       Vlans allowed on trunk
Fa0/1      1-4094

Port       Vlans allowed and active in management domain
Fa0/1      1-2,13,100,111,250

Port       Vlans in spanning tree forwarding state and not pruned
Fa0/1      2,13,100,111,250
Switch1#
```

You can see that the VTP domain name is "howtonetwork" and that the only trunking interface on the switch is fast 0/1. Please set all the switches to the same VTP domain name with either the legacy commands or the modern commands. Please also make sure all switches are set to VTP server (this should be the default but another user may have changed this).

Legacy:

```
Switch#vlan database
Switch(vlan)#vtp domain howtonetwork
```

Modern:

```
Switch(config)#vtp domain howtonetwork
```

And server commands:

```
Switch2(config)#vtp mode ?
  client      Set the device to client mode.
  server      Set the device to server mode.
  transparent Set the device to transparent mode.
```

2. To configure the switches for trunking on relevant ports, follow the below commands. You will not be able to enter the encapsulation command on a 2950 because it is dot1q, by default:

```
Switch#configure terminal
Switch1(config)#hostname Switch1
Switch1(config)#interface range fa0/1 - 2
Switch1(config-if-range)#switchport trunk encapsulation dot1q
Switch1(config-if-range)#switchport mode trunk

Switch#configure terminal
Switch1(config)#hostname Switch2
Switch2(config)#interface range fa0/1 - 2
Switch2(config-if-range)#switchport trunk encapsulation dot1q
Switch2(config-if-range)#switchport mode trunk

Switch#configure terminal
Switch1(config)#hostname Switch3
Switch3(config)#interface range fa0/1 - 2
Switch3(config-if-range)#switchport trunk encapsulation dot1q
Switch3(config-if-range)#switchport mode trunk
```

Please note — your ports on a 2950 may be numbered 1/1, 1/2, and so on. You can miss off the encapsulation command on the 2950. The range command may not work on your switch if it has an older IOS release so you will have to set the configs per interface.

You can now check which interfaces are set to trunking:

```
Switch1#sh int trunk

Port        Mode      Encapsulation  Status      Native vlan
Fa0/1       on        802.1q         trunking    1
Fa0/2       on        802.1q         trunking    1
```

3. To create VLANs on all switches:

```
Switch1(config)#vlan 2,3
Switch2(config)#vlan 2,3
Switch3(config)#vlan 2,3
```

You should then be able to see that VLANs 2 and 3 are part of the spanning tree:

```
Switch1#show interface trunk

Port        Mode      Encapsulation  Status      Native vlan
Fa0/1       on        802.1q         trunking    1
Fa0/2       on        802.1q         trunking    1
```

```
Port              Vlans allowed on trunk
Fa0/1             1-4094
Fa0/2             1-4094

Port              Vlans allowed and active in management domain
Fa0/1             1-3,13,100,111,250
Fa0/2             1-3,13,100,111,250

Port              Vlans in spanning tree forwarding state and not pruned
Fa0/1             1-3,13,100,111,250
Fa0/2             1-3,13,100,111,250
Switch1#
```

4. Check the switches to see which is the Root Bridge for VLANs 2 and 3. Some of the output is omitted and, of course, your output will be different due to MAC address numbers.

```
Switch2#show spanning-tree vlan 2

VLAN0002
  Spanning tree enabled protocol ieee
  Root ID    Priority    32768
             Address     0009.7c87.9081
             Cost        19
             Port        1 (FastEthernet0/1)
             Hello Time  2 sec  Max Age 20 sec   Forward Delay 15 sec

  Bridge ID  Priority    32770  (priority 32768 sys-id-ext 2)
             Address     0008.21a9.4f80
             Hello Time  2 sec  Max Age 20 sec   Forward Delay 15 sec
             Aging Time  300


Interface  Port ID                 Designated                 Port ID
Name       Prio.Nbr  Cost  Sts  Cost        Bridge ID          Prio.Nbr
---------- --------  ----  ---  ------ ----- ---------------- --------
Fa0/1      128.1      19   FWD      0 32768 0009.7c87.9081 128.13
Fa0/2      128.2      19   FWD     19 32770 0008.21a9.4f80 128.2
```

And now issue the same command on Switch3. The output is slightly different due to different versions of code:

```
Switch3#show spanning-tree vlan 2
VLAN0002
  Spanning tree enabled protocol ieee
  Root ID    Priority    32768
             Address     0009.7c87.9081
             Cost        19
             Port        1 (FastEthernet0/1)
             Hello Time  2 sec  Max Age 20 sec   Forward Delay 15 sec
```

```
Bridge ID  Priority    32770  (priority 32768 sys-id-ext 2)
           Address     000f.23a6.8940
           Hello Time  2 sec  Max Age 20 sec  Forward Delay 15 sec
           Aging Time  300

Interface        Role Sts Cost      Prio.Nbr Type
---------------  ---- --- --------- -------- -----------------------
Fa0/1            Root FWD 19        128.1    P2p
Fa0/2            Altn BLK 19        128.2    P2p
```

The spanning tree cost for a 100 Mbps interface is 19, and you can see that output in the Cost field.

You can issue a show interface fast 1/1 on Switch1 to verify the MAC address to see that it owns the MAC address allocated as the Root.

```
Swtch1#show int fast 1/1
FastEthernet1/1 is up, line protocol is up
  Hardware is Fast Ethernet, address is 0009.7c87.9081
```

5. Do the same for VLAN 3 to see where the root is.

```
Switch2#show spanning-tree vlan 3

VLAN0003
  Spanning tree enabled protocol ieee
  Root ID    Priority    32768
             Address     0009.7c87.9084
             Cost        19
             Port        1 (FastEthernet0/1)
             Hello Time  2 sec  Max Age 20 sec  Forward Delay 15 sec
```

The above MAC address belongs to Switch1 again.

6. Configure bridge priority on Switch2 and Switch3 for VLAN 2 and VLAN 3, respectively. We want Switch2 to be the root for VLAN2 and Switch3 to be the root for VLAN3. Here, we can use the trusty question mark to give us more information:

```
Switch2(config)#spanning-tree vlan 2 ?
  forward-time  Set the forward delay for the spanning tree
  hello-time    Set the hello interval for the spanning tree
  max-age       Set the max age interval for the spanning tree
  priority      Set the bridge priority for the spanning tree
  root          Configure switch as root
  <cr>

Switch2(config)#spanning-tree vlan 2 priority 4096
Switch3(config)#spanning-tree vlan 3 priority 4096
```

Now, we can issue the "show spanning-tree vlan #" command to check that the respective switches are the roots for the desired VLANs.

```
Switch2#show spanning-tree vlan 2
VLAN0002
  Spanning tree enabled protocol ieee
  Root ID    Priority    4098
             Address     0008.21a9.4f80
             This bridge is the root
             Hello Time  2 sec  Max Age 20 sec  Forward Delay 15 sec

  Bridge ID  Priority    4098   (priority 4096 sys-id-ext 2)
             Address     0008.21a9.4f80
             Hello Time  2 sec  Max Age 20 sec  Forward Delay 15 sec
             Aging Time  300

Interface  Port ID                   Designated               Port ID
Name       Prio.Nbr   Cost  Sts  Cost         Bridge ID       Prio.Nbr
---------- --------   ----  ---  ------ ----- -------------- --------
Fa0/1      128.1        19  FWD       0  4098 0008.21a9.4f80 128.1
Fa0/2      128.2        19  FWD       0  4098 0008.21a9.4f80 128.2
```

And if we do the same for VLAN3 on Switch3, we see that it is the root for that VLAN:

```
Switch3#show spanning-tree vlan 3
VLAN0003
  Spanning tree enabled protocol ieee
  Root ID    Priority    4099
             Address     000f.23a6.8940
             This bridge is the root
             Hello Time  2 sec  Max Age 20 sec  Forward Delay 15 sec

  Bridge ID  Priority    4099   (priority 4096 sys-id-ext 3)
             Address     000f.23a6.8940
             Hello Time  2 sec  Max Age 20 sec  Forward Delay 15 sec
             Aging Time  300

Interface       Role Sts Cost      Prio.Nbr Type
--------------- ---- --- --------- -------- -----
Fa0/1           Desg FWD 19         128.1   P2p
Fa0/2           Desg FWD 19         128.2   P2p
```

Running Configuration

```
Switch1#sh run
Building configuration...
--output truncated--
hostname Switch1
!
interface FastEthernet0/0
```

```
!
interface FastEthernet0/1
 switchport mode trunk
!
interface FastEthernet0/2
 switchport mode trunk
!
Switch2#sh run
Building configuration...
--output truncated--
hostname Switch2
!
spanning-tree vlan 2 priority 4096
!
!
!
!
!
interface FastEthernet0/0
!
interface FastEthernet0/1
 switchport mode trunk
!
interface FastEthernet0/2
 switchport mode trunk
!

Switch3#sh run
Building configuration...
--output truncated--
hostname Switch3
!
spanning-tree vlan 3 priority 4096
!
!
!
!
!
interface FastEthernet0/0
!
interface FastEthernet0/1
 switchport mode trunk
!
interface FastEthernet0/2
 switchport mode trunk
!
```

CHAPTER 14

Module 4 Labs

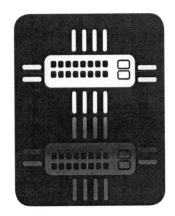

LAB 1: BASIC IP LAB — IP ADDRESSING

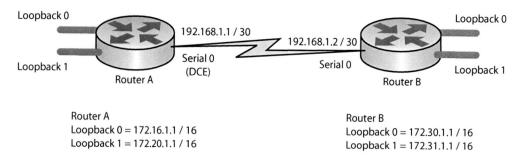

Router A
Loopback 0 = 172.16.1.1 / 16
Loopback 1 = 172.20.1.1 / 16

Router B
Loopback 0 = 172.30.1.1 / 16
Loopback 1 = 172.31.1.1 / 16

Figure 14–1: IP addressing

The physical topology is as shown in Figure 14–1.

Lab exercise

Your task is to configure the IP addressing as specified in Figure 14–1. Some of the commands we will use are discussed later, but we will enter them for practice.

Purpose

Every router will need to be configured with IP addresses and have to connect to another router either on the LAN or WAN. Being able to do this without looking at the walk-through is your eventual goal. This lab is the springboard for every other lab in the lab book.

Lab objectives

1. Configure the "enable password" to be "cisco".
2. Set the console password to be "letmein".
3. Configure telnet access to use the local username of "banbury" with the password "ccna".
4. Set the IP subnets for the loopback 0 and loopback 1 interfaces.
5. Set the IP subnet for the serial 0 interface.

Lab walk-through

1. To configure the "enable password" on a router, you need to do the following:

```
Router>enable
Router#configure terminal
Router(config)#hostname RouterA
RouterA(config)#enable password cisco ⇦ Configures the "enable
        password" or use an "enable secret password" (but not both)
RouterA(config)enable secret cisco ⇦ Configures a more secure
                            "enable password"
```

2. To configure the console password, you need to configure the console port. To do this, enter the following commands (in global config mode):

```
RouterA(config)#line console 0
RouterA(config-line)#password letmein
RouterA(config-line)#login ⇦ Whoever connects to the console port
                             will have to enter the password "letmein"
RouterA(config-line)#exit
RouterA(config)#
```

3. To set telnet access, you need to configure the VTY lines to allow telnet access: to do this type (from configuration mode):

```
RouterA(config)#line vty 0 4 ⇦ Enters the VTY line configuration
RouterA(config-line)#login local ⇦ This will use local usernames
                                 and passwords for telnet access
RouterA(config-line)#exit ⇦ Exit the VTY config mode
RouterA(config)#username banbury password ccna ⇦ Creates username
                      and password for telnet access (login local)
```

4. We now need to start setting the IP addresses on the loopback interfaces. As you will see from Figure 14–1, the subnet mask for the networks is represented by a /16 notation. This is actually a Class B mask (255.255.0.0) — the default for the address ranges we are using for the loopback interfaces. To apply an IP address to an interface, do the following:

```
RouterA(config)#interface loopback 0
RouterA(config-if)#ip address 172.16.1.1 255.255.0.0
RouterA(config-if)#interface loopback 1
RouterA(config-if)#ip address 172.20.1.1 255.255.0.0
```

5. Next, we need to configure the IP address for the interface serial 0. As this is a WAN link, it is good practice to conserve as many addresses as possible. So, as you will see in the network diagram in Figure 14–1, the serial interface is using a /30 mask; this is a 255.255.255.252 mask when written in dotted decimal format. By using this subnet mask, we reduce the available addresses from 255 per subnet to two available host addresses per subnet.

If the router does not accept this mask, you may need to enter the "ip subnet-zero" command to the router in config mode. However, as you will remember from the IP addressing/subnetting presentation we cannot use an address that is all 1s or all 0s, so the actual usable addresses are two. This mask is perfect for a WAN link, such as the one we are using in this lab, because no addresses are being wasted:

```
RouterA(config)#interface serial 0
RouterA(config-if)#ip address 192.168.1.1 255.255.255.252
```

```
RouterA(config-if)#clock rate 64000  ⇦ If this has the DCE cable attached
RouterA(config-if)#no shutdown       ⇦ This will initialize the
                  interface from the default state of down. This is only
                  necessary on physical, not logical (loopback) interfaces.
```

The following message should appear on the console session for router A:

```
00:15:51: %LINK-3-UPDOWN: Interface Serial0, changed state to down
```

The interface will not come up until router B's serial interface is up.

6. We will now follow all the above steps for router B.

```
Router B:
Router>enable
RouterB#config t
Router(config)#hostname RouterB
RouterB(config)#enable password cisco
```

or use an "enable secret password" (but not both).

```
RouterB(config)#enable secret cisco
```

Do not use the same password for both; otherwise, you will receive a warning message. In fact, it is best practice to just use the "enable secret":

```
The enable secret you have chosen is the same as your enable password.
This is not recommended. Re-enter the enable secret.
```

Configure the console password:

```
RouterB(config)#line console 0
RouterB(config-line)#password letmein
RouterB(config-line)#login
RouterB(config-line)#exit
RouterB(config)#
```

Configure the telnet password:

```
RouterB(config)#line vty 0 4
RouterB(config-line)#login local
RouterB(config-line)#exit
RouterB(config)#username banbury password ccna
```

Configure the loopback addresses:
```
RouterB(config)#interface loopback 0
RouterB(config-if)#ip address 172.30.1.1 255.255.0.0
RouterB(config-if)#interface loopback 1
RouterB(config-if)#ip address 172.31.1.1 255.255.0.0
```

Configure the serial addresses:

```
RouterB(config-if)#interface serial 0
RouterB(config-if)#ip address 192.168.1.2 255.255.255.252
RouterB(config-if)#no shutdown
```

7. You should see the interface come up on the console session:

```
00:31:21: %LINEPROTO-5-UPDOWN: Line protocol on Interface Serial0, changed
state to up
```

If router B has the DCE interface attached, then set the clock rate on that. You can issue the "show controllers serial 0" command to see if the cable is DTE or DCE.

You should now be able to ping router A from router B and vice versa.

```
RouterB#ping 192.168.1.1

Type escape sequence to abort.
Sending 5, 100-byte ICMP Echos to 192.168.1.1, timeout is 2 seconds:
!!!!!
Success rate is 100 percent (5/5), round-trip min/avg/max = 32/32/32 ms
RouterB#
```

If pings are not working, check the serial interfaces to make sure they are both up up with the "show ip interface brief" command.

```
RouterA#show ip interface brief
Interface    IP-Address    OK? Method    Status              Protocol

Ethernet0    unassigned    YES unset  administratively down down

Loopback0    172.16.1.1    YES manual  up                     up

Loopback1    172.20.1.1    YES manual  up                     up

Serial0      192.168.1.1   YES manual  up                     up

Serial1      unassigned    YES unset  administratively down down

RouterA#
```

Make sure you have put a clock rate on the correct interface, i.e., the DCE side. You can check with the "show controllers serial 0" command (if you are plugged into serial 0, that is).

```
RouterA#show controllers serial 0
HD unit 0, idb = 0x162890, driver structure at 0x168C18
buffer size 1524 HD unit 0, V.35 DCE cable, clockrate 64000
cpb = 0x2, eda = 0x2940, cda = 0x2800
RX ring with 16 entries at 0x4022800
00 bd_ptr=0x2800 pak=0x16A10C ds=0x4026108 status=80 pak_size=0
```

Make sure you have put the correct IP address on both sides and the subnet masks are the same. If all else fails and you cannot find what is wrong, look at the "show run" for both routers below. The commands on by default are in bold for Router As output. You should not need to enter them unless you have an old version of Cisco IOS.

You can copy and paste the configs below into your router at the "Router(config)#" prompt. Bear in mind that your router may have different interfaces. If, for example, your serial cable is plugged into serial 1, you will have to make the necessary changes to my configurations.

The exclamation marks are there to make the reading easier when you look at the show run.

Show runs

```
RouterA#show run
Building configuration...

Current configuration : 709 bytes
!
version 12.1
service timestamps debug uptime
service timestamps log uptime
no service password-encryption
!
hostname RouterA
!
enable secret 5 $1$rujI$BJ8GgiK8U9p5cdfXyApPr/
!
username banbury password 0 ccna
!
ip subnet-zero
!
interface Loopback0
 ip address 172.16.1.1 255.255.0.0
!
interface Loopback1
 ip address 172.20.1.1 255.255.0.0
!
interface Ethernet0
 no ip address
```

```
 shutdown
!
interface Serial0
 ip address 192.168.1.1 255.255.255.252
 clockrate 64000
!
interface Serial1
 no ip address
 shutdown
!
interface BRI0
 no ip address
 shutdown

ip classless
no ip http server
!
line con 0
 password letmein
 login
line aux 0
line vty 0 4
 login local
!
end

RouterA#

---
Router B:
RouterB#show run
Building configuration...

Current configuration : 697 bytes
!
version 12.1
service timestamps debug uptime
service timestamps log uptime
no service password-encryption
!
hostname RouterB
!
enable secret 5 $1$ydeA$MyfRKevOckjm7w/OornnB1
!
username banbury password 0 ccna
!
ip subnet-zero
!
interface Loopback0
 ip address 172.30.1.1 255.255.0.0
!
interface Loopback1
```

```
  ip address 172.31.1.1 255.255.0.0
 !
 interface Serial0
  ip address 192.168.1.2 255.255.255.252
 !
 interface Serial1
  no ip address
  shutdown
 !
 interface Ethernet0
  no ip address
  shutdown
 !
 interface BRI0
  no ip address
  shutdown

 !
 ip classless
 no ip http server
 !
 line con 0
  password letmein
  login
 line aux 0
 line vty 0 4
  login local
 !
 end

 RouterB#
```

LAB 2: NAT LAB — STATIC NAT

The physical topology is as shown in Figure 14–2.

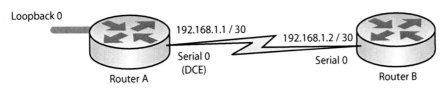

Router A
Loopback 0 = 172.16.1.1 / 16

Figure 14–2: Static NAT

Lab exercise

Your task is to configure the network in Figure 14–2 to allow the 172.16.1.1 host on the 172.16.1.0 LAN to access the Internet using address 10.0.0.1. The 10.0.0.1 would normally be a routable public address provided by your ISP (such as 80.1.1.1), but for this lab, we will use a private non-routable address. Please feel free to try the lab without following the lab walk-through section and then just check the notes for the NAT config.

Purpose

Being able to configure NAT is a fundamental CCNA skill. Any client who needs to access the Internet will want to use NAT. The key is to understand the clients' requirements and then design a solution to fit their needs.

Lab objectives

1. Use the IP addressing scheme depicted in Figure 14–2. Router A needs a clock rate on interface serial 0: set this to 64000.
2. Set telnet access for the router to use the local login permissions of username "banbury" and the password "ccna" (not needed for NAT, but added for practice purposes).
3. Put a static route on the router.
4. Configure the inside and outside NAT interfaces on the router.
5. Configure a static NAT translation.
6. Test the NAT translation.

Lab walk-through

1. To set the IP addresses to an interface, you will need to do the following:

```
Router#config t
Router(config)#hostname RouterA
```

```
RouterA(config)#
RouterA(config)#interface serial 0
RouterA(config-if)#ip address 192.168.1.1 255.255.255.252
RouterA(config-if)#clock rate 64000 ⇦ If this is the DCE side
RouterA(config-if)#no shutdown
RouterA(config-if)#ip nat outside ⇦ The outside NAT network
RouterA(config-if)#interface loopback 0 ⇦ No need for "no shutdown"
                                            on loopback interfaces
RouterA(config-if)#ip address 172.16.1.1 255.255.0.0
RouterA(config-if)#ip nat inside ⇦ The inside NAT network
RouterA(config-if)#^Z
RouterA#
Router B:
Router#config t
Router(config)#hostname RouterB
RouterB(config)#interface serial 0
RouterB(config-if)#ip address 192.168.1.2 255.255.255.252
RouterB(config-if)#no shutdown
RouterB(config-if)#exit
RouterB(config)#ip route 0.0.0.0 0.0.0.0 s0 ⇦ Static route
RouterB(config)#^Z
RouterB#
```

To set the clock rate on a serial interface (DCE connection only), you need to use the "clock rate #" command on the serial interface, where # indicates the speed:

```
RouterA(config-if)#clock rate 64000
```

Ping across the serial link now.

2. To set telnet access, you need to configure the VTY lines to allow telnet access: to do this type (from configuration mode):

```
RouterA(config)#line vty 0 4 ⇦ Enters the VTY line configuration

RouterA(config-line)#login local ⇦ This will use local usernames
 and passwords for telnet access

RouterA(config-line)#exit ⇦ Exit the VTY config mode

RouterA(config)#username banbury password ccna ⇦ Creates username
                        and password for telnet access (login local)
Router B:
RouterB(config)#line vty 0 4
RouterB(config-line)#login local
RouterB(config-line)#exit
RouterB(config)#username banbury password ccna
```

3. To set the "enable password" do the following:

    ```
    RouterA(config)#enable secret cisco ⇦ Sets the "enable password"
                                                      (encrypted)
    Router B:
    RouterB(config)#enable secret cisco
    ```

4. Configure a static NAT translation:

    ```
    RouterA(config)#ip nat inside source static 172.16.1.1 10.0.0.1

    Static NAT translation
    RouterA(config)#^Z
    ```

5. To see if NAT is working, we need to turn on a debug with "debug ip nat". Now imagine that the loopback address of 172.16.1.1 is a host on the LAN that wants to get out to the Internet. When the packet from the NATted LAN passes through the router, it will match the access-list and be statically translated to 10.0.0.1.

    ```
    RouterA#debug ip nat ⇦ Turn on the NAT debug
    RouterA#ping
    Protocol [ip]:
    Target IP address: 192.168.1.2 ⇦ Ping router B
    Repeat count [5]:
    Datagram size [100]:
    Timeout in seconds [2]:
    Extended commands [n]: y
    Source address or interface: loopback 0 ⇦ Source is the LAN
    Type of service [0]:
    Set DF bit in IP header? [no]:
    Validate reply data? [no]:
    Data pattern [0xABCD]:
    Loose, Strict, Record, Timestamp, Verbose[none]:
    Sweep range of sizes [n]:
    Type escape sequence to abort.
    Sending 5, 100-byte ICMP Echos to 192.168.1.2, timeout is 2 seconds:
    !!!!!
    Success rate is 100 percent (5/5), round-trip min/avg/max = 40/40/40 ms
    03:48:01: NAT: s=172.16.1.1->10.0.0.1, d=192.168.1.2 [35]
    03:48:01: NAT*: s=192.168.1.2, d=10.0.0.1->172.16.1.1 [35]
    03:48:01: NAT: s=172.16.1.1->10.0.0.1, d=192.168.1.2 [36]
    03:48:01: NAT*: s=192.168.1.2, d=10.0.0.1->172.16.1.1 [36]
    03:48:01: NAT: s=172.16.1.1->10.0.0.1, d=192.168.1.2 [37]
    03:48:01: NAT*: s=192.168.1.2, d=10.0.0.1->172.16.1.1 [37]
    03:48:01: NAT: s=172.16.1.1->10.0.0.1, d=192.168.1.2 [38]
    03:48:01: NAT*: s=192.168.1.2, d=10.0.0.1->172.16.1.1 [38]
    03:48:01: NAT: s=172.16.1.1->10.0.0.1, d=192.168.1.2 [39]
    03:48:01: NAT*: s=192.168.1.2, d=10.0.0.1->172.16.1.1 [39]
    ```

You can see that the NAT debug shows the source (s=) as the loopback interface 172.16.1.1 which is translated to 10.0.0.1. The destination (d=) is the serial address for router B 192.168.1.2. The * shows the returning packet that is translated back.

The numbers in brackets [35, etc.] are the IP identification numbers of the packets.

```
RouterA#show ip nat translations
Pro Inside global    Inside local    Outside local Outside global
-- 10.0.0.1          172.16.1.1        - - -          - - -
RouterA#
```

You can see from the NAT translation table above that the router is doing a one-to-one translation of the address.

6. Now please enter reload at the "Router#" prompt and type "yes" to confirm.

Show runs

```
RouterA#show run
Building configuration...

Current configuration : 757 bytes
!
version 12.1
no service single-slot-reload-enable
service timestamps debug uptime
service timestamps log uptime
no service password-encryption
!
hostname RouterA
!
ip subnet-zero
!
interface Loopback0
 ip address 172.16.1.1 255.255.0.0
 ip nat inside
!
interface Ethernet0
 no ip address
 shutdown
!
interface Ethernet1
 no ip address
 shutdown
!
interface Serial0
 ip address 192.168.1.1 255.255.255.252
```

```
 clock rate 64000
 ip nat outside
!
interface Serial1
 no ip address
 shutdown
!
ip nat inside source static 172.16.1.1 10.0.0.1
ip classless
no ip http server
!
line con 0
line aux 0
line vty 0 4
!
end

RouterA#

- - -

RouterB#show run
Building configuration...

Current configuration : 456 bytes
!
version 12.2
service timestamps debug uptime
service timestamps log uptime
no service password-encryption
!
hostname RouterB
!
ip subnet-zero
!
interface Serial0
 ip address 192.168.1.2 255.255.255.252
 !
interface Serial1
 no ip address
 shutdown
!
ip classless
ip route 0.0.0.0 0.0.0.0 Serial0
no ip http server
ip pim bidir-enable
!
line con 0
line aux 0
line vty 0 4
!
end
```

LAB 3: NAT LAB — NAT POOL

The physical topology is as shown in Figure 14–3.

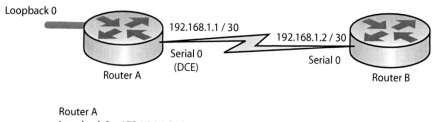

Figure 14–3: NAT pool

Lab exercise

Your task is to configure the network in Figure 14–3 to allow the hosts on the 172.16.0.0 LAN (we will simulate this with the loopback address and secondary address) to access the Internet using the NAT pool 10.0.0.1 to 10.0.0.10. Please feel free to try the lab without following the lab walk-through section.

Purpose

Being able to configure NAT is a fundamental CCNA skill. Any client who needs to access the Internet will want to use NAT. The key is to understand the client's requirements and then design a solution to fit his/her needs.

Lab objectives

1. Use the IP addressing scheme depicted in Figure 14–3. Router A needs a clock rate on interface serial 0: set this to 64000.
2. Set telnet access for the router to use the local login permissions of username "banbury" and the password "ccna" (optional).
3. Put a static route on the router.
4. Configure the inside and outside NAT interfaces on the router.
5. Configure a pool of addresses the router will use as a NAT pool.
6. Test the NAT config with a ping and debug.

Lab walk-through

1. To set the IP addresses for an interface, you will need to do the following:

```
Router#config t
Router(config)#hostname RouterA
RouterA(config)#
RouterA(config)#interface serial 0
RouterA(config-if)#ip address 192.168.1.1 255.255.255.252
RouterA(config-if)#clock rate 64000 ⇦ If this is the DCE side
RouterA(config-if)#no shutdown
RouterA(config-if)#ip nat outside ⇦ The outside NAT network
RouterA(config-if)#interface loopback 0  ⇦ No need for "no shutdown"
                                            on loopback interfaces
RouterA(config-if)#ip address 172.16.1.1 255.255.0.0
RouterA(config-if)#ip address 172.16.1.2 255.255.0.0 secondary
```

The secondary address will act as a second host on the LAN.

```
RouterA(config-if)#ip nat inside ⇦ The inside NAT network
RouterA(config-if)#^Z
RouterA#
Router B:
Router#config t
Router(config)#hostname RouterB
RouterB(config)#interface serial 0
RouterB(config-if)#ip address 192.168.1.2 255.255.255.252
RouterB(config-if)#no shutdown
RouterB(config-if)#exit
RouterB(config)#ip route 0.0.0.0 0.0.0.0 serial 0
RouterB(config)#^Z
RouterB#
```

To set the clock rate on a serial interface (DCE connection only) you need to use the "clock rate #" command on the serial interface, where # indicates the speed:

```
RouterA(config-if)#clock rate 64000
```

Ping across the serial link now.

2. To set telnet access, you need to configure the VTY lines to allow telnet access. To do this, type (from configuration mode):

```
RouterA(config)#line vty 0 4 ⇦ Enters the VTY line configuration

RouterA(config-line)#login local ⇦ This will use local usernames
                                     and passwords for telnet access

RouterA(config-line)#exit ⇦ Exit the VTY config mode
```

```
RouterA(config)#username banbury password ccna ⇔ Creates username
                          and password for telnet access (login local)
Router B:
RouterB(config)#line vty 0 4
RouterB(config-line)#login local
RouterB(config-line)#exit
RouterB(config)#username banbury password ccna
```

3. To set the "enable password", do the following:

```
RouterA(config)#enable secret cisco ⇔ Sets the "enable password"
                                           (encrypted)
Router B:
RouterB(config)#enable secret cisco
```

4. You need to configure a NAT pool and then tell the pool which access-list to access to determine what traffic you want to be NATted:

```
RouterA(config)#ip nat pool internet_out 10.0.0.1 10.0.0.10 prefix-length
24

(or you could have written "ip nat pool internet_out 10.0.0.1 10.0.0.10
netmask 255.255.255.0")

RouterA(config)#ip nat inside source list 1 pool internet_out

RouterA(config)#access-list 1 permit 172.16.0.0 0.0.255.255
RouterA(config)#^Z
```

5. To see if NAT is working, we need to turn on a debug with "debug ip nat". Now imagine that the loopback address of 172.16.1.1 is a host on the LAN that wants to get out to the Internet. When the packet from the NATted LAN passes through the router, it will match the access-list and be translated to an address from the NAT pool.

```
RouterA#debug ip nat ⇔ Turn on the NAT debug
RouterA#ping
Protocol [ip]:
Target IP address: 192.168.1.2 ⇔ Ping router B
Repeat count [5]:
Datagram size [100]:
Timeout in seconds [2]:
Extended commands [n]: y
Source address or interface: loopback 0 ⇔ Source is the LAN
Type of service [0]:
Set DF bit in IP header? [no]:
Validate reply data? [no]:
Data pattern [0xABCD]:
Loose, Strict, Record, Timestamp, Verbose[none]:
Sweep range of sizes [n]:
```

```
Type escape sequence to abort.
Sending 5, 100-byte ICMP Echos to 192.168.1.2, timeout is 2 seconds:
!!!!!
Success rate is 100 percent (5/5), round-trip min/avg/max = 40/40/40 ms
RouterA#
02:12:37: NAT: s=172.16.1.1->10.0.0.1, d=192.168.1.2 [20]
02:12:37: NAT*: s=192.168.1.2, d=10.0.0.1->172.16.1.1 [20]
02:12:37: NAT: s=172.16.1.1->10.0.0.1, d=192.168.1.2 [21]
02:12:37: NAT*: s=192.168.1.2, d=10.0.0.1->172.16.1.1 [21]
02:12:37: NAT: s=172.16.1.1->10.0.0.1, d=192.168.1.2 [22]
02:12:37: NAT*: s=192.168.1.2, d=10.0.0.1->172.16.1.1 [22]
02:12:37: NAT: s=172.16.1.1->10.0.0.1, d=192.168.1.2 [23]
02:12:37: NAT*: s=192.168.1.2, d=10.0.0.1->172.16.1.1 [23]
02:12:37: NAT: s=172.16.1.1->10.0.0.1, d=192.168.1.2 [24]
02:12:37: NAT*: s=192.168.1.2, d=10.0.0.1->172.16.1.1 [24]

RouterA#show ip nat translations
Pro Inside global      Inside local      Outside local      Outside
global
--- 10.0.0.1           172.16.1.1        ---                ---
RouterA#
```

You can see that the NAT debug shows the source (s=) as the loopback interface, which is translated to 10.0.0.1. The destination (d=) is the serial address for router B 192.168.1.2. The * shows the returning packet that is translated back.

The numbers in brackets [20, etc.] are the IP identification numbers of the packets.

If we want to check that the pool is allocating addresses correctly, we can source a second ping — this time from the secondary address. There should be another address allocated from the NAT pool.

```
RouterA#ping
Protocol [ip]:
Target IP address: 192.168.1.2
Repeat count [5]:
Datagram size [100]:
Timeout in seconds [2]:
Extended commands [n]: y
Source address or interface: 172.16.1.2
Type of service [0]:
Set DF bit in IP header? [no]:
Validate reply data? [no]:
Data pattern [0xABCD]:
Loose, Strict, Record, Timestamp, Verbose[none]:
Sweep range of sizes [n]:
Type escape sequence to abort.
Sending 5, 100-byte ICMP Echos to 192.168.1.2, timeout is 2 seconds:
!!!!!
```

```
Success rate is 100 percent (5/5), round-trip min/avg/max = 40/46/68 ms
RouterA#
04:09:23: NAT: s=172.16.1.2->10.0.0.2, d=192.168.1.2 [45]
04:09:23: NAT*: s=192.168.1.2, d=10.0.0.2->172.16.1.2 [45]
04:09:23: NAT: s=172.16.1.2->10.0.0.2, d=192.168.1.2 [46]
04:09:23: NAT*: s=192.168.1.2, d=10.0.0.2->172.16.1.2 [46]
04:09:23: NAT: s=172.16.1.2->10.0.0.2, d=192.168.1.2 [47]
04:09:23: NAT*: s=192.168.1.2, d=10.0.0.2->172.16.1.2 [47]
04:09:23: NAT: s=172.16.1.2->10.0.0.2, d=192.168.1.2 [48]
04:09:23: NAT*: s=192.168.1.2, d=10.0.0.2->172.16.1.2 [48]
04:09:23: NAT: s=172.16.1.2->10.0.0.2, d=192.168.1.2 [49]
04:09:23: NAT*: s=192.168.1.2, d=10.0.0.2->172.16.1.2 [49]
RouterA#show ip nat translations
Pro Inside global  Inside local  Outside local  Outside global
--- 10.0.0.1        172.16.1.1    ---            ---
--- 10.0.0.2        172.16.1.2    ---            ---
```

6. Now please enter reload at the "Router#" prompt and type "yes" to confirm.

Show runs

```
RouterA#show run
Building configuration...

Current configuration : 749 bytes
!
version 12.1
no service single-slot-reload-enable
service timestamps debug uptime
service timestamps log uptime
no service password-encryption
!
hostname RouterA
!
ip subnet-zero
!
interface Loopback0
 ip address 172.16.1.1 255.255.0.0
 ip address 172.16.1.2 255.255.0.0 secondary
 ip nat inside
!
interface Ethernet0
 no ip address
 shutdown
!
interface Ethernet1
 no ip address
 shutdown
!
interface Serial0
```

```
 ip address 192.168.1.1 255.255.255.252
 clockrate 64000
 ip nat outside
!
interface Serial1
 no ip address
 shutdown
!
ip nat pool internet_out 10.0.0.1 10.0.0.10 prefix-length 24
ip nat inside source list 1 pool internet_out
ip classless
no ip http server
!
access-list 1 permit 172.16.0.0 0.0.255.255
!
line con 0
line aux 0
line vty 0 4
!
end

RouterA#


- - -


RouterB#show run
Building configuration...

Current configuration : 456 bytes
!
version 12.2
service timestamps debug uptime
service timestamps log uptime
no service password-encryption
!
hostname RouterB
!
ip subnet-zero
!
interface Serial0
 ip address 192.168.1.2 255.255.255.252
 !
interface Serial1
 no ip address
 shutdown
!
interface TokenRing0
 no ip address
 shutdown
!
ip classless
ip route 0.0.0.0 0.0.0.0 Serial 0
```

```
no ip http server
ip pim bidir-enable
!
line con 0
line aux 0
line vty 0 4
!
end

RouterB#
```

LAB 4: NAT LAB — NAT OVERLOAD

The physical topology is as shown in Figure 14–4.

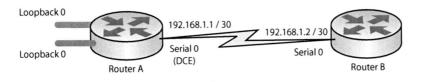

Router A
Loopback 0 = 172.16.1.129 / 26
Secondary = 172.16.1.65 /26

Figure 14–4: NAT overload

Lab exercise

Your task is to configure the network in Figure 14–4 to allow the hosts on the 172.16.1.128 subnet to access the Internet using the overloaded NAT address of 10.0.0.1. Hosts on the 172.16.1.64 subnet should not be natted. Please feel free to try the lab without following the lab walk-through section.

Purpose

Being able to configure NAT is a fundamental CCNA skill. Any client who needs to access the Internet will want to use NAT. The key is to understand the client's requirements and then design a solution to fit his needs. This lab helps you to understand NAT, access-lists, and VLSM.

Lab objectives

1. Use the IP addressing scheme depicted in Figure 14–4. Router A needs a clock rate on interface serial 0: set this to 64000.
2. Set telnet access for the router to use the local login permissions of username "banbury" and the password "ccna".
3. Put a static route on the router.
4. Configure the inside and outside NAT interfaces on the router.
5. Configure NAT overload.
6. Finally, test the NAT overload from loopback 0 and loopback 1.

Lab walk-through

1. To set the IP addresses for an interface, you will need to do the following:

```
Router#config t
Router(config)#hostname RouterA
RouterA(config)#
```

```
RouterA(config)#interface serial 0
RouterA(config-if)#ip address 192.168.1.1 255.255.255.252
RouterA(config-if)#clock rate 64000 ⇦ If this is the DCE side
RouterA(config-if)#no shutdown
RouterA(config-if)#ip nat outside ⇦ The outside NAT network
RouterA(config-if)#interface loopback 0 ⇦ No need for "no
                                      shutdown" on loopback interfaces
RouterA(config-if)#ip address 172.16.1.129 255.255.255.192
RouterA(config-if)#ip nat inside ⇦ The inside NAT network
RouterA(config-if)#interface loopback 1
RouterA(config-if)#ip address 172.16.1.65 255.255.255.192
RouterA(config-if)#ip nat inside
RouterA(config-if)#^Z
RouterA#
Router B:
Router#config t
Router(config)#hostname RouterB
RouterB(config)#interface serial 0
RouterB(config-if)#ip address 192.168.1.2 255.255.255.252
RouterB(config-if)#no shutdown
RouterB(config-if)#exit
RouterB(config)#ip route 0.0.0.0 0.0.0.0 serial 0
RouterB(config)#^Z
RouterB#
```

To set the clock rate on a serial interface (DCE connection only) you need to use the "clock rate #" command on the serial interface, where # indicates the speed:

```
RouterA(config-if)#clock rate 64000
```

Ping across the serial link now.

2. To set telnet access, you need to configure the VTY lines to allow telnet access: to do this type (from configuration mode):

```
RouterA(config)#line vty 0 4 ⇦ Enters the VTY line configuration

RouterA(config-line)#login local ⇦ This will use local usernames
                                    and passwords for telnet access

RouterA(config-line)#exit ⇦ Exit the VTY config mode

RouterA(config)#username banbury password ccna  ⇦ Creates username
                        and password for telnet access (login local)
Router B:
RouterB(config)#line vty 0 4
RouterB(config-line)#login local
RouterB(config-line)#exit
RouterB(config)#username banbury password ccna
```

3. To set the "enable password", do the following:

```
RouterA(config)#enable secret cisco ⇦ Sets the "enable password"
                                              (encrypted)
Router B:
RouterB(config)#enable secret cisco
```

4. You need to configure a NAT pool and then tell the pool which access-list to access to determine what traffic you want to be NATted:

```
RouterA(config)#ip nat pool internet_out 10.0.0.1 10.0.0.1 prefix-length
24 ⇦ The pool consists of one address
RouterA(config)#ip nat inside source list 1 pool internet_out overload ⇦
Tell the router to overload the pool (i.e. use PAT)
RouterA(config)#access-list 1 permit 172.16.1.128 0.0.0.63 ⇦ Match any
host on the 172.16.1.128 subnet
```

5. To see if NAT is working, we need to turn on a debug with "debug ip nat". Now imagine that the loopback address of 172.16.1.129 is a host on the LAN that wants to get out to the Internet. When the packet from the NATted LAN passes through the router, it will match the access-list and be translated to the overloaded NAT address.

```
RouterA#debug ip nat
IP NAT debugging is on
RouterA#ping
Protocol [ip]:
Target IP address: 192.168.1.2
Repeat count[5]:
Datagram size [100]:
Timeout  in seconds [2]:
Extended commands [n]: y
Source address  or interface: loopback0
Type of service [0]:
Set DF bit in IP header? [no]:
Validate reply data? [no]:
Data pattern [0xABCD]:
Loose, Strict, Record, Timestamp, Verbose[none]:
Sweep range of sizes [n]:
Type escape sequence to abort.
Sending 5, 100-byte ICMP Echos to 192.168.1.2, timeout is 2 seconds:
!!!!!
Success  rate is 100 percent (5/5), round-trip min/avg/max = 40/41/40ms
RouterA#

00:43:59: NAT:      s=172.16.1.129->10.0.0.1, d=192.168.1.2 [20]
00:43:59: NAT:      s=192.168.1.2, d=10.0.0.1->172.16.1.129 [20]
00:43:59: NAT:      s=172.16.1.129->10.0.0.1 d=192.168.1.2  [21]
00:43:59: NAT:      s=192.168.1.2, d=10.0.0.1->172.16.1.129 [21]
00:43:59: NAT:      s=172.16.1.129->10.0.0.1, d=192.168.1.2 [22]
```

```
00:43:59: NAT:        s=192.168.1.2, d=10.0.0.1->172.16.1.129 [22]
00:43:59: NAT:        s=172.16.1.129->10.0.0.1, d=192.168.1.2 [23]
00:43:59: NAT:        s=192.168.1.2, d=10.0.0.1->172.16.1.129 [23]
00:43:59: NAT:        s=172.16.1.129->10.0.0.1, d=192.168.1.2 [24]
00:43:59: NAT:        s=192.168.1.2, d=10.0.0.1->172.16.1.129 [24]

RouterA#show ip nat tran ⇔ Short for "translations"
Pro Inside global     Inside local      Outside local      Outside global
icmp 10.0.0.1:8759    172.16.1.129:8759 192.168.1.2:8759   192.168.1.2:8759
icmp 10.0.0.1:8760    172.16.1.129:8760 192.168.1.2:8760   192.168.1.2:8760
icmp 10.0.0.1:8761    172.16.1.129:8761 192.168.1.2:8761   192.168.1.2:8761
icmp 10.0.0.1:8762    172.16.1.129:8762 192.168.1.2:8762   192.168.1.2:8762
icmp 10.0.0.1:8763    172.16.1.129:8763 192.168.1.2:8763   192.168.1.2:8763

RouterA#
00:44:59: NAT: expiring 10.0.0.1 (172.16.1.129) icmp 8759 (8759)
00:44:59: NAT: expiring 10.0.0.1 (172.16.1.129) icmp 8760 (8760)
00:44:59: NAT: expiring 10.0.0.1 (172.16.1.129) icmp 8761 (8761)
00:44:59: NAT: expiring 10.0.0.1 (172.16.1.129) icmp 8762 (8762)
00:44:59: NAT: expiring 10.0.0.1 (172.16.1.129) icmp 8763 (8763)
```

You can see from the NAT translation table below that the router is allocating ports for the translations, in this example, ports 8759 to 8763.

Now ping from loopback 1, which does not match the access-list because it is in a different subnet. The address should not be NATted.

```
RouterA#ping
Protocol [ip]:
Target IP address: 192.168.1.2
Repeat count [5]:
Datagram size [100]:
Timeout in seconds [2]:
Extended commands [n]: y
Source address or interface: loopback 1
Type of service [0]:
Set DF bit in IP header? [no]:
Validate reply data? [no]:
Data pattern [0xABCD]:
Loose, Strict, Record, Timestamp, Verbose[none]:
Sweep range of sizes [n]:
Type escape sequence to abort.
Sending 5, 100-byte ICMP Echos to 192.168.1.2, timeout is 2 seconds:
!!!!!
Success rate is 100 percent (5/5), round-trip min/avg/max = 32/37/60 ms
RouterA#show ip nat tran
RouterA#
```

6. Now please enter reload at the "Router#" prompt and type "yes" to confirm.

Show runs

```
RouterA#show run
Building configuration...

Current configuration : 757 bytes
!
version 12.1
no service single-slot-reload-enable
service timestamps debug uptime
service timestamps log uptime
no service password-encryption
!
hostname RouterA
!
ip subnet-zero
!
interface Loopback0
 ip address 172.16.1.129 255.255.255.192
 ip nat inside
!
Interface Loopback1
 ip add 172.16.1.65 255.255.255.192
 ip nat inside
!
interface Ethernet0
 no ip address
 shutdown
!
interface Ethernet1
 no ip address
 shutdown
!
interface Serial0
 ip address 192.168.1.1 255.255.255.252
 ip nat outside
clock rate 64000
!
interface Serial1
 no ip address
 shutdown
!
ip nat pool internet_out 10.0.0.1 10.0.0.1 prefix-length 24
ip nat inside source list 1 pool internet_out overload
ip classless
no ip http server
!
access-list 1 permit 172.16.1.0 0.0.255.255
!
!
line con 0
line aux 0
```

```
line vty 0 4
!
end

RouterA#

- - -

RouterB#show run
Building configuration...

Current configuration : 456 bytes
!
version 12.2
service timestamps debug uptime
service timestamps log uptime
no service password-encryption
!
hostname RouterB
!
ip subnet-zero
!
interface Serial0
 ip address 192.168.1.2 255.255.255.252
 !
interface Serial1
 no ip address
 shutdown
!
interface TokenRing0
 no ip address
 shutdown
!
ip classless
!
ip route 0.0.0.0 0.0.0.0 Serial0

!
no ip http server
ip pim bidir-enable
!
line con 0
line aux 0
line vty 0 4
!
end

RouterB#
```

CHAPTER 15

Module 5 Labs

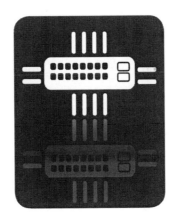

> **Note:** Please bear in mind that most networks in the real world consist of more than two routers. With the routing labs and, in fact, all the labs in the lab book, we are practicing most of the available commands and configurations used in the real world, but only on two or three routers.

An example is the OSPF labs; we would never normally use OSPF on two routers and certainly not use three different areas on two routers. We use various areas just so we understand how they operate and how to configure areas for the exam. There is a three-router topology in the back of the labs part of this book if you have three routers to use.

LAB 1: IP ROUTING PROTOCOL LAB — STATIC ROUTES

The physical topology is as shown in Figure 15–1.

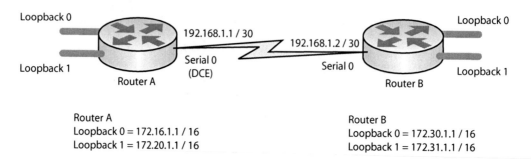

Router A
Loopback 0 = 172.16.1.1 / 16
Loopback 1 = 172.20.1.1 / 16

Router B
Loopback 0 = 172.30.1.1 / 16
Loopback 1 = 172.31.1.1 / 16

Figure 15–1: Static routes

Lab exercise

Your task is to configure the network in Figure 15–1 to allow full connectivity using the static routes. Please feel free to try the lab without following the lab walk-through section.

Text printed in a `monospaced font` indicates commands that can be entered on the router.

Purpose

The majority of small businesses have just one router that connects to another router provided by the service provider. These routers will only need to be configured with a very basic config including IP addresses and a static route to reach the ISP. This lab will show you just how do that.

Lab objectives

1. Use the IP addressing scheme depicted in Figure 15–1. Router A needs to have a clock rate on interface serial 0: set this to 64000.

2. Set telnet access for the router to use the local login permissions of username "banbury" and the password "ccna".

3. Configure the "enable password" to be "cisco".

   Configure the static routes to provide connectivity to all networks attached to the neighboring router, except the network used for the serial connection.

4. Ensure routing information is correct by checking the routing table for entries to your neighbor's networks.

5. Finally, try to ping all loopback interfaces of your neighbor, and then try to access your neighbor router via telnet.

Lab walk-through

1. To set the IP addresses on an interface, you will need to do the following:

```
Router#config t
Router(config)#hostname RouterA
RouterA(config)#interface serial 0
RouterA(config-if)#ip address 192.168.1.1 255.255.255.252
RouterA(config-if)#clock rate 64000
RouterA(config-if)#no shutdown
RouterA(config-if)#interface loopback 0
RouterA(config-if)#ip address 172.16.1.1 255.255.0.0
RouterA(config-if)#interface loopback 1
RouterA(config-if)#ip address 172.20.1.1 255.255.0.0
RouterA(config-if)#^Z
RouterA#
```

To set the clock rate on a serial interface (DCE connection only), you need to use the "clock rate #" command on the serial interface, where # indicates the speed:

```
RouterA(config-if)#clock rate 64000
```

2. To set telnet access, you need to configure the VTY lines to allow telnet access. To do this, type (from configuration mode):

```
RouterA(config)#line vty 0 4  ⇦ Enters the VTY line configuration
RouterA(config-line)#login local  ⇦ This will use local usernames
                                 and passwords for telnet access
RouterA(config-line)#exit  ⇦ Exit the VTY config mode

RouterA(config)#username banbury password ccna  ⇦ Creates username
                        and password for telnet access (login local)
```

3. To set the "enable password," do the following:

```
RouterA(config)#enable secret cisco  ⇦ Sets the "enable password"
                                        (encrypted)
```

4. To configure static routes on a router, there is only one step:

    ```
    RouterA(config)#ip route 172.30.0.0 255.255.0.0 192.168.1.2
    RouterA(config)#ip route 172.31.0.0 255.255.0.0 192.168.1.2
    ```

    The above command will configure a static route on router A. To get to the destination network of 172.30.0.0 and 172.31.0.0, use the next hop of 192.168.1.2. Instead of using the above commands, you can enter the ones below. This time the router is told to use an exit interface instead of a next hop. DO NOT USE BOTH THE ABOVE AND BELOW TOGETHER.

    ```
    RouterA(config)#ip route 172.30.0.0 255.255.0.0 serial 0
    RouterA(config)#ip route 172.31.0.0 255.255.0.0 serial 0
    ```

5. Next, we configure the same commands on router B.

    ```
    Set the IP addresses:
    Router#config t
    Router(config)#hostname RouterB
    RouterB(config)#interface serial 0
    RouterB(config-if)#ip address 192.168.1.2 255.255.255.252
    RouterB(config-if)#no shutdown
    RouterB(config-if)#interface loopback 0
    RouterB(config-if)#ip address 172.30.1.1 255.255.0.0
    RouterB(config-if)#interface loopback 1
    RouterB(config-if)#ip address 172.31.1.1 255.255.0.0
    RouterB(config-if)#^Z
    RouterB#
    ```

    Now make sure you can ping across the serial link. If you cannot, then check the configurations again.

    ```
    RouterA#ping 192.168.1.2

    Type escape sequence to abort.
    Sending 5, 100-byte ICMP Echos to 192.168.1.2, timeout is 2 seconds:
    !!!!!
    Success rate is 100 percent (5/5), round-trip min/avg/max = 28/31/32 ms
    ```

    ```
    Configure telnet access:
    RouterB(config)#line vty 0 4
    RouterB(config-line)#login local
    RouterB(config-line)#exit
    RouterB(config)#username banbury password ccna
    ```

    ```
    Configure the "enable secret password":
    RouterB(config)#enable secret cisco
    ```

Set the static route:

```
RouterB(config)#ip route 172.16.0.0 255.255.0.0 192.168.1.1
RouterB(config)#ip route 172.20.0.0 255.255.0.0 192.168.1.1
```

The above command will configure a static route on router B. To get to the destination network of 172.20.0.0 and 172.16.0.0, use the next hop of 192.168.1.1. Instead of using the above commands, you can enter the ones below. This time the router is told to use an exit interface instead of a next hop. **DO NOT USE BOTH THE ABOVE AND BELOW TOGETHER.**

```
Router B:
RouterB(config)#ip route 172.16.0.0 255.255.0.0 serial 0
RouterB(config)#ip route 172.20.0.0 255.255.0.0 serial 0
```

This command will configure a static route to the 172.20.0.0 or 172.16.0.0 network, but instead of having a next hop address, we have specified an exit interface to use.

6. Use the "show ip route" command to check that the static routes are in the routing table, and that the next hop address is correct.

```
RouterA#show ip route
Codes: C - connected, S - static, I - IGRP, R - RIP, M - mobile, B - BGP
D - EIGRP, EX - EIGRP external, O - OSPF, IA - OSPF inter area N1 - OSPF
NSSA external type 1, N2 - OSPF NSSA external type 2 E1 - OSPF external
type 1, E2 - OSPF external type 2, E - EGP
i - IS-IS, L1 - IS-IS level-1, L2 - IS-IS level-2, ia - IS-IS inter area
* - candidate default, U - per-user static route, o - ODR P - periodic
downloaded static route

Gateway of last resort is not set

C    172.16.0.0/16 is directly connected, Loopback0
C    172.20.0.0/16 is directly connected, Loopback1
S    172.31.0.0/16 [1/0] via 192.168.1.2
S    172.30.0.0/16 [1/0] via 192.168.1.2
     192.168.1.0/30 is subnetted, 1 subnets
C    192.168.1.0 is directly connected, Serial0
```

7. To test connectivity, you will need to use the "ping" command. And to logon to your neighbor's router, you need to use the "telnet" command:

```
RouterA#ping 172.30.1.1  ⇦ This will send a ping packet to the
   address specified; there should be five replies if everything is OK
Type escape sequence to abort.
Sending 5, 100-byte ICMP Echos to 172.30.1.1, timeout is 2 seconds:
```

```
!!!!!
Success rate is 100 percent(5/5),round-trip min/avg/max = 1/2/4 ms
RouterA#

RouterA#ping 172.31.1.1

Type escape sequence to abort.
Sending 5, 100-byte ICMP Echos to 172.31.1.1, timeout is 2 seconds:
!!!!!
Success rate is 100 percent (5/5), round-trip min/avg/max = 32/32/32 ms
RouterA#

RouterA#telnet 172.30.1.1 ⇦ This will open a telnet connection to
            your neighbor's router. If telnet access has been set up
            correctly, you should be presented with a login message.
            Type "exit" to quit a telnet session.
RouterA#telnet 172.30.1.1
Trying 172.30.1.1 ... Open


User Access Verification

Username: banbury
Password: ⇦ Password will not show as you type it
RouterB>exit

[Connection to 172.30.1.1 closed by foreign host]
RouterA#
Router B:
Do the same on router B:
RouterB#ping 172.16.1.1
RouterB#ping 172.20.1.1

RouterB#telnet 172.16.1.1
```

Show runs

```
RouterA#show run
Building configuration...

Current configuration : 704 bytes
!
version 12.1
no service single-slot-reload-enable
service timestamps debug uptime
service timestamps log uptime
no service password-encryption
!
hostname RouterA
!
username banbury password 0 ccna
```

```
!
ip subnet-zero
!
interface Loopback0
 ip address 172.16.1.1 255.255.0.0
!
interface Loopback1
 ip address 172.20.1.1 255.255.0.0
!
interface Ethernet0
 no ip address
 shutdown
!
interface Serial0
 ip address 192.168.1.1 255.255.255.252
 clockrate 64000
!
interface Serial1
 no ip address
 shutdown
!
ip classless
ip route 172.30.0.0 255.255.0.0 192.168.1.2
ip route 172.31.0.0 255.255.0.0 192.168.1.2
no ip http server
!
line con 0
line 1 8
line aux 0
line vty 0 4
 login local
!
end

RouterA#

---
RouterB# show run
Building configuration...

Current configuration : 678 bytes
!
version 12.1
no service single-slot-reload-enable
service timestamps debug uptime
service timestamps log uptime
no service password-encryption
!
hostname RouterB
!
username banbury password 0 ccna
!
```

```
ip subnet-zero
!
interface Loopback0
 ip address 172.30.1.1 255.255.0.0
!
interface Loopback1
 ip address 172.31.1.1 255.255.0.0
!
interface Ethernet0
 no ip address
 shutdown
!
interface Serial0
 ip address 192.168.1.2 255.255.255.252
!
interface Serial1
 no ip address
 shutdown
!
ip classless
ip route 172.16.0.0 255.255.0.0 192.168.1.1
ip route 172.20.0.0 255.255.0.0 192.168.1.1
no ip http server
!
line con 0
line aux 0
line vty 0 4
 login local
!
end
RouterB#
```

LAB 2: IP ROUTING PROTOCOL LAB — RIP VERSION 2

The physical topology is as shown in Figure 15–2.

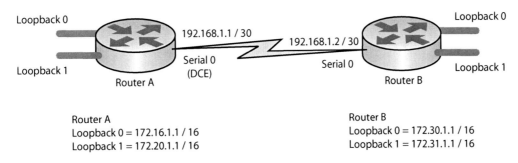

Router A
Loopback 0 = 172.16.1.1 / 16
Loopback 1 = 172.20.1.1 / 16

Router B
Loopback 0 = 172.30.1.1 / 16
Loopback 1 = 172.31.1.1 / 16

Figure 15–2: RIP v2

Lab exercise

Your task is to configure the network in Figure 15–2 to allow full connectivity using the routing protocol RIP version 2. Please feel free to try the lab without following the lab walk-through section.

Text printed in a `monospaced font` indicates commands that can be entered on the router.

Purpose

RIPv2 is fairly common in smaller networks. It is our first look at classless routing and will provide a valuable foundation for more advanced routing protocols later on.

Lab objectives

1. Use the IP addressing scheme depicted in Figure 15–2. Router A needs to be configured with a clock rate on interface serial 0. Set this to 64000.
2. Set telnet access for the router to use the local login permissions of username "banbury" and the password "ccna".
3. Configure the "enable password" to be "cisco".
4. Configure the routing protocol RIPv2 to advertise all networks attached to the router.
5. Ensure the routing information is correct by checking the routing table for entries of your neighbor's addresses.
6. Finally, try to ping all loopback interfaces of your neighbor, and then try to access your neighbor router via telnet.

Lab walk-through

1. To set the IP addresses on an interface you will need to do the following:

```
Router#config t
Router(config)#hostname RouterA
RouterA(config)#
RouterA(config)#interface serial 0
RouterA(config-if)#ip address 192.168.1.1 255.255.255.252
RouterA(config-if)#clock rate 64000 ⇦ If this is the DCE side
RouterA(config-if)#no shutdown
RouterA(config-if)#interface loopback 0  (no need for "no shutdown" on
loopback interfaces)
RouterA(config-if)#ip address 172.16.1.1 255.255.0.0
RouterA(config-if)#interface loopback 1
RouterA(config-if)#ip address 172.20.1.1 255.255.0.0
RouterA(config-if)#^Z
RouterA#
Router B:
Router#config t
Router(config)#hostname RouterB
RouterB(config)#
RouterB(config)#interface serial 0
RouterB(config-if)#ip address 192.168.1.2 255.255.255.252
RouterB(config-if)#no shutdown
RouterB(config-if)#interface loopback 0
RouterB(config-if)#ip address 172.30.1.1 255.255.0.0
RouterB(config-if)#interface loopback 1
RouterB(config-if)#ip address 172.31.1.1 255.255.0.0
RouterB(config-if)#^Z
RouterB#
```

2. To set the clock rate on a serial interface (DCE connection only) you need to use the "`clock rate #`" command on the serial interface, where # indicates the speed:

```
RouterA(config-if)#clock rate 64000
```

Ping across the serial link now.

3. To set telnet access you need to configure the VTY lines to allow telnet access: to do this type (from configuration mode):

```
RouterA(config)#line vty 0 4 ⇦ Enters the VTY line configuration
RouterA(config-line)#login local ⇦ This will use local usernames and
                                  passwords for telnet access
RouterA(config-line)#exit ⇦ Exit the VTY config mode
RouterA(config)#username banbury password ccna ⇦ Creates username and
                              password for telnet access (login local)
Router B:
RouterB(config)#line vty 0 4
RouterB(config-line)#login local
RouterB(config-line)#exit
RouterB(config)#username banbury password ccna
```

4. To set the "enable password", do the following:

```
RouterA(config)#enable secret cisco ⇦ Sets the "enable secret"
                                        password (encrypted)
Router B:
RouterB(config)#enable secret cisco
```

5. To configure RIP on a router, there are two steps: first, enable the routing protocol; and second, specify the networks to be advertised by RIP:

```
RouterA(config)#router rip ⇦ Enables RIP routing process
RouterA(config-router)#version 2 ⇦ Enable RIPv2
RouterA(config-router)#network 192.168.1.0
RouterA(config-router)#network 172.16.0.0
RouterA(config-router)#network 172.20.0.0 ⇦ Specifies the networks
    for RIPv2 to advertise; one network statement is needed for every
    network advertised.
Router B:
RouterB(config)#router rip
RouterB(config-router)#version 2
RouterB(config-router)#network 192.168.1.0
RouterB(config-router)#network 172.30.0.0
RouterB(config-router)#network 172.31.0.0
```

6. Use the "show ip route" command to determine if the networks being advertised by your neighbor's RIP process are in your routing table.

```
RouterA#show ip route
Codes: C - connected, S - static, I - IGRP, R - RIP, M - mobile, B - BGP D
- EIGRP, EX - EIGRP external, O - OSPF, IA - OSPF inter area
N1 - OSPF NSSA external type 1, N2 - OSPF NSSA external type 2
E1 - OSPF external type 1, E2 - OSPF external type 2, E - EGP
i - IS-IS, L1 - IS-IS level-1, L2 - IS-IS level-2, ia - IS-IS inter area *
- candidate default, U - per-user static route, o - ODR
P - periodic downloaded static route

Gateway of last resort is not set

C    172.16.0.0/16 is directly connected, Loopback0
C    172.20.0.0/16 is directly connected, Loopback1
R    172.31.0.0/16 [120/1] via 192.168.1.2, 00:00:05, Serial0
R    172.30.0.0/16 [120/1] via 192.168.1.2, 00:00:05, Serial0
     192.168.1.0/30 is subnetted, 1 subnets
C    192.168.1.0 is directly connected, Serial0
RouterA#
```

You can check that RIPv2 is enabled with the "show ip protocols" command on both sides.

```
RouterA#show ip protocols
Routing Protocol is "rip"
  Sending updates every 30 seconds, next due in 14 seconds
  Invalid after 180 seconds, hold down 180, flushed after 240
  Outgoing update filter list for all interfaces is not set
  Incoming update filter list for all interfaces is not set
  Redistributing: rip
  Default version control: send version 2, receive version 2
    Interface          Send  Recv  Triggered RIP  Key-chain
    Loopback0           2     2
    Loopback1           2     2
    Serial0             2     2
  Automatic network summarization is in effect
  Maximum path: 4
  Routing for Networks:
    172.16.0.0
    172.20.0.0
    192.168.1.0
  Routing Information Sources:
    Gateway          Distance      Last Update
    192.168.1.2        120         00:00:08
  Distance: (default is 120)

RouterA#
```

You can debug RIP packets with the "debug ip rip" command:

```
RouterA#debug ip rip
RIP protocol debugging is on
RouterA#
01:58:03: RIP: received v2 update from 192.168.1.2 on Serial0
01:58:03:      172.30.0.0/16 via 0.0.0.0 in 1 hops ⇐ Subnet mask
                                                       advertised
01:58:03:      172.31.0.0/16 via 0.0.0.0 in 1 hops
01:58:21: RIP: sending v2 update to 224.0.0.9 via Loopback0 (172.16.1.1)
01:58:21: RIP: build update entries
01:58:21:       172.20.0.0/16 via 0.0.0.0, metric 1, tag 0
01:58:21:       172.30.0.0/16 via 0.0.0.0, metric 2, tag 0
01:58:21:       172.31.0.0/16 via 0.0.0.0, metric 2, tag 0
01:58:21:       192.168.1.0/24 via 0.0.0.0, metric 1, tag 0
01:58:21: RIP: sending v2 update to 224.0.0.9 via Loopback1 (172.20.1.1)
01:58:21: RIP: build update entries
01:58:21:       172.16.0.0/16 via 0.0.0.0, metric 1, tag 0
01:58:21:       172.30.0.0/16 via 0.0.0.0, metric 2, tag 0
01:58:21:       172.31.0.0/16 via 0.0.0.0, metric 2, tag 0
01:58:21:       192.168.1.0/24 via 0.0.0.0, metric 1, tag 0
01:58:21: RIP: sending v2 update to 224.0.0.9 via Serial0 (192.168.1.1)
01:58:21: RIP: build update entries ⇐ Enter "un all" to turn off
```

If you add the "no auto-summary" command under the RIP config for both routers A and B, the router will then advertise the correct /30 mask for the 192.168.1.x network.

```
RouterA#config t
RouterA(config)#router rip
RouterA(config-router)#no auto-summary
RouterA(config-router)#^Z

RouterA#debug ip rip
RIP protocol debugging is on
RouterA#
01:26:41: RIP: received v2 update from 192.168.1.2 on Serial0
01:26:41:       172.30.0.0/16 via 0.0.0.0 in 1 hops
01:26:41:       172.31.0.0/16 via 0.0.0.0 in 1 hops
01:26:55: RIP: sending v2 update to 224.0.0.9 via Loopback0 (172.16.1.1)
01:26:55: RIP: build update entries
01:26:55:       172.20.0.0/16 via 0.0.0.0, metric 1, tag 0
01:26:55:       172.30.0.0/16 via 0.0.0.0, metric 2, tag 0
01:26:55:       172.31.0.0/16 via 0.0.0.0, metric 2, tag 0
01:26:55:       192.168.1.0/30 via 0.0.0.0, metric 1, tag 0
```

To test connectivity you will need to use the ping command, and to logon to your neighbor's router you need to use the telnet command:

```
RouterA#ping 172.30.1.1 ⇐ This will send a ping packet to the
 address specified; there should be five replies if everything is OK
RouterA#ping 172.30.1.1

Type escape sequence to abort.
Sending 5, 100-byte ICMP Echos to 172.30.1.1, timeout is 2 seconds:
!!!!!
Success rate is 100 percent (5/5), round-trip min/avg/max = 32/32/32 ms
RouterA#

RouterA#ping 172.31.1.1

RouterA#telnet 172.30.1.1 ⇐ This will open a telnet connection to
            your neighbor's router. If telnet access has been set up
            correctly you should be presented with a login message.
Router B:
RouterB#ping 172.16.1.1
RouterB#ping 172.20.1.1
RouterB#telnet 172.16.1.1
```

7. Now, please enter reload at the "Router#" prompt and type "yes".

Show runs

```
RouterA#show run
Building configuration...

Current configuration : 796 bytes
!
version 12.1
service timestamps debug uptime
service timestamps log uptime
no service password-encryption
!
hostname RouterA
!
enable secret 5 $1$rujI$BJ8GgiK8U9p5cdfXyApPr/
!
username banbury password 0 ccna
!
ip subnet-zero
!
interface Loopback0
 ip address 172.16.1.1 255.255.0.0
!
interface Loopback1
 ip address 172.20.1.1 255.255.0.0
!
interface Ethernet0
 no ip address
 shutdown
!
interface Serial0
 ip address 192.168.1.1 255.255.255.252
 clockrate 64000
!
interface Serial1
 no ip address
 shutdown
!
interface BRI0
 no ip address
 shutdown

 !
router rip
 version 2
 network 172.16.0.0
 network 172.20.0.0
 network 192.168.1.0
!
ip classless
no ip http server
!
```

```
line con 0
 !
line aux 0
line vty 0 4
 login local
 !
end

RouterA#

---


RouterB#show run
Building configuration...

Current configuration : 782 bytes
!
version 12.1
service timestamps debug uptime
service timestamps log uptime
no service password-encryption
!
hostname RouterB
!
enable secret 5 $1$ydeA$MyfRKevOckjm7w/OornnB1
!
username banbury password 0 ccna
!
ip subnet-zero
!
interface Loopback0
 ip address 172.30.1.1 255.255.0.0
!
interface Loopback1
 ip address 172.31.1.1 255.255.0.0
!
interface Serial0
 ip address 192.168.1.2 255.255.255.252
!
interface Serial1
 no ip address
 shutdown
!
interface Ethernet0
 no ip address
 shutdown
!
interface BRI0
 no ip address
 shutdown

!
```

```
router rip
 version 2
 network 172.30.0.0
 network 172.31.0.0
 network 192.168.1.0
!
ip classless
no ip http server
!
line con 0
 !
line aux 0
line vty 0 4
 login local
!
end

RouterB#
```

LAB 3: IP ROUTING PROTOCOL LAB — OSPF

The physical topology is as shown in Figure 15–3.

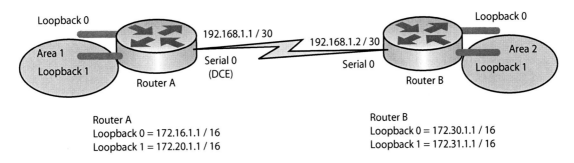

Router A
Loopback 0 = 172.16.1.1 / 16
Loopback 1 = 172.20.1.1 / 16

Router B
Loopback 0 = 172.30.1.1 / 16
Loopback 1 = 172.31.1.1 / 16

Figure 15–3: OSPF lab

Lab exercise

Your task is to configure the network in Figure 15–3 to allow full connectivity using the OSPF routing protocol. Please feel free to try the lab without following the lab walk-through section. Text printed in a monospaced font indicates commands that can be entered on the router.

Purpose

OSPF is a highly robust and scalable protocol and by far the most popular with medium-to-large companies. A good working knowledge of the protocol is vital to your success in the exam and as a Cisco engineer.

Lab objectives

1. Use the IP addressing scheme depicted in Figure 15–3. The student who is using router A needs to configure a clock rate on interface serial 0: set this to 64000.
2. Set telnet access for the router to use the local login permissions of username "banbury" and the password "ccna".
3. Configure the "enable password" to be "cisco".
4. Configure the OSPF routing protocol to advertise all networks attached to the router.
5. Ensure the routing information is correct by checking the routing table for entries of your neighbor's addresses.
6. Finally, try to ping all loopback interfaces of your neighbor, and then try to access your neighbor router via telnet.

Lab walk-through

1. To set the IP addresses to an interface, you will need to do the following:

```
Router#config t
Router(config)#hostname RouterA
RouterA(config)#
RouterA(config)#interface serial 0
RouterA(config-if)#ip address 192.168.1.1 255.255.255.252
RouterA(config-if)#clock rate 64000  ⇦ If this is the DCE side
RouterA(config-if)#no shutdown
RouterA(config-if)#interface loopback 0
RouterA(config-if)#ip address 172.16.1.1 255.255.0.0
RouterA(config-if)#interface loopback 1
RouterA(config-if)#ip address 172.20.1.1 255.255.0.0
RouterA(config-if)#^Z
RouterA#
Router B:
Router#config t
Router(config)#hostname RouterB
RouterB(config)#
RouterB(config)#interface serial 0
RouterB(config-if)#ip address 192.168.1.2 255.255.255.252
RouterB(config-if)#no shutdown
RouterB(config-if)#interface loopback 0
RouterB(config-if)#ip address 172.30.1.1 255.255.0.0
RouterB(config-if)#interface loopback 1
RouterB(config-if)#ip address 172.31.1.1 255.255.0.0
RouterB(config-if)#^Z
RouterB#
```

2. To set the clock rate on a serial interface (DCE connection only), you need to use the "clock rate #" command on the serial interface, where # indicates the speed:

```
RouterA(config-if)#clock rate 64000
```

Ping across the serial link now.

3. To set telnet access, you need to configure the VTY lines to allow telnet access: to do this type (from configuration mode):

```
RouterA(config)#line vty 0 4 ⇦ Enters the VTY line configuration

RouterA(config-line)#login local ⇦ This will use local usernames
                                 and passwords for telnet access
RouterA(config-line)#exit ⇦ Exit the VTY config mode
RouterA(config)#username banbury password ccna ⇦ Creates username
                        and password for telnet access (login local)
Router B:
```

```
RouterB(config)#line vty 0 4
RouterB(config-line)#login local
RouterB(config-line)#exit
RouterB(config)#username banbury password ccna
```

4. To set the "enable password" do the following:

```
RouterA(config)#enable secret cisco ⇔ Sets the "enable password"
                                        (encrypted)
Router B:
RouterB(config)#enable secret cisco
```

5. To configure OSPF on a router there are two steps: first, enable the routing protocol; and second, specify the networks to be advertised by OSPF:

```
RouterA(config)#router ospf 20 ⇔ Enables the OSPF routing process
RouterA(config-router)#network 172.20.0.0 0.0.255.255 area 1
RouterA(config-router)#network 192.168.1.0 0.0.0.3 area 0
RouterA(config-router)#network 172.16.0.0 0.0.255.255 area 0
    ⇔ Specifies the networks for OSPF to advertise; one network
       statement is needed for every network advertised.
Router B:
RouterB(config)#router ospf 20
RouterB(config-router)#network 192.168.1.0 0.0.0.3 area 0
RouterB(config-router)#network 172.30.0.0 0.0.255.255 area 0
RouterB(config-router)#network 172.31.0.0 0.0.255.255 area 2
```

You should see a console message telling you that the OSPF adjacencies have been formed. For the command to take you should come out of config mode with the ^Z or type "exit" twice.

```
RouterB#
02:38:57: %SYS-5-CONFIG_I: Configured from console by console
02:38:59: %OSPF-5-ADJCHG: Process 20, Nbr 172.20.1.1 on Serial0 from
LOADING to FULL, Loading Done
```

Use the "show ip route" command to determine if the networks being advertised by your neighbor's OSPF process are in your routing table.

```
RouterA#show ip route
Codes: C - connected, S - static, I - IGRP, R - RIP, M - mobile, B - BGP D
 - EIGRP, EX - EIGRP external, O - OSPF, IA - OSPF inter area
N1 - OSPF NSSA external type 1, N2 - OSPF NSSA external type 2
E1 - OSPF external type 1, E2 - OSPF external type 2, E - EGP
i - IS-IS, L1 - IS-IS level-1, L2 - IS-IS level-2, ia - IS-IS inter area *
 - candidate default, U - per-user static route, o - ODR
```

```
P - periodic downloaded static route

Gateway of last resort is not set

C    172.16.0.0/16 is directly connected, Loopback0
C    172.20.0.0/16 is directly connected, Loopback1
     172.31.0.0/32 is subnetted, 1 subnets
O IA    172.31.1.1 [110/65] via 192.168.1.2, 00:01:33, Serial0
     172.30.0.0/32 is subnetted, 1 subnets
O       172.30.1.1 [110/65] via 192.168.1.2, 00:01:33, Serial0
     192.168.1.0/30 is subnetted, 1 subnets
C       192.168.1.0 is directly connected, Serial0
RouterA#
```

You can issue a "show ip protocols" command to check on the OSPF configuration.

```
RouterA#show ip protocols
Routing Protocol is "ospf 20"
  Outgoing update filter list for all interfaces is not set
  Incoming update filter list for all interfaces is not set
  Router ID 172.20.1.1
  It is an area border router
  Number of areas in this router is 2. 2 normal 0 stub 0 nssa
  Maximum path: 4
  Routing for Networks:
    172.16.0.0 0.0.255.255 area 0
    172.20.0.0 0.0.255.255 area 1
    192.168.1.0 0.0.0.3 area 0
  Routing Information Sources:
    Gateway         Distance      Last Update
    172.31.1.1           110      00:05:48
    172.20.1.1           110      00:05:48
  Distance: (default is 110)

RouterA#
```

6. To test connectivity you will need to use the ping command, and to logon to your neighbor's router you need to use the telnet command:

```
RouterA#ping 172.30.1.1 ⇔ This will send a ping packet to the
                          address specified; there should be
                          five replies if everything is OK
RouterA#ping 172.30.1.1

Type escape sequence to abort.
Sending 5, 100-byte ICMP Echos to 172.30.1.1, timeout is 2 seconds:
!!!!!
Success rate is 100 percent (5/5), round-trip min/avg/max = 28/31/32 ms
RouterA#
RouterA#telnet 172.31.1.1 ⇔ This will open a telnet connection to
          your neighbor's router. If telnet access has been set up
          correctly you should be presented with a login message.
```

```
RouterA#telnet 172.31.1.1
Trying 172.31.1.1 ... Open

User Access Verification

Username: banbury
Password:
RouterB>exit

[Connection to 172.31.1.1 closed by foreign host]
RouterA#

RouterA#show ip ospf neighbor

Neighbor   ID Pri  State   Dead Time   Address   Interface
172.31.1.1 1   FULL/  -   00:00:29    192.168.1.2    Serial0
```

Test the following commands also:

```
show ip ospf database
show ip ospf interface
debug ip ospf packet
```

Router B:

Do the same with router B:

```
RouterB#ping 172.16.1.1
RouterB#ping 172.20.1.1
RouterB#telnet 172.16.1.1
```

7. Now please enter reload at the "Router#" prompt and type "yes".

Show runs

```
RouterA#show run
Building configuration...

Current configuration : 867 bytes
!
version 12.1
service timestamps debug uptime
service timestamps log uptime
no service password-encryption
!
hostname RouterA
!
enable secret 5 $1$rujI$BJ8GgiK8U9p5cdfXyApPr/
!
username banbury password 0 ccna
!
```

```
ip subnet-zero
!
interface Loopback0
 ip address 172.16.1.1 255.255.0.0
!
interface Loopback1
 ip address 172.20.1.1 255.255.0.0
!
interface Ethernet0
 no ip address
 shutdown
!
interface Serial0
 ip address 192.168.1.1 255.255.255.252
 clockrate 64000
!
interface Serial1
 no ip address
 shutdown
!
interface BRI0
 no ip address
 shutdown
!
router ospf 20
 log-adjacency-changes
 network 172.16.0.0 0.0.255.255 area 0
 network 172.20.0.0 0.0.255.255 area 1
 network 192.168.1.0 0.0.0.3 area 0
!
ip classless
no ip http server
!
line con 0
 password letmein
 login
line aux 0
line vty 0 4
 login local
!
end

RouterA#

---

RouterB#show run
Building configuration...

Current configuration : 853 bytes
!
version 12.1
```

```
service timestamps debug uptime
service timestamps log uptime
no service password-encryption
!
hostname RouterB
!
enable secret 5 $1$ydeA$MyfRKevOckjm7w/OornnB1
!
username banbury password 0 ccna
!
ip subnet-zero
!
interface Loopback0
 ip address 172.30.1.1 255.255.0.0
!
interface Loopback1
 ip address 172.31.1.1 255.255.0.0
!
interface Serial0
 ip address 192.168.1.2 255.255.255.252
!
interface Serial1
 no ip address
 shutdown
!
interface Ethernet0
 no ip address
 shutdown
!
interface BRI0
 no ip address
 shutdown
 !
router ospf 20
 log-adjacency-changes
 network 172.30.0.0 0.0.255.255 area 0
 network 172.31.0.0 0.0.255.255 area 2
 network 192.168.1.0 0.0.0.3 area 0
!
ip classless
no ip http server
!
line con 0
 password letmein
 login
line aux 0
line vty 0 4
 login local
!
end

RouterB#
```

LAB 4: IP ROUTING PROTOCOL LAB — EIGRP

The physical topology is as shown in Figure 15–4.

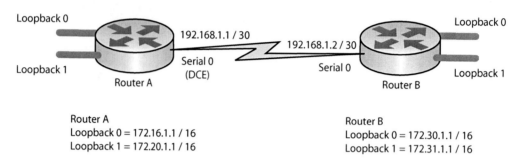

Router A
Loopback 0 = 172.16.1.1 / 16
Loopback 1 = 172.20.1.1 / 16

Router B
Loopback 0 = 172.30.1.1 / 16
Loopback 1 = 172.31.1.1 / 16

Figure 15–4: EIGRP lab

Lab exercise

Your task is to configure the network in Figure 15–4 to allow full connectivity using the EIGRP routing protocol. Please feel free to try the lab without following the lab walk-through section. Text written in monospaced type indicates commands that can be entered on the router.

Purpose

EIGRP is a very popular routing protocols and in wide use today. You will need to have a good working knowledge of it for the CCNA exam and as a Cisco engineer.

Lab objectives

1. Use the IP-addressing scheme depicted in Figure 15–4. The student who is using router A needs to configure a clock rate on interface serial 0: set this to 64000.
2. Set telnet access for the router to use the local login permissions of username "banbury" and the password "ccna".
3. Configure the "enable password" to be "cisco".
4. Configure the EIGRP routing protocol to advertise all networks attached to the router.
5. Ensure the routing information is correct by checking the routing table for entries of your neighbor's addresses.
6. Finally, try to ping all loopback interfaces of your neighbor, and then try to access your neighbor router via telnet.

Lab walk-through

1. To set the IP addresses on an interface, you will need to do the following:

```
Router#config t
Router(config)#hostname RouterA
```

```
RouterA(config)#
RouterA(config)#interface serial 0
RouterA(config-if)#ip address 192.168.1.1 255.255.255.252
RouterA(config-if)#clock rate 64000 ⇔ If this is the DCE side
RouterA(config-if)#no shutdown
RouterA(config-if)#interface loopback 0 ⇔ No "no shut" required
RouterA(config-if)#ip address 172.16.1.1 255.255.0.0
RouterA(config-if)#interface loopback 1
RouterA(config-if)#ip address 172.20.1.1 255.255.0.0
RouterA(config-if)#^Z
RouterA#
Router B:
Router#config t
Router(config)#hostname RouterB
RouterB(config)#
RouterB(config)#interface serial 0
RouterB(config-if)#ip address 192.168.1.2 255.255.255.252
RouterB(config-if)#no shutdown
RouterB(config-if)#interface loopback 0
RouterB(config-if)#ip address 172.30.1.1 255.255.0.0
RouterB(config-if)#interface loopback 1
RouterB(config-if)#ip address 172.31.1.1 255.255.0.0
RouterB(config-if)#^Z
RouterB#
```

2. To set the clock rate on a serial interface (DCE connection only), you need to use the "clock rate #" command on the serial interface, where # indicates the speed:

```
RouterA(config-if)#clock rate 64000
```

Ping across the serial link now.

3. To set telnet access, you need to configure the VTY lines to allow telnet access. To do this, type (from configuration mode):

```
RouterA(config)#line vty 0 4 ⇔ Enters the VTY line configuration

RouterA(config-line)#login local ⇔ This will use local usernames
                                     and passwords for telnet access
RouterA(config-line)#exit ⇔ Exit the VTY config mode
RouterA(config)#username banbury password ccna ⇔ Creates username and
                                  password for telnet access (login local)
Router B:
RouterB(config)#line vty 0 4
RouterB(config-line)#login local
RouterB(config-line)#exit
RouterB(config)#username banbury password ccna
```

4. To set the "enable password", do the following:

```
RouterA(config)#enable secret cisco ⇔ Sets the "enable password"
                                        (encrypted)
Router B:
RouterB(config)#enable secret cisco
```

5. To configure EIGRP on a router there are two steps: first, enable the routing protocol and second, specify the networks to be advertised by EIGRP.

```
RouterA(config)#router eigrp 20

RouterA(config-router)#network 192.168.1.0 ⇔ Specifies the networks
                        for EIGRP to advertise; one network statement
                        is needed for every network advertised
RouterA(config-router)#network 172.16.0.0
RouterA(config-router)#network 172.20.0.0
RouterA(config-router)#no auto-summary ⇔ This command prevents the
                        router from summarizing the 192.168.1.0 network
Router B:
RouterB(config)#router eigrp 20
RouterB(config-router)#network 192.168.1.0
RouterB(config-router)#network 172.30.0.0
RouterB(config-router)#network 172.31.0.0
RouterB(config-router)#no auto-summary
```

Use the "show ip route" command to determine if the networks being advertised by your neighbor's EIGRP process are in your routing table.

Without the "no auto-summary" command, the router would automatically summarize at the major subnet boundary. It is not so important for this lab. However, if you were using 10.0.0.0 addressing, the network details would be summarized to 10.0.0.0. Make sure you are aware of the "no auto-summary" command and when you would want to use it.

```
RouterA#show ip route
Codes: C - connected, S - static, I - IGRP, R - RIP, M - mobile, B - BGP,
D - EIGRP, EX - EIGRP external, O - OSPF, IA - OSPF inter area, N1 - OSPF
NSSA external type 1, N2 - OSPF NSSA external type 2, E1 - OSPF external
type 1, E2 - OSPF external type 2, E - EGP
i - IS-IS, L1 - IS-IS level-1, L2 - IS-IS level-2, ia - IS-IS inter area,
* - candidate default, U - per-user static route, o - ODR, P - periodic
downloaded static route

Gateway of last resort is not set
```

```
C    172.16.0.0/16 is directly connected, Loopback0
C    172.20.0.0/16 is directly connected, Loopback1
D    172.31.0.0/16 [90/2297856] via 192.168.1.2, 00:00:03, Serial0
D    172.30.0.0/16 [90/2297856] via 192.168.1.2, 00:00:03, Serial0
     192.168.1.0/30 is subnetted, 1 subnets
C        192.168.1.0 is directly connected, Serial0
RouterA#
```

You may also have a summary route in your routing table.

```
RouterA#show ip protocols

Routing Protocol is "eigrp 20"
  Outgoing update filter list for all interfaces is not set
  Incoming update filter list for all interfaces is not set
  Default networks flagged in outgoing updates
  Default networks accepted from incoming updates
  EIGRP metric weight K1=1, K2=0, K3=1, K4=0, K5=0
  EIGRP maximum hopcount 100
  EIGRP maximum metric variance 1
  Redistributing: eigrp 20
  Automatic network summarization is not in effect
  Maximum path: 4
  Routing for Networks:
    172.16.0.0
    172.20.0.0
    192.168.1.0
  Routing Information Sources:
    Gateway         Distance      Last Update
    (this router)         90      00:03:23
    192.168.1.2           90      00:02:08
  Distance: internal 90 external 170
```

6. To test connectivity, you will need to use the ping command and to logon to your neighbor's router, you need to use the telnet command:

```
RouterA#ping 172.30.1.1 ← This will send a ping packet to the address
specified; there should be five replies if everything is OK
Type escape sequence to abort.
Sending 5, 100-byte ICMP Echos to 172.30.1.1, timeout is 2 seconds:
!!!!!
Success rate is 100 percent (5/5), round-trip min/avg/max = 32/32/32 ms


RouterA#ping 172.31.1.1

RouterA#telnet 172.30.1. ⇐ This will open a telnet connection to
  your neighbor's router. If telnet access has been set up correctly,
  you should be presented with a login message.
  Trying 172.30.1.1 ... Open
```

```
User Access Verification

Username: banbury
Password:
RouterB>exit

[Connection to 172.30.1.1 closed by foreign host]
RouterA#
```

Router B:

Do the same on router B:

```
RouterB#ping 172.20.1.1
RouterB#ping 172.16.1.1
RouterB#telnet 172.20.1.1
```

Other commands to try:

```
debug ip eigrp
show ip eigrp neighbors
show ip eigrp topology
show ip eigrp interfaces
```

7. Now please enter reload at the "Router#" prompt and type "yes".

Show runs

```
RouterA#show run
Building configuration...

Current configuration : 838 bytes
!
version 12.1
service timestamps debug uptime
service timestamps log uptime
no service password-encryption
!
hostname RouterA
!
enable secret 5 $1$rujI$BJ8GgiK8U9p5cdfXyApPr/
!
username banbury password 0 ccna
!
ip subnet-zero
!
interface Loopback0
 ip address 172.16.1.1 255.255.0.0
!
interface Loopback1
```

```
 ip address 172.20.1.1 255.255.0.0
!
interface Ethernet0
 no ip address
 shutdown
!
interface Serial0
 ip address 192.168.1.1 255.255.255.252
 clockrate 64000
!
interface Serial1
 no ip address
 shutdown
!
interface BRI0
 no ip address
 shutdown

!
router eigrp 20
 network 172.16.0.0
 network 172.20.0.0
 network 192.168.1.0
 no auto-summary
 no eigrp log-neighbor-changes
!
ip classless
no ip http server
!
line con 0
 !
line aux 0
line vty 0 4
 login local
!
end

RouterA#

- - -

RouterB#show run
Building configuration...

Current configuration : 824 bytes
!
version 12.1
service timestamps debug uptime
service timestamps log uptime
no service password-encryption
!
hostname RouterB
```

```
!
enable secret 5 $1$ydeA$MyfRKevOckjm7w/OornnB1
!
username banbury password 0 ccna
!
ip subnet-zero
!
interface Loopback0
 ip address 172.30.1.1 255.255.0.0
!
interface Loopback1
 ip address 172.31.1.1 255.255.0.0
!
interface Serial0
 ip address 192.168.1.2 255.255.255.252
!
interface Serial1
 no ip address
 shutdown
!
interface Ethernet0
 no ip address
 shutdown
!
interface BRI0
 no ip address
 shutdown

!
router eigrp 20
 network 172.30.0.0
 network 172.31.0.0
 network 192.168.1.0
 no auto-summary
 no eigrp log-neighbor-changes
!
ip classless
no ip http server
!
line con 0
 !
line aux 0
line vty 0 4
 login local
!
end
```

CHAPTER 16

Module 6 Labs

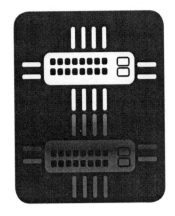

LAB 1: COPY STARTUP CONFIG USING TFTP

The physical topology is as shown in Figure 16–1.

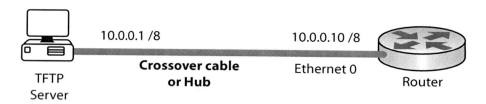

Figure 16–1: TFTP lab

Lab exercise

Your task is to configure the IP addressing as specified in Figure 16–1.

Text written in monospaced type indicates commands that can be entered on the router.

Purpose

Backing up the router's config is a crucial part of your back up and disaster avoidance procedures. You will also need to use a TFTP server if you want to upgrade your router's IOS. Familiarity with using a TFTP server is a fundamental skill for a Cisco engineer.

Lab objectives

1. Configure the router's Ethernet interface.
2. Put TFTP software onto your PC.
3. Connect the PC and router with a crossover cable or using a hub or switch.
4. Ping across the Ethernet link.
5. Copy the startup config from the router to the TFTP Server.

Lab walk-through

1. Configure the network shown in Figure 16–1. If you need help, look at the same as the other labs we have already configured.

   ```
   Router#config t
   RouterA(config)#interface fastethernet 0
   RouterA(config-if))#ip address 10.0.0.10 255.0.0.0
   RouterA(config-if)#no shut
   ```

2. Install TFTP software onto your PC, making it a TFTP server. You can find this from websites, such as www.solarwindsuk.net. Install the software on the root of your C drive.

3. Make sure the PC and the router are both on the same subnet. Change the IP address of the PC to 10.0.0.1 255.0.0.0. You can find how to do this on most common operating systems at www.wown.com.

4. Ping the PC from the router to confirm IP connectivity.

```
Router#ping 10.0.0.1
Type escape sequence to abort.
Sending 5, 100-byte ICMP Echos to 10.0.0.1, timeout is 2 seconds:
!!!!!
Success rate is 100 percent (5/5), round-trip min/avg/max = 32/32/32 ms
```

5. Copy the start up config to the tftp server:

```
Router#ping 10.0.0.1

Type escape sequence to abort.
Sending 5, 100-byte ICMP Echos to 10.0.0.1, timeout is 2 seconds:
!!!!!
Success rate is 100 percent (5/5), round-trip min/avg/max = 4/4/4 ms
Router#copy start tftp:
Address or name of remote host []? 10.0.0.1
Destination filename [router-confg]?
!!
421 bytes copied in 0.256 secs
Router#
```

6. Check the TFTP log to make sure the file has been received.

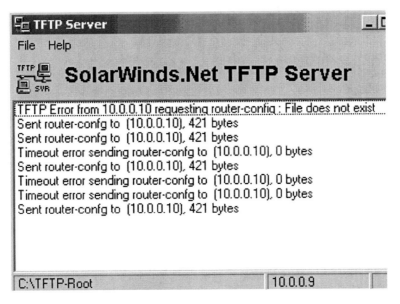

Figure 16–2: SolarWinds TFTP log

7. You can look for the config file on Windows explorer.

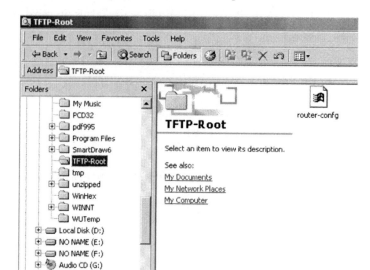

Figure 16–3: Finding the router config file

8. Reload the router. You can copy tftp:

```
Router#ping 10.0.0.1
Type escape sequence to abort.
Sending 5, 100-byte ICMP Echos to 10.0.0.1, timeout is 2 seconds:
!!!!!
Success rate is 100 percent (5/5), round-trip min/avg/max = 4/4/4 ms
Router#copy tftp: start
Address or name of remote host []? 10.0.0.1
Source filename []? router-confg * Note the spelling
Destination filename [startup-config]? * Just press Enter here
Accessing tftp://10.0.0.1/router-confg...Accessing tftp://10.0.0.1/router-
confg...
Loading router-confg .from 10.0.0.1 (via Ethernet0): !
[OK - 421/4096 bytes]
[OK]
421 bytes copied in 37.980 secs (11 bytes/sec)
Router#
00:18:04: %SYS-5-CONFIG_NV_I: Nonvolatile storage configured from
tftp://10.0.0.1/router-confg by console
```

ALWAYS, *ALWAYS* NAME THE ROUTER'S STARTUP CONFIG AS "startup-config". DOING OTHERWISE WILL PREVENT THE ROUTER FROM BOOTING CORRECTLY.

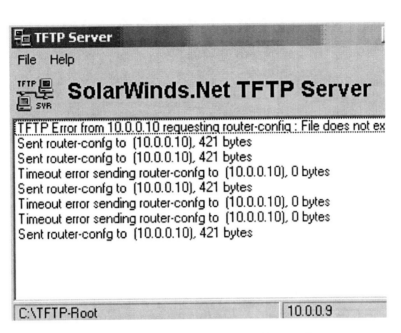

Figure 16–4: The TFTP log shows the transfer

LAB 2: TRACEROUTE FROM ROUTER A TO ROUTER B

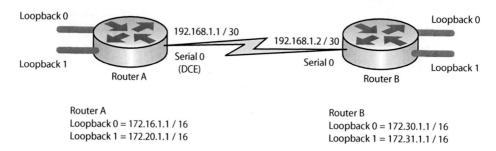

Router A
Loopback 0 = 172.16.1.1 / 16
Loopback 1 = 172.20.1.1 / 16

Router B
Loopback 0 = 172.30.1.1 / 16
Loopback 1 = 172.31.1.1 / 16

Figure 16–5: Performing a traceroute

Lab exercise

Performing a traceroute to Router B.

Using the network from Figure 16–5, traceroute to one of the loopback interfaces on Router B. This command will ideally be used from Router A to Router C in a three-router lab (see the back of the book).

Purpose

The traceroute command is a very valuable part of your troubleshooting toolkit. Make sure you use the traceroute command on the three-router labs later in the book.

Lab walk-through

From the privileged mode, type in the loopback address of Router B.

```
RouterA#traceroute 172.30.1.1

Type escape sequence to abort.
Tracing the route to 172.20.1.1

  1 RouterA (192.168.1.2) 16 msec *  16 msec
RouterA#
```

LAB 3: ARP, CDP, PING, AND TELNET LAB

The physical topology is shown in Figure 16–6.

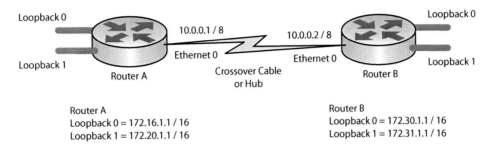

Router A
Loopback 0 = 172.16.1.1 / 16
Loopback 1 = 172.20.1.1 / 16

Router B
Loopback 0 = 172.30.1.1 / 16
Loopback 1 = 172.31.1.1 / 16

Figure 16–6: ARP, CDP, and Telnet lab

Lab exercise

Your task is to configure the network in Figure 16–6 to check for an ARP entry, CDP neighbor, and to test the ping command and the telnet command. Please feel free to try the lab without following the lab walk-through section.

Purpose

This lab explores some TCP and CDP fundamentals. ARP issues are very common and the capacity to check ARP entries will be very useful to you in your career as a Cisco engineer.

Lab objectives

1. Use the IP addressing scheme depicted in Figure 16–6. We are using Ethernet interfaces connected by a crossover cable or a switch for this lab.
2. Set telnet access for the router to use the local login permissions of username "banbury" and the password "ccna".
3. Configure the "enable password" to be "cisco".
4. Check the ARP entry on Router A. Ping Router B and check the ARP entry again.
5. Check CDP neighbor details.
6. Telnet from Router A to Router B.

Lab walk-through

1. To set the IP addresses on an interface you will need to do the following:

```
Router#config t
Router(config)#hostname RouterA
RouterA(config)#interface fastethernet 0
RouterA(config-if)#ip address 10.0.0.1 255.0.0.0
```

```
RouterA(config-if)#no shutdown
RouterA(config-if)#interface loopback 0
RouterA(config-if)#ip address 172.16.1.1 255.255.0.0
RouterA(config-if)#interface loopback 1
RouterA(config-if)#ip address 172.20.1.1 255.255.0.0
RouterA(config-if)#^Z
RouterA#
Router B:
Router#config t
Router(config)#hostname RouterB
RouterB(config)#
RouterB(config)#interface fastethernet 0
RouterB(config-if)#ip address 10.0.0.2 255.0.0.0
RouterB(config-if)#no shutdown
RouterB(config-if)#interface loopback 0
RouterB(config-if)#ip address 172.30.1.1 255.255.0.0
RouterB(config-if)#interface loopback 1
RouterB(config-if)#ip address 172.31.1.1 255.255.0.0
RouterB(config-if)#^Z
RouterB#
```

2. To set telnet access, you need to configure the VTY lines to allow telnet access. To do this, type (from configuration mode):

```
RouterA(config)#line vty 0 4 ✱ Enters the VTY line configuration
RouterA(config-line)#login local ✱ This will use local usernames
                                 and passwords for telnet access
RouterA(config-line)#exit ✱ Exit the VTY config mode
RouterA(config)#username banbury password ccna ✱ Creates username
                        and password for telnet access (login local)
Router B:
RouterB(config)#line vty 0 4
RouterB(config-line)#login local
RouterB(config-line)#exit
RouterB(config)#username banbury password ccna
```

3. To set the "enable password" do the following:

```
RouterA(config)#enable secret cisco ✱ Sets the "enable password"
                                       (encrypted)
Router B:
RouterB(config)#enable secret cisco
```

4. To configure a default route, there is one simple step (from configuration mode):

```
RouterA(config)#ip route 0.0.0.0 0.0.0.0 fastethernet 0 ✱ For all
               unknown addresses send the packet out of Ethernet 0
Router B:
RouterB(config)#ip route 0.0.0.0 0.0.0.0 fastethernet 0
```

5. To test the connection, you will need to first check that the link is up. To do this, use the "show interface" command (see below):

Make sure that Ethernet 0 is up and line protocol is up.

```
RouterA#show interface fastethernet 0
Ethernet0 is up, line protocol is up
  Hardware is Lance, address is 0000.0c3d.d469 (bia 0000.0c3d.d469)
  Internet address is 10.0.0.1/8
  MTU 1500 bytes, BW 10000 Kbit, DLY 1000 usec,
     reliability 255/255, txload 1/255, rxload 1/255
  Encapsulation ARPA, loopback not set
Router B:
RouterB#show interface fastethernet 0
Next, ping your neighbor's Ethernet interface: this will test if the link
is OK:
RouterA#ping 10.0.0.2

Type escape sequence to abort.
Sending 5, 100-byte ICMP Echos to 10.0.0.2, timeout is 2 seconds:
.!!!! * The first ping failed while the ARP reply came back
         from router A
Success rate is 80 percent (4/5), round-trip min/avg/max = 1/1/1 ms.
RouterA#show arp
Protocol  Address          Age (min)  Hardware Addr   Type   Interface
Internet  10.0.0.2                 0  0050.5460.f1f8  ARPA   Ethernet0
Internet  10.0.0.1                 -  0010.7b80.63a3  ARPA   Ethernet0
RouterA#
Router B:
RouterB#ping 10.0.0.1
```

Your hardware address will obviously be different from the one on my routers!

6. To test CDP, we simply need to enter the "show cdp neighbor" command. Bear in mind that the spelling is US English and that you will have a different output, depending upon what device you are connected to.

```
RouterA#show cdp neighbor
Capability Codes: R - Router, T - Trans Bridge, B - Source Route Bridge S
- Switch, H - Host, I - IGMP, r - Repeater

Device ID  Local Intrfce  Holdtme   Capability  Platform  Port ID
RouterB    Eth 0            172          R        2500      Eth 0
RouterB    Ser 0            172          R        2500      Ser 0
RouterA#
```

7. Finally, telnet from Router A to Router B.

```
RouterA#telnet 10.0.0.2
Router B:
RouterB#telnet 10.0.0.1
```

LAB 4: CONFIGURING A ROUTER AS A DHCP SERVER

Physical topology is as follows:

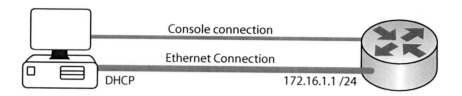

Figure 16–7: DHCP server

Lab exercise

Your task is to configure the router to issue an IP address to the host via DHCP. Please feel free to try the lab without following the Lab walk-through section.

Purpose

Configuring a router to act as a DHCP server is now included in the CCNA exam. You may well also have to carry out this task as a network engineer whilst on site.

Lab objectives

1. Use the IP addressing scheme depicted in the diagram above. You will need to connect the router to the PC via crossover cable unless you have a switch you can use.
2. Set the IP address on the router fast Ethernet interface as `172.16.1.1 /24`.
3. Set the PC to search for an IP address via DHCP.
4. Configure a DHCP pool on the router for network `172.16.1.0 /24`.
5. Add an excluded address on the router and add TCP settings (optional).
6. Finally to test that DHCP is working renew the IP address on the PC.

Lab walk-through

1. To set the IP addresses to an interface you will need to do the following:

```
Router#conf t
Router(config)#interface fast 0/0 * Check if your route is modular
Router(config)#ip address 172.16.1.1 255.255.255.0
```

2. Enable DHCP on your router and set the address pool (from configuration mode) :-

```
Router(config)#service DHCP * Turn DHCP on

Router(config)#ip dhcp pool pool1 * Name your pool pool1
```

```
Router(dhcp-config)#network 172.16.1.0 255.255.255.0 * This is
                                                       your DHCP pool
Router(dhcp-config)#lease 3 * 3-day lease on the IP address

Router(dhcp-config)#ip dhcp excluded-address 172.16.1.1

Router(config)#exit * router drops back to config mode
Optional Commands
Router(config)#ip dhcp pool pool1
Router(dhcp-config)#dns-server 24.196.64.39 24.196.64.40
Router(dhcp-config)#default-router 10.10.10.254
Router(dhcp-config)#domain-name mydomain.com
Router(dhcp-config)#ctrl + z
Router#
```

3. To configure the PC to use DHCP, do the following (this is on Windows XP):

    Go to Network Connections, right click, and press "Properties."

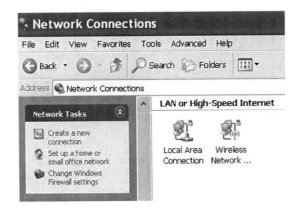

Press on TCP / IP and ensure the network card is set to 'obtain IP address automatically.'

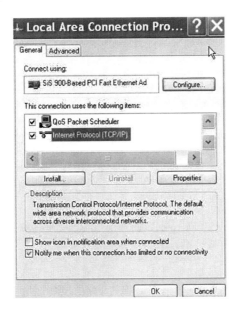

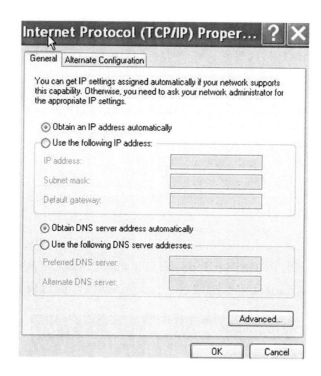

Go back to the network connections icon, right click, and press Repair which will enable a DHCP broadcast.

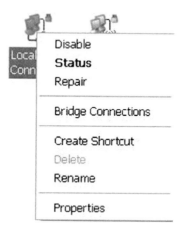

Now open a command prompt and issue the "ipconfig/all" command to check the TCP/IP settings on the network card.

```
Ethernet adapter Local Area Connection:

        Connection-specific DNS Suffix  . : mydomain.com
        Description . . . . . . . . . . . : SiS 900-Based PCI Fast Eth
ter
        Physical Address. . . . . . . . . : 00-14-2A-A8-22-81
        Dhcp Enabled. . . . . . . . . . . : Yes
        Autoconfiguration Enabled . . . . : Yes
        IP Address. . . . . . . . . . . . : 172.16.1.2
        Subnet Mask . . . . . . . . . . . : 255.255.255.0
        Default Gateway . . . . . . . . . : 10.10.10.254
        DHCP Server . . . . . . . . . . . : 172.16.1.1
        DNS Servers . . . . . . . . . . . : 24.196.64.39
                                            24.196.64.40
        Lease Obtained. . . . . . . . . . : 20 November 2007 08:20:03
        Lease Expires . . . . . . . . . . : 23 November 2007 08:20:03

C:\Documents and Settings\bigjobs>
```

Now check the DHCP settings allocated on the router.

```
Router#show ip dhcp binding
Bindings from all pools not associated with VRF:
IP address Client-ID/ Lease expiration Type
Hardware address/
User name
172.16.1.2 0100.142a.a822.81 Dec 09 2006 10:13 PM
```

You can see the IP address allocated from the pool and the correct MAC address. The router has added 01 to the front of the MAC when it wants to reserve an address.

Show run

```
Current configuration : 860 bytes
!
! Last configuration change at 22:19:11 UTC Wed Dec 6 2006
!
version 12.3
service timestamps debug datetime msec
service timestamps log datetime msec
no service password-encryption
!
hostname Router
!
boot-start-marker
boot-end-marker
!
!
mmi polling-interval 60
no mmi auto-configure
no mmi pvc
mmi snmp-timeout 180
no aaa new-model
ip subnet-zero
```

```
!
!
ip dhcp excluded-address 172.16.1.1
!
ip dhcp pool pool1
network 172.16.1.0 255.255.255.0
dns-server 24.196.64.39 24.196.64.40
default-router 10.10.10.254
domain-name mydomain.com
lease 3
!
ip cef
ip audit po max-events 100
!
interface FastEthernet0/0
ip address 172.16.1.1 255.255.255.0
speed auto
interface Serial0/0
no ip address
shutdown
no fair-queue
!
ip classless
no ip http server
no ip http secure-server
!

line con 0
line aux 0
line vty 0 4
!
end
```

CHAPTER 17

Module 7 Labs

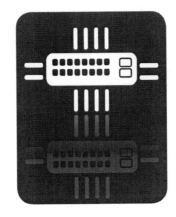

LAB 1: BASIC NETWORK SECURITY — ACCESS-LISTS (STANDARD)

The physical topology is as shown in Figure 17–1.

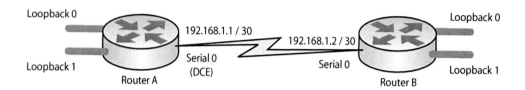

Figure 17–1: Standard access-list

Lab exercise

Your task is to configure the network in Figure 17–1 to allow full connectivity using a default route. Then you will need to configure an access-list to deny connections from your neighbor's network on their loopback 0. Please feel free to try the lab without following the lab walk-through section. Text written in monospaced type indicates commands that can be entered on the router.

Purpose

Access-lists are a fundamental way of protecting the router and are also a very useful troubleshooting tool. Standard access-lists allow you to filter traffic based upon source address or network and are a great introduction before moving onto the more sophisticated extended access-list.

Lab objectives

1. Use the IP addressing scheme depicted in Figure 17–1. Router A (if it is the DCE) needs to have a clock rate on interface serial 0: set this to be 64000.
2. Set telnet access for the router to use the local login permissions of username "banbury" and the password "ccna".
3. Configure the "enable secret password" to be "cisco".
4. Configure a default route to allow full connectivity.
5. Configure an access-list to deny any connection from the neighboring router's loopback 0 interface, whilst still allowing all other traffic through.
6. Finally, to test that the access-list is working you will need to use the extended ping command.

Lab walk-through

1. To set the IP addresses on an interface, you will need to do the following:

```
Router#config t
Router(config)#hostname RouterA
RouterA(config)#interface serial 0
RouterA(config-if)#ip address 192.168.1.1 255.255.255.252
RouterA(config-if)#clock rate 64000
RouterA(config-if)#no shutdown
RouterA(config-if)#interface loopback 0
RouterA(config-if)#ip address 172.16.1.1 255.255.255.0
RouterA(config-if)#interface loopback 1
RouterA(config-if)#ip address 172.20.1.1 255.255.255.0
RouterA(config-if)#
RouterA#
Router B:
Router#config t
Router(config)#hostname RouterB
RouterB(config)#interface serial 0
RouterB(config-if)#ip address 192.168.1.2 255.255.255.252
RouterB(config-if)#no shutdown
RouterB(config-if)#interface loopback 0
RouterB(config-if)#ip address 172.30.1.1 255.255.255.0
RouterB(config-if)#interface loopback 1
RouterB(config-if)#ip address 172.31.1.1 255.255.255.0
RouterB(config-if)#
RouterB#
```

Optional — To set the clock rate on a serial interface (DCE connection only) you need to use the "`clock rate #`" command on the serial interface, where # indicates the speed:

```
RouterA(config-if)#clock rate 64000
```

Ping across the serial interface now. If you wait until the access-list is in place you will struggle to troubleshoot the problem. It could be a serial link or access-list issue.

2. To set telnet access, you need to configure the VTY lines to allow telnet access. To do this, type (from configuration mode):

```
RouterA(config)#line vty 0 4 ⇔ Enters the VTY line configuration
RouterA(config-line)#login local ⇔ This will use local usernames
                                and passwords for telnet access
RouterA(config-line)#exit ⇔ Exit the VTY config mode
RouterA(config)#username banbury password ccna ⇔ Creates username
                          and password for telnet access (login local)

Router B:
RouterB(config)#line vty 0 4
RouterB(config-line)#login local
```

```
RouterB(config-line)#exit
RouterB(config)#username banbury password ccna
```

3. To set the "enable password", do the following:

```
RouterA(config)#enable secret cisco ⇦ Sets the "enable password"
                                           (encrypted)
Router B:
RouterB(config)#enable secret cisco
```

4. To configure a default route, there is one simple step (from configuration mode):

```
RouterA(config)#ip route 0.0.0.0 0.0.0.0 serial 0 ⇦ For all
                    unknown addresses send packet out of serial 0
Router B:
RouterB(config)#ip route 0.0.0.0 0.0.0.0 serial 0
```

5. To configure an access-list, there are two steps: first, specify the networks to permit or deny and second, apply the access-list to an interface:

```
RouterA(config)#access-list 1 deny 172.30.1.0 0.0.0.255 ⇦ Deny the
                network specified; remember to use a wildcard mask
RouterA(config)#access-list 1 permit any ⇦ Permit everything else
RouterA(config)#interface serial 0
RouterA(config-if)#ip access-group 1 in ⇦ Assign the access-list to
            the interface and the direction of traffic to be checked
Router B:
RouterB(config)#access-list 1 deny 172.16.1.0 0.0.0.255
RouterB(config)#access-list 1 permit any
RouterB(config)#interface serial 0
RouterB(config-if)#ip access-group 1 in
```

6. To test the access-list, you need to use an extended ping. The extended ping allows you to specify a different source address for the ping instead of using the IP address assigned to the exiting interface:

```
RouterA#ping ⇦ Press Enter here
Protocol [ip] : ⇦ Press Enter here
Target IP address : 192.168.1.2
Repeat count [5] :
Datagram size [100] :
Timeout in seconds [2] :
Extended commands [n]  : y
Source address or interface : 172.16.1.1
Type of service [0] :
Set DF bit in IP header? [no] :
```

```
Validate reply data? [no] :
Data pattern [0xABCD] :
Loose, Strict, Record, Timestamp, Verbose[none] :
Sweep range of sizes [n] :
Type escape sequence to abort.
Sending 5, 100-byte ICMP Echos to 172.16.1.1, timeout is 2 seconds:
U.U.U ⇦ Traffic from 172.16.1.0 network blocked by acl on router B
Success rate is 0 percent (0/5)
```

Note: *Your response may be .... instead of U U U U*

```
RouterA#ping
Protocol [ip] :
Target IP address : 192.168.1.2
Repeat count [5] :
Datagram size [100] :
Timeout in seconds [2] :
Extended commands [n] : y
Source address or interface : 172.20.1.1
Type of service [0] :
Set DF bit in IP header? [no] :
Validate reply data? [no] :
Data pattern [0xABCD] :
Loose, Strict, Record, Timestamp, Verbose[none] :
Sweep range of sizes [n] :
Type escape sequence to abort.
Sending 5, 100-byte ICMP Echos to 172.20.1.1, timeout is 2 seconds:
!!!!! ⇦ Traffic from 172.20.0.0 network permitted by acl
Success rate is 100 percent (5/5), round-trip min/avg/max = 32/32/32 ms
Router B:
RouterB#ping
Protocol [ip] :
Target IP address : 192.168.1.1
Repeat count [5] :
Datagram size [100] :
Timeout in seconds [2] :
Extended commands [n] : y
Source address or interface : 172.30.1.1
Type of service [0] :
Set DF bit in IP header? [no] :
Validate reply data? [no] :
Data pattern [0xABCD] :
Loose, Strict, Record, Timestamp, Verbose[none] :
Sweep range of sizes [n] :
Type escape sequence to abort.
Sending 5, 100-byte ICMP Echos to 172.30.1.1, timeout is 2 seconds :
U.U.U ⇦ Traffic from 172.30.1.0 network denied by acl
Success rate is 0 percent (0/5)#
RouterB#ping
Protocol [ip] :
Target IP address : 192.168.1.1
Repeat count [5] :
Datagram size [100] :
```

```
Timeout in seconds [2] :
Extended commands [n] : y
Source address or interface : 172.31.1.1
Type of service [0] :
Set DF bit in IP header? [no] :
Validate reply data? [no] :
Data pattern [0xABCD] :
Loose, Strict, Record, Timestamp, Verbose[none] :
Sweep range of sizes [n] :
Type escape sequence to abort.
Sending 5, 100-byte ICMP Echos to 172.31.1.1, timeout is 2 seconds :
!!!!! ⇐ Traffic from 172.31.0.0 network permitted by acl
Success rate is 100 percent (5/5), round-trip min/avg/max = 32/32/32 ms
Try the following commands:
RouterA#show ip access-lists
RouterA#show access-lists
RouterA#show run interface serial 0 ⇐ This command may not work
                                   in the exam (so use "show run" instead).
```

Show runs

```
RouterA#show run
Building configuration...

Current configuration : 810 bytes
!
version 12.1
service timestamps debug uptime
service timestamps log uptime
no service password-encryption
!
hostname RouterA
!
enable secret 5 $1$jjQo$YJXxLo.EZm9t6Sq4UYeCvO
!
username banbury password 0 ccna
!
ip subnet-zero
!
interface Loopback0
 ip address 172.16.1.1 255.255.255.0
!
interface Loopback1
 ip address 172.20.1.1 255.255.255.0
!
interface Serial0
 ip address 192.168.1.1 255.255.255.252
 ip access-group 1 in
 clockrate 64000
!
interface Serial1
 no ip address
```

```
 shutdown
!
interface Ethernet0
 no ip address
 shutdown
!
interface BRI0
 no ip address
 shutdown

!
ip classless
ip route 0.0.0.0 0.0.0.0 Serial0
no ip http server
!
access-list 1 deny    172.30.1.0 0.0.0.255
access-list 1 permit any
!
line con 0
line aux 0
line vty 0 4
 login local
!
end

RouterA#

- - -

RouterB#show run
Building configuration...

Current configuration : 791 bytes
!
version 12.1
service timestamps debug uptime
service timestamps log uptime
no service password-encryption
!
hostname RouterB
!
enable secret 5 $1$HrXN$ThplDHEZdnCbbeA/Ie67E1
!
username banbury password 0 ccna
!
ip subnet-zero
!
interface Loopback0
 ip address 172.30.1.1 255.255.255.0
!
interface Loopback1
 ip address 172.31.1.1 255.255.255.0
```

```
!
interface Ethernet0
 no ip address
 shutdown
!
interface Serial0
 ip address 192.168.1.2 255.255.255.252
 ip access-group 1 in
!
interface Serial1
 no ip address
 shutdown
!
interface BRI0
 no ip address
 shutdown

!
ip classless
ip route 0.0.0.0 0.0.0.0 Serial0
no ip http server
!
access-list 1 deny    172.16.1.0 0.0.0.255
access-list 1 permit any
!
line con 0
line aux 0
line vty 0 4
 login local
!
end

RouterB#
```

LAB 2: BASIC NETWORK SECURITY — ACCESS-LISTS (EXTENDED)

The physical topology is as shown in Figure 17–2.

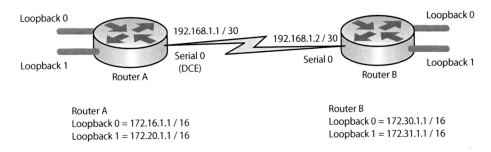

Figure 17–2: Extended access-list

Lab exercise

Your task is to configure the network in Figure 17–2 to allow full connectivity using a default route. Then you will need to configure an access-list to deny telnet connections into router A and Web (HTTP) traffic into router B. Please feel free to try the lab without following the lab walk-through section.

Text written in monospaced type indicates commands that can be entered on the router.

Purpose

Extended access-lists are one of the foundation skills of any competent CCNA. You will be expected to be able to configure one to protect a client's network from certain types of traffic. The number one tip for access-lists is to practice over and over again and also write it out on paper in rough before you configure it (these are two tips I know).

Lab objectives

1. Use the IP addressing scheme depicted in Figure 17–2. The student who is using router A needs to configure a clock rate on interface serial 0: set this to 64000.

2. Set telnet access for the router to use the local login permissions of username "banbury" and the password "ccna".

3. Configure the "enable password" to be "cisco".

4. Configure a default route to allow full connectivity.

5. Configure an access-list to deny any telnet connection from the neighboring router, whilst still allowing all other traffic through.

6. Finally, to test that the access-list is working you will need to telnet to your neighbor's router.

Lab walk-through

1. To set the IP addresses on an interface, you will need to do the following:

```
Router#config t
Router(config)#hostname RouterA
RouterA(config)#interface serial 0
RouterA(config-if)#ip address 192.168.1.1 255.255.255.252
RouterA(config-if)#clock rate 64000
RouterA(config-if)#no shutdown
RouterA(config-if)#interface loopback 0
RouterA(config-if)#ip address 172.16.1.1 255.255.0.0
RouterA(config-if)#interface loopback 1
RouterA(config-if)#ip address 172.20.1.1 255.255.0.0
RouterA(config-if)#^Z
RouterA#
Router B:
Router#config t
Router(config)#hostname RouterB
RouterB(config)#interface serial 0
RouterB(config-if)#ip address 192.168.1.2 255.255.255.252
RouterB(config-if)#no shutdown
RouterB(config-if)#interface loopback 0
RouterB(config-if)#ip address 172.30.1.1 255.255.0.0
RouterB(config-if)#interface loopback 1
RouterB(config-if)#ip address 172.31.1.1 255.255.0.0
RouterB(config-if)#^Z
RouterB#
```

2. To set the clock rate on a serial interface (DCE connection only), you need to use the "clock rate #" command on the serial interface, where # indicates the speed:

```
RouterA(config-if)#clock rate 64000
```

Ping across the serial link now.

3. To set telnet access you need to configure the VTY lines to allow telnet access. To do this type (from configuration mode):

```
RouterA(config)#line vty 0 4 ⇦ Enters the VTY line configuration
RouterA(config-line)#login local ⇦ This will use local usernames
                                 and passwords for telnet access
RouterA(config-line)#exit ⇦ Exit the VTY config mode
RouterA(config)#username banbury password ccna ⇦ Creates username
                     and password for telnet access (login local)
Router B:
RouterB(config)#line vty 0 4
RouterB(config-line)#login local
RouterB(config-line)#exit
RouterB(config)#username banbury password ccna
```

4. To set the "enable password" do the following:

```
RouterA(config)#enable secret cisco ⇦ Sets the "enable password"
                                           (encrypted)
Router B:
RouterB(config)#enable secret cisco
To configure a default route there is one simple step (from configuration
mode):
RouterA(config)#ip route 0.0.0.0 0.0.0.0 serial 0 ⇦ For all
                    unknown addresses, send the packet out of serial 0
Router B:
RouterB(config)#ip route 0.0.0.0 0.0.0.0 serial 0
```

5. To configure an access-list, there are two steps: first, specify the networks to permit or deny and second, apply the access-list to an interface:

```
RouterA(config)#access-list 100 deny tcp any any eq 23 ⇦ Deny any
                                      TCP connection using telnet
RouterA(config)#access-list 100 permit ip any any ⇦ Permit
                                           everything else
RouterA(config)#interface serial 0
RouterA(config-if)#ip access-group 100 in ⇦ Assign the access-list
        to the interface and the direction of traffic to be checked
Router B:
RouterB(config)#access-list 100 deny tcp any any eq 80
RouterB(config)#access-list 100 permit ip any any
RouterB(config)#interface serial 0
RouterB(config-if)#ip access-group 100 in
```

6. To test this access-list, you will need to telnet to your neighbor's router. If the access-list is working the connection will be denied:

```
RouterA#telnet 192.168.1.2 80 ⇦ Telnet using port 80 to test
Trying 192.168.1.2 ...
% Destination unreachable; gateway or host down
Router B:
RouterB#telnet 192.168.1.1
Trying 192.168.1.1 ...
% Destination unreachable; gateway or host down
```

7. To make sure the access-list is doing its job, remove the access-list from the serial interface and try the telnet connection again. Router B must have the "ip http server" command added, just so we can test the telnet on port 80.

```
Router B:
RouterB#config t
RouterB(config)#interface serial 0
RouterB(config-if)#no ip access-group 100 in ⇦ Remove the
                    access-list from the interface on Router B
```

```
RouterB(config-if)#exit
RouterB(config)#ip http server ⇐ Will permit telnet on port 80
Router A:
RouterA#telnet 192.168.1.2 80 ⇐ Telnet from router A to B
Trying 192.168.1.2, 80 ... Open

exit ß Type "exit"

HTTP/1.0 501 Not Implemented
Date: Mon, 01 Mar 1993 00:17:40 UTC
Content-type: text/html
Expires: Thu, 16 Feb 1989 00:00:00 GMT

<H1>501 Not Implemented</H1>

[Connection to 192.168.1.2 closed by foreign host]
RouterA#
Router A:
RouterA#config t
RouterA(config)#interface serial 0
RouterA(config-if)#no ip access-group 100 in ⇐ Remove the
                          access-list from the interface on Router A
RouterA(config-if)#
Router B:
RouterB#telnet 192.168.1.1 ⇐ Telnet from Router B to A
RouterB#telnet
02:03:55: %SYS-5-CONFIG_I: Configured from console by console192.168.1.1
Trying 192.168.1.1 ... Open

User Access Verification

Username: banbury
Password:
RouterA>
```

The telnet connection should be successful now because the access-list is no longer in use.

Show runs

```
RouterA#show run
Building configuration...

Current configuration : 799 bytes
!
version 12.1
service timestamps debug uptime
service timestamps log uptime
no service password-encryption
!
hostname RouterA
```

```
!
enable secret 5 $1$jjQo$YJXxLo.EZm9t6Sq4UYeCvO
!
username banbury password 0 ccna
!
ip subnet-zero
!
interface Loopback0
 ip address 172.16.1.1 255.255.0.0
!
interface Loopback1
 ip address 172.20.1.1 255.255.0.0
!
interface Serial0
 ip address 192.168.1.1 255.255.255.252
 ip access-group 100 in
 clockrate 64000
!
interface Serial1
 no ip address
 shutdown
!
interface Ethernet0
 no ip address
 shutdown
!
interface BRI0
 no ip address
 shutdown

!
ip classless
ip route 0.0.0.0 0.0.0.0 Serial0
no ip http server
!
access-list 100 deny tcp any any eq telnet
access-list 100 permit ip any any
!
line con 0
line aux 0
line vty 0 4
 login local
!
end

---

RouterB#show run
Building configuration...

Current configuration : 781 bytes
!
```

```
version 12.1
service timestamps debug uptime
service timestamps log uptime
no service password-encryption
!
hostname RouterB
!
enable secret 5 $1$HrXN$Thp1DHEZdnCbbeA/Ie67E1
!
username banbury password 0 ccna
!
ip subnet-zero
!
interface Loopback0
 ip address 172.30.1.1 255.255.0.0
!
interface Loopback1
 ip address 172.31.1.1 255.255.0.0
!
interface Ethernet0
 no ip address
 shutdown
!
interface Serial0
 ip address 192.168.1.2 255.255.255.252
 ip access-group 100 in
 !
interface Serial1
 no ip address
 shutdown
!
interface BRI0
 no ip address
 shutdown

!
ip classless
ip route 0.0.0.0 0.0.0.0 Serial0
no ip http server
!
access-list 100 deny tcp any any eq www
access-list 100 permit ip any any
!
line con 0
line aux 0
line vty 0 4
 login local
!
end

RouterB#
```

LAB 3: BASIC NETWORK SECURITY — ACCESS-LISTS (NAMED)

The physical topology is shown in Figure 17–3.

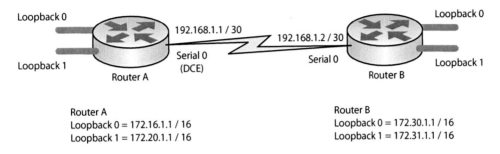

Router A
Loopback 0 = 172.16.1.1 / 16
Loopback 1 = 172.20.1.1 / 16

Router B
Loopback 0 = 172.30.1.1 / 16
Loopback 1 = 172.31.1.1 / 16

Figure 17–3: Named access-list

Lab exercise

Your task is to configure the network in Figure 17–3 to allow full connectivity using a default route. Then you will need to configure a named access-list to permit pings from loopback 0 on router B to loopback 0 on router A and telnet traffic to loopback 1 on router A only. Any other traffic will be denied (which is done by default). Please feel free to try the lab without following the lab walk-through section.

Text written in monospaced type indicates commands that can be entered on the router.

Purpose

Named access-lists are one of the foundation skills of any competent CCNA. You will be expected to be able to configure one to protect a client's network from certain types of traffic. The number one tip for access-lists is to practice over and over again and also write it out on paper in rough before you configure it (these are two tips I know).

Lab objectives

1. Use the IP addressing scheme depicted in Figure 17–3. The student who is using router A needs to configure a clock rate on interface serial 0: set this to 64000.

2. Set telnet access for the router to use the local login permissions of username "banbury" and the password "ccna".

3. Configure the "enable password" to be "cisco".

4. Configure a default route to allow full connectivity.

5. Configure an access list on Router A to permit ICMP from 172.30.1.1 to 172.16.1.1 and telnet to 172.20.1.1 only.

6. Finally, to test that the access-list is working you will need to telnet to your neighbor's router.

Lab walk-through

1. To set the IP addresses on an interface, you will need to do the following:

```
Router#config t
Router(config)#hostname RouterA
RouterA(config)#interface serial 0
RouterA(config-if)#ip address 192.168.1.1 255.255.255.252
RouterA(config-if)#clock rate 64000
RouterA(config-if)#no shutdown
RouterA(config-if)#interface loopback 0
RouterA(config-if)#ip address 172.16.1.1 255.255.0.0
RouterA(config-if)#interface loopback 1
RouterA(config-if)#ip address 172.20.1.1 255.255.0.0
RouterA(config-if)#^Z
RouterA#
Router B:
Router#config t
Router(config)#hostname RouterB
RouterB(config)#interface serial 0
RouterB(config-if)#ip address 192.168.1.2 255.255.255.252
RouterB(config-if)#no shutdown
RouterB(config-if)#interface loopback 0
RouterB(config-if)#ip address 172.30.1.1 255.255.0.0
RouterB(config-if)#interface loopback 1
RouterB(config-if)#ip address 172.31.1.1 255.255.0.0
RouterB(config-if)#^Z
RouterB#
```

2. To set the clock rate on a serial interface (DCE connection only), you need to use the "clock rate #" command on the serial interface, where # indicates the speed:

```
RouterA(config-if)#clock rate 64000
```

Ping across the serial link now.

3. To set telnet access, you need to configure the VTY lines to allow telnet access. To do this type (from configuration mode):

```
RouterA(config)#line vty 0 4 ⇔ Enters the VTY line configuration
RouterA(config-line)#login local ⇔ This will use local usernames
                                 and passwords for telnet access
RouterA(config-line)#exit ⇔ Exit the VTY config mode
RouterA(config)#username banbury password ccna ⇔ Creates
         username and password for telnet access (login local)
Router B:
```

```
RouterB(config)#line vty 0 4
RouterB(config-line)#login local
RouterB(config-line)#exit
RouterB(config)#username banbury password ccna
```

4. To set the "enable password", do the following:

```
RouterA(config)#enable secret cisco ⇐ Sets the "enable password"
                                              (encrypted)
Router B:
RouterB(config)#enable secret cisco
To configure a default route, there is one simple step (from configuration
mode):
RouterA(config)#ip route 0.0.0.0 0.0.0.0 serial 0 ⇐ For all
                    unknown addresses send the packet out of serial 0
Router B:
RouterB(config)#ip route 0.0.0.0 0.0.0.0 serial 0
```

5. To configure an access-list there are two steps: first, specify the networks and traffic to permit or deny and second, apply the access-list to an interface:

```
RouterA#config t
RouterA(config)#ip access-list extended secure_LAN ⇐ Go into names
access-list config
RouterA(config-ext-nacl)#permit icmp host 172.30.1.1 host 172.16.1.1
RouterA(config-ext-nacl)#permit tcp any host 172.20.1.1 eq telnet
RouterA(config-ext-nacl)#exit
RouterA(config)#interface serial 0
RouterA(config-if)#ip access-group secure_LAN in ⇐ Assign the
      access-list to the interface and the direction of traffic to be
      checked
Router B:
To test this access-list you will need to telnet to your neighbor's
router: if the access-list is working the connection will be denied:
RouterB#telnet 192.168.1.1 ⇐ Telnet to the serial interface
Trying 192.168.1.1 ...
% Destination unreachable; gateway or host down

RouterB#telnet 172.20.1.1 ⇐ Telnet to loopback 1 will work
Trying 172.20.1.1 ... Open

User Access Verification

Password:
```

Now test the ICMP deny statement by pinging loopback 0 from the serial on router B.

```
RouterB#ping 172.16.1.1

Type escape sequence to abort.
```

```
Sending 5, 100-byte ICMP Echos to 172.16.1.1, timeout is 2 seconds:
U.U.U
Success rate is 0 percent (0/5)
RouterB#
Now, ping from source interface 172.30.1.1, which should be permitted.
RouterB#ping
Protocol [ip]:
Target IP address: 172.16.1.1
Repeat count [5]:
Datagram size [100]:
Timeout in seconds [2]:
Extended commands [n]: y
Source address or interface: 172.30.1.1
Type of service [0]:
Set DF bit in IP header? [no]:
Validate reply data? [no]:
Data pattern [0xABCD]:
Loose, Strict, Record, Timestamp, Verbose[none]:
Sweep range of sizes [n]:
Type escape sequence to abort.
Sending 5, 100-byte ICMP Echos to 172.16.1.1, timeout is 2 seconds:
!!!!!
Success rate is 100 percent (5/5), round-trip min/avg/max = 32/32/32 ms
```

Show runs

```
RouterA#show run
Building configuration...

Current configuration : 831 bytes
!
version 12.1
no service single-slot-reload-enable
service timestamps debug uptime
service timestamps log uptime
no service password-encryption
!
hostname RouterA
!
ip subnet-zero
!
interface Loopback0
 ip address 172.16.1.1 255.255.0.0
!
interface Loopback1
 ip address 172.20.1.1 255.255.0.0
!
interface Ethernet0
 no ip address
 shutdown
!
```

```
interface Ethernet1
 no ip address
 shutdown
!
interface Serial0
 ip address 192.168.1.1 255.255.255.252
 clockrate 64000
 ip access-group secure_LAN in
!
interface Serial1
 no ip address
 shutdown
!
ip classless
ip route 0.0.0.0 0.0.0.0 Serial0
no ip http server
!
!
ip access-list extended secure_LAN
 permit icmp host 172.30.1.1 host 172.16.1.1
 permit tcp any host 172.20.1.1 eq telnet
!
line con 0
line aux 0
line vty 0 4
 password cisco
 login
!
end

RouterA#

---

RouterB#show run
Building configuration...

Current configuration : 574 bytes
!
version 12.2
service timestamps debug uptime
service timestamps log uptime
no service password-encryption
!
hostname RouterB
!
ip subnet-zero
!
interface Loopback0
 ip address 172.30.1.1 255.255.0.0
!
interface Loopback1
```

```
 ip address 172.31.1.1 255.255.0.0
!
interface Serial0
 ip address 192.168.1.2 255.255.255.252
 !
interface Serial1
 no ip address
 shutdown
!
interface TokenRing0
 no ip address
 shutdown
!
ip classless
ip route 0.0.0.0 0.0.0.0 Serial0
no ip http server
ip pim bidir-enable
!
line con 0
line aux 0
line vty 0 4
!
end

RouterB#
```

CHAPTER 18

Module 8 Labs

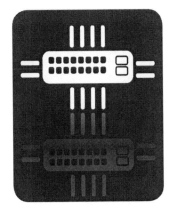

LAB 1: WAN LAB — POINT-TO-POINT PROTOCOL (PPP)

The physical topology is shown in Figure 18–1.

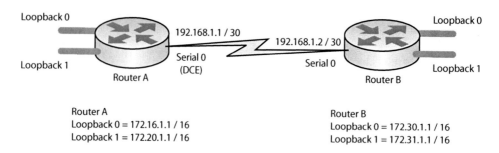

Router A
Loopback 0 = 172.16.1.1 / 16
Loopback 1 = 172.20.1.1 / 16

Router B
Loopback 0 = 172.30.1.1 / 16
Loopback 1 = 172.31.1.1 / 16

Figure 18–1: PPP lab

Lab exercise

Your task is to configure the network in Figure 18–1 to allow full connectivity using the PPP (point-to-point protocol) of WAN. Please feel free to try the lab without following the lab walk-through section.

Text written in monospaced type indicates commands that can be entered on the router.

Purpose

Not all networks run the default encapsulation of HDLC. Many companies use PPP, especially for ISDN connections. PPP is popular due to improved security features.

Lab objectives

1. Use the IP-addressing scheme depicted in Figure 18–1. Router A needs to have a clock rate on interface serial 0: set this to 64000.
2. Set telnet access for the router to use the local login permissions of username "banbury" and the password "ccna".
3. Configure the "enable password" to be "cisco".
4. Configure PPP on the serial interface to provide connectivity to your neighbor. Enable CHAP authentication
5. Configure a default route to allow full IP connectivity.
6. Finally, test that the PPP link is up and working by sending a ping across the link.

Lab walk-through

1. To set the IP addresses on an interface, you will need to do the following:

```
Router#config t
Router(config)#hostname RouterA
RouterA(config)#
RouterA(config)#interface serial 0
RouterA(config-if)#ip address 192.168.1.1 255.255.255.252
RouterA(config-if)#clock rate 64000
RouterA(config-if)#no shutdown
RouterA(config-if)#interface loopback 0
RouterA(config-if)#ip address 172.16.1.1 255.255.0.0
RouterA(config-if)#interface loopback 1
RouterA(config-if)#ip address 172.20.1.1 255.255.0.0
RouterA(config-if)#^Z
RouterA#
Router B:
Router#config t
Router(config)#hostname RouterB
RouterB(config)#
RouterB(config)#interface serial 0
RouterB(config-if)#ip address 192.168.1.2 255.255.255.252
RouterB(config-if)#no shutdown
RouterB(config-if)#interface loopback 0
RouterB(config-if)#ip address 172.30.1.1 255.255.0.0
RouterB(config-if)#interface loopback 1
RouterB(config-if)#ip address 172.31.1.1 255.255.0.0
RouterB(config-if)#^Z
RouterB#
```

To set the clock rate on a serial interface (DCE connection only) you need to use the "clock rate #" command on the serial interface, where # indicates the speed:

```
RouterA(config-if)#clock rate 64000
```

Ping across the serial link now.

2. To set PPP CHAP authentication, you need to set a username and password on each router. The username must match the hostname of the calling router exactly:

```
RouterA(config)#username RouterB password cisco ⇦ Creates username
                                                  and password for PPP CHAP
Router B:
RouterB(config)#username RouterA password cisco
```

3. To set the "enable password," do the following:

```
RouterA(config)#enable secret cisco ⇦ Sets the "enable password"
                                        (encrypted)
Router B, etc.:
RouterB(config)#enable secret cisco
```

4. We now need to configure PPP as the WAN link for this lab. To enable PPP, you will need to do the following:

```
RouterA(config)#interface serial 0

RouterA(config-if)#encapsulation ppp ⇦ This will change the
                                         encapsulation type to be PPP.
RouterA(config-if)#ppp authentication chap ⇦ Use CHAP to
                                               authenticate.
Router B:
RouterB(config)#interface serial 0
RouterB(config-if)#encapsulation ppp
RouterB(config-if)#ppp authentication chap
```

5. To configure a default route, there is one simple step (from configuration mode):

```
RouterA(config)#ip route 0.0.0.0 0.0.0.0 serial 0 ⇦ For all unknown
                         addresses, send the packet out of serial 0.
Router B:
RouterB(config)#ip route 0.0.0.0 0.0.0.0 serial 0
```

6. To test the PPP connection, you will need to first check that the link is up. To do this use the "show interface" command:

```
RouterA#show interface serial 0

RouterA#show interface serial 0
Serial0 is up, line protocol is up
  Hardware is HD64570
  Internet address is 192.168.1.1/30
  MTU 1500 bytes, BW 1544 Kbit, DLY 20000 usec,
    reliability 255/255, txload 1/255, rxload 1/255
  Encapsulation PPP, loopback not set
[Some output omitted...]
Router B:
RouterB#show interface serial 0

RouterB#show interface serial 0
Serial0 is up, line protocol is up
  Hardware is HD64570
  Internet address is 192.168.1.2/30
  MTU 1500 bytes, BW 1544 Kbit, DLY 20000 usec,
    reliability 255/255, txload 1/255, rxload 1/255
  Encapsulation PPP, loopback not set
LCP Open
  Open: IPCP, CDPCP
```

Make sure that serial 0 is up and the line protocol is up.

Next, ping your neighbor's serial interface: this will test if the link is up:

```
RouterA#ping 192.168.1.2

Type escape sequence to abort.
Sending 5, 100-byte ICMP Echos to 192.168.1.2, timeout is 2 seconds:
!!!!!
Success rate is 100 percent (5/5), round-trip min/avg/max = 28/31/32 ms
Router B:
RouterB#ping 192.168.1.1
```

If everything is OK, you will receive five replies and have a 100 percent success rate.

```
Type escape sequence to abort.
Sending 5, 100-byte ICMP Echos to 192.168.1.1, timeout is 2 seconds:
!!!!!
Success rate is 100 percent (5/5), round-trip min/avg/max = 28/31/32 ms
```

7. To test the PPP negotiation, you can shut the serial interface and then no shut it with the "debug ppp authentication" and "debug ppp negotiation" commands on. You can see the CHAP challenge taking place and the line coming up as you read the debug.

```
RouterB#config t
RouterB(config)#debug ppp authentication
RouterB(config)#debug ppp authentication
RouterB(config)#interface s0
RouterB(config-if)#shut
RouterB(config-if)#
01:41:37: %LINK-5-CHANGED: Interface Serial0, changed state to
administratively down
RouterB(config-if)#
01:41:37: Se0 IPCP: Remove link info for cef entry 192.168.1.1
01:41:37: Se0 IPCP: State is Closed
01:41:37: Se0 CDPCP: State is Closed
01:41:37: Se0 PPP: Phase is TERMINATING
01:41:37: Se0 LCP: State is Closed
01:41:37: Se0 PPP: Phase is DOWN
01:41:37: Se0 IPCP: Remove route to 192.168.1.1
RouterB(config-if)#
01:41:38: %LINEPROTO-5-UPDOWN: Line protocol on Interface Serial0, changed
state to down
RouterB(config-if)#no shut
RouterB(config-if)#^Z

RouterB#
01:41:46: %SYS-5-CONFIG_I: Configured from console by console
01:41:46: %LINK-3-UPDOWN: Interface Serial0, changed state to up
01:41:46: Se0 PPP: Treating connection as a dedicated line
01:41:46: Se0 PPP: Phase is ESTABLISHING, Active Open
01:41:46: Se0 PPP: Authorization NOT required
01:41:46: Se0 LCP: O CONFREQ [Closed] id 184 len 15
```

```
01:41:46: Se0 LCP:    AuthProto CHAP (0x0305C22305)
01:41:46: Se0 LCP:    MagicNumber 0x093B9E12 (0x0506093B9E12)
01:41:46: Se0 LCP: I CONFREQ [REQsent] id 84 len 15
01:41:46: Se0 LCP:    AuthProto CHAP (0x0305C22305)
01:41:46: Se0 LCP:    MagicNumber 0x00698D38 (0x050600698D38)
01:41:46: Se0 LCP: O CONFACK [REQsent] id 84 len 15
01:41:46: Se0 LCP:    AuthProto CHAP (0x0305C22305)
01:41:46: Se0 LCP:    MagicNumber 0x00698D38 (0x050600698D38)
01:41:48: Se0 LCP: TIMEout: State ACKsent
01:41:48: Se0 LCP: O CONFREQ [ACKsent] id 185 len 15
01:41:48: Se0 LCP:    AuthProto CHAP (0x0305C22305)
01:41:48: Se0 LCP:    MagicNumber 0x093B9E12 (0x0506093B9E12)
01:41:48: Se0 LCP: I CONFREQ [ACKsent] id 85 len 15
01:41:48: Se0 LCP:    AuthProto CHAP (0x0305C22305)
01:41:48: Se0 LCP:    MagicNumber 0x00698D38 (0x050600698D38)
01:41:48: Se0 LCP: O CONFACK [ACKsent] id 85 len 15
01:41:48: Se0 LCP:    AuthProto CHAP (0x0305C22305)
01:41:48: Se0 LCP:    MagicNumber 0x00698D38 (0x050600698D38)
01:41:48: Se0 LCP: I CONFACK [ACKsent] id 185 len 15
01:41:48: Se0 LCP:    AuthProto CHAP (0x0305C22305)
01:41:48: Se0 LCP:    MagicNumber 0x093B9E12 (0x0506093B9E12)
01:41:48: Se0 LCP: State is Open
01:41:48: Se0 PPP: Phase is AUTHENTICATING, by both
01:41:48: Se0 CHAP: O CHALLENGE id 180 len 28 from "RouterB"
01:41:48: Se0 CHAP: I CHALLENGE id 180 len 28 from "RouterA"
01:41:48: Se0 PPP: Sent CHAP SENDAUTH Request to AAA
01:41:48: Se0 CHAP: I RESPONSE id 180 len 28 from "RouterA"
01:41:48: Se0 PPP: Phase is FORWARDING, Attempting Forward
01:41:48: Se0 PPP: Phase is AUTHENTICATING, Unauthenticated User
01:41:48: Se0 PPP: Sent CHAP LOGIN Request to AAA
01:41:48: Se0 PPP: Received SENDAUTH Response from AAA = PASS
01:41:48: Se0 CHAP: O RESPONSE id 180 len 28 from "RouterB"
01:41:48: Se0 PPP: Received LOGIN Response from AAA = PASS
01:41:48: Se0 PPP: Phase is FORWARDING, Attempting Forward
01:41:48: Se0 PPP: Phase is AUTHENTICATING, Authenticated User
01:41:48: Se0 CHAP: O SUCCESS id 180 len 4
01:41:48: Se0 CHAP: I SUCCESS id 180 len 4
01:41:48: Se0 PPP: Phase is UP
01:41:48: Se0 IPCP: O CONFREQ [Closed] id 2 len 10
01:41:48: Se0 IPCP:    Address 192.168.1.2 (0x0306C0A80102)
01:41:48: Se0 CDPCP: O CONFREQ [Closed] id 2 len 4
01:41:48: Se0 CDPCP: I CONFREQ [REQsent] id 2 len 4
01:41:48: Se0 CDPCP: O CONFACK [REQsent] id 2 len 4
01:41:48: Se0 CDPCP: I CONFACK [ACKsent] id 2 len 4
01:41:48: Se0 CDPCP: State is Open
01:41:48: Se0 IPCP: I CONFREQ [REQsent] id 2 len 10
01:41:48: Se0 IPCP:    Address 192.168.1.1 (0x0306C0A80101)
01:41:48: Se0 IPCP: O CONFACK [REQsent] id 2 len 10
01:41:48: Se0 IPCP:    Address 192.168.1.1 (0x0306C0A80101)
01:41:48: Se0 IPCP: I CONFACK [ACKsent] id 2 len 10
01:41:48: Se0 IPCP:    Address 192.168.1.2 (0x0306C0A80102)
01:41:48: Se0 IPCP: State is Open
```

```
01:41:48: Se0 IPCP: Install route to 192.168.1.1
01:41:48: Se0 IPCP: Add link info for cef entry 192.168.1.1
01:41:49: %LINEPROTO-5-UPDOWN: Line protocol on Interface Serial0, changed
state to up
RouterB#un all
All possible debugging has been turned off
```

Show runs

```
RouterA#show run
Building configuration...

Current configuration : 739 bytes
!
version 12.1
service timestamps debug uptime
service timestamps log uptime
no service password-encryption
!
hostname RouterA
!
enable secret 5 $1$jjQo$YJXxLo.EZm9t6Sq4UYeCv0
!
username RouterB password cisco
!
ip subnet-zero
!
interface Loopback0
 ip address 172.16.1.1 255.255.0.0
!
interface Loopback1
 ip address 172.20.1.1 255.255.0.0
!
interface Serial0
 ip address 192.168.1.1 255.255.255.252
 encapsulation ppp
 ppp authentication chap
 clockrate 64000
!
interface Serial1
 no ip address
 shutdown
!
interface Ethernet0
 no ip address
 shutdown
!
interface BRI0
 no ip address
 shutdown
```

```
!
ip classless
ip route 0.0.0.0 0.0.0.0 Serial0
no ip http server
!
line con 0
line aux 0
line vty 0 4
 login local
!
end

RouterA#

---


RouterB#show run
Building configuration...

Current configuration : 721 bytes
!
version 12.1
service timestamps debug uptime
service timestamps log uptime
no service password-encryption
!
hostname RouterB
!
enable secret 5 $1$HrXN$ThplDHEZdnCbbeA/Ie67E1
!
username RouterA password cisco
!
ip subnet-zero
!
interface Loopback0
 ip address 172.30.1.1 255.255.0.0
!
interface Loopback1
 ip address 172.31.1.1 255.255.0.0
!
interface Ethernet0
 no ip address
 shutdown
!
interface Serial0
 ip address 192.168.1.2 255.255.255.252
 encapsulation ppp
 ppp authentication chap
!
interface Serial1
 no ip address
 shutdown
```

```
!
interface BRIO
 no ip address
 shutdown

!
ip classless
ip route 0.0.0.0 0.0.0.0 Serial0
no ip http server
!
line con 0
line aux 0
line vty 0 4
 login local
!
end

RouterB#
```

LAB 2: BASIC FRAME RELAY

Lab exercise

Your task is to configure the network in Figure 18–2 to allow full connectivity using frame relay. In order to complete the lab, you will have to use three routers—two as hosts and one as the frame relay router/switch. Configuring a frame relay switch can be a little tricky, but you will never be expected to use this for the CCNA. It is purely for use in a lab environment.

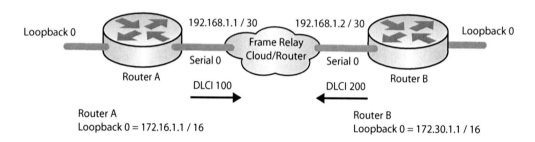

Figure 18–2: Basic frame relay

If you do not have a third router to use as a frame switch, then just practice inputting the commands on a router without being able to test it. **The DCE cables are always plugged into the frame relay switch.**

One last thing to bear in mind is that you may have plugged your cables into different interfaces than the one shown in Figure 18–2. You need to draw out your own lab diagram marking your own ports.

Text written in `monospaced type` indicates commands that can be entered on the router.

Purpose

Frame relay is still widely used all around the world and is still an area you could be tested on in the CCNA exam.

Lab objectives

1. Use the IP addressing scheme depicted in Figure 18–2. The frame switch will have the DCE interfaces so will need to have the clock rate command added
2. Configure frame relay on the serial interfaces of Routers A and B.
3. Configure the frame relay switch.
4. Configure RIP on Routers A and B to allow for end-to-end connectivity.
5. Test the link by pinging across.

Lab walk-through

1. Set the IP address and encapsulation type on the routers:

```
Router#config t
Router(config)#hostname RouterA
RouterA(config)#interface serial 0
RouterA(config-if)#ip add 192.168.1.1 255.255.255.252
RouterA(config-if)#no shut
RouterA(config-if)#encapsulation frame-relay
RouterA(config-if)#frame-relay interface-dlci 100
RouterA(config-if)#interface loopback 0
RouterA(config-if)#ip address 172.16.1.1 255.255.0.0
```

*Note — your router may show a different prompt at the dlci input.

```
Router B:
Router#config t
Router(config)#hostname RouterB
RouterB(config)#interface serial 0
RouterB(config-if)#ip add 192.168.1.2 255.255.255.252
RouterB(config-if)#no shut
RouterB(config-if)#encapsulation frame-relay
RouterB(config-if)#frame-relay interface-dlci 200
RouterB(config-if)#interface loopback 0
RouterB(config-if)#ip address 172.30.1.1 255.255.0.0
```

2. We need to configure RIP to allow all networks to see each other.

```
RouterA#config t
RouterA(config)#router rip
RouterA(config-router)#version 2
RouterA(config-router)#network 192.168.1.0
RouterA(config-router)#network 172.16.0.0
Router B:
RouterB#config t
RouterB(config)#router rip
RouterB(config-router)#version 2
RouterB(config-router)#network 192.168.1.0
RouterB(config-router)#network 172.30.0.0
```

3. We need to configure the frame relay switch. Just copy and paste the config and change the interface if you are not using the same ones we have here.

```
Router#config t

Router(config)#hostname FrameSwitch
FrameSwitch(config)#frame-relay switching ⇦ Make the router a
                                              frame switch

FrameSwitch(config)#interface serial 0
```

```
FrameSwitch(config-if)#clock rate 64000
FrameSwitch(config-if)#encapsulation frame-relay
FrameSwitch(config-if)#frame-relay intf-type dce ⇐ Interface is
                                                     the DCE
FrameSwitch(config-if)#frame-relay route 100 interface serial 1 200
         ⇐ Send traffic from dlci 100 out of interface serial 1
            as dlci 200.
FrameSwitch(config-if)#no shut
FrameSwitch(config-if)#interface Serial 1
FrameSwitch(config-if)#clock rate 64000
FrameSwitch(config-if)#encapsulation frame-relay
FrameSwitch(config-if)#frame-relay intf-type dce
FrameSwitch(config-if)#frame-relay route 200 interface serial 0 100
FrameSwitch(config-if)#no shut
```

4. Ping from router A to the loopback on router B.

```
RouterA#ping 172.30.1.1

Type escape sequence to abort.
Sending 5, 100-byte ICMP Echos to 172.30.1.1, timeout is 2 seconds:
!!!!!
Success rate is 100 percent (5/5), round-trip min/avg/max = 60/60/60 ms
RouterA#
```

If you cannot ping, then go to the troubleshooting module (Module 9). Check that:

- The interfaces are up up.
- Clock rate is configured on the frame switch DCE interfaces.
- The encapsulation is set to frame relay on all interfaces.
- The interfaces have been "no shut".
- You have put the correct frame relay route statements on the correct interfaces.
- You have configured the correct RIP routes.

5. Check for frame relay connectivity.

```
RouterA#show frame-relay map
Serial0 (up): ip 192.168.1.2 dlci 100(0x64,0x1840), dynamic,
              broadcast, status defined, active
RouterA#

RouterA#show frame-relay pvc

PVC Statistics for interface Serial0 (Frame Relay DTE)
```

	Active	Inactive	Deleted	Static
Local	1	0	0	0
Switched	0	0	0	0
Unused	0	0	0	0

```
DLCI = 100, DLCI USAGE = LOCAL, PVC STATUS = ACTIVE, INTERFACE = Serial0

   input pkts 20          output pkts 20          in bytes 1838
   out bytes 1898         dropped pkts 0          in FECN pkts 0
   in BECN pkts 0         out FECN pkts 0         out BECN pkts 0
   in DE pkts 0           out DE pkts 0
   out bcast pkts 10       out bcast bytes 858
   pvc create time 00:07:57, last time pvc status changed 00:03:23

RouterA#show frame-relay lmi

LMI Statistics for interface Serial0 (Frame Relay DTE) LMI TYPE = CISCO
   Invalid Unnumbered info 0        Invalid Prot Disc 0
   Invalid dummy Call Ref 0         Invalid Msg Type 0
   Invalid Status Message 0         Invalid Lock Shift 0
   Invalid Information ID 0         Invalid Report IE Len 0
   Invalid Report Request 0         Invalid Keep IE Len 0
   Num Status Enq. Sent 47          Num Status msgs Rcvd 48
   Num Update Status Rcvd 0         Num Status Timeouts 0

RouterA#

RouterA#debug frame-relay lmi
Frame Relay LMI debugging is on
Displaying all Frame Relay LMI data
RouterA#
00:46:38: Serial0(out): StEnq, myseq 53, yourseen 52, DTE up
00:46:38: datagramstart = 0xE3EEA4, datagramsize = 13
00:46:38: FR encap = 0xFCF10309
00:46:38: 00 75 01 01 01 03 02 35 34
00:46:38:
00:46:38: Serial0(in): Status, myseq 53
00:46:38: RT IE 1, length 1, type 1
00:46:38: KA IE 3, length 2, yourseq 53, myseq 53
00:46:48: Serial0(out): StEnq, myseq 54, yourseen 53, DTE up
00:46:48: datagramstart = 0xE3EEA4, datagramsize = 13
00:46:48: FR encap = 0xFCF10309
00:46:48: 00 75 01 01 01 03 02 36 35
00:46:48:
00:46:48: Serial0(in): Status, myseq 54
00:46:48: RT IE 1, length 1, type 1
00:46:48: KA IE 3, length 2, yourseq 54, myseq 54
00:46:58: Serial0(out): StEnq, myseq 55, yourseen 54, DTE up
00:46:58: datagramstart = 0xE3EEA4, datagramsize = 13
00:46:58: FR encap = 0xFCF10309
00:46:58: 00 75 01 01 00 03 02 37 36
00:46:58:
00:46:58: Serial0(in): Status, myseq 55
00:46:58: RT IE 1, length 1, type 0
00:46:58: KA IE 3, length 2, yourseq 55, myseq 55
00:46:58: PVC IE 0x7 , length 0x6 , dlci 100, status 0x2 , bw 0
RouterA#un all
```

```
All possible debugging has been turned off
RouterA#
```

Watch the myseq and yourseq incrementing; "status 0x2" means that the PVC is operational.

```
RouterA#show ip route
Codes: C - connected, S - static, I - IGRP, R - RIP, M - mobile, B - BGP
       D - EIGRP, EX - EIGRP external, O - OSPF, IA - OSPF inter area
       N1 - OSPF NSSA external type 1, N2 - OSPF NSSA external type 2
       E1 - OSPF external type 1, E2 - OSPF external type 2, E - EGP
       i - IS-IS, L1 - IS-IS level-1, L2 - IS-IS level-2, ia - IS-IS inter
area
       * - candidate default, U - per-user static route, o - ODR
       P - periodic downloaded static route

Gateway of last resort is not set

C    172.16.0.0/16 is directly connected, Loopback0
R    172.30.0.0/16 [120/1] via 192.168.1.2, 00:00:12, Serial0
     192.168.1.0/30 is subnetted, 1 subnets
C    192.168.1.0 is directly connected, Serial0
RouterA#
```

Try all of these commands on Router B also.

Show runs

```
RouterA#show run
Building configuration...

Current configuration : 726 bytes
!
version 12.1
service timestamps debug uptime
service timestamps log uptime
no service password-encryption
!
hostname RouterA
!
enable secret 5 $1$jjQo$YJXxLo.EZm9t6Sq4UYeCvO
!
username banbury password 0 ccna
!
ip subnet-zero
!
interface Loopback0
 ip address 172.16.1.1 255.255.0.0
!
interface Serial0
```

```
 ip address 192.168.1.1 255.255.255.252
 encapsulation frame-relay
 frame-relay interface-dlci 100
!
interface Serial1
 no ip address
 shutdown
!
interface Ethernet0
 no ip address
 shutdown
!
interface BRI0
 no ip address
 shutdown

!
router rip
 version 2
 network 172.16.0.0
 network 192.168.1.0
!
ip classless
no ip http server
!
line con 0
line aux 0
line vty 0 4
 login local
!
end

RouterA#

---

RouterB#show run
Building configuration...

Current configuration : 633 bytes
!
version 12.1
service timestamps debug uptime
service timestamps log uptime
no service password-encryption
!
hostname RouterB
!
ip subnet-zero
!
interface Loopback0
 ip address 172.30.1.1 255.255.0.0
```

```
!
interface Serial0
 ip address 192.168.1.2 255.255.255.252
 encapsulation frame-relay
 frame-relay interface-dlci 200
!
interface Serial1
 no ip address
 shutdown
!
interface Ethernet0
 no ip address
 shutdown
!
interface BRI0
 no ip address
 shutdown

!
router rip
 version 2
 network 172.30.0.0
 network 192.168.1.0
!
ip classless
no ip http server
!
line con 0
line aux 0
line vty 0 4
!
end

RouterB#


---


FrameSwitch#show run
Building configuration...

Current configuration : 685 bytes
!
version 12.1
service timestamps debug uptime
service timestamps log uptime
no service password-encryption
!
hostname FrameSwitch
!
ip subnet-zero
!
frame-relay switching
```

```
!
interface Ethernet0
 no ip address
 shutdown
!
interface Serial0
 no ip address
 encapsulation frame-relay
 clockrate 64000
 frame-relay intf-type dce
 frame-relay route 100 interface Serial1 200
!
interface Serial1
 no ip address
 encapsulation frame-relay
 clockrate 64000
 frame-relay intf-type dce
 frame-relay route 200 interface Serial0 100
!
interface BRI0
 no ip address
 shutdown

!
ip classless
no ip http server
!
line con 0
line aux 0
line vty 0 4
!
end
```

LAB 3: FRAME RELAY SUB-INTERFACES

Lab exercise

Your task is to configure the network in Figure 18–3 to allow full connectivity using frame relay. In order to complete the lab, you will have to use three routers—two as hosts and one as the frame relay router/switch. Configuring a frame relay switch can be a little tricky, but you will never be expected to use this for the CCNA. It is purely for use in a lab environment.

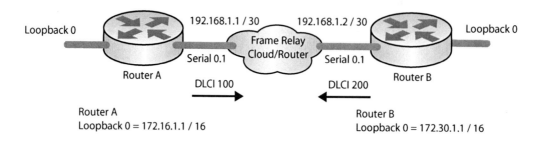

Figure 18–3: Frame relay sub-interfaces

Frame relay sub-interfaces overcome split horizon issues allowing more than one network to be attached to one physical interface. The physical interface can be divided down into one or more sub-interfaces.

Text written in monospaced type indicates commands that can be entered on the router.

Lab objectives

1. Use the IP-addressing scheme depicted in Figure 18–3. The frame switch will have the DCE interfaces so will need to have the clock rate command added.
2. Configure frame relay on the serial interfaces of Routers A and B.
3. Configure the frame relay switch.
4. Configure RIP on Routers A and B to allow for end-to-end connectivity.
5. Test the link by pinging across.

Purpose

Frame relay sub-interfaces are in very common use. Sub-interfaces allow multiple PVCs to terminate on one physical interface. We will only have one PVC per interface in this lab, but you will practice using sub-interfaces.

Lab walk-through

1. Set the IP address and encapsulation type on the routers:

```
Router#config t
Router(config)#hostname RouterA
RouterA(config)#interface serial 0
RouterA(config-if)#encapsulation frame-relay
RouterA(config-if)no shut
RouterA(config)#interface serial 0.1 point-to-point
RouterA(config-subif)#ip add 192.168.1.1 255.255.255.252
RouterA(config-subif)#frame-relay interface-dlci 100 ⇦ You may need
 to exit to config-if after this command.
RouterA(config-fr-dlci)#interface loopback 0 (You may have a different
prompt here.)
RouterA(config-if)#ip address 172.16.1.1 255.255.0.0
Router B:
Router#config t
Router(config)#hostname RouterB
RouterB(config)#interface serial 0
RouterB(config-if)#encapsulation frame-relay
RouterB(config-if)#no shut
RouterB(config-if)#interface serial 0.1 point-to-point
RouterB(config-subif)#ip add 192.168.1.2 255.255.255.252
RouterB(config-subif)#frame-relay interface-dlci 200
RouterB(config-fr-dlci)#interface loopback 0
RouterB(config-if)#ip address 172.30.1.1 255.255.0.0
```

2. We need to configure RIP to allow all networks to see each other.

```
RouterA#config t
RouterA(config)#router rip
RouterA(config-router)#version 2
RouterA(config-router)#network 192.168.1.0
RouterA(config-router)#network 172.16.0.0
Router B:
RouterB#config t
RouterB(config)#router rip
RouterB(config-router)#version 2
RouterB(config-router)#network 192.168.1.0
RouterB(config-router)#network 172.30.0.0
```

3. We need to configure the frame relay switch. Just copy the config and change the interface if you are not using the same ones we have here.

```
Router#config t
Router(config)#hostname FrameSwitch
FrameSwitch(config)#frame-relay switching (Make the router a frame
switch.)
FrameSwitch(config)#interface serial 0
FrameSwitch(config-if)#no ip address
```

```
FrameSwitch(config-if)#clock rate 64000
FrameSwitch(config-if)#encapsulation frame-relay
FrameSwitch(config-if)#frame-relay intf-type dce (Make the interface DCE.)
FrameSwitch(config-if)#frame-relay route 100 interface serial 1 200
            ⇦ Send traffic from dlci 100 out of interface serial 0
                as dlci 200
FrameSwitch(config-if)#no shut
FrameSwitch(config-if)#interface Serial 1
FrameSwitch(config-if)#no ip address
FrameSwitch(config-if)#encapsulation frame-relay
FrameSwitch(config-if)#frame-relay intf-type dce
FrameSwitch(config-if)#frame-relay route 200 interface serial 0 100
FrameSwitch(config-if)#clock rate 64000
FrameSwitch(config-if)#no shut
```

4. Ping from Router A to the loopback on Router B.

```
RouterA#ping 172.30.1.1

Type escape sequence to abort.
Sending 5, 100-byte ICMP Echos to 172.30.1.1, timeout is 2 seconds:
!!!!!
Success rate is 100 percent (5/5), round-trip min/avg/max = 60/60/60 ms
RouterA#
```

If you cannot ping, then go to the module on troubleshooting.

5. Check for frame relay connectivity.

```
RouterA#show frame-relay map
Serial0 (up): ip 192.168.1.2 dlci 100(0x64,0x1840), dynamic,
            broadcast, status defined, active
RouterA#

RouterA#show frame-relay pvc

PVC Statistics for interface Serial0 (Frame Relay DTE)

              Active    Inactive    Deleted    Static
Local           1          0           0          0
Switched        0          0           0          0
Unused          0          0           0          0

DLCI = 100, DLCI USAGE = LOCAL, PVC STATUS = ACTIVE, INTERFACE = Serial0

  input pkts 20          output pkts 20        in bytes 1838
  out bytes 1898         dropped pkts 0        in FECN pkts 0
  in BECN pkts 0         out FECN pkts 0       out BECN pkts 0
  in DE pkts 0           out DE pkts 0
  out bcast pkts 10       out bcast bytes 858
  pvc create time 00:07:57, last time pvc status changed 00:03:23
```

```
RouterA#show frame-relay lmi

LMI Statistics for interface Serial0 (Frame Relay DTE) LMI TYPE = CISCO
  Invalid Unnumbered info 0          Invalid Prot Disc 0
  Invalid dummy Call Ref 0           Invalid Msg Type 0
  Invalid Status Message 0           Invalid Lock Shift 0
  Invalid Information ID 0           Invalid Report IE Len 0
  Invalid Report Request 0           Invalid Keep IE Len 0
  Num Status Enq. Sent 47            Num Status msgs Rcvd 48
  Num Update Status Rcvd 0           Num Status Timeouts 0
RouterA#


RouterA#debug frame-relay lmi
Frame Relay LMI debugging is on
Displaying all Frame Relay LMI data
RouterA#
00:46:38: Serial0(out): StEnq, myseq 53, yourseen 52, DTE up
00:46:38: datagramstart = 0xE3EEA4, datagramsize = 13
00:46:38: FR encap = 0xFCF10309
00:46:38: 00 75 01 01 01 03 02 35 34
00:46:38:
00:46:38: Serial0(in): Status, myseq 53
00:46:38: RT IE 1, length 1, type 1
00:46:38: KA IE 3, length 2, yourseq 53, myseq 53
00:46:48: Serial0(out): StEnq, myseq 54, yourseen 53, DTE up
00:46:48: datagramstart = 0xE3EEA4, datagramsize = 13
00:46:48: FR encap = 0xFCF10309
00:46:48: 00 75 01 01 01 03 02 36 35
00:46:48:
00:46:48: Serial0(in): Status, myseq 54
00:46:48: RT IE 1, length 1, type 1
00:46:48: KA IE 3, length 2, yourseq 54, myseq 54
00:46:58: Serial0(out): StEnq, myseq 55, yourseen 54, DTE up
00:46:58: datagramstart = 0xE3EEA4, datagramsize = 13
00:46:58: FR encap = 0xFCF10309
00:46:58: 00 75 01 01 00 03 02 37 36
00:46:58:
00:46:58: Serial0(in): Status, myseq 55
00:46:58: RT IE 1, length 1, type 0
00:46:58: KA IE 3, length 2, yourseq 55, myseq 55
00:46:58: PVC IE 0x7 , length 0x6 , dlci 100, status 0x2 , bw 0
RouterA#un all
All possible debugging has been turned off
RouterA#


RouterA#show ip route
Codes: C - connected, S - static, I - IGRP, R - RIP, M - mobile, B - BGP
       D - EIGRP, EX - EIGRP external, O - OSPF, IA - OSPF inter area
       N1 - OSPF NSSA external type 1, N2 - OSPF NSSA external type 2
       E1 - OSPF external type 1, E2 - OSPF external type 2, E - EGP
       i - IS-IS, L1 - IS-IS level-1, L2 - IS-IS level-2, ia - IS-IS inter
area
```

```
        * - candidate default, U - per-user static route, o - ODR
        P - periodic downloaded static route

Gateway of last resort is not set

C    172.16.0.0/16 is directly connected, Loopback0
R    172.30.0.0/16 [120/1] via 192.168.1.2, 00:00:12, Serial0
     192.168.1.0/30 is subnetted, 1 subnets
C        192.168.1.0 is directly connected, Serial0
RouterA#
```

Try all these commands on Router B also.

Show runs

```
RouterA#show run
Building configuration...

Current configuration : 781 bytes
!
version 12.1
service timestamps debug uptime
service timestamps log uptime
no service password-encryption
!
hostname RouterA
!
enable secret 5 $1$jjQo$YJXxLo.EZm9t6Sq4UYeCv0
!
username banbury password 0 ccna
!
ip subnet-zero
!
interface Loopback0
 ip address 172.16.1.1 255.255.0.0
!
interface Serial0
 no ip address
 encapsulation frame-relay
!
interface Serial0.1 point-to-point
 ip address 192.168.1.1 255.255.255.252
 frame-relay interface-dlci 100
!
interface Serial1
 no ip address
 shutdown
!
interface Ethernet0
 no ip address
 shutdown
```

```
!
interface BRI0
 no ip address
 shutdown

!
router rip
 version 2
 network 172.16.0.0
 network 192.168.1.0
 !
ip classless
no ip http server
!
line con 0
line aux 0
line vty 0 4
 login local
!
end

RouterA#

---

RouterB#show run
Building configuration...

Current configuration : 688 bytes
!
version 12.1
service timestamps debug uptime
service timestamps log uptime
no service password-encryption
!
hostname RouterB
!
ip subnet-zero
!
interface Loopback0
  ip address 172.30.1.1 255.255.0.0
!
interface Serial0
 no ip address
 encapsulation frame-relay
!
interface Serial0.1 point-to-point
  ip address 192.168.1.2 255.255.255.252
  frame-relay interface-dlci 200
!
interface Serial1
 no ip address
```

```
 shutdown
!
interface Ethernet0
 no ip address
 shutdown
!
interface BRI0
 no ip address
 shutdown

!
router rip
 version 2
 network 172.30.0.0
 network 192.168.1.0
!
ip classless
no ip http server
!
line con 0
line aux 0
line vty 0 4
!
end

RouterB#

---

FrameSwitch#show run
Building configuration...

Current configuration : 685 bytes
!
version 12.1
service timestamps debug uptime
service timestamps log uptime
no service password-encryption
!
hostname FrameSwitch
!
ip subnet-zero
!
frame-relay switching
!
interface Ethernet0
 no ip address
 shutdown
!
interface Serial0
 no ip address
 encapsulation frame-relay
```

```
 clockrate 64000
 frame-relay intf-type dce
 frame-relay route 100 interface Serial1 200
!
interface Serial1
 no ip address
 encapsulation frame-relay
 clockrate 64000
 frame-relay intf-type dce
 frame-relay route 200 interface Serial0 100
!
interface BRI0
 no ip address
 shutdown

!
ip classless
no ip http server

!
line con 0
line aux 0
line vty 0 4
!
end
FrameSwitch#
```

CHAPTER 19

Advanced Labs

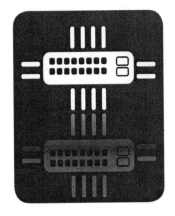

LAB 1: OSPF WITH THREE ROUTERS

The physical topology is as shown in Figure 19–1.

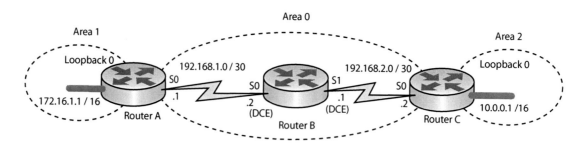

Figure 19–1: Advanced OSPF lab

Lab exercise

Your task is to configure the network in Figure 19–1 to allow full connectivity using OSPF. Router A should see routes for and be able to ping the loopback interface on router C and vice versa. Please feel free to try the lab without following the lab walk-through section.

Text written in `monospaced font` indicates commands that can be entered on the router.

Lab objectives

1. Use the IP addressing scheme depicted in Figure 19–1.
2. Set telnet access for the router to use the local login permissions of username "`banbury`" and the password "`ccna`".
3. Configure the "`enable password`" to be "`cisco`".
4. Configure IP addressing on all three routers.
5. Configure OSPF areas 0, 1, and 2.
6. Finally, test that the link is up and working by sending a ping across the link.

Purpose

Being able to configure and troubleshoot three routers will enable you to easily tackle issues that will arise in the lab.

Lab walk-through

1. To set the IP addresses on an interface, you will need to do the following:

```
Router#config t
Router(config)#hostname RouterA
RouterA(config)#
```

```
RouterA(config)#interface serial 0
RouterA(config-if)#ip address 192.168.1.1 255.255.255.252
RouterA(config-if)#no shutdown
RouterA(config-if)#interface loopback 0 ⇦ "no shut" not needed
RouterA(config-if)#ip address 172.16.1.1 255.255.0.0
RouterA(config-if)#^Z
RouterA#
Router B:
Router#config t
Router(config)#hostname RouterB
RouterB(config)#
RouterB(config)#interface serial 0
RouterB(config-if)#ip address 192.168.1.2 255.255.255.252
RouterB(config-if)#clock rate 64000 ⇦ If this is the DCE side
RouterB(config-if)#no shutdown
RouterB(config-if)#interface serial 1
RouterB(config-if)#ip address 192.168.2.1 255.255.255.252
RouterB(config-if)#clock rate 64000 ⇦ If this is the DCE side
RouterB(config-if)#no shutdown
RouterB(config-if)#^Z
RouterB#
Router C:
Router#config t
Router#(config)#hostname RouterC
RouterC(config)#
RouterC(config)#interface serial 0
RouterC(config-if)#ip address 192.168.2.2 255.255.255.252
RouterC(config-if)#no shutdown
RouterC(config-if)#interface loopback 0 ⇦ "no shut" not needed
RouterC(config-if)#ip address 10.0.0.1 255.255.0.0
RouterC(config-if)#^Z
RouterC#
```

Ping across the serial link now from A to B and then B to C You will not be able to ping from A to C until you configure a routing protocol.

2. To set telnet access, you need to configure the VTY lines to allow telnet access. To do this, type (from configuration mode):

```
RouterA(config)#line vty 0 4 ⇦ Enters the VTY line configuration
RouterA(config-line)#login local ⇦ This will use local usernames
                              and passwords for telnet access
RouterA(config-line)#exit ⇦ Exit the VTY config mode
RouterA(config)#username banbury password ccna ⇦ Creates username
                    and password for telnet access (login local)
Router B:
RouterB(config)#line vty 0 4
RouterB(config-line)#login local
RouterB(config-line)#exit
RouterB(config)#username banbury password ccna
```

```
Router C:
RouterC(config)#line vty 0 4
RouterC(config-line)#login local
RouterC(config-line)#exit
RouterC(config)#username banbury password ccna
```

3. To set the "enable password" do the following:

```
RouterA(config)#enable secret cisco ← Sets the "enable
password"(encrypted).
Router B:
RouterB(config)#enable secret cisco
Router C:
RouterC(config)#enable secret cisco
```

4. To configure OSPF on a router, there are two steps: first, enable the routing protocol and second, specify the networks to be advertised by OSPF:

```
RouterA(config)#router ospf 20 ⇦ Enables the OSPF routing process
RouterA(config-router)#network 192.168.1.0 0.0.0.3 area 0
RouterA(config-router)#network 172.16.0.0 0.0.255.255 area 1
    ⇦ Specifies the networks for OSPF to advertise; one network
      statement is needed for every network advertised
Router B:
RouterB(config)#router ospf 20
RouterB(config-router)#network 192.168.1.0 0.0.0.3 area 0
RouterB(config-router)#network 192.168.2.0 0.0.0.3 area 0
Router C:
RouterC(config)#router ospf 20
RouterC(config-router)#network 192.168.2.0 0.0.0.3 area 0
RouterC(config-router)#network 10.0.0.0 0.0.255.255 area 2

As you complete the configuration you should see the OSPF process loading.

03:19:29: %OSPF-5-ADJCHG: Process 20, Nbr 192.168.2.1 on Serial0 from
LOADING to FULL, Loading Done
```

5. Make sure all the interfaces on the routers are up up with the "show ip interface brief" command.

```
RouterA#show ip interface brief
Interface       IP-Address      OK? Method Status                 Protocol
Ethernet0       unassigned      YES unset  administratively down   down
Loopback0       172.16.1.1      YES manual up                      up
Serial0         192.168.1.1     YES manual up                      up
Serial1         unassigned      YES unset  administratively down   down
```

Make sure you can see all of the networks including the loopback interfaces.

```
RouterA#show ip route
Codes: C - connected, S - static, I - IGRP, R - RIP, M - mobile, B - BGP
       D - EIGRP, EX - EIGRP external, O - OSPF, IA - OSPF inter area
       N1 - OSPF NSSA external type 1, N2 - OSPF NSSA external type 2
       E1 - OSPF external type 1, E2 - OSPF external type 2, E - EGP
       i - IS-IS, L1 - IS-IS level-1, L2 - IS-IS level-2, ia - IS-IS inter
area
       * - candidate default, U - per-user static route, o - ODR
       P - periodic downloaded static route

Gateway of last resort is not set

Gateway of last resort is not set

C    172.16.0.0/16 is directly connected, Loopback0
     10.0.0.0/32 is subnetted, 1 subnets
O IA    10.0.0.1 [110/129] via 192.168.1.2, 00:00:07, Serial0
     192.168.1.0/30 is subnetted, 1 subnets
C        192.168.1.0 is directly connected, Serial0
     192.168.2.0/30 is subnetted, 1 subnets
O        192.168.2.0 [110/128] via 192.168.1.2,00:00:07, Serial0
```

Check the protocol settings:

```
RouterA#show ip protocols
Routing Protocol is "ospf 20"
  Outgoing update filter list for all interfaces is not set
  Incoming update filter list for all interfaces is not set
  Router ID 172.16.1.1
  It is an area border router
  Number of areas in this router is 2. 2 normal 0 stub 0 nssa
  Maximum path: 4
  Routing for Networks:
    172.16.0.0 0.0.255.255 area 1
    192.168.1.0 0.0.0.3 area 0
  Routing Information Sources:
    Gateway          Distance      Last Update
    10.0.0.1              110      00:03:54
    192.168.2.1          110      00:03:54
    172.16.1.1           110      00:03:54
  Distance: (default is 110)
```

Ping the loopback interfaces:

```
RouterA#ping 10.0.0.1
Type escape sequence to abort.
Sending 5, 100-byte ICMP Echos to 10.0.0.1, timeout is 2 seconds:
!!!!!
Success rate is 100 percent (5/5), round-trip min/avg/max = 56/64/76 ms
RouterA#
```

6. Now reload the routers.

Show runs

```
RouterA#show run
Building configuration...

Current configuration : 697 bytes
!
version 12.1
no service single-slot-reload-enable
service timestamps debug uptime
service timestamps log uptime
no service password-encryption
!
hostname RouterA
!
enable secret 5 $1$SJxM$QL6.HXWDKQJBbfBa.tOg/0
!
username banbury password 0 ccna
!
ip subnet-zero
!
interface Loopback0
 ip address 172.16.1.1 255.255.0.0
!
interface Ethernet0
 no ip address
 shutdown
!
interface Serial0
 ip address 192.168.1.1 255.255.255.252
!
interface Serial1
 no ip address
 shutdown
!
router ospf 20
 log-adjacency-changes
 network 172.16.0.0 0.0.255.255 area 1
 network 192.168.1.0 0.0.0.3 area 0
!
ip classless
no ip http server
!
line con 0
line aux 0
line vty 0 4
 login local
!
end
```

```
-----

RouterB#show run
Building configuration...
!
version 12.1
no service single-slot-reload-enable
service timestamps debug uptime
service timestamps log uptime
no service password-encryption
!
hostname RouterB
!
enable secret 5 $1$C2Wp$S2ox/WQFXjyshkwnFX6Iu0
!
username banbury password 0 ccna
!
ip subnet-zero
!
interface Ethernet0
 no ip address
 shutdown
!
interface Serial0
 ip address 192.168.1.2 255.255.255.252
 clockrate 64000
!
interface Serial1
 ip address 192.168.2.1 255.255.255.252
 clockrate 64000
!
interface BRI0
 no ip address
 shutdown
!
router ospf 20
 log-adjacency-changes
 network 192.168.1.0 0.0.0.3 area 0
 network 192.168.2.0 0.0.0.3 area 0
!
ip classless
no ip http server
!
line con 0
line aux 0
line vty 0 4
 login local
!
end

RouterB#
---
```

```
RouterC#show run
Building configuration...

Current configuration : 726 bytes
!
version 12.1
service timestamps debug uptime
service timestamps log uptime
no service password-encryption
!
hostname RouterC
!
enable secret 5 $1$1AZx$UzhYsYlIpc7I4vJI3ZI4U.
!
username banbury password 0 cisco
!
ip subnet-zero
!
interface Loopback0
 ip address 10.0.0.1 255.255.0.0
!
interface Ethernet0
 no ip address
 shutdown
!
interface Serial0
 ip address 192.168.2.2 255.255.255.252
!
interface Serial1
 no ip address
 shutdown
!
interface BRI0
 no ip address
 shutdown

!
router ospf 20
 log-adjacency-changes
 network 10.0.0.0 0.0.255.255 area 2
 network 192.168.2.0 0.0.0.3 area 0
!
ip classless
no ip http server
!
line con 0
line aux 0
line vty 0 4
 login local
!
end
RouterC#
```

LAB 2: OSPF WITH ACCESS-LIST

Lab exercise

Your task is to configure the network in Figure 19–2 to allow full connectivity using OSPF. Router A is to block ICMP from Router C, and Router C is to deny any traffic on port 80. Please feel free to try the lab without following the lab walk-through section.

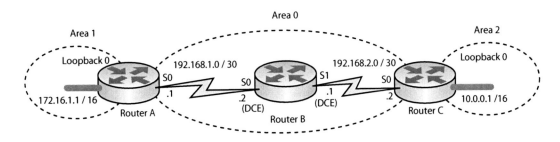

Figure 19–2: OSPF with access-list

Text written in monospaced type indicates commands that can be entered on the router.

Purpose

A three-router lab is the typical scenario you will face in the CCNA exam. You must be comfortable with configuring three routers with a basic config and then applying a routing protocol and access-list.

Lab objectives

1. Use the IP-addressing scheme depicted in Figure 19–2.
2. Set telnet access for the router to use the local login permissions of username "banbury" and the password "ccna".
3. Configure the "enable password" to be "cisco".
4. Configure IP addressing on all three routers.
5. Configure OSPF areas 0, 1, and 2.
6. Add an access-list on the serial interfaces of both routers A and C. Router A is to block all ping traffic from network 192.168.2.0. Router C is to block all DNS traffic from any network.

Lab walk-through

1. Follow the configuration from the previous lab.

2. Configure the access-lists on both Routers A and C and apply them to the serial interfaces.

```
RouterA(config)#
RouterA(config)#access-list 100 deny icmp 192.168.2.0 0.0.0.255 any
RouterA(config)#access-list 100 permit ip any any
RouterA(config)#interface serial 0
RouterA(config-if)#ip access-group 100 in

RouterC(config)#access-list 100 deny tcp any any eq 80
RouterC(config)#access-list 100 permit ip any any
RouterC(config)#ip http server
RouterC(config)#interface serial 0
RouterC(config-if)#ip access-group 100 in
```

3. Telnet from Router A to Router C. A normal telnet will work. However, a telnet on port 53 (DNS) will fail.

```
RouterA#telnet 192.168.2.2
Trying 192.168.2.2 ... Open

User Access Verification

Username: ← Press Ctrl+Shift+6 (all together) and then "X"
RouterA#

RouterA#telnet 192.168.2.2 80
Trying 192.168.2.2, 80 ... Open

exit
HTTP/1.0 501 Not Implemented
Date: Mon, 01 Mar 1993 00:22:17 UTC
Content-type: text/html
Expires: Thu, 16 Feb 1989 00:00:00 GMT

<H1>501 Not Implemented</H1>


[Connection to 192.168.2.2 closed by foreign host]
```

4. Now ping Router A from Router C. The ping from the serial interface (the blocked network) will fail. A ping from loopback 0 (10.0.0.1) will however, work.

```
RouterC#ping 192.168.1.1

Type escape sequence to abort.
Sending 5, 100-byte ICMP Echos to 192.168.1.1, timeout is 2 seconds:
U.U.U
Success rate is 0 percent (0/5)

RouterC#ping
Protocol [ip]:
Target IP address: 192.168.1.1
```

```
Repeat count [5]:
Datagram size [100]:
Timeout in seconds [2]:
Extended commands [n]: y
Source address or interface: 10.0.0.1
Type of service [0]:
Set DF bit in IP header? [no]:
Validate reply data? [no]:
Data pattern [0xABCD]:
Loose, Strict, Record, Timestamp, Verbose[none]:
Sweep range of sizes [n]:
Type escape sequence to abort.
Sending 5, 100-byte ICMP Echos to 192.168.1.1, timeout is 2 seconds:
!!!!!
Success rate is 100 percent (5/5), round-trip min/avg/max = 60/60/64 ms
RouterC#
```

Show runs

```
RouterA#show run
Building configuration...

Current configuration : 900 bytes
!
version 12.1
no service single-slot-reload-enable
service timestamps debug uptime
service timestamps log uptime
no service password-encryption
!
hostname RouterA
!
enable secret 5 $1$rujI$BJ8GgiK8U9p5cdfXyApPr/
!
username banbury password 0 ccna
!
ip subnet-zero
!
interface Loopback0
 ip address 172.16.1.1 255.255.0.0
!
interface Loopback1
 ip address 172.20.1.1 255.255.0.0
!
interface Ethernet0
 no ip address
 shutdown
!
interface Serial0
 ip address 192.168.1.1 255.255.255.252
 ip access-group 100 in
```

```
!
interface Serial1
 no ip address
 shutdown
!
router ospf 20
 log-adjacency-changes
 network 172.16.0.0 0.0.255.255 area 1
 network 192.168.1.0 0.0.0.3 area 0
!
ip classless
no ip http server
!
access-list 100 deny  icmp 192.168.2.0 0.0.0.255 any
access-list 100 permit ip any any
!
line con 0
 password letmein
 login
line 1 8
line aux 0
line vty 0 4
 login local
!
end

---


RouterB#show run
Building configuration...

Current configuration : 827 bytes
!
version 12.1
no service single-slot-reload-enable
service timestamps debug uptime
service timestamps log uptime
no service password-encryption
!
hostname RouterB
!
enable secret 5 $1$oXft$UMJZc/BQzbfpeHVCApF3H0
!
username banbury password 0 ccna
!
ip subnet-zero
!
interface Loopback0
 ip address 172.30.1.1 255.255.0.0
!
interface Loopback1
 ip address 172.31.1.1 255.255.0.0
```

```
!
interface Ethernet0
 no ip address
 shutdown
!
interface Serial0
 ip address 192.168.1.2 255.255.255.252
 clockrate 64000
!
interface Serial1
 ip address 192.168.2.1 255.255.255.252
 clockrate 64000
!
router ospf 20
 log-adjacency-changes
 network 192.168.1.0 0.0.0.3 area 0
 network 192.168.2.0 0.0.0.3 area 0
!
ip classless
no ip http server
!
line con 0
 password letmein
 login
line aux 0
line vty 0 4
 login local
!
end

RouterB#

  ---


RouterC#show run
Building configuration...

Current configuration:
!
version 11.3
service timestamps debug uptime
service timestamps log uptime
no service password-encryption
!
hostname RouterC
!
enable secret 5 $1$1AZx$UzhYsYlIpc7I4vJI3ZI4U.
!
username banbury password 0 cisco
ip subnet-zero
!
!
```

```
interface Loopback0
 ip address 10.0.0.1 255.255.0.0
!
interface Ethernet0
 no ip address
 shutdown
!
interface Serial0
 ip address 192.168.2.2 255.255.255.252
 ip access-group 100 in
 no ip mroute-cache
!
interface Serial1
 no ip address
 shutdown
!
router ospf 20
 network 10.0.0.0 0.0.255.255 area 2
 network 192.168.2.0 0.0.0.3 area 0
!
ip classless
!
access-list 100 deny    tcp any any eq www
access-list 100 permit ip any any
!
line con 0
line 1 16
line aux 0
line vty 0 4
 login local
!
end

RouterC#
```

CHAPTER 20

Epilog

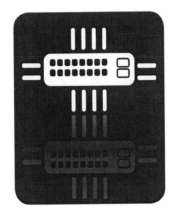

DID YOU FIND ANY MISTAKES?

The labs in this book have been checked by several CCNPs and CCIEs, as well as the hundreds of students who have attended www.NetworksInc.co.uk CCNA boot camps. We think that they are as close to perfect as possible, but in the unlikely event you find an error, please let us know. help@howtonetwork.net

ARE YOU READY FOR THE EXAM?

You are ready for the practical part of the CCNA test when:

- You can configure all the labs without looking at the instructions.
- You can replace the suggested IP addressing scheme with your own.
- You can configure and troubleshoot all the labs using three routers.

If it helps, remember that the best Cisco experts in the world all logged onto a router for the first time once and probably sat there confused. Being a good network engineer just means you have put in time and effort doing the same thing over and over again until it becomes second nature.

Try all the labs above with the following IP addressing scheme. Which routing protocols cannot be used with the addressing scheme below? Do you need to use any special commands to get the /16 mask advertised?

If you have a second serial interface, then swap the cables to that interface to avoid only configuring the clock rate on one interface every time.

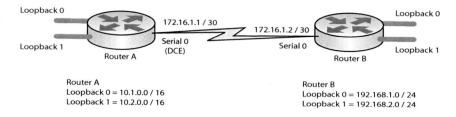

Router A
Loopback 0 = 10.1.0.0 / 16
Loopback 1 = 10.2.0.0 / 16

Router B
Loopback 0 = 192.168.1.0 / 24
Loopback 1 = 192.168.2.0 / 24

Figure 20–2: Alternative topology

If you have access to a third router, you can go through all the labs using the topology in Figure 20–1. Put all the access-lists on routers A and C to start with and just use router B as the hub router in the middle.

It is important that you swap the DCE cable around and use different IP addressing schemes. If you just use the ones I have used, you may struggle in the exam when you are presented with different IP addresses.

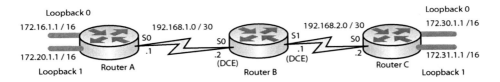

Figure 20–2: Three-router topology

PART 3

APPENDICES

APPENDIX A

The Easy Way to Subnet

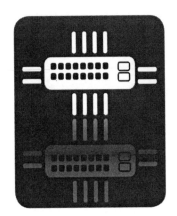

Subnetting is easy, really easy in fact. Even if you do not understand how it all works the first or the hundredth time, if you follow the system outlined in this book you will come to the correct answer every time without fail.

By the end of this guide you will be well on the way to being able to answer most subnetting questions in your head in seconds. Make sure you have read through the manual before you launch into this appendix. I am presuming you have read through that at least once and understood some of the fundamentals, such as powers of 2 and binary mathematics.

 IN THE EXAM:

When you reach the subnetting questions in the exam — RELAX! Take three deep breaths to get some extra oxygen into your brain and just follow the steps you have learned here.

CLASS C SUBNETTING

Here are the possible Class C subnets:

Bits	Subnet mask	CIDR	Subnets	Hosts
0	255.255.255.0	/24	1 network	254
1	255.255.255.128	/25	2	126
2	255.255.255.192	/26	4	62
3	255.255.255.224	/27	8	30
4	255.255.255.240	/28	16	14
5	255.255.255.248	/29	32	6
6	255.255.255.252	/30	64	2

Logic tells us that the more host bits we steal, the more subnets we have, but the less hosts we have available per subnet.

We know from the manual that we need to follow five simple steps in order to answer any subnetting question. The five steps are:

1. How many subnets?

   2 to the power of masked bits.

2. How many hosts per subnet?

   2 to the power of unmasked bits − 2.

3. What are the valid subnets?

   256 minus the rightmost non-zero subnet.

4. What are the valid hosts per subnet?

5. What is the broadcast address of the subnet?

The first subnet of a Class C address we can use involves taking one bit of the remaining eight host bits. If you are not sure of what is happening with the binary numbers, then go back to the manual. For the quick method we will not have time to write things down in binary.

Example 1: `255.255.255.128` or `/25`

I know we are not supposed to have one bit for subnetting, but there are exceptions. It is a slightly awkward to start with the exception, but we need to address it some time and there is no time like the present. You would use this subnet if you wanted two subnets each containing 126 hosts on a Class C subnet.

The Subnetting Secrets Chart© works for the IP subnet-zero example. We can use the zero subnet, which is the first bit off, and the second subnet, which is the first bit on.

Subnets	0	128
First host	1	129
Last host	126	254
Broadcast	127	255

We have taken one bit to use for subnets, so tick down one place on the top subnets column, giving us the value 128, which gives us the subnet mask `255.255.255.128` (which is useful if you had only been given the /25 mask). You can then tick one place down on the lower subnets column to show that we have two subnets. We have seven bits left for the hosts, so tick down seven places on the "Hosts minus 2" column to reveal that we have 126 (128 – 2) hosts per subnet.

Super Subnetting Chart™

	Bits	128	64	32	16	8	4	2	1
Subnets		✓							
128	✓								
192									
224									
240									

	Subnets	Hosts minus 2								
248										
252										
254										
255										
Powers of 2										
2	✓	✓								
4		✓								
8		✓								
16		✓								
32		✓								
64		✓								
128		✓								
256										
512										
1024										
2048										
4096										
8192										
16,384										

So, if in the exam you were asked which subnet host 192.168.12.68 /25 is in, you would simply follow the above steps and see that host number 68 is within subnet 192.168.12.0.

Subnet 1 192.168.12.0 hosts 1–126 (broadcast 127).
Subnet 2 192.168.12.128 hosts 129–254 (broadcast 255).

If the above example does not make sense at the moment, then leave it for now and come back to it later. It will still be here and will make more sense after you go through the examples below.

Example 2: 255.255.255.192 or /26

We can rely on the Subnetting Secrets Chart© here as well.

1. How many subnets?
   We know that the default Class C mask is 24 bits or 255.255.255.0 and that this example is using a /26 mask, which means two bits have been stolen after the default mask. We

can tick two boxes down the top subnets column of the Subnetting Secrets Chart© to get to the 192 box to determine the subnet mask value of 255.255.255.192.

Next we can click down two boxes on the Subnetting Secrets Chart© subnets column, giving us four subnets.
2^2 = 4

So we have four subnets.

Super Subnetting Chart™

	Bits	128	64	32	16	8	4	2	1
Subnets		✓	✓						
128	✓								
192	✓								
224									
240									
248									
252									
254									
255									
Powers of 2	Subnets	Hosts minus 2							
2	✓	✓							
4	✓	✓							
8		✓							
16		✓							
32		✓							
64		✓							
128									
256									
512									
1024									
2048									
4096									
8192									
16,384									

2. How many hosts per subnet?

    We have six bits at the top of the Subnetting Secrets Chart© left unchecked. So we know we have six bits left for the hosts. We can now tick down six host boxes on the powers-of-2 column to get 64 minus 2. We have put this next to the original two ticks to save space.

    You can refer to the Subnetting Secrets© videos if you really want to see how this process works.

    You can find them at: www.subnetting-secrets.com or at www.howtonetwork.net.
    2^6 – 2 = 62

3. What are the valid subnets?

    We take the subnet number (in this case 192) away from 256.

    256 – 192 = 64, or we tick two places across the top bits row because we ticked down two on the subnets column. We will use the subnet zero throughout this guide, which will allow us to use the 0 and the subnet, which is 192 in this case.

    0, 64, 128, 192. So each subnet number would end in:
    x.x.x.0
    x.x.x.64
    x.x.x.128
    x.x.x.192

4. What are the valid hosts per subnet/broadcast address?

    We can actually answer questions four and five at the same time.

Subnets	0	64	128	192
First host	1	65	129	193
Last host	62	126	190	254
Broadcast	63	127	191	255

That was fairly simple, was it not? If you follow the Subnetting Secrets Chart©, you cannot go wrong.

If you were asked in the exam which subnet host 192.16.150.76 /26 is in, you would see that it is within subnet 192.16.150.64 because 192.16.150.0 is too low and 192.16.150.128 is too high. The subnets would be:

Subnet 1 = 192.16.150.0 hosts 1 – 62 (63 is the broadcast).

Subnet 2 = 192.16.150.64 hosts 65 – 126 (127 is the broadcast).*

Subnet 3 = 192.16.150.128 hosts 129 – 190 (191 is the broadcast).

Subnet 4 = 192.16.150.192 hosts 193 – 254 (255 is the broadcast).

The * in all the examples indicates the correct subnet (i.e., the subnet the host address is in).

Example 3: Which subnet is host 200.100.206.99 /27 in?

We have taken one more bit for subnetting. You know that to get to /24 requires a subnet mask of 255.255.255.0, i.e., 24 binary bits. We need to add 3 to 24 to get to 27, so now you have to tick down three bits from the top subnets column to get 224. The subnet mask for /27 is, therefore, 255.255.255.224.

1. How many subnets?

   2^3 = 8

   Tick down three boxes on the lower subnets column, giving us eight subnets.

Super Subnetting Chart™

	Bits	128	64	32	16	8	4	2	1
Subnets		✓	✓	✓					
128	✓								
192	✓								
224	✓								
240									
248									
252									
254									
255									
Powers of 2	Subnets	Hosts minus 2							
2	✓	✓							
4	✓	✓							
8	✓	✓							
16		✓							
32		✓							
64									
128									
256									

512								
1024								
2048								
4096								
8192								
16,384								

2. How many hosts per subnet?

    We have five remaining bits for the hosts. Tick down five places on the powers-of-2 chart to give us 32, and take away 2.

    $2^5 - 2 = 30$

    So we have eight subnets, each with 30 hosts.

3. What are the valid subnets?

    We take 224 away from 256, or tick three across the very top bits row.

    $256 - 224 = 32$

    0, 32, 64, 96, 128, 160, 192, 224

    So our subnets are going up in increments of 32.

4. What are the valid hosts per subnet/broadcast address?

Subnets	0	32	64	96	128	160	192	224
First host	1	33	65	97	129	161	193	225
Last host	30	62	94	126	158	190	222	254
Broadcast	31	63	95	127	159	191	223	255

The above boxes represent the last octet, so if you wanted to write the subnets out in full you would have:

200.100.206.0

200.100.206.32

200.100.206.64 (we still have not reached the .99 host).

200.100.206.96 * the .99 **host must be in here since the next subnet is too high.**

200.100.206.128 We could carry on subnetting, but there is no point as we have the answer.

Can you see how simple the process is? You must be careful to tick the right boxes on the Subnetting Secrets Chart© to start with or your entire subnetting results will be wrong.

Example 4: What is the broadcast address for host 192.200.200.167 /28?
(This question is just a distraction because we simply follow the same process and the correct answer will be revealed.)

We can see that we have to convert the /28 address into a subnet mask. The subnet mask for /24 is 255.255.255.0 and we need to add 4 to 24 to get 28. We have stolen four bits for subnetting, so you need to tick down four boxes on the upper subnets column to get to 240. Our subnet mask is 255.255.255.240.

Tick 128, 192, 224, and then 240.

How many subnets?
You should know the drill now. Tick down four boxes on the powers-of-2 subnets chart.

Super Subnetting Chart™

	Bits	128	64	32	16	8	4	2	1
Subnets		✓	✓	✓	✓				
128	✓								
192	✓								
224	✓								
240	✓								
248									
252									
254									
255									
Powers of 2	Subnets	Hosts minus 2							
2	✓	✓							
4	✓	✓							
8	✓	✓							
16	✓	✓							
32									
64									
128									
256									
512									
1024									
2048									

4096								
8192								
16,384								

How many hosts per subnet?

We have 4 bits left for the hosts.

$2^4 - 2 = 14$

So we have 16 subnets, each containing 14 hosts.

What are the valid subnets?

$256 - 240 = 16$, or tick four along the very top.

So, our subnets are going up in increments of 16 (starting at 0).

0, 16, 32, 48, 64, 80, up to 240

What are the valid hosts per subnet/broadcast address?

Our subnets are:

192.200.200.0 hosts 1 – 14 (15 is the broadcast)

192.200.200.16 hosts 17 – 30 (31 is the broadcast)

Multiply 16 by 10 next to save time (recommended for the exam).

192.200.200.160 hosts 161 – 174 (175 is the broadcast).*

192.200.200.176

So, following the same process we can see that the broadcast address for host 192.200.200.167 is 192.200.200.175 and the subnet address is 192.200.200.160.

Example 5: Which subnet is host 200.100.55.86 /29 in?

By now you should be familiar with ticking down on the Subnetting Secrets Chart©. Make sure you continue to use it for the examples. We need to work out how many to add to /24 to get to /29; the answer is 5, of course. So tick down column five to get your mask of 255.255.255.248.

Super Subnetting Chart™

	Bits	128	64	32	16	8	4	2	1
Subnets		✓	✓	✓	✓	✓			
128	✓								
192	✓								
224	✓								
240	✓								
248	✓								
252									
254									
255									
Powers of 2	Subnets	Hosts minus 2							
2	✓	✓							
4	✓	✓							
8	✓	✓							
16	✓								
32	✓								

How many subnets?

2^5 = 32 subnets.

How many hosts per subnet?

2^3 − 2 = 6

What are the valid subnets?

256 − 248 = 8, or tick five across the top.

So we will go up in increments of 8. We do not have the space to count up all the way to 248 in multiples of 8. In the exam you will not have time to do it either. So, you can skip to the number closest to the subnet you are being asked about such as 40, 80, 120, etc. Just make sure the number is divisible by 8.

What are the valid hosts per subnet / broadcast address?

Subnets	0	8	16	24	etc.	80	88	etc.	248
First host	1	9	17	25	etc.	81	89	etc.	249
Last host	6	14	22	30	etc.	86	94	etc.	254
Broadcast	7	15	23	31	etc.	87	95	etc.	255

The subnets are:

200.100.55.0

200.100.55.8, etc., but we really want to get to host 88, so I will multiply 8 by 10 to jump ahead.

200.100.55.80 hosts 81 – 86 (broadcast 87).*

200.100.55.88

Host 200.100.55.86 is in subnet 200.100.55.80.

Example 6

Which subnet is host 210.25.200.165 /30 in?

We use a 30-bit subnet mask for subnets that only need two hosts. A point-to-point connection is ideal for this.

You should now write out your own Subnetting Secrets Chart© to get into the habit you will need for the exam. There is a blank Subnetting Secrets Chart© available for you to download for printing out at: http://www.howtonetwork.net/public/1337.cfm. You do need to write it out by hand in IT exams or interviews though.

We need to get to /30 from the default /24 mask, so tick down six in the top subnet column, giving you a mask of 255.255.255.252.

How many subnets?
$2^6 = 64$

How many hosts per subnet?
$2^2 - 2 = 2$

What are the valid subnets?
$256 - 252 = 4$, or tick six places across the top row.
0, 4, 8, 12, 16, etc., up to 248

 IN THE EXAM:

Be careful not to go up to 8 and then double it, i.e., 4, 8, 16. This is a very common mistake to make when a person is under pressure.

What are the valid hosts per subnet/broadcast address?

Subnets	0	4	8	12	16	etc.	160	164	etc.	252
First host	1	5	9	13	17	etc.	161	165	etc.	253
Last host	2	6	10	14	18	etc.	162	166	etc.	254
Broadcast	3	7	11	15	19	etc.	163	167	etc.	255

Be careful not to spend an age counting up in multiples of 4 in the exam. I always look at the host number (165 in this example) and multiply the subnets 4 or 8 by 10. If we need to get to host 165, I would multiply 16 by 10 giving the subnet 160 (which is a still a multiple of 4).

Subnet 210.25.200.160 hosts 161 – 162 (broadcast 163).
Subnet 210.25.200.164 hosts 165 – 166 (broadcast 167).*
Subnet 210.25.200.168.

CLASS B SUBNETTING

The principles for subnetting Class B addresses are exactly the same as for Class C. You just need to remember that the default subnet mask for Class B addresses is 255.255.0.0. So, the subnetting will take place from the third octet onwards.

Here are all the possible Class B subnets:

Bits	Subnet mask	CIDR	Subnets	Hosts
0	255.255.0.0	/16	1 (network)	65534
1	255.255.128.0	/17	2	32766
2	255.255.192.0	/18	4	16382
3	255.255.224.0	/19	8	8190
4	255.255.240.0	/20	16	4094
5	255.255.248.0	/21	32	2046
6	255.255.252.0	/22	64	1022
7	255.255.254.0	/23	128	510
8	255.255.255.0	/24	256	254
9	255.255.255.128	/25	512	126
10	255.255.255.192	/26	1024	62
11	255.255.255.224	/27	2048	30
12	255.255.255.240	/28	4096	14
13	255.255.255.248	/29	8192	6
14	255.255.255.252	/30	16384	2

Example 1: 255.255.128.0 or /17.

We need to get the hard one out of the way first. Let's just treat this like a normal subnet. The usual rules do not apply.

We can use the 0 subnet on the third octet as long as we have some bits turned on, on the fourth octet. Unfortunately, you have to think in binary to understand this example.

The /17 indicates that we have added one bit to the default /16 mask to use for subnetting. Tick down one column in the upper subnets column, giving us the mask 255.255.128.0.

Super Subnetting Chart™

	Bits	128	64	32	16	8	4	2	1 (+8)
Subnets		✓							
128	✓								
192									
224									
240									
248									
252									
254									
255									
Powers of 2	Subnets	Hosts minus 2							
2	✓	✓							
4		✓							
8		✓							
16		✓							
32		✓							
64		✓							
128		✓							
256		✓							
512		✓							
1024		✓							
2048		✓							
4096		✓							
8192		✓							
16,384		✓							
32,768		✓							
65,536									

How many subnets?

We can have 0 and 128, so we get 2^1 = 2. You can see this by the one tick we have added to the lower subnets column (for the 1 bit we have stolen).

How many hosts per subnet?

We have seven bits left on the third octet and eight on the fourth (hence the + 8 in the Subnetting Secrets Chart©), giving us 15 host bits all together.

2^15 − 2 = 32,766

We cannot really follow the rest of the subnetting questions for the 128 mask because the /17 mask is the exception. We do know though that we can have 0 on the third octet as long as we have no bits turned on on the fourth octet.

Subnet	0.0	128.0
First host	0.1	128.1
Last host	127.254	255.254
Broadcast	127.255	255.255

So if our host address was 120.100.55.86 /17, our subnets would be:

120.100.0.0 hosts 0.1 − 127.254 (broadcast 127.255).*

120.100.128.0 hosts 128.1 − 255.254 (broadcast 255.255).

The above host is in subnet 120.100.0.0.

Example 2: What subnet is host 150.200.155.23 /18 in?

The trick is to remember that we are still subnetting on the third octet. The default mask for Class B is 255.255.0.0 which is 16 binary bits. We need to add 2 to 16 to get to our /18 mask, so tick down two on the top subnets column. Our subnet mask is 255.255.192.0.

This will leave six host bits on the third octet and another eight on the fourth octet (6 + 8 = 14 host bits).

Super Subnetting Chart™

	Bits	128	64	32	16	8	4	2	1 (+ 8)
Subnets		✓	✓						
128	✓								
192	✓								
224									
240									
248									
252									
254									
255									
Powers of 2	Subnets	Hosts minus 2							
2	✓	✓							
4	✓	✓							
8		✓							
16		✓							
32		✓							
64		✓							
128		✓							
256		✓							
512		✓							
1024		✓							
2048		✓							
4096		✓							
8192		✓							
16,384		✓							

How many subnets?

$2^2 = 4$ (indicated by ticking down two on the powers of 2 subnets column).

How many hosts per subnet?

For this question you are going to have to use your imagination to extend the Subnetting Secrets Chart©. The bits all represent the octet we are subnetting. If we subnet across two subnets, we will need to remember how many host bits are left.

In this example, we have stolen two bits from the third octet, which leaves six bits on the third octet plus eight on the fourth octet, giving us 14 bits. Tick down 14 host bits on the hosts column.

$2^{\wedge}14 - 2 = 16,382$

What are the valid subnets?

$256 - 192 = 64$ (or tick two across the top row).

0, 64, 128, 192

What are the valid hosts per subnet/broadcast address?

Subnets	0.0	64.0	128.0	192.0
First host	0.1	64.1	128.1	192.1
Last host	63.254	127.254	191.254	255.254
Broadcast	63.255	127.255	191.255	255.255

The above numbers are the third and fourth octets. You could write out the entire subnet (as below) but this does take a lot longer.

So our subnets are:

150.200.0.0 hosts 0.1 – 63.254 (broadcast 150.200.63.255).

150.200.64.0 hosts 64.1 – 127.254 (broadcast 150.200.127.255).

150.200.128.0 hosts 128.1 – 191.254 (broadcast 150.200.191.255)* **our host is here.**

150.200.192.0 hosts 192.1 – 255.254 (broadcast 150.200.255.255.

Host 155.23 is within the host numbers 128.1 – 191.254 on subnet 3.

Example 3: Which subnet is host 160.24.67.200 /19 in?

Can you write out your own Subnetting Secrets Chart© for this one?

What do we have to add to /16 to get the mask of /19, and how many bits do we tick down and across the top?

1. How many subnets?

   $2^{\wedge}3 = 8$

2. How many hosts per subnet?

   $2^{\wedge}13 - 2 = 8190$

3. What are the valid subnets?

   $256 - 224 = 32$ (or tick three across the top).

   0, 32, 64, 96, 128, 160, 192, 224

4. What are the valid hosts per subnet/broadcasts?

Subnets	0.0	32.0	64.0	96.0	128.0	160.0	192.0	224.0
First host	0.1	32.1	64.1	96.1	128.1	160.1	192.1	224.1
Last host	31.254	63.254	95.254	127.254	159.254	191.254	223.254	255.254
Broadcast	31.255	63.255	95.255	127.255	159.255	191.255	223.255	255.255

Can you look at the table above and see which subnet host 67.200 is in? The answer is: subnet 160.24.64.0 contains host 160.24.67.200.

What if you had been asked what the broadcast address for this subnet is?

Example 4: Which subnet is host 192.50.100.200 /20 in?

Write out a Subnetting Secrets Chart© again.

How many do we tick down to get to /20 from /16 default mask? And tick the same number across the top to get the increment.

1. How many subnets?
   2^4 = 16
2. How many hosts per subnet?
   2^12 – 2 = 4094
3. What are the valid subnets?
   256 – 240 = 16
   0, 32, 64, 96, 128, 160, 192, 224
4. What are the valid hosts per subnet/broadcasts?

Subnets	0.0	16.0	32.0	48.0	64.0	80.0	96.0	112.0	etc.	240.0
First host	0.1	16.1	32.1	48.1	64.1	80.1	96.1	112.1		240.1
Last host	15.254	31.254	47.254	63.254	79.254	95.254	111.254	127.254		255.254
Broadcast	15.255	31.255	47.255	63.255	79.255	95.255	111.255	127.255		255.255

We are looking for host 100.200 which is in the 96.0 subnet.
Host 192.50.100.200 is in the 192.50.96.0 subnet.

Example 5: Which subnet is host 180.22.56.65 /21 in?

Follow the procedure for the previous examples to determine the correct mask for the /21 subnet.

1. How many subnets?

   2^5 = 32

2. How many hosts per subnet?

   2^11 – 2 = 2046

3. What are the valid subnets?

   256 – 248 = 8

   0, 8, 16, 24, 32, 40 ..., etc., 248, or in full:

   180.22.0.0

   180.22.8.0

   180.22.16.0, etc.

4. What are the valid hosts per subnet / broadcasts?

Subnets	0.0	8.0	16.0	24.0	32.0	40.0	48.0	56.0	etc.
First host	0.1	8.1	16.1	24.1	32.1	40.1	48.1	56.1	
Last host	7.254	15.254	23.254	31.254	39.254	47.254	55.254	63.254	
Broadcast	7.255	15.255	23.255	31.255	39.255	47.255	55.255	63.255	

Subnets	192.0	200.0	208.0	216.0	224.0	232.0	240.0	248.0
First host	192.1	200.1	208.1	216.1	224.1	232.1	240.1	248.1
Last host	199.254	207.254	215.254	223.254	231.254	239.254	247.254	255.254
Broadcast	199.255	207.255	215.255	223.255	231.255	239.255	247.255	255.255

We cannot fit all of the available subnets in and in the exam you will just want to find the answer as quickly as possible. Anything before or after the relevant subnet is of no concern to you (apart from working out the correct subnet).

The correct subnet for the host 180.22.56.65 is 180.22.56.0.

Are you starting to understand how it all works now? You may have understood this in the first go or it may take what seems like an age for it to sink in. How long it takes has nothing to do with how clever you are. Previous IT experience will help but a lot of it will be down to when you last studied and whether the left or right side of your brain dominates.

Do not force it in. Just follow the process over and over and you will get it, guaranteed.

One more thing. Do not be surprised if it clicks into place all of a sudden and then goes away again. This is very common and a sign that the information is passing from short- to long-term memory. It will come back again.

Example 6: Which subnet is host 180.100.60.85 /23 in?

Use the Subnetting Secrets Chart© to determine the subnet mask and subnet increment, etc.

1. How many subnets?

   $2^7 = 128$

2. How many hosts per subnet?

   $2^9 - 2 = 510$

3. What are the valid subnets?

   $256 - 254 = 2$

   0, 2, 4, 6, 8, etc., 250, 252, 254

4. What are the valid hosts per subnet/broadcast?

Subnets	0.0	2.0	4.0	6.0	etc.	60.0	etc.	254.0
First host	0.1	2.1	4.1	6.1		60.1		254.1
Last host	1.254	3.254	5.254	7.254		61.254		255.254
Broadcast	1.255	3.255	5.255	7.255		61.255		255.255

You could jump from 6.0 to 60.0 which would hit the 60.85 host straightaway as the next subnet would be 62.0. Host 180.100.60.85 is in subnet 180.100.60.0.

Example 7: Which subnet is host 130.100.200.121 /24 in?

No, your eyes do not deceive you. Do not look at this subnet and think Class C, it is in this instance eight bits of subnetting being used for a Class B address. Do not ponder too long over it, just follow the usual procedure.

Use the Subnetting Secrets Chart.

1. How many subnets?

   $2^8 = 256$

2. How many hosts per subnet?

   $2^8 - 2 = 254$

3. What are the valid subnets?

$256 - 255 = 1$

0, 1, 2, 3, 4, 5 and so on up to 255.

4. What are the valid hosts per subnet / broadcast?

Subnets	0.0	1.0	2.0	3.0	etc.	254.0	255.0
First host	0.1	1.1	2.1	3.1		254.1	255.1
Last host	0.254	1.254	2.254	3.254		254.254	255.254
Broadcast	0.255	1.255	2.255	3.255		254.255	255.255

So, if you just keep counting up in increments of 1, you will reach subnet `200.0`. Host `130.100.200.121` is therefore in subnet `130.100.200.0`.

Example 8: Which subnet is host `191.20.56.65 255.255.255.128` in?

This one is a bit easier because the (/25) subnet is written out in long hand for you already. Nine bits have been taken for use on the subnet. This is another tricky example which does not fit neatly into the usual formula we use. Instead of taking the 128 away from 256 to get the valid subnets we use the 255.

We are also allowed to have a 0 in the third octet if we have a bit turned on, on the fourth octet. For each value such as subnet 10 you get `10.0` and then `10.128`. If you remember that you will be fine

.

1. How many subnets?

$2^9 = 512$

2. How many hosts per subnets?

$2^7 - 2 = 126$

3. What are the valid subnets?

$256 - 255 = 1$

0, 1, 2, 3, 4, 5, etc., 255

Because we are subnetting on the fourth octet we can actually use the 0 subnet on the third octet. This is possible because if we have a bit turned on on the fourth octet we do not have all the hosts bits off. We can also use 255 on the last octet.

If this does not make much sense at the moment there is no need for concern. It is very doubtful if you will come across this in exams or interviews but then again it is a useful subnet for use in the real world so you never know! You can write this out in binary later when you have time.

What are the valid hosts per subnet / broadcast?

Subnets	0.0	0.128	1.0	1.128	2.0	2.128	etc.	255.0	255.128
First host	0.1	0.129	1.1	1.129	2.1	2.129		255.1	255.129
Last host	0.126	0.254	1.126	1.254	2.126	2.254		255.126	255.254
Broadcast	0.127	0.255	1.127	1.255	2.127	2.255		255.127	255.255

Host 191.20.56.65 is on subnet 191.20.56.0. There is not room to fill in every subnet value above, but you can see that the subnets would go up as follows:

191.20.55.0

191.20.55.128

191.20.56.0*

191.20.56.128

191.20.57.0, etc.

Example 9: Which subnet is host 180.100.1.220 /27 in?

We have skipped a subnet. The principles are exactly the same. Remember to use the Subnetting Secrets Chart© to save time and to insure that your answer is correct. You are hitting the fourth octet in this example so you would just tick down three places (because you cannot fit in the eight bits on the third octet on the chart.

Super Subnetting Chart™

	Bits	128	64	32	16	8	4	2	1
Subnets		✓	✓	✓					
128	✓								
192	✓								
224	✓								
240									
248									
252									
254									
255									
Powers of 2	Subnets	Hosts minus 2							
2	✓	✓							
4	✓	✓							

8	✓	✓							
16	✓	✓							
32	✓	✓							
64	✓								
128	✓								
256	✓								
512	✓								
1024	✓								
2048	✓								
4096									
8192									
16,384									

1. How many subnets?

   $2^{11} = 2048$

2. How many hosts per subnet?

   $2^5 - 2 = 30$

3. What are the valid subnets?

   $256 - 224 = 32$

   `0.0, 0.32, 0.64, 0.96, etc., 255.32, 255.64, etc., 255.192, 255.224`

4. What are the valid hosts per subnet/broadcast?

As before, if all of this does not make much sense, then let me assure you that this is normal. This is all based upon binary mathematics but because as we are using the fast decimal method it will just never look right. Keep on working through the examples and it will eventually make perfect sense—honest!

We can manipulate the third octet due to the fact that we can have bits on and off on the fourth octet. There are too many subnets to write out but we can write out some of them.

Subnets	0.0	0.32	0.64	0.96	0.128	0.160	0.192	0.224
First host	0.1	0.33	0.65	0.97	0.129	0.161	0.193	0.225
Last host	0.30	0.62	0.94	0.126	0.158	0.190	0.222	0.254
Broadcast	0.31	0.63	0.95	0.127	0.159	0.191	0.223	0.255

The above example works because as long as we can have bits turned on, on the fourth octet we can have all the bits off on the third octet.

Next we can turn bits on, on the third octet.

Subnets	1.0	1.32	1.64	1.96	1.128	1.192	1.224
First host	1.1	1.33	1.65	1.97	1.129	1.193	1.225
Last host	1.30	1.62	1.94	1.126	1.190	1.222	1.254
Broadcast	1.31	1.63	1.95	1.127	1.191	1.223	1.255

We can continue subnetting until we get up to the number 255 in the third octet. We can go all the way up to subnet 255.224 since subnet zero is allowed.

```
1.1.1.1.1.1.1.1|1.1.1.1.1.1.1.1|1.1.1.1.1.1.1.1|1.1.0.1.1.1.1.1
Subnet -------------------------------------------------| Host bits
```

All the subnet bits we can turn on are on. We cannot have 1.1.1 for the first three subnet bits since this is the number 224, which is our subnet. When we turn on the last five bits (the host bits), this is a broadcast on the 255.192 subnet.

Subnets	255.0	255.32	255.64	255.96	255.128	255.160	255.192	255.224
First host	255.1	255.33	255.65	255.97	255.129	255.161	255.193	255.225
Last host	255.30	255.62	255.94	255.126	255.158	255.190	255.222	255.254
Broadcast	255.31	255.63	255.95	255.127	255.159	255.191	255.223	255.255

Host 180.100.1.220 is on subnet 180.100.1.192.

Example 10: Which subnet is host 150.60.200.107 /28 in?

Use the Subnetting Secrets Chart© again. (The mask will be 255.255.255.240.) The chart will have to be used to represent the last octet. Taking the 12 masked bits we have stolen, we have to presume we have ticked across the first eight bits for the third octet and have spilled over to the fourth octet and tick the last remaining four bits.

Super Subnetting Chart™

	Bits	128	64	32	16	8	4	2	1
Subnets		✓	✓	✓	✓				
128	✓								
192	✓								
224	✓								
240	✓								
248									

	Subnets	Hosts minus 2								
252										
254										
255										
Powers of 2	Subnets	Hosts minus 2								
2	✓	✓								
4	✓	✓								
8	✓	✓								
16	✓	✓								
32	✓									
64	✓									
128	✓									
256	✓									
512	✓									
1024	✓									
2048	✓									
4096	✓									
8192										
16,384										

1. How many subnets?

   2^12 = 4096

2. How many hosts per subnet?

   2^4 – 2 = 14

3. What are the valid subnets?

   256 – 240 = 16

   0, 16, 32, 48, 64, 80, 96, etc., 208, 224, 240

4. What are the valid hosts per subnet/broadcast?

The same rules apply as in the previous example. We can have all the bits off on the third octet as long as we have subnet bits on, on the fourth octet.

Here are the first subnets:

Subnets	0.0	0.16	0.32	0.48	0.64	0.96	etc.	0.240
First host	0.1	0.17	0.33	0.49	0.65	0.97		0.241
Last host	0.14	0.30	0.46	0.62	0.94	0.111		0.254
Broadcast	0.15	0.31	0.47	0.63	0.95	0.112		0.255

Here are more subnets:

Subnets	1.0	1.16	1.32	1.48	1.64	1.80	1.96	1.112
First host	1.1	1.17	1.33	1.49	1.65	1.81	1.97	1.113
Last host	1.14	1.30	1.46	1.62	1.78	1.94	1.110	1.126
Broadcast	1.15	1.31	1.47	1.63	1.79	1.95	1.111	1.127

Here are some more subnets:

Subnets	200.48	200.64	200.80	200.96	200.112	200.128	200.144	200.160
First host	200.49	200.65	200.81	200.97	200.113	200.129	200.145	200.161
Last host	200.62	200.78	200.94	200.110	200.126	200.142	200.158	200.174
Broadcast	200.63	200.79	200.95	200.111	200.127	200.143	200.159	200.175

Here are the last subnets.

Subnets	255.0	255.16	255.32	255.48	255.64	etc.	255.223	255.240
First host	255.1	255.17	255.33	255.49	255.65		255.224	255.241
Last host	255.14	255.30	255.46	255.62	255.78		255.338	255.254
Broadcast	255.15	255.31	255.47	255.63	255.79		255.239	255.255

Host 150.60.200.107 is on subnet 150.60.200.96. The full details for the subnet are: Subnet 150.60.200.96 hosts 97–110 broadcast 111.

www.HowToNetwork.net has a handy free subnet calculator you can download. I do not recommend relying on one to learn how to subnet, but it is a useful tool to check your working out.

Subnetting in your head

You can actually do subnetting without writing a thing down. It does take a bit of practice but you will be able to see the question and know the right answer without even seeing the available answers.

Let's use an example:

What subnet is 192.168.10.90 255.255.255.192 in?

Can you take 192 away from 256 in your head?

You should come to 64. If you start with the first subnet as 0 then 64, the next is 128 and the last is 192. You can see the host number is 90 which is less than 128 and more than 64, so we know it is in the .64 subnet somewhere.

Host 192.168.10.90 is in subnet 192.168.10.64.

Another example:

What subnet is 172.16.20.112 255.255.255.224 in?

Take 224 away from 256, giving you 32. We can keep adding 32 until we come to the subnet containing 112 as an address. Not 32, not 64, could be in 96 and 96 plus 32 is 128. Bingo! It is in the 172.16.20.96 subnet.

Any of the subnets taken away from 256 will come to 2, 4, 8, 16, 32, 64, or 128. The more examples you do, you will remember what taken away from 256 equals what. You will instantly know that 256 – 224 = 32 or that 256 – 240 = 16. Once you have the result of that simple mental calculation you have everything you need. Simple, is it not?

Subnetting is like riding a bicycle, the more you practice the more natural it becomes. You will get to a point where you can look at an IP address and subnet mask and know which subnet it belongs to.

CLASS A SUBNETTING

The principles are exactly the same for Class A subnetting as they are for Class B and Class C. We just have more host bits available. We are going to keep this section fairly short since by now you have everything you need to answer any subnetting question.

Bits	Subnet mask	CIDR	Subnets	Hosts
0	255.0.0.0	/8	1	16,777,216
1	255.128.0.0	/9	2	8,388,606
2	255.192.0.0	/10	4	4,194,302
3	255.224.0.0	/11	8	2,097,150
4	255.240.0.0	/12	16	1,048,574
5	255.248.0.0	/13	32	524,286
6	255.252.0.0	/14	64	262,142
7	255.254.0.0	/15	128	131,070
8	255.255.0.0	/16	256	65,534
9	255.255.128.0	/17	512	32,766
10	255.255.192.0	/18	1024	16,382
11	255.255.224.0	/19	2048	8190

12	255.255.240.0	/20	4096	4094
13	255.255.248.0	/21	8192	2046
14	255.255.252.0	/22	16,384	1022
15	255.255.254.0	/23	32,768	510
16	255.255.255.0	/24	65,536	254
17	255.255.255.128	/25	131,072	126
18	255.255.255.192	/26	262,144	62
19	255.255.255.224	/27	524,288	30
20	255.255.255.240	/28	1,048,576	14
21	255.255.255.248	/29	2,097,152	6
22	255.255.255.252	/30	4,194,304	2

Example 1: Which subnet is 10.100.100.93 /10 in?

Remember that the default subnet mask for a Class A address is 255.0.0.0 (or /8) so we have 24 bits available for hosts or to use for subnetting. We will need to add two host bits to the Subnetting Secrets Chart© to get to the /10 value and to calculate the subnet and hosts per subnet.

Super Subnetting Chart™

	Bits	128	64	32	16	8	4	2	1 (+ 16)
Subnets		✓	✓						
128	✓								
192	✓								
224									
240									
248									
252									
254									
255									
Powers of 2	Subnets	Hosts minus 2							
2	✓	✓							
4	✓	✓							
8		✓							
16		✓							
32		✓							
64		✓							
128		✓							

256		✓							
512		✓							
1024		✓							
2048		✓							
4096		✓							
8192		✓							
16,384		✓							
32,768		✓							
65,536		✓							
131,072		✓							
262,144		✓							
524,288		✓							
1,048,576		✓							
2,097,152		✓							
4,194,304		✓							

1. How many subnets?

   $2\wedge2 = 4$

2. How many hosts per subnets?

   $2\wedge22 - 2 = 4,194,302$

3. What are the valid subnets?

   $256 - 192 = 64$

   0, 64, 128, 192, or if you want to write out the last three octets:

   `0.0.0, 64.0.0, 128.0.0, 192.0.0`

4. What are the valid hosts per subnet/broadcast?

Subnets	10.0.0.0	10.64.0.0	10.128.0.0	10.192.0.0
First host	10.0.0.1	10.64.0.1	10.128.0.1	10.192.1
Last host	10.63.254	10.127.255.254	10.191.255.254	10.255.255.254
Broadcast	10.63.255	10.127.255.255	10.191.255.255	10.255.255.255

Host `10.100.100.93` is in subnet `10.64.0.0`.

Note: Exams such as the CCNA are usually pretty fair, so I would be surprised if Cisco gives you a subnetting question that will clearly take a considerable time to work out (such as working out powers of 2 to 22 places, as above). It is always better to train using the hard questions though, and then the exam questions will appear easy to you.

Example 2: Which subnet is host 10.210.204.70 /12 in?

How many bits are we using for subnetting here? Are we subnetting on the first, second, or third octet?

1. How many subnets?

    2^4 = 16

2. How many hosts per subnet?

    2^20 – 2 = 1,048,574

3. What are the valid subnets?

    256 – 240 = 16

    10.0.0.0

    10.16.0.0

    10.32.0.0 etc.

    10.176.0.0

    10.192.0.0

    10.208.0.0, etc.

    10.224.0.0

    10.240.0.0

4. What are the valid hosts per subnet/broadcast?

Subnets	10.0.0.0	10.16.0.0	10.32.0.0	etc.	10.208.0.0	10.224.0.0
First host	10.0.0.1	10.16.0.1	10.32.0.1		10.208.0.1	10.224.0.1
Last host	10.15.255.254	10.31.255.254	10.47.255.254		10.223.255.254	10.255.255.254
Broadcast	10.15.255.255	10.31.255.255	10.47.255.255		10.223.255.255	10.255.255.255

Host 10.210.204.70 is in subnet 10.208.0.0.

Example 3: Which subnet is host 10.200.100.107 /20 in?

Use the Subnetting Secrets Chart© again. Remember that we will have to use the chart for the overspill bits from the third octet. You would have ticked eight bits for the subnets in the second octet, leaving four bits to tick on the chart for the third octet.

1. How many subnets?

    2^12 = 4096

2. How many hosts per subnet?

    2^12 – 2 = 4094

3. What are the valid subnets?

256 − 240 = 16

I have written them out in full this time but I could have just as easily written 0.0, 16.0, 32.0, etc.

10.0.0.0

10.0.16.0

10.0.32.0

10.0.48.0, etc.

10.1.0.0

10.1.16.0, etc.

10.1.240.0

10.2.0.0

10.2.16.0, etc. up to

10.255.240.0

4. What are the valid hosts per subnet / broadcast?

We can use 0 in the third octet as before — as long as we turn on a subnet bit in the second octet. We could start with 0 in the second octet if we wished as long as we turned on a bit on the third octet.

There are far too many to write out here so we will have to skip most of the subnets.

Subnets	10.0.0.0	10.0.16.0	10.0.32.0	etc.	10.0.224.0	10.0.240.0
First host	10.0.0.1	10.0.16.1	10.0.32.1		10.0.224.1	10.0.240.1
Last host	10.0.15.254	10.0.31.254	10.0.47.254		10.0.239.254	10.0.255.254
Broadcast	10.0.15.255	10.0.31.255	10.0.47.255		10.0.239.255	10.0.255.255

Some more subnets:

Subnets	10.1.0.0	10.1.16.0	10.1.32.0	etc.	10.1.224.0	10.1.240.0
First host	10.1.0.1	10.1.16.1	10.1.32.1		10.1.224.1	10.1.240.1
Last host	10.1.15.254	10.1.31.254	10.1.47.254		10.1.239.254	10.1.255.254
Broadcast	10.1.15.255	10.1.31.255	10.1.47.255		10.1.239.255	10.1.255.255

Some more subnets:

Subnets	10.200.48.0	10.200.64.0	10.200.80.0	10.200.96.0	10.200.112.0
First host	10.200.48.1	10.200.64.1	10.200.80.1	10.200.96.1	10.200.112.1
Last host	10.200.63.254	10.200.79.254	10.200.95.254	10.200.111.254	10.200.127.254
Broadcast	10.200.63.255	10.200.79.255	10.200.95.255	10.200.111.255	10.200.127.255

Host 10.200.100.107 is in subnet 10.200.96.0.

Subnet 10.200.96.0 hosts 10.200.96.1–10.200.111.254 (broadcast 10.200.111.255).
It can get fairly hard when working out Class A subnets with what are traditionally thought of as Class B or Class C addresses. I would recommend working at these examples over and over until they start to make sense.

Example 4: Which subnet is host 20.100.55.3 /26 in?

Use the Subnetting Secrets Chart© again.
1.   How many subnets?
    $2^{18} = 262,144$
2.   How many hosts per subnet?
    $2^6 - 2 = 62$
3.   What are the valid subnets?
    256 – 192 = 64
    20.0.0.0
    20.0.0.64
    20.0.0.128, etc.
    20.0.14.192
    20.0.15.0, etc.
4.   What are the valid hosts per subnet/broadcast?

The subnet values need to be added to the second, third, and fourth octets. The last octet must be multiples of 64, and 0 is permitted as long as there are bits turned on on the second and third octets. Below are the starting subnets.

Subnets	20.0.0.0	20.0.0.64	20.0.0.128	20.0.0.192	20.0.1.0
First host	20.0.0.1	20.0.0.65	20.0.0.129	20.0.0.193	20.0.1.1
Last host	20.0.0.62	20.0.0.126	20.0.0.190	20.0.0.254	20.0.1.62
Broadcast	20.0.0.63	20.0.0.127	20.0.0.191	20.0.0.255	20.0.1.63

And more subnets:

Subnets	20.100.54.128	20.100.54.192	20.100.55.0	20.100.55.64	20.100.55.128
First host	20.100.54.129	20.100.54.193	20.100.55.1	20.100.55.65	20.100.55.129
Last host	20.100.54.190	20.100.54.254	20.100.55.62	20.100.55.126	20.100.55.190
Broadcast	20.100.54.191	20.100.54.255	20.100.55.63	20.100.55.127	20.100.55.191

We can continue counting up but to get to the subnet containing host 20.100.55.3 would take some time. It is to be found in subnet 20.100.55.0.

Subnet 20.100.55.0 hosts 20.100.55.1–20.100.55.62 (broadcast = 20.100.55.63).

HOW MANY SUBNETS? / HOW MANY HOSTS?

The second type of question you will be asked in the exam is to take a standard IP address and subnet mask and subnet it down further to provide X amount of subnets with X amount of hosts per subnet.

Example 1

Your client has been given address 192.168.1.0 /24 and requires four subnets and each subnet must be able to provide at least ten hosts.

Use the Subnetting Secrets Chart© and tick down the lower subnets column next to the powers of 2 until you reach a value that will give you a minimum of four subnets.

Super Subnetting Chart™

	Bits	128	64	32	16	8	4	2	1
Subnets									
128	✓								
192	✓								
224									
240									
248									

Powers of 2	Subnets	Hosts minus 2									
252											
254											
255											
Powers of 2	Subnets	Hosts minus 2									
2	✓	✓									
4	✓	✓									
8		✓									
16		✓									
32		✓									
64		✓									
128											
256											
512											
1024											
2048											
4096											
8192											
16,384											

Ticking down two boxes gives you the required four subnets. You can now tick down two on the upper subnets column two boxes to generate the correct subnet of 255.255.255.192 (or /26).

You have stolen two bits from the last octet to generate the subnet mask leaving six for hosts. Tick down six boxes on the hosts column to find out how many hosts per subnet you have.

You have 62 (64 − 2) hosts per subnet, which more than what meets the requirement the client needs.

Example 2

You have address 200.100.20.0 /24 and the client wants to break this down to at least nine subnets each having at least ten hosts per subnet.

Here you need to generate AT LEAST nine subnets but not waste subnets.

Tick down the powers of 2 subnet column until you reach the closest number possible to nine without wasting subnets.

Super Subnetting Chart™

Bits	128	64	32	16	8	4	2	1
Subnets								
128	✓							
192	✓							
224	✓							
240	✓							
248								
252								
254								
255								

Powers of 2	Subnets	Hosts minus 2							
2	✓	✓							
4	✓	✓							
8	✓	✓							
16	✓	✓							
32									
64									
128									
256									
512									
1024									
2048									
4096									
8192									
16,384									

The closest we can get is 16 because eight are not sufficient.

Tick down four places on the upper subnets column to generate a subnet mask of
255.255.255.240.

You have taken four bits from the last subnet, leaving four for hosts.
16 − 2 gives us 14 hosts per subnet, which is sufficient.

Example 3

Your client has IP address 130.100.0.0 /16 and requires 30 subnets each having at least 1000 hosts. Generate a subnet mask that meets this requirement.

Same deal, but remember that we are taking bits from the third octet.

Super Subnetting Chart™

	Bits	128	64	32	16	8	4	2	1 (+ 8)
Subnets									
128	✓								
192	✓								
224	✓								
240	✓								
248	✓								
252									
254									
255									
Powers of 2	Subnets	Hosts minus 2							
2	✓	✓							
4	✓	✓							
8	✓	✓							
16	✓	✓							
32	✓	✓							
64		✓							
128		✓							
256		✓							
512		✓							
1024		✓							
2048		✓							
4096									
8192									
16,384									

We have to tick down five boxes in the powers-of-2 subnet column to get the value of 32, which is as close as we can get to 30 subnets. This leaves three bits in the third octet and eight bits in the fourth octet for hosts (eleven bits).

Five ticks down in the upper subnets column gives us a subnet of 255.255.248.0. Tick down eleven places in the hosts column giving us 2046 hosts per subnet. Easy peasy.

CONGRATULATIONS!

Well done on getting this far. Subnetting is one of those necessary skills for network engineers, and yet it is also one of the most neglected skills. If you can confidently subnet, you will insure yourself that you will be a useful addition to any network team or to prospective clients as a network consultant.

Make sure you periodically review both books and videos to keep your subnetting skills sharp. One last piece of advice—make sure you can write down the Subnetting Secrets Chart© by hand for use in IT exams or interview.

Paul Browning—November 2009

SUBNETTING RESOURCES

You can find more information at:
www.subnetting.org and www.subnetting-secrets.com

DO YOU WANT TO BE A CISCO ENGINEER?

Why not join us for an online Cisco training course. www.howtonetwork.net provides excellent online Cisco training courses to help you pass your Cisco exams and make a success of your career as a Cisco engineer.

There are videos, practice exams, flash study cards, a live rack of Cisco routers and a very friendly discussion forum. Why not come over now and say "hi."

Many thanks,

Paul Browning
help@howtonetwork.net
Phone (worldwide):+44 870 0670622
Phone (UK): 0800 083 6277
Fax (worldwide): +44 870 4584011
Fax (UK): 0870 4584011

APPENDIX B

Answers for the Module Summary Questions

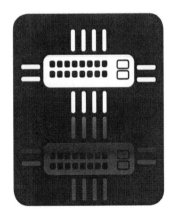

Module 1

1. MAC address
2. WWW, POP3, SMTP, and FTP
3. Determines the best path for data to take, segments to packets, and logical addressing
4. Data, Segment, Packet, Frame, Bit
5. Core, Distribution, and Access
6. Normally when connecting like to like equipment — such as hub to hub, PC to PC.
7. Pin 1 to pin 3 and pin 2 to pin 6
8. Gigabit Ethernet 1000 BaseT
9. Transport layer
10. Presentation layer

Module 2

1. enable
2. show version
3. show ip interface brief
4. 9600 bits per second, 8 data bits, parity none, stop bits 1, flow control none
5. show history
6. Try another COM port.
7. copy running-config startup-config (or copy run start)
8. power-on self-test (POST)
9. Flash memory
10. Trivial File Transfer Protocol (TFTP)

Module 3

1. Stores MAC addresses, filters and forwards traffic, prevents loops
2. STP
3. Store and forward
4. Frame tagging
5. ISL
6. VTP Server
7. 100 Mbps
8. VTP pruning
9. Server, client and transparent
10. switchport mode trunk

Module 4

Summary answers

1. 11100000
2. 10
3. 192-223
4. 10.x.x.x, 172.16.x.x–172.31.x.x, 192.168.x.x
5. /30
6. 192.168.2.128
7. 255.255.255.252
8. 199 and 11000111
9. IPv6 uses 16-bit hexadecimal number fields representing a 128-bit address
10. Multicasting

Answers for the conversion exercises

1. **Convert 1111 to hex and decimal**

   Hex = F

   Decimal = 15

2. **Convert 11010 to hex and decimal**

   Hex = 1A

   Decimal = 26

3. **Convert 10000 to hex and decimal**

   Hex = 10

   Decimal = 16

4. **Convert 20 to binary and hex**

   Binary = 10100

   Hex = 14

5. **Convert 32 to binary and hex**

   Binary = 100000

   Hex = 20

6. **Convert 101 to binary and hex**

   Binary = 1100101

   Hex = 65

7. **Convert A6 from hex to binary and decimal**
   Binary = 10100110
   Decimal = 166

8. **Convert 15 from hex to binary and decimal**
   Binary = 10101
   Decimal = 21

9. **Convert B5 from hex to binary and decimal**
   Binary = 10110101
   Decimal = 181

Module 5

1. Path determination and packet switching
2. 120
3. Classful
4. 14 is the maximum (same as RIP)
5. LSA
6. show ip route
7. EIGRP
8. Converged
9. Next hop address
10. EIGRP

Module 6

1. Connectionless
2. Telnet
3. ICMP
4. Traceroute
5. ARP
6. copy startup-config tftp:
7. show cdp neighbor
8. DNS
9. ip host RouterB 172.16.1.1
10. Telnet

Module 7

1. banner motd
2. 100-199
3. 0.0.255.255
4. 23
5. 80
6. ip access-group {number} in/out
7. DNS
8. service password-encryption
9. 'established'
10. ip access-class 100 in/out

Module 8

1. CPE – Customer premise equipment
2. LCP – Link Control Protocol
3. CHAP
4. 'show controllers serial x'
5. LMI
6. show ip interface brief
7. Every 10 seconds
8. Demarcation point
9. 2.048 Mb
10. HDLC

Module 10

1. Wireless client, access point, and access switch
2. Reflection, scattering, absorption, and attenuation
3. Ad-hoc and infrastructure
4. An access point and multiple clients
5. Two or more BSSs from the same sub-network
6. Centralized security management, scalablity, increased reach
7. 802.11
8. Open-system and shared-key
9. WEP, WPA and WPA2
10. AES (advanced encryption standard)

Module 11

1. No
2. On the router or your PC / laptop
3. ip http server and ip http secure-server
4. 15
5. Yes
6. No, you need 6 Mb
7. Internet Explorer 5.5 or higher and Java Virtual Machine

Lightning Source UK Ltd.
Milton Keynes UK
UKOW012217091211

183488UK00001B/1/P